MUSLIM BROTHERHOODS IN NINETEENTH-CENTURY AFRICA

AFRICAN STUDIES SERIES

MUSLIM BROTHERHOODS IN NINETEENTH-CENTURY AFRICA

B. G. MARTIN

CAMBRIDGE UNIVERSITY PRESS

CAMBRIDGE

LONDON · NEW YORK · MELBOURNE

Published by the Syndics of the Cambridge University Press
The Pitt Building, Trumpington Street, Cambridge CB2 1RP
Bentley House, 200 Euston Road, London NW1 2DB
32 East 57th Street, New York, NY 10022, USA
296 Beaconsfield Parade, Middle Park, Melbourne 3206, Australia

First published 1976

Printed in the United States of America
Typeset, printed, and bound by
Vail-Ballou Press, Inc., Binghamton, New York

Library of Congress Cataloging in Publication Data

Martin, Bradford G

Muslim brotherhoods in nineteenth-century Africa.

(African studies series; 18)

Bibliography: p.

Includes index.

1. Sufism – Africa – History. 2. Africa – History – 19th century.   I. Title.
II. Series.
BP188.8.A44M37   297'.4   75-35451
ISBN 0 521 21062 3

For Philip and Jenny

Contents

Preface

This book about sufi brotherhoods derives from my interest in African Islam, which I have taught or been concerned with for some time. It occurred to me that several short studies of sufi groups and their chiefs in East, North, and West Africa – based on the groups' common historical background, tied together by their attachment to "political" mysticism, and amplified by discussions on allied subjects – might be useful. It seemed appropriate to contrast these groups, so that their contribution to African Islam might be reevaluated or, in some cases, discussed for the first time. Hence this book employs an informal comparative method – largely historical, but with an occasional contribution from other disciplines, such as politics, literary studies, anthropology, or Islamic theology. I believe that it is essential for historians of Africa to adopt such interdisciplinary techniques in order to give suitable explanations for the problems they encounter. (See the programmatic statement of the editors of this series in the front papers of this book.)

When I started writing this study, I thought I would find that the leaders of the brotherhoods I wanted to investigate used their organizations in much the same way – that, for example, in the case of jihad or military operations in which they engaged, the brotherhoods would invariably furnish the structural underpinning that the leaders needed. This was not the case; certain leaders exploited the brotherhood structure more than others. For example, their ideas of "holy war" (jihad) were quite different. I also found that dedication to mysticism in no way hindered many of them from being practical leaders of causes, quite as much as being mystics or intellectuals, and that most of them had expressed their ideas in writing. Also, most of them were very much in the contemporary intellectual mainstream; they rejected blind imitation of what earlier thinkers had done. They very often showed their great intellectual independence over such matters as *hijra* ("removal," "withdrawal"), particularly in the face of a colonial takeover by some alien power, and expressly opted for a form of juridical freedom (*ijtihad*) when it was appropriate.

Another theme that runs through these pages, and now appears much larger than I had originally thought possible, is that of Islamic millennialism and mahdism. Here is a subject that deserves for itself a complete study – applied to the African continent – but that can only be touched on peripherally here. I hope that some other writer may take this subject up and exploit it. Much can be inferred about African mahdi figures from the writings of Norman Cohn, Peter Worsley, and A. F. C. Wallace. One day a full account of African mahdis, of whom there are so many, will be written.

Another interrelated theme that appears and reappears in this book is that of Pan-Islam – of Ottoman Turkish interest in the Muslim Africa of the late nineteenth century. This was particularly true in Arabic-speaking areas of the continent, or where Islam was gaining ground. Thus many of the leaders of brotherhoods treated here looked hopefully to Istanbul for moral and political support. Sometimes they obtained it, sometimes not, although it is now clearer that the farther they were from Istanbul, the higher their hopes were raised. Once again, this is a theme that demands an exhaustive study, which this book cannot claim to make.

To deal more effectively with the interconnected issues and problems treated here, I have deliberately avoided European sources wherever I could do so. I was determined to use them only in a confirmatory manner to support what I found in Arabic (or occasionally in Turkish) materials. Among such sources, I have used the writings of chiefs of brotherhoods whenever I could find them, in order to read about their ideas, theories, and convictions in their own words. This has not always been easy, for much of this material is still uncollected or otherwise inaccessible. All the same, this study attempts, in a limited way, to explain and synthesize a series of problems in hope that it may some day contribute to a fuller understanding of the development of Islam in Africa.

In translating Arabic (and a few Turkish) words and names, I have simplified the standard practice by omitting subscripts and long marks, but I have retained k for a front k (*kaf*), q for a back k (*qaf*). An apostrophe stands for both *'ayn* and *hamza*.

Among many other people who have helped me with this book, I would like to thank Norman Bennett, who gave me the idea for it, and John Paden, J. R. Willis, Mervyn Hiskett, Idris el-Hareir, David Robinson, Mallam 'Abd al-Qadir Datti, Harry Norris, Shaykh 'Umar 'Abdallah, and Hans Panofsky, who have furnished me with material. I should also like to thank Ivor Wilks, Robert Ferrell, Tom Whitcomb, John Paden, Phyllis Martin, and J. R. Willis for their helpful criticism. Additionally, I would like to thank Karen Ford, Mrs. John Sbordone, and Debra Chase for their typing, and Joyce Hendrixson for her useful suggestions and kindly assistance. My thanks are also due to my editor, Jack Goody, and the staff of the Cambridge University Press. Finally, I claim the errors in this book as my own.

B. G. Martin

Bloomington, Indiana
August 1976

Abbreviations

BCEHSAOF
Bulletin du Comité des Hautes Études de l'Afrique Occidentale Français
BIFAN
Bulletin de l'Institut Fondamentale de l'Afrique Noire
BNP
Bibliothèque Nationale, Paris
BSOAS
Bulletin of the School of Oriental and African Studies
CADRB
Research Bulletin, Centre of Arabic Documentation
EI¹   EI²
Encyclopedia of Islam, first or second editions
IJAHS
International Journal of African Historical Studies
JAH
Journal of African History
JAOS
Journal of the American Oriental Society
JHSN
Journal of the Historical Society of Nigeria
JRAS
Journal of the Royal Asiatic Society
JRGS
Journal of the Royal Geographical Society
MW
Muslim World
RA
Revue Africaine
REI
Revue des Études Islamiques
RHM
Revue d'Histoire Maghrebine
RMM
Revue du Monde Musulman
TNR
Tanzania Notes and Records

Introduction

Roughly defined, sufi orders or brotherhoods (*tariqa,* pl. *turuq,* "way" or "path") are hierarchically organized mystical organizations. Theoretically, all sufi orders are branches from the trunk of the Qadiriya, founded in the twelfth century by the saint 'Abd al-Qadir al-Jilani (unless they are "neosufi" brotherhoods or Muhammadiya *tariqas* such as the Ahmadiya, Sanusiya, and Tijaniya, founded only about the end of the eighteenth century or just after). These depended on direct inspiration from the Prophet to the founder of the order.

There had already been schools of mysticism and, of course, many individual mystics in both the Muslim and non-Muslim worlds. The creation and spread of sufi orders, however, introduced a collective and organized spirit into mysticism. By later medieval times, sufi orders had thoroughly permeated Islam. At a guess, between 1500 and 1800, perhaps 60 to 80 percent of all Muslims in Egypt, North Africa, and the Muslim portions of West and East Africa belonged to some sufi order. As the numbers of sufis attached to brotherhoods grew, the orders grew increasingly powerful and influential. In particular, certain urban orders developed very fully. Most contemporary orders are descended from brotherhoods originally developed in two main regions: in Iraq, Syria, Iran, and Central Asia, or separately in western North Africa.

In the East, such famous orders as the Qadiriya (founded by 'Abd al-Qadir al-Jilani or Kaylani, d. 1166); the Rifa'iya (founded by al-Rifa'i, d. 1182); the Chishtiya (so called after Mu'in al-Din Chishti, d. 1236), a famous Indian order; and the Naqshbandiya (named for Baha' al-Din Naqshband, d. 1389), which has inspired a number of suborders, emerged. A famous North African order, which has since had many offshoots, is the Shadhiliya, named for al-Hasan al-Shadhili (d. 1258).[1]

Significantly, sufi brotherhoods cut cross kinship groups, classes, professions, and lineages, serving to integrate these units vertically. Important in maintaining the existence of these voluntary mystical organizations were individual members' experiences in congregational *hadras* or *dhikrs.* In a *dhikr* circle (here *dhikr* means the frequent "mention" of God), the participants commonly sang hymns, recited formulas, and brought themselves to the brink of collective ecstasy by

1

techniques of controlled breathing or bodily motion. Hyperventilation, or states of consciousness approaching the threshold of hyperventilation, could be induced by these collective rites. Under these circumstances, the carbon dioxide–oxygen balance in the brain is altered, creating a greater susceptibility to visions or hallucinations.[2]

Owing to the intensity of these emotional experiences in the *dhikr* circle, a brotherhood could generate much love and devotion – not only among the brothers (*ikhwan* or *ahbab*) themselves, but between them and their spiritual director and leader (their *shaykh* or *murshid*). Thus one *dhikr* circle, joined to others in the neighborhood and – in the case of a big order – throughout the land, created a cohesive body of men (women were occasionally admitted to *tariqas*, but not by the majority of orders). With its members having social and worldly preoccupations as well as spiritual ones, an order could be oriented toward political purposes. This was more the case with the popular orders – where the emotional dependence of the brothers on their director was greater, and where they were politically more passive. Among "intellectual" orders such as Ottoman or Egyptian Khalwatiya, there was less dependence, less coherence of this sort.[3] Loyalty, enthusiasm, and commitment to the order are obvious presuppositions for political activity. Likewise, the degree of control exercised over an order by its *shaykh* was significant. If his control was complete, then the "convertibility" of the organization to political – or even military – roles was the easier. Yet it must be stressed that no brotherhood has any inherent tendency towards political action, no special call to defend Islam, nor to participate in what has been called "primary resistance."[4] Being essentially mystical organizations, orders did not deviate from their original reasons for existing without strong pressure external to the order. Yet at various times in the past, some of them had good reason to do just that.

Such was the situation at the end of the eighteenth century. At that time, sufi orders throughout the Islamic world could not but share the fear of many Muslims that their society was threatened by Europe. The continuing loss of lands regarded as Islamic territory underlined these attitudes; the Napoleonic invasion of Egypt confirmed them. A trend then came into being that had as its goal the defense of Islam. Brotherhoods proliferated and became more influential, both politically and socially, than ever before. A religious revival simultaneously got under way, triggered by underlying considerations, two of which were a broad social decline and Ottoman military weakness.[5]

The resurgence of organized sufism[6] in the political arena after a long period of quiescence may be matched with another important phenomenon, on which it had some bearing. This was the reemer-

gence – after many centuries – of the idea of the caliphate.[7] When the
last Abbasids were overrun by the Mongols in 1258, the caliphate, by
some uncertain process, passed into the political armory of the
Mamluks of Egypt. When the Mamluks were pushed off the stage by
the Ottoman Turks in 1517, Sultan Selim I inherited the caliphate,
which was to be of more use to his descendants than to him. Until the
last quarter of the eighteenth century, the issue remained dormant. At
that time, Europeans, basing their views on a series of misunderstand-
ings over the relative positions of the Christian pope and Ottoman
sultan, began to see the Turkish ruler as a "Muslim pontiff" – as the
religious head of Sunni Islam. Soon after 1800, Ottoman rulers discovered that they could score some minor political gains against their
European adversaries as "caliphs," by playing their religious cards.[8]

Without falling into any of these European errors, the Muslim world
was also inescapably drawn – as the nineteenth century opened –
toward the Ottoman sultan. This happened for the simple reason that
about 1825, he was the sole major Islamic ruler who still functioned as
such. There were no longer any Great Moguls in India; their rule had
been taken over by Britain. The 'Alawi Sharif dynasty of Morocco had
only a local impact, though in the eyes of purists, its credentials for
the caliphate were better than those of the Ottomans. In Persia, the
Safavids had passed from the scene and had been supplanted by Nadir
Shah and the uncertain Qajar line, but the Qajar dynasty was not a
Sunni one. Like the Sharifs of Morocco, they were too isolated, too
feeble to possess much weight on the international stage. Hence the
Ottomans were in a class by themselves.

Further, the capital cities and provinces of many formerly independent Muslim states were constantly being invaded or colonized by
Europeans. In 1830, for the first time, the French took over a large
Muslim population when they commenced the conquest of Algeria.
They did the same in Tunis in 1881, then with Morocco in 1912. At
the end of the 1870s, the British were well along with their semi-
permanent occupation of Egypt. They followed their Egyptian take-
over with an invasion of the Sudan in the 1880s and 1890s. Throughout
the nineteenth century, greater or smaller Muslim populations were
being transferred to European colonial rule, particularly in Africa.
Hence it was not surprising that these Muslims, deprived of their
normal style of government and cut off from their fellows, should look
toward Istanbul for political guidance and, indeed, political help.
Istanbul and the Ottoman sultan were the only sources to which they
could look and still hope for some as yet unspecified sort of political
support against involuntary colonial status. As always, they tended
to see their own plight in religious colors, as part of an ongoing

struggle between Christian intruders and the Islamic polity directed – morally at least – by the sultan-caliph.

Within Muslim areas that had been occupied by the French, the British, the Dutch, or by the Russians in the Caucasus and Central Asia, these political hopes and aspirations directed to Turkey were almost universal. The more remote from Istanbul, the stronger the aspirations and the greater the reverence for the Ottoman ruler. Thus the Islamic periphery looked toward the Ottomans at the center – a center that paid little attention to them until the 1850s, after the winning of the Crimean War by the Turks and their allies. The sultan himself and the "Young Ottomans" of a slightly later era discovered the "lost Muslims" beyond the Turkish frontiers and at last began to pay some heed to their cries for political aid. Sultan 'Abd al-Majid (ruling 1839 to 1861) may have been the first Ottoman ruler to consider these issues seriously.[9] In a letter written in 1858 to the Mai of Bornu, far away on the southern side of the Sahara, the sultan's deputy, the Pasha of Tripoli, informed the Mai that, as a Muslim, he would be "gratified" to know of the defeat of the Russian Tsarist regime. In reply, the Mai stated that he "took pleasure" in calling himself the "*Mütevelli* [deputy governor] of Bornu Province," as if it were a remote yet integral part of the Ottoman state.[10] Similar ideas of "attaching" themselves to Ottoman rule circulated among the even more distant Sumatrans of Atjeh, who were at that time fighting the Dutch.[11]

By 1880, the earlier Ottoman policy of ignoring foreign Muslims was formally discarded. The aspirations of non-Turkish Muslims in Asia and Africa who had come under colonial rule now got a hearing at Yildiz Palace. The new sultan, 'Abd al-Hamid II, sometimes welcomed his visitors personally. He put them up at Yildiz Palace or in adjoining guesthouses so as to pick their brains and consult them about Islamic problems, or rather, Pan-Islamic issues. It was 'Abd al-Hamid, in fact, who discovered just how useful foreign Muslims could be; he had little to do but listen to them and furnish them with minimal financial support. In return he obtained an unexpectedly good stick with which to beat those colonial powers who were always pressing Turkey to make some "reform" or other or to accept yet another politically inspired loan. As much as anything, the Pan-Islamic policy was useful to Turkey because of its scare value. 'Abd al-Hamid was perpetually suspected by the diplomats and intelligence services of the European powers of carrying out constant "machinations" aimed at them – at the French in Algeria and Tunisia, at the British in India or Afghanistan, or at the Russians in Turkestan.

Considerable light is thrown on 'Abd al-Hamid's genuine – yet at the same time, limited – activities in this field by the reports sent to the

Foreign Office in London by the eminent Hungarian orientalist Arminius (or Hermann) Vambéry.[12] A Hungarian patriot who hated both the Austrians and the Germans, Rashid Efendi (as Vambéry called himself on his frequent trips to Turkey) was quite willing to sell information about Turkey to the British (and perhaps about the British to Turkey). Evidently 'Abd al-Hamid had great trust in Vambéry, conversing with him without much attempt to conceal his thoughts. From Vambéry's reports (c. 1889–1902), there was apparently an unbroken stream of Muslim visitors to Yildiz Palace from remote Islamic places. Vambéry claims that he heard about or saw "*sheikhs* from the Sudan and Darfur"; travelers from India, Zanzibar, and Java; "mullas and hadjis"; as well as "eminent *moulwies*" [sic] from India coming and going, often staying at two semisecret guesthouses on the palace grounds called Hind Tekkesi and Bukhara Tekkesi. On their departures, they set off for their homelands armed with letters from the caliph to local Muslim rulers or other prominent people. Vambéry speaks of emissaries to the Libyan Sanusis, to the Amir of Afghanistan, to the Sudanese Mahdi, to "Swat, Java, and all parts of India." At the same time that 'Abd al-Hamid II (whom Vambéry described in one report as a "secret-monger par excellence" who "delights particularly in these doings") maintained a network of pilgrims, emissaries, and personal agents, he also tried to enlist the help of intellectuals, publicists, and Muslim clericals for his purposes. Indeed, one of these publicists, Ahmad Faris al-Shidyaq, editor of *Ceva'ib*, had been recruited before 'Abd al-Hamid's accession. Among Muslim intellectuals, the caliph was aided by Jamal al-Din al-Afghani and the South Arabian *shaykh* from Zufar, Sayyid Fadl ibn 'Alawi (who had a long history of opposition to Britain).[13]

More important than these men, however, were heads of certain sufi orders whom 'Abd al-Hamid won over to the Pan-Islamic idea. Here the threads of the caliphate and brotherhood themes intertwine. Crossing with them was another strand, pointed out by Hourani – the use of Arabs (after c. 1880) to influence Muslim political developments, particularly in Arabic-speaking areas in Africa. The two most significant Arab heads of *tariqas* recruited by 'Abd al-Hamid for his cause in Africa were the Syrian Abu'l-Huda al-Sayyadi (director of the Rifa'iya order, which had many adherents in Africa) and the Libyan Muhammad bin Muhammad b. Hamza Zafir al-Madani, chief of the Madaniya brotherhood.

The writings of both of these men include fulsome praise for 'Abd al-Hamid II. In a book entitled *Da'i al-Rashad li-sabil al-ittihad wa'l-inqiyad*, Abu'l-Huda describes the Ottoman rulers as the "perfection of the monarchs of Islam," and suggests that they are the direct heirs of the Prophet. "May God sustain their sultanate in every age and time and [safeguard] it against the schemes of infidels and corrupters," he wrote.[14] Muhammad Zafir al-Madani speaks similar language in his *Nur al-sati' wa Burhan al-Qati'*, where he expresses his hopes for the victory of 'Abd al-Hamid's armies, divine protection for his reign, and the "covering of his state with glory."[15] Unfortunately for the Pan-Islamic idea, Shaykh Abu'l-Huda and Muhammad Zafir's personal rivalry was such that they were unable to coordinate their policies, and their hosannas to the sultan were matched in number by diatribes written by their helpers and allies in the form of polemical pamphlets against each other.[16] Hence the sultan was unable to derive much advantage from what was, from his standpoint, a very good idea. In South Arabia and East Africa at least, the caliph undoubtedly got more help from such sufis and political advisers as Sayyid Fadl ibn 'Alawi, a long-term resident at Yildiz and an adviser who could tell his master much about the politics of the Indian Ocean area. As Hourani says:

> The Arabs were the largest Muslim group in the Empire, and the one most able, by the extension of their language throughout the *umma,* to win support for the Sultan-Caliph in Africa and Asia. In particular, they were the key to Africa: through them, the empire might be able to resist European control of the African territories, perhaps to win new lands where Islam was spreading. The Pan-Islamic propaganda was carried on mainly through the medium of the Arabic language and with the help of men of Arab origin.[17]

Thus we find that 'Abd al-Hamid tried to make contact with the Moroccan Sharifian sultan Hasan I in the 1880s through his *Shaykh al-Islam* and later through diplomatic channels. In East Africa the Yashru-tiya, like the Madaniya a branch of the Shadhili order, had vague ties to the sultan. This was also true of Shaykh Uways in Somalia and his rival, Muhammad 'Abdallah Hasan. The rulers of Zanzibar, particularly Sultan 'Ali, looked to Istanbul. Even the Amir 'Abd al-Karim in the Rif of Morocco, although he had no connection with 'Abd al-Hamid, was nonetheless attracted to Turkey – to the Pan-Islamic legacy – which impelled him about 1914 to join the post-Hamidian "Special Forma-tions" created by the Committee of Union and Progress.

A symptom of serious social dislocation and emergent political dis-turbance in the Islamic regions of Africa (as in the Muslim world generally) in the nineteenth century was the prevalence of the mahdist idea. This was a perpetual Islamic millennial scheme that customarily emerged just before the turn of every Islamic century (e.g., in 1785–6 and 1881–2, or 1200 and 1300 of the Hijra). Of course, the best known of these episodes is the anti-Turkish (really anti-Egyptian, anti-

European) rising of the Sudanese Mahdi Muhammad Ahmad ibn 'Abdallah as the Islamic version of the Christian savior, "who will come to
fill the world with justice, as it was previously filled with tyranny and
oppression." To borrow David Pocock's words, Islamic societies in
Africa were:

> being subjected to a gathering flood of external experience which
> finally increased beyond the "stretch" of the indigenous categories
> which might render it meaningful. The social forms of communication
> appear inadequate. The society is as near to atomization as it could
> be. The last resort is a new stress upon the individual as that society
> conceives it, an emphasis upon history, upon individual possession
> by spirits, upon the individually inspired leader.[18]

Hence about the year 1785, there were many such episodes. In Algeria,
the careers of Bu Dali and Muhammad ibn Sharif (discussed in
Chapter 2) illustrate this point. They exploited the proper date; their
movements were grounded in political oppression, famine, and
plagues. These two men were certainly "primitive" Darqawis, which
provided both of them with some organizational support for their
military and political enterprises. There was a similar movement about
the same time in the Caucasus, where the Abkhaz Muslim leader
Imam Mansur fought the Russians.[19] And there is no doubt that the
cause of Usuman dan Fodio was helped along by sincere expectations
in Hausaland that he might turn out to be the mahdi.

The year 1300/1881–2 not only brought the messianic movement in
the Sudan but also saw great hopes aroused in Libya by the Sanusi
leader Muhammad al-Mahdi al-Sanusi – one of whose names was
surely given him by his father in anticipation of the use he might have
for it. If circumstances were right, he could proclaim himself a mahdi.
This he never did. Another episode, in northern Nigeria in the 1850s
(where the timing was thirty years off), was the case of Ibrahim Sharif
al-Din (also known as *al-Dabbaba* or *Abu Sha'ir*), who created widespread millennial disturbances and counseled the population to follow
him – like the Pied Piper – to the East to await the appearance of the
"Expected Mahdi."[20]

Such revitalization movements, to use the terminology of Anthony
F. C. Wallace, can easily be broken down into multiple episodes. To
describe them,Wallace uses the phrases "equilibrium, increasing stress,
and cultural distortion" followed by a second "equilibrium," or "steady
state."[21] His ideas and terminology are quite as applicable to Islamic
Africa as to his original example, the Iroquois of eastern North
America. Brotherhoods might or might not participate in "revitalization
movements." But they often did so, as in the episodes of Bu Dali and

Muhammad ibn Sharif or in the case of the Rahmaniya brotherhood's 1871 eastern Algerian uprising (now known to have had Ottoman support) against the French. (The millennial component of this uprising was not very evident.)[22]

I

The eight sufi brotherhoods and their leaders discussed below can be separated into three categories. Category One includes a pair of militant resisters and ideologues, the Somali chief Muhammad 'Abdallah Hasan and al-Hajj 'Umar from Futa Toro in Senegal. Category Two comprises five moderates, who taught mysticism, carried on jihads, and instituted social reforms. They are Usuman dan Fodio (of northern Nigeria); the Algerian Amir 'Abd al-Qadir; a Libyan reformer, Muhammad 'Ali al-Sanusi; Shaykh Uways al-Barawi, of the East African Banadir coast and Zanzibar; and Shaykh Ma'ruf, of Moroni in the Comoro Islands, between Madagascar and Mozambique. The final category includes a Mauritanian, Shaykh Ma' al-'Aynayn, a conservative sufi leader very little affected by the changing world of the nineteenth century. The first and second categories show interesting differences within their ranks, whereas the third stands apart from the others.

Muhammad 'Abdallah Hasan (erroneously named the "Mad Mullah"), who was endowed with much force and authority, fully shared these characteristics of leadership with al-Hajj 'Umar, the West African Tijani leader. In Somalia, the Salihi dervishes of Muhammad 'Abdallah Hasan fought first against Ethiopians and recalcitrant Somalis and then, on a bigger scale, against the British and Italians. Al-Hajj 'Umar fought an incidental conflict with France and then attacked the Bambara, in a war of revenge and conversion. In both cases the adherence of local Muslims to the Salihi or Tijani orders was stressed, and the internal organization of the two orders had some military relevance. However deep the commitments of both men to mysticism at the beginnings of their careers, they became increasingly politicized, more devoted to their own ideologies (which can be traced in both cases from their Arabic writings), and more and more despotic and authoritarian with their own followers. With al-Hajj 'Umar, departure from sufism caused serious psychological troubles to emerge. Both men were well educated and versed in Islamic theology and can be described as intellectuals and writers of distinction.

Like the majority of the moderate sufis noted here, Muhammad 'Abdallah Hasan was influenced by the eighteenth-century Egyptian sufi revival – through the reformer Ahmad ibn Idris al-Fasi and, separately, by the Wahhabis, another facet of the same religious rebirth. Al-Hajj 'Umar was likewise touched by this revival, but through a different channel – that of the Khalwatiya, the parent order of the Tijaniya. Neither man was much affected by millennial factors, although the Somali chief was often wrongly called a mahdi in the European press of the time – a tag that has been picked up by a careless Egyptian writer.[23] Al-Hajj 'Umar had millennial qualities foisted on him by some of his extreme followers (who named him "the *Wazir* of the *Mahdi*"), but he never espoused this idea himself.[24] Both al-Hajj 'Umar and Muhammad 'Abdallah Hasan employed their sufi orders as tools to mobilize their own societies either against the Bambara or against the Italians or British, attempting to create secure enclaves where their distinctive kinds of Islam could function undisturbed.

The second category includes moderate sufis – leaders of jihads who were forced into that role, social reformers, teachers of mysticism, and theologians. It comprises a number of Qadiris – Usuman dan Fodio, Amir 'Abd al-Qadir, and Shaykh Uways al-Barawi. Not that this sufi order had any monopoly over moderation in political or mystical style; these three personalities had serious commitments to mysticism and were inherently less politically oriented – far less aggressive – than al-Hajj 'Umar or Muhammad 'Abdallah Hasan. Like them are the Shadhili (more accurately Yashruti) Shaykh Ma'ruf of Moroni, in the Comoro Islands, and Muhammad 'Ali al-Sanusi, a teacher and reformer, essentially a pacific figure. All five men were touched by the eighteenth-century sufi revival to a greater or lesser extent. Usuman dan Fodio was influenced by the Khalwatiya through his teacher, Jibril bin 'Umar, whereas the Amir 'Abd al-Qadir met and studied with a Naqshbandi – the Iraqi Shaykh Khalid, of Shahrazur. Shaykh Uways was in touch with Qadiri headquarters in Baghdad, and Shaykh Ma'ruf was in contact with the headquarters of his order in Palestine and subject to similar pro-Ottoman influences from there.

Muhammad 'Ali al-Sanusi was long the leading figure in his own brotherhood, an organization that was part of a cluster of sufi orders (made up of the Mirghaniya, Rashidiya, and Ahmadiya) that was inspired by the great teacher and mystic Ahmad ibn Idris al-Fasi (d. 1836). All of these orders emerged from Arabia in the 1840s or after. Al-Sanusi had the advantage of being taught personally by Ahmad ibn Idris in Mecca and in Yemen.

Endowed with greater sensitivity, greater personal amiability, and more devotion to purely religious matters than al-Hajj 'Umar or Muhammad 'Abdallah Hasan, Usuman dan Fodio could retire from public affairs and his jihad to spend the rest of his life with his students and mystical practices. In Syria, after 1853, Amir 'Abd al-Qadir did much the same thing, although the degree of his political interests was broader. These same characteristics may be observed in Shaykhs Uways and Ma'ruf, and certainly in al-Sanusi. Their ability to attract students – to evoke respect and even reverence from their contemporaries – was remarkable. Likewise, their independence, moderation, and openness allowed them to promote change in the legal and social arenas. Usuman, al-Sanusi, and the Amir all wanted the old way of juridical imitation (*taqlid*) broken down in favor of a new flexibility (*ijtihad*) – a characteristic which they shared with al-Hajj 'Umar.

Two related issues are those of *hijra* ("migration") and jihad (often translated as "holy war"). In theory, migration must precede a conflict against powers inimical to Islam. These theoretical preoccupations can be seen with five of the eight leaders under discussion. With Usuman dan Fodio, a new doctrine of *hijra* and jihad was given its latest expression by Muhammad 'Abdallah Hasan. Under foreign colonial pressures or attacks from "unbelievers," Muslims must migrate, regroup themselves under their own leaders, then fight back to defend their societies and culture and to prevent their values from being overwhelmed and destroyed by the armed intrusions of non-Muslims.

It is also within this group of five men that millennialism was most common. Usuman's jihad and his prolific writing was heavily influenced by his expectations of a coming mahdi. If 'Abd al-Qadir rejected these ideas, many of his Algerian rivals took them up and touted them to win followers. Here the relation between climatic disasters, wars, famines, and epidemics on the one hand and political action of millennial inspiration on the other is closest.[25] The same cluster of ideas is apparent with Shaykh Uways in East Africa. He called himself "Master of the Time" (*sahib al-waqt*), which hints that he may have considered himself the advance agent of a mahdi; the Mecca Letter Affair also betrays a clear millennial component. Most prominent is the millennial facet of the Sanusi order after its founder's death; that he should have named his son and successor Muhammad al-Mahdi speaks for itself. Al-Sanusi lent his son a political option for the approaching turn of the fourteenth Islamic century in 1882. Like the Sudanese mahdi, he could have announced himself as the "expected savior," but he did not.

If Shehu dan Fodio. Shaykh Ma'ruf, and Shaykh Uways had little or no contact with the Turks, the matter is quite otherwise with al-Sanusi and Amir 'Abd al-Qadir. Contrary to what many European writers have claimed, al-Sanusi had only minor disagreements with the Ottomans, and his successors were fairly close to Turkey. In the era before Pan-Islam, Amir 'Abd al-Qadir had difficulty in interesting Istanbul in his military and political plight. He tried, but he failed to do so because of the Porte's liking for Ahmad Bey of Constantine. That he should turn to the "sultan-caliph" for assistance is nevertheless symptomatic of Istanbul's rising prestige for distant Muslims, who were being overtaken by colonial aggression. Al-Hajj 'Umar had no contact with the Turks that can be traced, but Muhammad 'Abdallah Hasan was an admirer of the Ottomans and even dedicated a long poem to the last sultan of Turkey.

The last category, represented by Ma' al-'Aynayn, stands by itself. Ma' al-'Aynayn was a traditional Saharan religious leader of a type that can be identified far into the past. No intellectual on the plane of Usuman dan Fodio or al-Hajj 'Umar, he was nevertheless a skilled politician and prolific author. Like many medieval writers of the Maghrib, Ma' al-'Aynayn was fascinated by magic – its potentialities, powers, and properties. This interest of his did not hinder him from emerging into the outside world, with a short pilgrimage to Mecca, and building a real attachment to the sharifian rulers of Morocco. Ma' al-'Aynayn was also a Qadiri and an admirer of the Ottomans (whose virtues he glorified in one of his texts). Highly conservative, he disapproved of the changes in law and theology that found expression in the *taqlid-ijtihad* controversy. All the same, he did support more effective central rule in Morocco over some decades. If he were interested in the idea of the mahdi, he appears to have viewed it abstractly and made no actual use of it. Finally, like Amir 'Abd al-Qadir and al-Hajj 'Umar, he was involved in a military clash with the French.

In spite of their minor divergences, the eight brotherhood leaders discussed here with their organizations have far more features in common than features that set them apart from each other. Hence they may be considered fairly representative for the Africa of the nineteenth century.

CHAPTER 1

Usuman dan Fodio and the Fulani
Jihad in Northern Nigeria

In 1800, one of the more significant Muslim leaders in West Africa was Usuman dan Fodio (usually arabicized as 'Uthman ibn Fudi). Known as the "Shehu" in his own country, Usuman reformed Islam. He was a spiritual leader, a writer, and an intellectual. His teachings were new, and his writings were both numerous and influential; many of them are still read in West Africa.[1] The Shehu's plans for political and social reform largely succeeded, bringing new Islamic states – outgrowths of his revolutionized Islamic community – into being in Hausaland and its adjoining areas. Usuman's career is now better understood. His thought and actions are also well recorded, and the greater part of his writings in Arabic have been recovered.

Various writers have noted differing interpretations of the "holy war" (jihad) in the Hausa states and Usuman's role in it. The German africanist Adolph Brass saw the jihad as a materialistically motivated political clash between Hausas and Fulanis. Brass claims that the Fulanis of northern Nigeria "used a religious motive as . . . convenient camouflage for their political ends . . . raids, and campaigns of plunder."[2] The Russian author Olderogge sees the jihad as a peasant revolt against an oppressive upper class. To him, "Uthman dan Fodio was not concerned with altering the old structure of society. In the place of the fallen Hausa kings was now the Fulani clan nobility . . . the preaching of Uthman dan Fodio assumed the character of a mahdist movement."[3]

An Anglo-Nigerian scholar, Abdallahi Smith, sees the movement as representing more "than the attempt of a few underprivileged and determined men to seize political power for their own benefit. . . . It was also an important intellectual movement, involving in the minds of its leaders a conception of the ideal society and a philosophy of revolution."[4]

The essential features of this movement are no longer in doubt. The Fulani jihad was directed by three Muslim reformers – Usuman dan Fodio at their head, aided by his son Muhammad Bello and his brother Abdallahi. It echoed a contemporary political and intellectual movement then going on in the Middle East – the sufi response to Wahhabi reform in Arabia. More significantly, it was a locally rooted effort di-

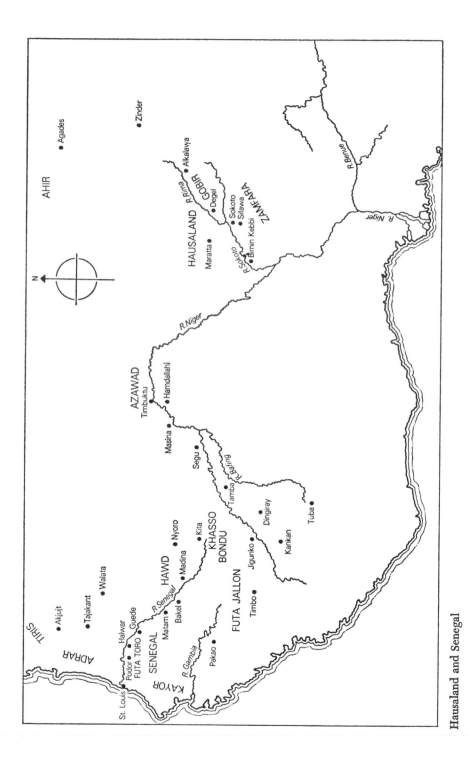

Hausaland and Senegal

rected toward Islamic reform, not revival. It stressed an altered Muslim value system, emphasizing a legalistic, intellectualized, "urban" Islam. Usuman's movement also embodied a millennial component that facilitated its acceptance among the people of northern Nigeria, who were at that time troubled by climatic disasters. To some extent, the movement depended on the ideology of the Qadiri brotherhood and may have been influenced at long range by the Kunta *shaykhs* of the Azawad (near Timbuktu). In their efforts, the reformers were aided by convinced Muslims who repudiated the current religious and political accommodation to non-Muslim belief systems and opposed religious syncretism. They also opposed Hausa (Habe) oppression, slave raiding, and arbitrary taxation.

All three reformers were gifted and dedicated men, possessing good educations. They reached a high level of sophistication and learning. Further, they wrote so profusely over such a broad range of subjects, not merely the jihad itself, that much of their thinking and inspiration becomes clear from their writings.

Usuman dan Fodio was born at Maratta near Galmi in northern Hausaland on 15 December 1754. His younger brother Abdallahi was born in 1766 and his son Muhammad Bello in 1781. They belonged to a Muslim clerical clan (Torodbe) of professional religious teachers. They were descendants of cattle nomads – migrants who entered Hausaland from the west, probably in the fifteenth century. All three men had been educated in the traditional Torodbe-Fulani manner of the time.[5] The Torodbe lived lives in many ways indistinguishable from those of the surrounding Fulani nomads. The Torodbe teaching clans were mostly settled, but they occasionally lived among their cattle during periods of good pasturage. To the surrounding Hausa population, then, the words *Torodbe, Toronkawa,* and *Torodo* were virtually identical with *Fulani.*

Usually the word *Torodbe* is derived from Futa Toro, a region in Senegal, but there are other explanations for the term.[6] One of them is that *Torodbe* means those who "go begging in company." Another theory suggests that the Torodbe were a social catch-all category, including slaves and ex-slaves from Futa Toro and adjoining regions, remnants of peoples ground up in wars, or individuals who wished to rise socially and politically. Many of them accepted Islam, taught it, and spread it. By doing so, they turned themselves into a class of Muslim learned men.[7]

Through their Muslim interests, it is alleged, the Torodbe found a way out of their social isolation and political subordination. In Futa Toro and Futa Jallon, at the end of the seventeenth century, they began to stir. Aware of their superior learning, they were already politically uni-

fied from years of harassment from hostile neighbors. They waited for
an appropriate moment to strike back at the surrounding non-Muslims.
About 1725, a militant group of Torodbe tried to seize political control
in Futa Jallon, led by the "Faqih Ibrahim," as Muhammad Bello called
him. After a number of political reversals in the region during the eighteenth century, the Torodbe of Futa Toro and Futa Jallon ultimately
expelled pagan or semi-islamized Fulani and other groups from their
lands, establishing small Islamic states. Later, under Faqih Sulayman
Bal and then 'Abd al-Qadir bi-Hammadi (c. 1776) and his successor
Muhammad al-Amin (c. 1812), the Torodbe triumphed. There is no
doubt that these examples were known to Usuman dan Fodio and his
circle, who derived a certain inspiration from them.[8]

In West Africa, the Torodbe intellectuals were not isolated from
political or cultural developments in other parts of the Islamic world.
They possessed a strong educational tradition of their own that, in the
case of some individuals, reached high levels. In the seventeenth and
eighteenth centuries, the careers of such writers as Muhammad b.
Muhammad al-Kashinawi of Katsina and Muhammad al-Tahir b. Ibrahim al-Fallati of Bornu illustrate this point.[9] Such men went on the
pilgrimage to Mecca and sometimes sojourned for long periods in
Egypt or elsewhere, where they absorbed cosmopolitan Islamic ideas.
Frequently their value systems were drawn from the "high" Muslim
culture that they had observed abroad and that they favored on returning home. As they were a minority among the Hausas, they often led
difficult lives. Occasionally their circumstances turned them inward
toward mysticism, at other times outward into political activity. The
self-image of the Torodbe militants was one of a spiritual aristocracy
deprived of its rightful place in society. As Last points out, the Torodbe
and Fulani clerics of this sort were in touch with each other over life-
spans and long distances; they remained politically cohesive.[10]

In Hausaland, the Torodbe had long observed the gulf between the
kind of Islam in which they believed and the kind they preached, and
the prevailing syncretism and accommodation. Existing within such a
social environment, they noticed every day those "unstable conditions
of society" mentioned by Abdallahi Smith – a sea of pagan or slightly
islamized Hausas surrounding small islands of "political Muslims"
(Fulani, Taureg, Arabs, even a few Muslim Hausas).[11] These groups,
awaiting the same political changes as had happened further west,
looked for Muslim guidance in their daily lives and followed Islamic
law as best they could. They looked forward to a time when formal
Muslim government and social institutions might exist, under an imam
or caliph. The numbers of militants, or "political Muslims," had been

increasing throughout Hausaland during the eighteenth century, certainly from ongoing migration from the west. Once their numbers had grown sufficiently, the militants were willing to risk a revolution against the established Hausa powers, those "syncretic" Habe rulers, to create the kind of Islamic ambiance they wanted. The pious and well read among them looked back to the Islamic states of the past (such as the Abbasids) or the period of the first four caliphs as meritorious precedents and compared them with the badly flawed society of their own era. With its overtaxation and "improper" customs, Habe rule exemplified to them the inevitable by-products of an erratic and irreligious government. By 1760 or before, the "political Muslims" of Hausaland were ready to accept a leader who would direct such a revolution.

Once that leader appeared, supported by an enlarged Muslim party (or even a majority), his task was quite clear. Syncretism and the more obvious sorts of non-Muslim customs such as uncanonical taxes and institutions would be forcibly dismantled. This had been the usual Torodbe political objective since the start of the eighteenth century. If the ruler, such as a Habe prince, continued to be partly Muslim or a pagan, then the standard of his subjects' Islam would automatically fall short of the Torodbe ideal. Everywhere, the level of Islam had to be revised upward. Already, a sort of accommodationist Islam had become entrenched in Hausaland:

> Islam had grown from being the faith of a coterie of scholars and foreigners to being the generally established religion of the people. . . . But the non-Muslim elements . . . not only the pagans, but also those who retained their traditional beliefs along with their Islam – were still strong enough to support syncretic practices and make it necessary for the ruler . . . to be the head of both faiths . . . only scholars and foreigners remained "pure" Muslims.[12]

Usuman dan Fodio was the man who exactly suited the role of leader for a revolutionary Islamic community. He came from an appropriate Torodbe clan whose ancestors had entered Hausaland during the fifteenth century. Scholarship, study, and books were familiar to him. Usuman's father, Muhammad, made him learn the *Qur'an* by heart. He then mastered Arabic grammar, the fundamentals of Maliki law, and Muslim tradition.[13] By the time he was twenty, Usuman was well acquainted with Arabic verse and metrics. He also studied rhetoric, the history of Islam, and some of the more familiar works of Arabic literature. If neither Usuman nor his brother Abdallahi became great poets in Arabic, they developed into competent and cultivated writers of Arabic prose. Following Torodbe custom, they studied under learned members of their own clan – their uncles – at least one of whom had made the pilgrimage to Mecca.

Learned as they were, Usuman's uncles were soon supplanted as teachers by a Tuareg from Agades in the southern Sahara. This was the widely traveled Jibril bin 'Umar al-Aqdasi, who had twice made the pilgrimage and also spent long periods in Egypt. Jibril initiated Usuman, Abdallahi, and Muhammad Bello into three sufi orders, the Qadiriya, Khalwatiya, and Shadhiliya.[14] Further, Jibril was much concerned with "sin" among his contemporaries. At home in Agades, he had agitated the local political scene by outspoken preaching against wine-drinking, those who embezzled the property of orphans, and merchants who took excessive interest. Jibril was persuaded that the commission of certain "gross sins" turned a Muslim into an unbeliever.[15] As Usuman frequently notes, Jibril's views put him close to the doctrines of the medieval Muslim theological schools of the Khawarij and the Mu'tazila. Yet Jibril was doubtless the dominant influence in Usuman's life. Although Usuman sometimes disagreed with him over his radical tendencies, he gives him credit for initiating a campaign against "evil practices in this Sudanic land of ours." Muhammad Bello, too, had high praise for Jibril, echoing the opinions of his father and uncle:

> Jibril, *Shaykh* of *shaykhs* in our country
>   Blessings are what he confers in great number
> He disperses the gloom of error
>   Like a lamp shedding light over the land.[16]

Like so many earlier members of his clan, Usuman dan Fodio might have chosen a quiet career – reading, teaching, or discussing fine points of Arabic grammar with his students. That he did not follow this course can be ascribed to his teachers, particularly Jibril. Jibril's radical opinions and new ideas excited Usuman and stirred him deeply. Usuman began to think about Islamic reform, together with the suppression of uncanonical practices that he abhorred. From one of Jibril's unidentified writings, Muhammad Bello quotes a passage about religious "mixing," expressing views that Usuman soon made his own:

> As to what is happening in the Sudanic countries, concerning the syncretists, mixers of Islamic acts with actions of unbelief, such are the majority of the kings of those countries and their troops. This is not innovation nor change, nor substitution, nor the adoption of custom. Rather, it is unbelief which hangs over them. For we have never heard that they had abandoned it in any way. And, if we had heard that they had, did they not add to their oppression the light of

fasting and prayer? Did they not mouth [the phrase], "There is no god but God?" Hence the ignorant and unknowing amongst them believed that they were Muslims, which they surely were not.[17]

Under Jibril's influence, the Shehu started preaching about these themes from about the age of twenty. He traveled from his home at Degel (near Sokoto), attacking abuses, often in company with his brother Abdallahi after about 1774. At this period in his life, Usuman was already deeply committed to sufism. At some time in the 1770s, he composed a poem that begins:

> Is there a way by which I can
>   Go quickly to Madina
> To visit the grave of Muhammad al-Hashimi?[18]

Al-Masri has shown that the remainder of this poem – too long for inclusion here – is full of sufi vocabulary and imagery, demonstrating its author's knowledge of and wholehearted involvement in Islamic mysticism. The Shehu's primary attachment tied him to the Qadiri order, then to the Khalwati and Shadhili sufi organizations; ties to all three of them were given to him by Jibril bin 'Umar (see pp. 24–5).[19]

After a decade of the Shehu's itinerant teaching and preaching, the majority of Hausa rulers were well aware of him. At least once, Usuman boldly approached the powerful Habe ruler of Gobir, Bawa Jangwarzo, to explain his views. Writing about this visit later, Abdallahi noted that Usuman dan Fodio had expounded to the Sarkin Gobir "sound Islam, ordered him to keep it, and establish justice within his domains."[20] These exhortations evidently had little effect on a hard-bitten warrior-king who had struggled for years to keep his state together. Bawa's inflexible character is revealed by a Hausa praise poem:

> Iron chieftain, causer of terror
>   Son of Alasan, owner of the drum
> Causer of terror, iron gate of the town . . .
>   Bawa, son of Babari, the son of Alasan
> Forked pole which supports the roof
>   Bawa, it is you who begin to conquer the town
> Son of Alasan, the Wealthy One
>   My brothers, come, let us follow the Wealthy One
> That we may obtain horses to mount.[21]

The tone of seriousness and determination now used by the Shehu was already creating widespread anxiety and apprehension among many Habe rulers, not only Bawa. They reacted in a predictable way. In 1788, the king of Gobir invited Muslim learned men to celebrate an important Islamic festival. On this occasion, it is claimed that Bawa conspired with his courtiers to murder Usuman. This they failed to do, as they were greatly outnumbered by the assembled clerics.[22] Usuman dan Fodio's standing was much enhanced by this episode after news of the plot leaked out. Henceforth, Bawa and his successors treated the Shehu with less liking but more respect; this was particularly so when they heard that the Shehu and his community were stockpiling weapons. Like their masters, the religious personnel attached to the court of Gobir treated Usuman with suspicion and reserve, few of them joining his reform movement or entering his community.

In spite of the hostile attitudes of Bawa and other rulers and their clerical minions, the Shehu was not deterred from preaching. He also continued to write and circulate poetry in Arabic and Fulfulde and to write pamphlets in Arabic, the latter aimed at a different and more literate audience.[23]

About 1789 and again in 1794 Usuman began to have mystical experiences that influenced him permanently. Both these visions and powerful millennial and climatic factors (both discussed on pp. 25–8) probably made him more ready than before to try conclusions with the king of Gobir. Although the Shehu had had earlier mystical experiences, these were of great intensity:

> When I reached the age of thirty-six, God stripped the veil from my sight, the inperfection from my hearing and sense of smell, the flatness from my taste, the knots from my hands, and the heaviness from my feet and body. I saw things far away like near things and heard distant sounds like close ones. I smelt the good smell of the worshipper of God, sweeter than any sweetness, and the bad odor of the sinful man, more repugnant than any putrefaction.[24]

After 1794, another similar experience convinced Usuman dan Fodio that he possessed divine support. Not surprisingly, the founder of the Qadiri brotherhood, 'Abd al-Qadir al-Jilani, figured largely in the Shehu's mystical vision:

> When I reached the age of forty, five months, and some days, God drew me to him. I found there Our Master Muhammad . . . with the companions and prophets and the saints. . . . Then came the Intermediary, the Lord of Men and Jinns, 'Abd al-Qadir al-Jilani, bringing a green robe embroidered with the phrase, "There is no god but God and Muhammad is His Messenger," . . . He tied around me the Sword of God to draw against his foes.[25]

Like Cromwell before Edgehill, Usuman after 1794 seems to have become slowly convinced that a military confrontation with Bawa or one of his successors was inevitable. He could not avoid a clash with Bawa's son Nafata or his grandson Yunfa. Although the Shehu did have some personal contact with Yunfa – whose tutor he was for a short interval and whom he is alleged to have helped to the throne – the political divergences between the Muslims and the Gobir dynasty had become unbridgable. Whereas the more tolerant Bawa had granted considerable freedom to the community, Nafata wanted to regain control of the Muslims and reincorporate them into Gobir. Since approximately 1784, the community had been allowed to wear turbans or veils and to convert non-Muslims to Islam freely. Yet in 1797 or 1798 Nafata decreed a halt to such conversion and prohibited the wearing of any distinctive Muslim styles in dress.[26]

It is generally agreed that the rising tension between Gobir and Usuman dan Fodio was catalyzed by Nafata's decree. Having armed his followers, the Shehu made ready to leave Gobir. He planned to carry out a *hijra* – a migration – like that of the Prophet, on the basis of the Qur'anic injunction," Migrate . . . for God's earth is wide."[27] Although two further visions of 'Abd al-Qadir made Usuman hesitate, he soon transferred his headquarters from Degel to Gudu, north and west of Degel. Gudu was just on, or beyond, the confines of Gobir. Having made his *hijra* – doubtless viewed as an act of rebellion by the king – Usuman grasped its implications clearly. Migration was invariably followed by "holy war," jihad. All the same, the Shehu did not wish to provoke a break with either Nafata or Yunfa. The final breach came through an act undertaken by Abdallahi dan Fodio, who freed some Muslim prisoners from Gobir's control either by force or by a threat of force. Another issue at the time was the aggressive behavior of 'Abd al-Salam, a supporter of the Shehu's at Gimbana. Similar provocation came from the Gobirawa, Yunfa's troops. The result was outright war, for which neither side was fully prepared.[28]

From the date of the *hijra*, 21 February 1804, the jihad lasted about four years. Just before, the Shehu had had still another vision of 'Abd al-Qadir al-Jilani, which seemed to tell him that the time for migration had come. Initially, the Shehu's soldiers had some successes, taking the towns of Matankari and Birnin Konni. Traditionally Birnin Konni was the place where the Shehu's ancestors had settled on their arrival from Futa Toro. In June 1804, there was a major battle at Tabkin Kwotto (Lake Kwotto) near Gudu. The Gobir side was heavily defeated; Yunfa fled. Abdallahi dan Fodio commemorated this clash in verse:

> Then they lined up and
> Beat their drums . . .
> Until we could see each other

   And we came nearer and nearer
They shot at us: we shot at them
   Then they turned their backs and scattered
I saw that their cloud had passed from before
   The Sun of Islam
Which shone by the help of Him
   Who caused the Prophet to conquer the enemy
At Badr, with all the angels assembled
   How many men of note did we throw to the ground?
Axeblades split their heads
   How many armed men were stretched out
By our swords and arrows?[29]

This victory brought the Shehu new allies, fence-sitters who had waited to see how things would turn out before committing themselves. Mostly nomadic Fulani, these recruits were less interested in the objectives of the jihad than in the loot they could obtain. They tended to raid whenever possible. Indispensable as their military services were to Usuman dan Fodio, they were controllable only with difficulty. As the Shehu knew well, they lent little moral luster to the jihad and offered Min little help in other ways.[30]

Although the Shehu was essentially a mystic, a scholar, and a teacher, that did not mean that he was unaware of what war was like or what tactics ought to be used in battle. The following passage yields insight into contemporary military tactics in the Western Sudan. Here the effectiveness of the Fulani cavalry and archers with poisoned arrows is revealed:

> The best scheme is that the infantry should arm themselves with large shields (*diraq*) and carry long lances and javelins sharpened for penetration. They should line up in ranks and group themselves, with their lance ends on the ground. Every man should kneel, so that his left knee touches the soil, holding his round shield (*tars*) before him. Behind stand selected archers who shoot at the enemy's horses and men in chain mail (*duru'*) behind their bowmen. If the enemy attacks the Muslims, the footsoldiers should not budge from their positions: no man should stand up. When the enemy is close, the archers must shoot, the infantry should launch their javelins and shoot their bows in the encounter. They should then run right and left so that the Muslim cavalry can charge from behind them. . . . Concentration is the first thing in victory: the beginning of defeat is dispersion.[31]

By the end of 1804 and the first months of 1805, the Shehu's men moved up the River Rima to attack Alkalawa, the capital of Gobir. At

Tsuntsua, the Muslims were beaten off and lost many men; the Gobir forces won easily. Usuman's men regrouped to attack Birnin Kebbi, which they captured in 1805. In the same year, they gathered more support from Muslim leaders in the big towns of Kano and Katsina, and from Zamfara, the traditional enemy of Gobir. They also won territory in the south and west: Yauri, Borgu, and the Dendi country along the Niger.

At the end of 1805, after a decisive victory at Fafara, the Muslims launched their second attack on Alkalawa, which was prolonged into a siege lasting almost two years. Yunfa died making a last stand in his palace. Gobir resistance was now over, and with it the Habe will to fight had expired. To all practical purposes, the Shehu had won the war.

The Shehu's last remaining political problem concerned a conflict with the state of Bornu, which had become involved in the jihad through military aid it had extended to certain Habe amirs on the eastern fringes of Hausaland. The energetic ruler of Bornu, Muhammad al-Amin al-Kanemi, wrote repeatedly to the Shehu and Muhammad Bello to ask why their Fulani followers were trying to create an internal uprising within Bornu. Much of the correspondence that ensued between him and the Torodbe rulers at the new capital of Sokoto is preserved in Bello's account of the jihad, his *Infaq al-Maysur*. In 1809, the armies of the empire of Sokoto (which had supplanted the former capital at Gwandu) clashed several times with al-Kanemi's forces. Birnin Gazargamu, the chief city of Bornu, was taken three times by the Fulanis, who failed to hold it. By 1810, the jihad had run its course. The contest between Sokoto and Bornu was obviously a draw. Even so, minor raiding went on for many years.[32]

Once the jihad was over, the Shehu only lived for another seven years. He had realized many of his goals, but others had eluded him. He was particularly disappointed by the moral letdown after victory. Disillusioned, he retired to Sifawa, near Sokoto, having divided the state in two. The western part and the former capital, Gwandu, went to his brother Abdallahi; the larger eastern section, including Sokoto, was the portion of his son Muhammad Bello. The Shehu devoted the rest of his life to study, mysticism, and to teaching his many students. He died at Sifawa on 20 April 1817 at the age of sixty-three and was buried at Sokoto.

Writings, Opinions, and Doctrines

Usuman dan Fodio's actions and thought may be divided into several categories. These touch on sufi matters, issues relevant to the jihad (in-

cluding mahdism and climatic factors), and his concerns with theology
and jurisprudence. It is not always easy to separate these themes neatly
for purposes of analysis. To these three categories, it is worth adding
comments about the Shehu's personality and his teaching.

Among his own instructors, Usuman was most heavily influenced by
Jibril bin 'Umar of Agades. Jibril added a hatred of syncretism and an
awareness of significant currents of contemporary Muslim thought to
Usuman's desire to reform local Islam. Through Jibril, Usuman became
a member of the Khalwati sufi order.[33] This was an important connection, although it is doubtful that Usuman was a practicing Khalwati
for very long. During his long sojourn in Egypt – and perhaps in the
cities of Mecca and Madina as well – Jibril had been in touch with the
Khalwatiya. He had joined it in Cairo. There, the order was still much
influenced by Muhammad al-Hifnawi, a Shaykh of the Azhar (d. 1768).
Jibril was actually taught by Hifnawi's pupil Ahmad al-Dardir (d.
1786), one of the most prominent Khalwatis of the day. Like their
predecessor Mustafa al-Bakri (d. 1748), these two men spearheaded
the Khalwati revival in Egypt. The Khalwati order was part of a
broader sufi front. It was both part of a sufi response to the criticisms
of the Wahhabis, and, simultaneously, a reply to European political
encroachment against the lands of Islam. Two such episodes were the
Ottoman-Russian Wars of 1768–74 and 1787–92.[34]

It can be assumed that Jibril told his pupil Usuman of the details of
recent political developments, which he had heard about in Egypt and
the Hijaz, and that he discussed contemporary political trends with
him. Thus the Sokoto leaders were aware of what was going on in the
outer world, even if their information was second-hand. Usuman's zeal
for Islamic reform in Hausaland was certainly strengthened by his
teacher's adherence to the Khalwati brand of reforming sufism. So far
there is no evidence to suggest that Jibril was in any way "commis-
sioned" by his Khalwati mentors in Cairo to launch an Islamic revival
in the Western Sudan, although some authors claim that Jibril tried to
raise a jihad in Agades about 1790.[35] In a remote sense, then, it may
be claimed that the Fulani jihad was an echo of political events in the
Middle East. It is equally certain that political, social, and economic
issues in Hausaland loomed far larger for the reformers.

Through his loyalties to the Qadiri and Khalwati orders, Usuman
espoused a moderate sufi way, adhering to a middle ground in reform
without going to the contemporary extreme of Wahhabism. This is
worth mentioning because certain scholars have mistakenly attributed
the timing and vigor of the Fulani jihad to Wahhabi influence. Usuman's choice, rejecting Wahhabism, was wholly consonant with his
moderation in political and theological matters.[36]

If Usuman remained a practicing Khalwati only briefly, he was firmly attached to the Qadiriya. In his case it was a deep personal belief, unlike al-Hajj 'Umar Tal's ideological commitment to the Tijani doctrine. The profundity of Usuman's attachment to the Qadiriya is revealed by his visions (see p. 20) when he was thirty-six (c. 1789) and forty (c. 1794) and again in 1804, when he commenced the jihad. It is significant that not only the Prophet, but also 'Abd al-Qadir al-Jilani – the founder of the Qadiri order – appeared in his visions of 1794 and 1804. In the first vision, al-Jilani crowned him with a turban and girded him with the "Sword of God, to draw against His enemies." Thus, Usuman was convinced in the Cromwellian sense that he had been chosen by God to carry out a jihad. One of his means for self-mobilization was the Qadiri sufi order. Precisely how he envisaged the use of the order to mobilize others in the jihad is obscure. However, the leaders and probably a portion of the soldiers in the armies included many Qadiris. Usuman was personally identified with the order, and he certainly attended sufi gatherings at intervals, out of conviction and for the sake of organizational morale.

A totally unexpected factor, which functioned in favor of Shehu dan Fodio's movement, was the matter of mahdism. In the Hausa-speaking regions, a large segment of the population had long believed that the Muslim years 1200/1785–6 or 1204/1789–90 would see cataclysmic events. This belief was noted at the same time in the Muslim-populated areas of the Caucasus, where the Imam Mansur was resisting the Russians, and in Algeria, where a mahdi appeared. Usuman certainly believed this himself, with complete sincerity.[37]

In eighteenth-century Hausaland, constant rumors circulated about the coming of a mahdi. Some of Usuman's followers believed that he was the mahdi or, at least, a *mujaddid* (a "renewer" of Islam), who, in theory, would appear about the turn of every Islamic century. At first the Shehu did not discourage these millennial speculations, because of their use to his emerging movement. Later, Usuman was at pains to deny that he was the mahdi. Yet he had become too proficient at politics not to see the benefits that could be gained by orchestrating the mahdi theme. Once the jihad had started, Usuman dispatched delegations to the major Hausa towns (c. 1805) to tell the inhabitants that the advent of the mahdi was imminent and that the jihad would continue until the mahdi manifested himself.[38]

Hence millennial ideas became of much importance for the Fulani movement. In Hausaland, the *hijra* year 1200/1785–6 became the focus of peculiarly intense expectations. "Twelve centuries," it was said, and "twelve caliphs" had come and gone, but the mahdi had not yet shown himself. In the minds of the people, the concept of a savior was intertwined with their hopes for a "renovator" (*mujaddid*). This was no new trend; it had been fermenting in the region for centuries. The era close to the millennium of the *hijra* (1000 H./1591–2) had probably witnessed the episode of Shaykh Mahmud al-Baghdadi. Al-Baghdadi "showed proofs of spiritual power . . . his companions preached that he was the Expected *Mahdi* . . . a great battle took place, between him and the learned men of the land in which he was killed and his following broken up."[39] Even before the sixteenth century, prophecies had been current about the coming of a "renewer." Muhammad Bello preserves the following prophecy, allegedly spoken by a Fulani lady, Umm Hani bint Muhammad al-'Abdusi (d. 1455):

> There will appear in this Sudanic land one of God's saints who will renew religion, revive orthodoxy, and create a religious community. The fortunate will follow him and spread his fame in distant places. . . . One of his signs will be that he will not tend cattle as the Fulani custom is. Whoever lives until that time should follow him.[40]

Further, according to the celebrated Egyptian writer al-Suyuti (d. 1504 A.D.), the thirteenth Muslim century – the year 1200 or 1204 – would witness the coming of the mahdi. Al-Suyuti publicized his opinions in several small treatises, which were eagerly read and discussed throughout the Muslim world, including Hausaland. These pamphlets were known to Usuman dan Fodio, who was in agreement with the truth of al-Suyuti's statements and shared in the general tension and expectation.[41]

Hence an atmosphere of approaching disaster, of political events unrolling against a backdrop of doom, was significant to the jihad. Usuman capitalized on it. Yet if his actions look like opportunism, they were spurred by his utter conviction. An indication of the weight ascribed by the Shehu (and by his audience) to these matters is the number of times he wrote about it. He composed at least ten short treatises about mahdis before, during, and after the jihad. Some of their titles are meaningful: "A Warning to the Community . . . about the Signs of the Hour," or the "Duration of the World." Once the jihad was over, the Shehu soft-pedaled the theme of a savior. In his *Tanbih al-Fahim* of 1808, he wrote, "Based on al-Suyuti's assumptions, what we said repeatedly in our preaching at assemblies was, that the time for the advent of the *Mahdi* had come. Yet, upon investigation, we must admit that we do not know the time with any certainty."[42]

Climatic matters were also of significance. It is very probable that cyclical natural disasters played a role in sustaining the perpetual millennial beliefs of the people of Hausaland and its vicinity. From 1968 to 1974, for example, a six-year drought decimated men and animals in the *sahil,* the transitional zone along the southern fringes of the Sahara. Those who were to survive the drought had to migrate. Similar episodes, some of long duration, were noted in the nineteenth and early twentieth centuries. In 1913 and 1914, a severe two-year drought (called *kakalawa,* "thinness") brought ruin to Bornu and the Hausa states. Another severe drought and famine (*banga banga,* "swollen stomachs") lasted for about a year around 1855. It had been preceded by another in 1847. In the eighteenth century, there had been catastrophic droughts from the end of the 1740s into the 1750s, lasting in some places more than ten years. About 1790, a bad famine and its aftermath brought severe losses in crops and animals to Kano and Bornu and provoked a mass exodus from Agades. Other similar episodes are recorded for the sixteenth and seventeenth centuries, as far back as the 1540s.[43] Not only did these events create severe economic and demographic dislocation; they cannot have failed to cause credulous elements in the population to believe that the end of the world was near – that the catastrophes they had witnessed were the prelude to something far worse. The disasters of the 1740s and 1750s and of 1790 are cases in point; such well-rooted popular attitudes probably brought many adherents to the Shehu's cause.[44]

In the light of such droughts and famines, some of Usuman dan Fodio's poems in Fulfulde take on new significance. Speaking of himself, his own estimate of his mission, and the reality of the coming mahdi, Usuman says some revealing things to a nonliterate public – one that knew no Arabic and could be reached only by word of mouth:

> I have been given the attributes of the Mahdi . . .
>   Because our time is the time of the Mahdi . . .
> Observe that I am not the . . . Mahdi
>   Yet I have been clothed with his mantle
> In keeping with the pattern
>   For every era has a Mahdi, and it is already a
> Thousand years or more . . .
>   Like the wind heralding the raincloud
> So precisely am I, in relation to the Mahdi.[45]

According to Mervyn Hiskett, Usuman dan Fodio

> awaited the Mahdi to unravel the tangle of the times. . . . He saw the world as almost having run its course. Whatever reforms he might introduce . . . they were but a temporary expedient. Mankind had reached the point where it was no longer salvable by human agency. . . . Hope lay only in the ultimate millenium . . . to prepare for the Mahdi was to play his appointed part in the divine order.[46]

Pending the advent of the mahdi, the Shehu had very clear ideas of the new society he hoped to usher into existence. It is clear that he foresaw – as did many of his followers – some sort of new Islamic Golden Age, harking back to the time of the Four Orthodox Caliphs in the seventh century A.D. His vision of this remote period was quite untroubled by any awareness of irreversible historical change. Usuman assumed that, under the right circumstances, this remote Islamic past might be reconstituted. It has been suggested that his views on this point were based on his reading of certain post-Abbasid writers who held these opinions.[47] In any case, Usuman dan Fodio saw his own Hausa-Fulani society as a most imperfect replica of that distant vision. In his writing, there occasionally emerges the voice of an exasperated intellectual irritated by the unrewarding gyrations of contemporary semi-Muslims of northern Nigeria. It is expressed more than once in his descriptions (sometimes of great ethnographic interest) of the syncretic doings of the inhabitants.

Among the real culprits, in the Shehu's opinion, who distorted local Islam into a travesty of the real thing, were diviners, spell-mongers, hawkers of talismans, and purveyors of other sorts of dubious magic. Another category of dangerous individuals, having a slightly higher level of instruction and a smattering of theological education, were able to read texts of Maliki law but deliberately misconstrued its essential points. These were the "venal mallams" so often slated by the Shehu, Abdallahi, and Muhammad Bello. Attacking the first sort of pseudo-Muslim, Usuman condemns "mixers" who dabble in forbidden things:

> Among those syncretists who claim that they are Muslims and carry out the practices of Islam . . . [are those] who worship trees by sacrifices to them, make offerings, and daub them with dough. They are unbelievers. . . . [There are others] who claim that they possess knowledge of the Unseen through written magic or by sand-writing, from the positions of the stars, or the language of the birds and their movements. . . . There are persons who place cotton and wool on stones, along the roads, under trees, or at a crossroads. . . . Those who practice black magic [try] to separate those who love each other, or husband and wife: all of that is unbelief.[48]

Elsewhere, the Shehu specifically warns against the use of the current styles in black magic: "O my brothers, do not employ black magic, such as talismans or incantations, or letters the meanings of which are unknown, or books with the name of God, the *Qur'an*, of names of the prophets, for the sake of love or hatred."[49]

The "venal mallams" and the magical practitioners merged into another culpable group – the quietists, so often attacked by the Shehu. If the "venal mallams" were opportunists who openly sold themselves and their "knowledge" to kings so as to gain a livelihood, the quietists were compromisers who desired to prolong their comfortable existences as court counselors. Like the others their attitude was one as old as Islam in West Africa. When Islam was the religion of a minority, it was natural that they should be forced into such a role. Later, when a larger proportion of the population had become Muslim, Usuman accused them of abandoning whatever vision of a better and more progressive society they might have had for the sake of material comforts. The Shehu believed that they should have long since dropped their passivity and assumed more militant attitudes, like his own, so as to play a more constructive social function. Usuman was convinced that these mallams were duty-bound to urge on their sponsoring rulers a different, more "orthodox" Islamic style. By failing to criticize openly, they condoned serious social abuses. Of course, Usuman's view overlooked the political reality of mixed Muslim and pagan states. In such cases the Habe rulers were the heads of two different religious systems, indeed different value systems, which looked in opposite directions. Gobir was a state of exactly this kind.

Right from his twenties, Usuman had pursued his attacks on such dubious local governments, when he traveled from Degel with his brother Abdallahi to Zamfara, Kebbi, and throughout Gobir. At that time, he had tilted verbally at obvious social evils, invariably on religious grounds. What these were had already been indicated by Jibril b. 'Umar, under whose somewhat puritanical influence Usuman and his brother had come by this time:

> That is abandonment of the Holy Law
>   Nakedness with women, and the mixing which goes on
> Swindling the orphan, taking more than four wives
>   Is similar, like taking women in raids –
> An imitation of the people of the Age of Ignorance
>   Likewise making improper changes in the laws
> Without guidance from prominent men of religion
>   That is an imitation of their ignorant ancestors –
> Make no mistake.[50]

Later, the Shehu denounced the same abuses in his pamphlets. Particularly offensive to him was what he deemed to be deliberate and flagrant perversion of Islamic government by rulers who called themselves Muslims. Usuman accused them of perpetual oppression and extortion against their own subjects. He claimed that they appointed corrupt judges. The kings themselves took bribes and enforced un-

canonical taxation. Too often, they merely confiscated their subjects'
money and property. Sometimes they enslaved Muslims. That freeborn Muslims could not be enslaved was a basic principle of Islamic
law. It was his emphasis on such issues that attracted his first followers
to the Shehu. From Usuman's continuing attacks on such problems,
one can only conclude that they were both real and widespread.

Thomas Hodgkin has summed up the administrative changes actually made by the Shehu once he had won the jihad – changes indicating what he wished to substitute for the old Habe system he despised:

> As regards the structure of the [Sokoto] Caliphate, the Shehu be-
> lieved in and attempted to establish, an essentially simple, nonex-
> ploitative type of system. His views on the subject are set out in
> *Bayan wujub al-Hijra* . . . and elsewhere. The bureaucracy should
> be limited to a loyal and honest vizier, judges, a chief of police, and
> a collector of taxes. Local administration should be in the hands of
> governors [amirs] . . . drawn from the scholarly class, selected for
> their learning, piety, integrity, and sense of justice. . . . The *Amirs*
> were in most cases scholars and probably all except one [Ya'qub in
> Bauchi] Fulani. The geographical scale of the Caliphate combined
> with the principle of delegation [*tafwid*] meant that individual
> *amirs* enjoyed considerable power, so that . . . the new Fulani
> *Amir* might be said to be the old Hausa *Sarki* writ large.[51]

Mervyn Hiskett suggests that a conflict between sedentary Hausa
cultivators and encroaching Fulani pastoralists may have played an
underlying but significant role in the jihad. Also, it probably contributed to the governmental overturn of which Hodgkin speaks. If
both ethnic groups coveted limited areas of good land – the one for
grazing, the other for agriculture – then the traditional hospitality extended by Habe chiefs to migratory Fulani and their animals may have
been stretched to the breaking point. When the jihad started, many
leading Fulani personalities joined the Shehu's forces to attack the
existing Habe amirates. Later, some of these leaders were appointed
as new amirs in the same places. Hiskett supplies evidence of such
events at Zaberma in northern Hausaland and at Hadejia between
Kano and Bornu. This latent conflict, he claims, may have been accelerated by the unscrupulousness of Habe chiefs who on occasion enslaved both Fulanis and freeborn Muslims. At the time, they may have
been aided by access to superior imported firearms from Europe.[52]
Whether these muskets came into Hausaland from the coasts or were
brought in via the Saharan routes is uncertain.

Various theological ideas and currents were interwoven with the
Shehu's political acts. To understand this side to the jihad, some dis-

cussion of Usuman's intellectual matrix may be useful. His espousal of a moderate, reforming sufism has already been discussed. In addition, his admiration for Muhammad al-Maghili and attachment to the Kunta *shaykhs* of the Azawad region near Timbuktu deserves comment.

To justify the jihad, Usuman looked beyond purely legal matters to historical precedents. Locally, the situation in the Niger Valley kingdom of Songhay under Sonni 'Ali (King of Songhay, c. 1464-93) was clearly analogous to his own. Sonni 'Ali wanted to maintain a political balance within his state between Muslims and non-Muslims. He tried to rule without relinquishing all control to the Muslim clerical class. Thus his motives in dealing with Muslim militants resembled those of Bawa Jangwarzo of Gobir. On his overthrow in 1493, Sonni 'Ali was replaced by a Muslim ruler, Askiya Muhammad. In his entourage, the Askiya had an Algerian Muslim adviser, Muhammad al-Maghili (d. 1504). In his dialogues about Islam with the Askiya, al-Maghili explained at great length and detail that islamization had to be complete, eschewing accommodation or compromise with local cults. Al-Maghili denounced any such accommodation as a travesty of Islam.[53]

Because of al-Maghili's unyielding attitudes over these points and because the doings of Sonni 'Ali were so similar to the actions of Bawa, Nafata, and Yunfa of Gobir, al-Maghili's books were read constantly by the Shehu, his son, and his brother. Al-Maghili became one of their favorite authors. His writings were scrutinized by the Shehu for helpful precedents and suggestions. In addition to his writings, al-Maghili had introduced members of the Kunta clan of Timbuktu to the Qadiri brotherhood. One of Usuman's own ties to the Qadiriya order came through al-Maghili and the Kuntas. Finally, al-Maghili had openly and consistently attacked "false men of learning" – those "venal mallams" and badly educated, self-serving clerics who supported Bawa and his like.

Usuman dan Fodio's attachment to the Qadiriya, his devotion to the principles enunciated by al-Maghili, and his zeal for reform were reinforced by his ties to the Kunta *shaykhs*. This clerical dynasty, established in the Azawad district adjoining Timbuktu, was certainly one of the most significant groups of Qadiri intellectuals and leaders in the entire western Sudan. One of the Kuntas, Sidi al-Mukhtar (1729–1811), who in 1757 took over leadership of his clan, created nothing less than a great spiritual empire in the Sahara.[54] He had an unequaled reputation for sanctity and for remarkable religious powers. For this reason, his influence was soon felt over a huge area, from Ahir in the eastern *sahil* through the Tuareg lands to the Niger and the Senegal basins and north toward the Wadi Dra'a on the borders of Morocco. Sidi al-Mukhtar al-Kunti, it was rumored, could fly through the air, raise the dead, move instantly over vast spaces, comprehend the "speech" of solids, see superhuman distances, find lost objects, and aim deadly imprecations at long range. Finally, he was celebrated as a skilled rainmaker, a matter of much moment in those drought-prone regions.[55]

Like Jibril bin 'Umar and the Khalwatiya, al-Kunti had a great impact on Usuman and his circle. They saw themselves as his spiritual, if not his political, vassals. Al-Kunti sent several emissaries to obtain news of the progress of the jihad and lent the Shehu firm moral support. Though geography may have hindered close relations, they were cordial, as the following lines by Usuman show:

> Take my greetings to al-Mukhtar
>   Our Illumination in these regions
> Tell him to store up good things
>   In This World and the Next
> Alive or in spiritual form,
>   Give him, O Sharif, our salutations.[56]

Muhammad Bello also describes Sidi al-Mukhtar al-Kunti as a "learned jurist, a sufi traditionalist, a pious saint, the Pivot, Intermediary, and Familiar of God, famous east and west . . . the last of the sufi *Imams*."[57] That Bello should heap such fulsome praise on al-Mukhtar – terminology he normally reserved for his father – testifies to his affection for and unlimited admiration of this distant Qadiri personality. It has been suggested that al-Mukhtar, wielding his undoubted influence, had a strong impact on the timing and certain of the theological aspects of the jihad, as he did with other jihads in the Western Sudan. The evidence is suggestive rather than compelling, as it concerns influences of an intangible spiritual kind.

If Usuman dan Fodio was influenced by Jibril bin 'Umar, al-Maghili, and Sidi al-Mukhtar, he was also swayed by the medieval theologian al-Ghazali (d. 1111), as he says himself.[58] He was also a continual reader of al-Sha'rani, a sixteenth-century Egyptian theologian and mystic (d. 1565). A number of theological and legal views held by Usuman coincide with the opinions of these scholars.[59] Aside from the position and role of Muslim clerics, the issues of the *mujaddid* and the mahdi (discussed briefly above), the concept of migration (*hijra*), and the debate over the liberal or conservative interpretation of Islamic law (*taqlid* vs. *ijtihad*) merit brief discussion.

The Shehu gave a full treatment to the migration issue in a long treatise completed in 1806, his *Bayan wujub al-Hijra* ("Explanation of the Need for Migration"). Here he skillfully elaborates arguments from the *Qur'an* and tradition about the necessity of leaving an "unbelieving country" for a Muslim-controlled area. Real Muslims must take this obligation seriously:

> And what we have been saying from the beginning of this chapter is – that migration from the land of unbelief is imperative for all Muslims, with only two exceptions . . . the physically incapacitated and those who are [actually] hindered from departing. . . . O my brothers, migration is incumbent upon you from the land of unbelief to the Land of Islam, so that you may gain Paradise.[60]

In his *Bayan*, he makes it clear that jihad should follow migration in quick succession. He also differentiates between who is and is not a Muslim. Those who live within the "Land of Islam" are Muslims, particularly if their ruler is also a Muslim. From a place having a non-Muslim ruler, a *hijra* must soon begin. The need for a *hijra* is linked by the Shehu to allegiance rendered by the Muslim community to an imam or caliph, a religious and political head of state. Having once pledged their loyalty to such a man, the community must subsequently follow his orders. If need be, it must make war on "unbelieving rulers." Muslims who choose to stay behind in enemy territory are indistinguishable from non-Muslims.[61]

There is little original here. What is new and remarkable is Usuman's rigor and consistency in the application of concepts he took from extant legal sources. He demonstrates a militant yet logical and carefully legalistic attitude, most of it based on familiar Maliki texts. He then applies these opinions to Gobir and other Habe states. Later in the nineteenth century, this same *hijra* argument, similarly expressed, became a standard doctrine for Muslim leaders in Africa (and elsewhere) when threatened by European colonial encroachments. It was so used by the Algerian amir 'Abd al-Qadir (see Chapter 2), by the Mauritanian leader Ma' al-'Aynayn (see Chapter 5), and by Muhammad 'Abdallah Hasan in Somalia (see Chapter 7), with little change. Usuman dan Fodio deserves credit as the first Muslim African thinker to elaborate this theme in coherent fashion.

Although it sounds dry and academic, a debate raged in Hausaland (c. 1800) between some intellectuals who favored blind imitation of earlier scholars in theological and legal practice and others who advocated new attitudes of more liberal and adventurous personal interpretations. The first attitude is called *taqlid,* the contrary, *ijtihad.* Surprisingly, this debate, often acrimonious, had considerable political relevance.[62] By the end of the eighteenth century a liberal current was flowing from the Middle East, aimed at a loosening of old intellectual structures and interpretations within Sunni Islam. In this field, matters had moved little over several centuries past. Usuman was in sympathy with the new current. Further, his opponents, whether quietists or "venal mallams" or many of those he defined as "pseudo-Muslims," were vociferously in favor of *taqlid*. These conservative attitudes discouraged latitude in interpretation, so vital as underpinning for the Shehu's opinions about political and legal issues. Out of logical consistency, Usuman eventually abandoned *taqlid*, invariably so favorable to the status quo. As he grew more mature, he saw the merits of the liberal position, even though he hoped that "imitators" in law and theology might be inspired to do better. In his *Hisn al-Afham* (1810), the Shehu quotes verses by another Fulani theologian:

> The majority of practitioners of *taqlid*
> Shall they not be saved on Judgment Day?
> When one dreads the blade and the earthquake
> Amid the rending catastrophes to come?[63]

Later, Usuman dan Fodio moved further to the juridical left, breaking through the barriers of both blind imitation and liberal interpretation. He seems to suggest the abolition of the usual demarcation lines between Sunni schools of law in favor of a uniform code for all Sunni Muslims. In one late composition, he asks:

> Whatever came from Muhammad was not known as a "school of law": it was called His Divine Law. . . . Does God in His Book or His Prophet in the *Sunna* make it necessary to rely on a single law school or one liberal interpreter (*mujtahid*) in particular? We have not heard of a single person among the learned men of the past who directed anyone to follow a specific school of law.[64]

If al-Sha'rani had already enunciated several of these points, the Shehu reformulated them and drew important inferences from them. About fifty years after the Shehu's death, the compilers of a new Ottoman law code (the *Mecelle* of 1870) assembled just such a pragmatic compilation of legal decisions, selected from all relevant schools.[65]

An issue of lesser significance than jihad or migration or how to interpret Islamic law deserves mention because of the large amount of time and energy the Shehu and his associates spent writing or discussing it. This is the question of sin, and its corollary, apostasy from Islam. Again, these matters are closely connected to the Shehu's definition of *Muslim* and to the questions of *hijra* and "holy war." In his *Shifa' al-Ghalil*, the Shehu had criticized his old master Jibril for excessive zeal – Jibril had said that a Muslim who committed "gross sins" was no longer a Muslim. Usuman rejected this view as too radical. It is indeed reminiscent of the views of the Kharijites in early Islam, which the Shehu points out. It may reflect some old residual Kharijite opinions that crossed the Sahara to West Africa. Here again, the Shehu showed his typical moderation. He did, however, exploit this issue against the Habe rulers.[66] As Hiskett says, he was "searching for legal justifications . . . for what were in the end subjective decisions."[67]

Something about Usuman dan Fodio as a man, as a scholar and teacher, and as a spiritual leader remains to be said. Much of this information comes from his son Muhammad Bello. Despite Bello's natural admiration, his account seems to ring true. Bello describes his father's nocturnal teaching sessions as follows:

> Every Thursday night, he came out to preach to the people, about what they wanted to hear. Many people came to these gatherings – only God knows their number. On other nights, he came out after the evening prayers to instill knowledge and explain strange things. After the afternoon prayers, he came out to teach, to comment on the *Qur'an*, to instruct in law, tradition, or Sufism.[68]

Here Bello comments on his father's style in public:

> I used to watch him when he came out to the people. . . . When he arrived at a gathering, he greeted them, so that all present could hear him. When he went up to his chair, he saluted all of them three times in a cheerful way, with a relaxed expression. . . . He never became irritated or showed resentment or boredom, although some of those present exhibited bad manners. . . . He never embarassed any person who attended, neither important *shaykhs* nor envious men of learning.[69]

Finally, Bello sums up the Shehu's achievements:

> Know that he grew up modestly, in a godly manner, possessing good traits . . . in the end attaining a high position. People came to him from East and West. He instructed the learned class and raised the banner of religion, reviving the *Sunna* and extinguishing blameworthy innovation. . . . [He] was an upholder of the Right, a man of sound vision, practised in the teaching of enigmatic things, the carrier of the flag of study . . . greatly liked by high and low, the Renewer (*mujaddid*) of the turn of this [Muslim] century, an eloquent speaker and accomplished poet.[70]

An ultimate tribute to his success was that Usuman found many imitators throughout West Africa. One of them was Ahmadu Seku of Masina; another was al-Hajj 'Umar Tal (see Chapter 3).

Opposition to French Colonialism in Algeria: 'Abd al-Qadir, His Predecessors and Rivals

The career of the Algerian amir 'Abd al-Qadir offers both remarkable similarities and striking contrasts to the life of Usuman dan Fodio (Chapter 1). The most obvious difference arises from the arrival in Algeria of European invaders – Frenchmen – which led to a protracted colonial war, 1830–47. Although there was no millennial dimension to the aristocratic 'Abd al-Qadir's movement, many of his forerunners and rivals in Algeria did not hesitate to spread millennial ideas among the people. Almost certainly, they set in motion disturbing prophecies, many of which predicted dire events after the turn of the thirteenth Muslim century (1785). In Algeria and elsewhere in North Africa, the millennial hopes of the population were constantly renewed by fears of pestilence, famine, infestation by locusts, and earthquake. Parallel events also occurred in Hausaland.

Like Usuman dan Fodio, Amir 'Abd al-Qadir wrote about the need for Muslims to migrate (*hijra*) from regions under the military occupation or political control of "unbelievers" and also about the necessity of a "holy war" (*jihad*) against them. Here the amir had the aid – rather, the occasional help – of a branch of the Qadiri order (the Mukhtariya) traditionally directed by a member of his own family. Like some other branches of the Qadiri order, the Mukhtariya was at least touched by the sufi revival in the east during the end of the eighteenth century. On the pilgrimage, 'Abd al-Qadir himself encountered a minor yet significant figure in the "new wave" of Islamic mysticism and reform, the Naqshbandi Shaykh Khalid of Shahrazur.[1]

Usuman dan Fodio had never been concerned with the doings of other brotherhoods; but 'Abd al-Qadir and his Qadiri following had to battle the Tijanis of 'Ayn Madi in southwestern Algeria (for discussion of another branch of the Tijanis, see Chapter 3). Unfortunately for the hopes of many Algerian Muslim moderates who wanted interbrotherhood cooperation so as to concert resistance to France, the Tijanis and Qadiris split. This division had also been fostered by the Ottoman Turks before they left Algeria in 1830. The political gulf between Tijanis and Qadiris proved too wide to bridge. The amir, who was seen as the leader of resistance to French colonial encroachment, had his task rendered still more difficult by the millennial ambitions of such

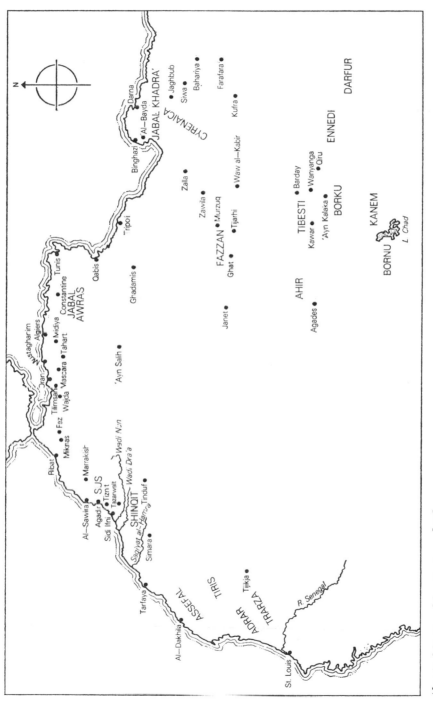

Algeria, Morocco, Mauritania, and Libya

minor leaders as Bu Ma'aza and the Tayyibiya, who might have made
common cause with him. They failed to do this, or they waited until
it was too late for any effective opposition.

Amir 'Abd al-Qadir had further difficulties with the Ottoman Turks.
The former holders of Algerian overrule distrusted 'Abd al-Qadir –
probably because of an incident that had involved his father. Hence
the Ottomans shortsightedly supported the hopeless cause of their
faithful Bey, Ahmad of Constantine. Because of Tijani opposition and
Turkish distrust, compounded by his own errors, the amir failed to
unite any sizable part of Algerian Muslim society for long. The result
of his failure was the breakdown of Muslim efforts to oppose France.
A partial collapse of Algerian Muslim society and culture ensued.
What armed opposition to France did exist was driven from the settled
north of Algeria into the southern deserts. Here isolated risings and
episodes of militant opposition to colonial rule continued for a long
period – as late as 1904 – despite French military efforts to suppress
the rebels and stifle leaks of information about the revolts.[2]

In the history of nineteenth-century Algeria, the event that dwarfs all
others is the French invasion of 1830. The history of this invasion is
well known; it was triggered by the celebrated "flywhisk incident,"
when the last Turkish dey, Hüseyin, struck the French consul, Deval.
It continued with a French landing at Sidi Faraj near Algiers in June
1830, and it terminated with a series of bloody battles ending in the
capture of Algiers itself a month later.[3]

The pretext for the conquest was a business affair of some Jewish
merchants of Algiers. They made deliveries of grain to France under
the Directory, for which they were not paid. The Dey himself had lent
money to these merchants and had repeatedly pressed the French for
repayment. During a tense audience in April 1827, the Dey struck the
French consul across the face with his flywhisk. The negotiations that
followed with France failed and were succeeded by a blockade after a
French truce vessel was mistakenly fired upon.[4]

At one point, France considered enlisting the services of Muhammad
'Ali, the Pasha of Egypt, to conquer the Maghrib; but the Polignac
ministry rejected this plan in favor of a military expedition against
Algiers. Essentially, this decision was a matter of internal French
politics. A successful invasion and capture of Algiers would lend the
monarchy of Charles X a luster it needed badly; the opposition would
be silenced, and an impressive victory would help to win a forthcoming election. Within France, the largest group interested in such
a conquest was made up of the capitalists and businessmen of Marseille, who believed that a takeover of Algeria would be to their
advantage. When Algiers was taken by the French on 5 July 1830, the

Bourbon monarchy had already collapsed. The new government found itself embarrassed by a colonial enterprise for which it had made no preparations, which it wanted to break off, in a country about which it knew virtually nothing.[5]

What would France do with its new acquisition? A number of alternatives stood open. It could abandon the enterprise and return Algeria to Ottoman rule. It could hand it over to the local Muslims, or other European countries might be invited to share in it. Alternatively, France could continue to hold it. In the latter case, if Algeria were to be a permanent possession, how would the French establish themselves in the land?

Eventually, French business and settler interests had the last word; the July Monarchy under Louis Philippe decided to retain Algeria and colonize it. After an interval, large numbers of European settlers began to arrive. They took over much of the desirable agricultural land adjoining the big cities and major ports, where French rule was reinforced by a military presence. Tension began to grow between the French military and settlers on the one hand and Algerian Muslims on the other. Sporadic fighting broke out. After nearly four years of hesitation (c. 1834), France decided to undertake a full-scale conquest of Algeria. This decision was made in the light of national pride, desires for economic expansion, and hopes for decisive military conquest.[6]

Local opposition became manifest as the tempo of French encroachment increased. Fighting became relentless and ferocious. This was not only so because of the loss of lands and homes by Muslims, but because of the huge ethnic, cultural, and religious gulf separating the two sides. In spite of the guerrilla aspect of the warfare between the French and Algerians, the outcome could be predicted. The French would win in the end because of their technological superiority. By 1847, after thirteen years of campaigning (broken by a truce from 1837 to 1839), the back of Algerian resistance seemed broken with the defeat and surrender of Amir 'Abd al-Qadir. Yet the French spent huge sums in Algeria; they were forced to increase their armies to large dimensions, and they had to fight a costly minor conflict with Morocco. French casualties were sometimes heavy. French hopes for a quick conquest were illusory, too. Intermittent warfare and resistance to the conquerors continued on for many years, until 1904. By this time, the French had crushed a revolt by the Kabyles of eastern Algeria in 1871 and exiled its leaders to New Caledonia (this revolt had at least the moral support of the Ottoman Turks). They had also suppressed many local uprisings in the south and west. One of these, the revolt of the Awlad Sidi Shaykh, went on from 1864 to 1902, when it was "pacified." Even then, one of its leaders, Bu 'Imama, went on fighting until 1904.[7] Most of the larger risings (which were fairly frequent in the Algerian-Moroccan border regions) were put down by the middle 1880s. The size and dimensions of the outbreaks lessened, but armed opposition never entirely stopped. It was resumed again by the Algerians on a country-wide scale in 1954, and it was successfully concluded by them. In 1962, the French left the country.

Looking at the earlier phases of local opposition to French colonial enterprise in Algeria, French and other European historians (with some exceptions) have focused their attention on the activities of the colonizers in the land. Only more recently, with the growth of Algerian nationalist historiography, have Muslim motivations, forces, and leaders been given the scrutiny they deserve. This is also true of the religious considerations that gave external motivation to the first Algerian resistance. A majority of nineteenth-century Algerians saw their conflict with France in terms of defense of their religion and culture, but never in modern nationalist terms. Mass nationalism, in the contemporary sense, was a development that only came to Algeria after 1900.

It is worth considering for a moment the way in which the Algerian religious situation of 1830 had come into being. Because of the unique religious circumstances in North Africa after around 1300, Islamic societies there followed a different line of development from those of eastern Islam. In the Maghrib, political movements led by charismatic figures and supported by groups of mystics came to be of great significance. These rapidly became mass movements. Soon nearly every man in the land belonged to some sufi organization or other. This fact had important political implications.[8]

By 1500, from end to end of the Maghrib, both in the cities and the countryside, there existed widespread networks of sufi centers. Here dead saints under their whitewashed cupolas attracted visitors and pilgrims by their *baraka* (spiritual powers). At these *zawiyas*, their live descendants arbitrated contests over water rights, inheritances or grazing lands. Alternatively, they might operate schools in the cities or in rural places, either for elementary education, or occasionally to teach advanced students in the Islamic sciences or Maliki law. Many of these sufi centers attracted adherents and drew students from a wide area. Here and there existed dynasties of sufi *shaykhs* who maintained their ties to certain *zawiyas* for generations. A *zawiya* of this sort was that of the family of 'Abd al-Qadir near Mascara (al-Mu'askar) in western Algeria, as will be shown below in more detail.

Through their leadership, standing, and authority many such *shaykhs* of North African sufi centers were propelled into politics. This was another striking difference between them and many *zawiyas* of eastern mystics. In the East many – but not all – sufis were concerned with moral guidance, psychological or even rudimentary medical assistance, or the organization of ecstatic rites (dhikrs or hadras) for their members. A landmark often cited by historians of the Maghrib for the emergence of such sufis into politics is the Maraboutic Crisis at the end of the fifteenth century. At this time, the political leadership of the Marinids and the Banu Wattas sultans failed before a Spanish and Portuguese invasion. The agitated population turned to the only other alternative leadership available, that of the sufi shaykhs and marabouts (murabits) and the leaders of brotherhoods. These men soon found themselves assuming ambitious political roles or undertaking serious military tasks. In Morocco after 1500 two dynasties of this sort emerged in turn, the Sa'dis and the Filalis. They claimed to be descendants of the Prophet (sharifs) and entered the battleground of politics directly from their zawiyas.[9]

In Algeria and in the borderlands between Algeria and Morocco, the identical role played by certain Moroccan sufis was assumed by the Ottoman Turks. Turkey had first established herself in Algeria in 1516. Within a few decades, she exerted firm control over the Algerian coastline as far west as the Tilimsan-Wajda region. Inland, the Ottomans were powerful as far as 300 miles south of the Mediterranean coast. As long as the Muslim populations of these regions remained convinced that the Turks were acting the part of "champions of Islam" – that the Turks were holding the hostile Spanish Christians at arm's length – the local sufis of Tilimsan and Oran (Wahran) acquiesced and cooperated with the superior Ottoman power, exercised by pashas, deys, beys, and through their local military forces, janissaries, or sipahis.[10]

Only with Ottoman military decline, which became visible by the end of the seventeenth century, did Algerian sufis and other segments of the population begin to have second thoughts about the political utility of Turks in their country.[11] The resident Turks (and their children by Algerian mothers known as the kuloğlular, quloghlis, or kuroughlis) had become a special privileged class, sometimes exacting and tyrannical. Moreover, they were beginning to fail in the duty for which they had first been welcome in Algeria – hindering European Christian interference there. By 1700, many Algerians had come to think that bad Turkish government, compounded by crushing taxation (a large part of which went to Istanbul) was too high a political price to pay. As yet there was no open revolt; for example, in 1749, a Spanish expedition under O'Reilly landed near Oran. It was driven off with difficulty by the Bey of the city in alliance with certain prominent families of the neighborhood. One participant was Amir

'Abd al-Qadir's great-grandfather, who was killed in the fighting.[12] This episode underscored growing Ottoman inefficiency.

At the same time that Turkish military weakness was becoming patent – during the reign of Sultan Ahmad III (1703–36) – the Turkish regency at Algiers discovered that its seaborne jihad, its piratical activities and corsairing, were increasingly counterproductive. They misfired frequently and attracted European reprisals, sometimes on an impressive scale. To make up the revenue lost by failing captures at sea, the dey and his subordinates tried to obtain more money by the only practical method they knew – stepping up the taxation in some places and ordering new tax levies in others (often regions that had not been taxed before or had been dealt with very lightly).[13]

Hence by 1800, much of the population of Algeria, rural or urban, no longer appreciated the Ottoman presence in the country. Turkish tax-collecting drives (organized like small-scale military expeditions) alienated the country people. In the towns, the obnoxious behavior of Turkish troops was equally offensive.[14] Politically, the non-Turkish Muslims in Algeria began to grope toward their earlier, traditional leaders – the sufis and the *shaykhs* of *zawiyas*. From these quarters, they hoped to glimpse some signs of leadership, to hear of some method for ejecting the burdensome Turks from the country. This is not to suggest that they were opposed to them on any nationalistic grounds but merely that they found their fellow Muslims increasingly oppressive.

Soon after 1800, a series of uprisings broke out in western Algeria. From the degree of violence they evidenced and from the broad areas concerned they testify eloquently to a considerable degree of social disturbance. Some of the blame for this unrest may be laid to the irritation of the populace at the Ottoman Turks, but other factors were at work also. Inflation was one, and others were food shortages, invasions of locusts, and frequent epidemics of bubonic plague brought into the country by returning pilgrims from the Hijaz. Famines of a local nature frequently took place. Further, it seems quite likely that the Moroccan government wanted to probe the military readiness of the Algerian Turks; their weakness was known in the sharifian state. Might this not be the moment to expel them from western Algeria? Moreover, there was a serious earthquake at Oran at the end of the 1790s.[15] Bubonic plague was made worse by occasional outbreaks of smallpox; other issues that exacerbated an already serious situation were rising prices of staple foods and confused internal migrations of starving people. All of this had severe political and demographic repercussions. The population in many parts of Algeria was decimated, and the survivors began to entertain millennial hopes and expectations. Prophecies (doubtless of Moroccan inspiration) about the expulsion of the Turks from the Maghrib began to circulate among the people.[16] As in Hausaland and in the Caucasus, the approaching Muslim year 1200/1785–6 was believed by many to herald profound, perhaps apocalyptic, change.

Against this somber background of war, pestilence, and profound social disturbance, two rebels appeared – al-Hajj Muhammad al-Ahrash and Muhammad ibn Sharif. They both emerged in diffcrent parts of the country at the same time and are said to have belonged to the same brotherhood, the Darqawa or Darqawiya.[17] Largely, their movements were based on local resentment of Ottoman authority, with a millennial component (and perhaps clandestine Moroccan aid) thrown in. Assistance from Tunisia may also have been a factor. Significantly, these uprisings prefigure the activities of Amir 'Abd al-Qadir and demonstrate many factors in common with his movement. Some of the same tribes who later supported him participated in them, and they took place in the same or adjoining areas. Their timing, at the start of the thirteenth Islamic century, certainly made them appear as the forerunners of new things to the Algerian public, large segments of which were now much moved by eschatological symbolism.

Al-Hajj Muhammad al-Ahrash (otherwise known as "Bu Dali") was a Moroccan who went to the Hijaz on pilgrimage.[18] On his return (c. 1799) from the East, he stopped in Egypt, at that moment under attack by the French. He gathered a force of Tunisians and other Maghribis – of whom there was a large colony in late eighteenth-century Cairo – to fight the invaders. Herc Bu Dali won fame for his personal gallantry. After leaving Egypt, Bu Dali stopped at Tunis, making the acquaintance of the Bey, Abu Muhammad Hammuda Pasha. According to the *Tuhfat al-za'ir*, the Bey entrusted him with the role of fomenting an insurrection against the Ottoman Bey of Constantine and gave him money for that purpose. So far the evidence is insufficient to suggest that Hammuda Pasha's scheme fit into any simultaneous Moroccan plan for western Algeria. Yet the hostility of both the eastern and western neighbors of the Turkish Regency to the Ottomans is well known.[19]

In provoking a rising, Bu Dali's Darqawi connections were significant. He also called himself *Sahib al-Waqt*, "Master of the Time," hinting that he might be a mahdi or at least the precursor of a mahdi. He was also able to take advantage of the anti-Turkish mood of the people, at the same time playing on their millennial expectations. He soon won resounding military successes. Hundreds of Kabyle tribesmen joined his forces. About 1218/1803–4, Bu Dali ambushed the incautious Bey of Constantine and massacred his army in a narrow defile. Despite the rage of the Dey at Algiers over this disaster, which was followed by intensified Ottoman military activity against him, Bu Dali was able to hold out in the mountains of eastern Algeria for a long time. Much of that region was in perpetual uproar over his raiding and resistance to the Dey in Algiers. However, when the Dey enlisted a *qa'id* who knew the country and led a new army against him, Bu Dali fled westward toward the Oran region, where he joined Muhammad ibn Sharif. At this point, he vanished from history. A number of different versions exist of his final exploits and his flight to Morocco.[20]

Another figure very much like Bu Dali was Muhammad ibn Sharif (whose full name was Abu Muhammad 'Abd al-Qadir ibn al-Sharif al-Falliti), a Kassana Berber from the Wadi'l-'Abd district east and south of Oran.[21] He had studied at the *zawiya* of 'Abd al-Qadir's family at al-Qaytana, and he was personally acquainted with 'Abd al-Qadir's father. On leaving al-Qaytana he went to Fez, where he met the great sufi *shaykh* al-'Arabi al-Darqawi and joined his brotherhood. At this time, al-Darqawi was an important political ally of the sultan of Morocco.[22] As a result of this connection, perhaps, Muhammad ibn Sharif returned in 1217/1802–3 to his own district – among the Kassana, Himyan, and Shafi'i tribes – proclaiming himself the "Expected Mahdi." He obtained quick support from the impoverished local people, who were only too willing to sack and plunder under his leadership when he laid waste to adjoining areas. Informed of Muhammad ibn Sharif's activities, the Bey of Oran raised an army against the rebel. But Muhammad ibn Sharif was too powerful for the Bey, who was heavily defeated by the insurrectionists on the Plain of Gharis (or Eghris) between Mascara and al-Qaytana. The beaten Bey fled to Oran for cover. As they pressed their pursuit, Ibn Sharif's men obtained much booty. Eventually they besieged Oran. A relief army was sent overland from Algiers by the Dey, commanded by 'Ali Agha. Along the route, in the Wadi Shalif, the army was so harassed by hostile tribesmen and fell so short of food and water that it had to turn back to Algiers.[23]

Although the "Mahdi" Muhammad ibn Sharif had been unable to take Oran, he was "recognised by the people from Tilimsan to Midiya (Médéa)." Ibn Sharif stayed in the neighborhood of Oran and Tilimsan until 1226/1811–2, when the Dey of Algiers dispatched another army to the western provinces, commanded this time by the energetic Muhammad Bey al-Muqallish. Using a subtler and more conciliatory policy than his predecessor, Muhammad Bey managed to divide Muhammad ibn Sharif's following and then defeat him. Ibn Sharif fled to Morocco and took refuge with the Banu Yaznasin (Snassen) tribe, where he later died.[24]

In both insurrections, Muhammad ibn Sharif's as well as Bu Dali's, there was great tension between the shaky authority of the Dey at Algiers and the local political forces. In addition, western Algeria just before the rising had been hard hit by natural calamities. It was into this situation that the Darqawiya entered, doubtless preceded by the customary prophetic propaganda. The organization of the new brotherhood may have served, too, as the framework for the revolt of the peasant population, the ra'iya. As there may have been Tunisian and Moroccan influence with Bu Dali, there is more than a hint of Moroccan support behind Muhammad al-Sharif. According to the Moroccan historian al-Nasiri al-Salawi, when Muhammad ibn Sharif took Tilimsan he significantly ordered the khutba (the Friday prayer for the sovereign) to be said in the name of the Sharifian Sultan Sulayman ibn Muhammad.[25] Other, and more immediate causes of which the Moroccans could take advantage were the "bad faith" of the Bey of Oran and his reckless execution of a number of Darqawis – an order that traditionally dressed in rags, despised kings and sultans, and scorned "great men of the world." Finally, the Moroccans were probably considering strategic matters; they may have wanted to test the readiness of the Ottoman defenses near Tilimsan and Oran. This part of the old Ziyanid state had been fought over by the Moroccans and Algerian Turks since at least 1550.[26]

In the southwestern part of Algeria, within the southern part of Oran Beylik, there were still other disturbances going on between 1785 and 1827. These concerned the Tijani brotherhood of 'Ayn Madi and the Ottoman authorities.[27] In these areas, along the fringes of the Sahara and the neighboring oases, there is no evidence that the population had any particular millennial preoccupations. All the same, there was a definite mood of opposition to Turkish methods of collecting tribute and taxes and to their heavy-handed military style. The Tijani order had manifested hostility to the Turks since its foundation in 1781. Sensing this political danger, Muhammad al-Kabir, the Bey of Oran, in 1785 and again in 1788 had sent expeditions to collect taxes and take tribute, hoping to overawe the population of 'Ayn Madi. The Tijani center was just within the confines of his beylik. In 1789, Ahmad al-Tijani, the founder of the order, fearing ruin from the Dey and the government at Algiers, fled 'Ayn Madi for that asylum of Algerian dissidents, Morocco. At Fez, he was welcomed by the sharifian ruler. When their father died in 1815, Tijani's two sons came back to 'Ayn Madi. Very soon the Turks returned also. They made two more forays in 1820 and 1822 against the Tijani center. By now, 'Ayn Madi was well fortified. This fact, and its remoteness from Turkish bases nearer the coast like Titteri and Oran, preserved it from more frequent attack.[28]

Muhammad al-Tijani, the eldest son of Ahmad al-Tijani, was propelled into action by the continued hostility of the local Turkish beys. About 1826 he began to talk openly against the Regency, telling the people of the southwestern districts to "obey him and drop their allegiance to the government."[29] Soon after, Muhammad al-Tijani came to Mascara to seek recruits for future military operations against the Turks. The leaders of the Banu Hashim tribe, many of them Qadiris and close to 'Abd al-Qadir's father, Muhyi al-Din (both were then away on the pilgrimage), agreed with Muhammad al-Tijani to confront the Bey of Oran. The immediate grievance of the Banu Hashim was a dispute over taxes. Hearing of an impending alliance between the Banu Hashim and the Tijanis, the Bey of Oran rightly feared a large-scale uprising. In 1827, the two sides fought on the Plain of Gharis. Before the battle, the Bey had suborned some of the Banu Hashim to desert. When they did, Muhammad al-Tijani and a loyal fraction of the Banu Hashim were defeated. This defection and defeat was most serious. The equivocal behavior of the Banu Hashim effectively prevented any future cooperation between Amir 'Abd al-Qadir and the Tijanis. After 1830 this split worked to the benefit of the French.[30]

Between the Tijani debacle of 1827 and the invasion of 1830, there seem to have been few serious disturbances in Algeria. Perhaps this was a peace of exhaustion. Under Hüseyin Dey (1818–30), the Regency continued in semi-independence, "a sort of republic dominated by the Turkish military elite."[31] However, it is not certain whether the umbilical cord that tied the frequently unpredictable Algerian regime to the home government at Istanbul still functioned. This was the right the deys possessed, to send annual recruiting expeditions into Anatolia, to Izmir or to Istanbul, to enlist replacements for the Algerian Janissary Corps. After Mahmud II's annihilation of the Janissary Corps (1826), it is unclear whether Algerian recruitment campaigns continued within Turkey as they had before. It is possible that the deys obtained troops elsewhere.[32]

In 1830 Algeria was hardly a socially or politically united country. It had real tensions among its social classes, and equally genuine ethnic differences between its local Arabs and Berbers and imported Turks or near-Turks (*Kuloğlular*). There was also a sectarian difference between these two elements, Arabs and Berbers being Malikis and the Turks and *Kuloğlular* being Hanafis. Yet the country still possessed a distinct Muslim culture drawn from its peculiar ethnic blend, a culture that was surprisingly uniform. Nor could the Algerian Regency be described as a "colonial" government, because of its age and prestige and because of its Islamic basis. These cultural and religious factors bridged the gap between the Turkish military élite and other Muslims. The Ottomans had no intention of settling any part of its Anatolian populations in Algeria nor carrying out any intensive or systematic exploitation of Arabs and Berbers there. In many places these two groups had a great deal of autonomy.[33] A significant point brought out by Émerit is the relative efficiency of the educational system and the prevalence of literacy. It was rather high, and compared favorably to contemporary France.[34]

The Algerian economy in 1830 was little different from other Middle Eastern economies of that era. It was mostly based on subsistence agriculture and nomadism. By the time the French arrived Muslim corsairing was virtually dead, like the Christian counter-corsairing and privateering from Malta and some Italian ports, which had helped to keep it alive. Corsairing had moved to Tunis for a short interval before it was finally suppressed there in 1819.[35]

On the appearance of the French, the old spirit of Muslim resistance to a foreign governing class – which was already reviving after 1700 – was turned against the Christian invaders. By 1830, a revival of earlier Algerian Muslim attitudes reminiscent of those of the Moroccans in the fifteenth and sixteenth centuries may be discerned. Encountering yet another foreign conqueror who aimed to impose his rule by force, the Algerian people turned to their traditional leaders, the sufi *shaykhs* and chiefs of *zawiyas*. For a brief interval before they were ground down by the weight of French troops and weapons, these leaders reasserted the control they had relinquished to the Ottoman Turks in the sixteenth century. Apart from Ahmad Bey of Constantine, a holdover from the Ottoman regime who fought the French tenaciously, the most effective, most famous, and certainly most learned leader of the traditional local opposition was Amir 'Abd al-Qadir of Al-Qaytana near Oran.

According to his son Muhammad in the *Tuhfat al-Za'ir*, Amir 'Abd al-Qadir was born on 23 Rajab 1222/25 September 1807 at the family settlement of al-Qaytana on the Wadi al-Hammam ("Pigeon River").[36] This dry river bed meanders through the western end of the Plain of Gharis west of Mascara and finally enters the Mediterranean just east of Oran at a place called al-Maqta' (or La Macta, the scene of a clash between the French and 'Abd al-Qadir in 1835). Al-Qaytana (or La Guetna, as the French called it) is approximately eight miles directly west of Mascara.[37]

The family of 'Abd al-Qadir was both long established and very prominent in western Algeria. They claimed to be of Arab origin, descendants of the Prophet Muhammad through his grandson al-Hasan and then through Idris ibn 'Abdallah, an 'Alid and the supposed founder of the city of Fez in Morocco. These claims of 'Abd al-Qadir's family to be *sharifs* have been contested by some experts.

A family tradition has it that the lineage descends from an Andalusian *sharif* named 'Abd al-Qawi (fl. 1350), the Lord of Tafarsit in the Rif of eastern Morocco.[38] A seventeenth-century ancestor, Ahmad al-Mukhtar, was a Qadiri, and the family branch of the Qadiriya at al-Qaytana takes its name from him. This Mukhtariya suborder is not to be confused with the more famous Mukhtariya of the Kunta *shaykhs* of the Azawad near Timbuktu.

In the middle of the eighteenth century, a member of the lineage was killed before Oran, fighting the Spaniards alongside the Turkish bey of Oran.[39] This ancestor (Muhammad al-Mujahid) was succeeded as head of the local *zawiya* of the Mukhtariya by his son Mustafa (c. 1747–98). Mustafa inaugurated a family tradition of going to the East to study. He also enhanced his prestige by having himself confirmed as head of the *zawiya* at al-Qaytana (perhaps with the title of *muqaddam*) by the chief of the *sharifs* at Baghdad, who was also the head of the Qadiriya there. Mustafa ibn Muhammad also took the opportunity to study with the well-known sufi, linguist, and lexicographer Murtada al-Zabidi in Cairo. Zabidi was a prominent Muslim reformer and intellectual of the late eighteenth century.[40]

On his return from the pilgrimage, al-Hajj Mustafa laid out a new Qadiri settlement and founded an enlarged *zawiya* at al-Qaytana in 1206/1791–2. About this time, Mustafa was making much publicity for his branch of the Qadiriya. His relations with the local Turks were apparently good, for he had Muhammad Bey, the Ottoman *veli* of Mascara, as one of his students; "*amirs* and others" often visited his establishment. Mustafa died in Cyrenaica in 1798 as he was returning from his second pilgrimage.[41]

Al-Hajj Mustafa's successor in charge of the *zawiya* was his son Muhyi al-Din, 'Abd al-Qadir's father. Muhyi al-Din lived from 1776 to 1834. His career was very much a copy of those of his father and grandfather. Nevertheless, his spiritual merits were recognized and appreciated by his contemporaries, many of whom came great distances to learn the sufi way and accept the rites of the Qadiriya from him. Muhyi al-Din's additions to and rebuilding of the new *zawiya* of al-Qaytana, along with his great increased following, amounted to a revival of the Mukhtariya. It had some unexpected and lasting political results.[42]

In the mid-1820s the local representatives of the Dey of Algiers suddenly became very suspicious of the *shaykh*'s intentions. Perhaps they thought that the Qadiris of al-Qaytana might attempt a revolt like the Tijanis in the south. According to the *Tuhfa*, Muhya al-Din was denounced to the Bey of Oran (Hasan Bey, governing 1817–30) by "an envious person." The Bey forced Shaykh Muhyi al-Din and his family to go to Oran and to live there under conditions of house arrest for a short time. After several months had elapsed, the Bey and his minions became convinced that Muhyi al-Din harbored no dangerous political aims, and he was released. He now handed over control of his *zawiya* to his eldest son, Muhammad Sa'id, for he found it expedient to go on the pilgrimage. He took 'Abd al-Qadir with him and set off for the Hijaz about 1241/1825–6, first going by land to Tunis and from there to Alexandria by ship.[43]

Far from the unwelcome attentions of the Bey of Oran, Muhyi al-Din and 'Abd al-Qadir made the pilgrimage twice and visited Damascus and Baghdad. In Damascus, they stopped for a while to study a book of traditions in the classes of the famous 'Abd al-Rahman al-Kuzbari at the Umayyad Mosque. In Damascus also, they encountered the important Naqshbandi leader Diya' al-Din Khalid al-Shahrazuri. Father and son spent some weeks with him, and 'Abd al-Qadir is said to have taken the tie (*wird*) of the Naqshbandiya from Shaykh Khalid.[44]

The significance of this encounter is hard to assess. However, Shaykh Khalid was an important "reviver" of the Naqshbandiya. He made important contributions to nineteenth-century Islamic thought, particularly in the matter of its defense against European encroachments; some of Shaykh Khalid's writings advocate a general revival of Islam.[45] Thus, Shaykh Khalid exercised direct influence on the Shaykh Shamil Daghistani, a Naqshbandi chief who fought a prolonged war against the Russians in the Caucasus in the nineteenth century. The same sort of influence may be seen in sporadic Naqshbandi uprisings against the Tsarist regime in the Ferghana Valley in Central Asia during the 1890s.[46] At any rate, Khalid's impact on 'Abd al-Qadir – assuming there was any – may not have been very crucial. On the other hand, his grandfather, al-Hajj Mustafa, had met the celebrated Zabidi in Cairo. Thus his family had been exposed to some important contemporary intellectuals and, very probably, to some of their ideas.

At Baghdad, Muhyi al-Din (and doubtless 'Abd al-Qadir) were granted Qadiri cloaks by Mahmud al-Jaylani, the head of the order and a descendant of the founder. Both of them also received some sort of written certificates (*ijaza*). In the case of Muhyi al-Din, the *ijaza* doubtless confirmed him as chief of the Mukhtariya branch of the order, perhaps with the rank of *muqaddam*.[47] Unfortunately, these documents cannot be traced and probably no longer exist.

About 1828, on their way back from the East, 'Abd al-Qadir and his father stopped in Algiers to call on the Dey, who received them "with honor and respect."[48] The political overtones to this visit emphasize Muhyi al-Din's caution in dealings with the Ottoman power. Despite his unfortunate experiences with the Bey of Oran, the leader of the Qadiriya of al-Qaytana took care to be on outwardly friendly terms with the Regency as long as it existed.[49]

Within two years of their return to al-Qaytana, the Algerian political situation altered radically with the French invasion and the unbelievably sudden downfall of the Regency. After 1830, the hopes of 'Abd al-Qadir and his father for a quiet life like that of their predecessors were dashed. Soon after the invasion, Algerian Muslims came to realize that if the undecided French tried to hold any area in Algeria permanently, they might later attempt to conquer the entire country. If they did so, their rule might be far less bearable than that of the Turks.

An incident that gave a foretaste of future French colonial methods was furnished in 1831 by the Duc de Rovigo, a French official in Algiers. In building a military highway through an old part of the city, de Rovigo's road-makers dug recklessly through two Muslim cemeteries that were still in use, scattering the skulls and bones of former beys, deys, and notables in every direction.[50] And as Émerit has shown, certain Maltese "men of affairs" in Algiers and elsewhere were making a business of buying up human bones (perhaps from these very cemeteries) and shipping them to Marseille, where they were used in the refining of sugar.[51] As a petty measure of revenge, perhaps for French casualties in the invasion, de Rovigo also took over a number of mosques in the city, like the Kachawa Mosque, and converted them into Catholic churches.[52] When these doings became known in Algiers and elsewhere in the country, they created a wave of shock and disbelief.

Muslim public opinion quickly hardened against the French. This sudden change was based on popular hatred and scorn as much as violent acts of the invaders. Even so, there was some hesitation over what to do; in the east of Algeria, the Turkish Bey Ahmad was still in control at Constantine. In the region of Algiers and in a number of ports, including Oran in the west, there were Muslims who were prepared to collaborate with the French. Their attitude may have been based on self-interest, passivity, or some old political clash; the Tijaniya of the southwest was a case in point. However, those Algerians of the center and west who chafed under foreign control were those who ultimately accepted 'Abd al-Qadir as their leader. Their willingness to obey him was accelerated by what Muhammad ibn 'Abd al-Qadir in his *Tuhfa* described as the policy of a "weak government with few resources."[53] Such a government would promote personal hatreds among its political adversaries and foment intrigues. The technique of "divide and rule," according to the author of the *Tuhfa*, was typical of the Ottoman regime in its last decade and of the beginnings of French control. Executions and atrocities masked indecision and uncertainty. When de Rovigo and others massacred a small tribe near Algiers, broke safe-conducts issued to tribal chiefs coming to negotiate, and killed Muslims merely on suspicion, the Muslim majority turned away from the French; accommodation with the invaders was no longer possible.[54] On the French side, there was a distinct willingness to show a strong hand against a people who were considered "inferior." A clear racist tone emerged here, coupled with a wish to test the new French weapons of the time. Behind the French colonial government and the military were pressures from settlers, would-be migrants from Europe, and land speculators, who wanted to manipulate French military power for their own purposes.

Muhammad ibn 'Abd al-Qadir has more to say about the hardening of opinion of the Algerian side:

> When the wheel of trade stopped, when agriculture was suspended and the carpet of safety rolled up . . . the governing classes, the *sharifs*, the hereditary holy men, the learned and the notables began to look for an individual who combined within himself the conditions of the *amir*ship, so as to take an oath to him and join forces.[55]

Clearly, sizable segments of the middle and upper classes of the traditional Muslim Algerian society, and many tribesmen too, felt themselves and their way of life threatened. The next move was resistance, a jihad against the Christians. This was a traditional response such as had last been seen in the Maghrib on a large scale in the fifteenth and sixteenth centuries. But it was by no means a blind traditionalism, for its leader, 'Abd al-Qadir, showed great flexibility and a pragmatic willingness to accept European ideas and innovations.

Who would now play the role of "Champion of Islam" against the French? For western Algeria and many persons elsewhere, there could be only one answer: Muhyi al-Din, the chief of the Qadiriya. This was an easy choice for the "governing classes, *sharifs*, hereditary holy men, *'ulama*, and notables" in many places. Among the tribes of the Oran Plateau and the Plain of Gharis, there was a nucleus of tribes already bound to Muhyi al-Din by ties of instruction and guidance in the sufi way of the Qadiriya. Linked by these largely informal bonds were the Banu Hashim, the Gharaba, the Banu 'Amir, and Awlad Sidi Shaykh, with some other minor groups. There was also a strong contemporary impression that since the Darqawiya had failed against the Turks and the Tijanis too, the time of the Qadiriya to prove itself had come. For western Algerians, this choice was in no way surprising. It reflected the high standing of the order, the fame of its *zawiya* at al-Qaytana, and the excellence of the long lineage of leaders of the Mukhtariya branch. As a well-established and deeply rooted Muslim institution, it was expected to furnish the necessary leadership at a time of crisis.

A more conservative person than Shaykh Muhyi al-Din could hardly have been found. He had always lived in an atmosphere of devotion and rectitude. Yet having gone on the pilgrimage, he was no provincial. Above all, he was a descendant of the Prophet, and he was thought to possess those powers, that *baraka*, which would put him in touch with the invisible order of nature so familiar to mystics. At will, he could communicate with the Prophet or with 'Abd al-Qadir al-Jilani. These qualities gave him a special advantage that would guard his fellow Muslims and grant them special guidance in the coming struggle. Such a man was indispensable to contemporary Algerian Muslim society, shaken as it was by a quick and unbelievable sequence of events – the disappearance of the Turks, then the arrival of the French in force. Muhyi al-Din was just the man to shore up its autonomy and self-confidence. In this role, he and his son Abd al-Qadir were almost interchangeable individuals, sharing fully in the same ancestry, education, *baraka,* and prestige.

Muhyi al-Din at first refused to lead. As he was nearly sixty, he did not want the part that was being thrust upon him. In disappointment, a delegation from Mascara and Tilimsan set off to the sharifian ruler at Fez with a request that he annex their districts to Morocco, along with Oran and its vicinity, and so forestall a French occupation. Mawla'i 'Abd al-Rahman quickly agreed to this, dispatching his cousin 'Ali ibn Sulayman to Tilimsan with instructions to convert it into the capital of a new "Amirate of the Central Maghrib." At the same time, Moroccan cavalry penetrated as far east as Milyana near Algiers, to reconnoiter. Elsewhere, sharifian agents lost no time in collecting taxes. Even so the attitude of the Algerian Muslims toward the Moroccans was uncertain; they certainly preferred them to the French, but would they be any better than the Turks? Would not Fez regard western Algeria as anything more than a new province to exploit? When the *'ulama* of Tilimsan sent a request to Morocco for aid, the *'ulama* of the Moroccan capital rejected it.[56] At this time and later, there were many ambiguities in the relationship between Fez and the Algerians. In the light of later events, many Moroccans and Algerians alike must have regretted their inability to cooperate. But this issue was soon settled by the French; those elements in France that were interested in holding Algeria decided to keep the Moroccans out, pending a decision about the future of the country. Naturally, these were the spokesmen for the settlers, land speculators, and interested businessmen, who combined to exercise formidable political pressure in Paris. Thus the scheme of "limited occupation" was pushed aside slowly in favor of harsher plans to crush Algerian Muslim opposition. Eventually, the Moroccans had no choice but to withdraw from Tilimsan and the other towns they had occupied, after French diplomacy had exerted a maximum of compulsion on the sharifian ruler.

Meanwhile, Muhyi al-Din had gone to Tilimsan himself. Perhaps he wanted to keep in touch with the Moroccans there. He was also concerned with teaching his local students and, perhaps, with keeping a truce between two factions in the town. On his return to al-Qaytana (early in 1832?), the political situation had changed. Some of the Banu Hashim and the Banu 'Amir pressed him a second time to become their leader, to take the title of amir, and to guide the jihad. This time, Muhyi al-Din refused to assume the amirate, but agreed to direct a jihad.[57]

Very quickly the French general Pierre Boyer at Oran (known as "Pedro the Cruel" to the local Spaniards for his frequent executions of Algerians) began to feel new pressures from the Muslim opposition headed by Muhyi al-Din, ably seconded by 'Abd al-Qadir.[58] In May 1832 two battles took place under the walls of the Citadel of Oran – one at Khanq al-Nitah (or Nattah) and the other at Burj Ra's al-Ayn.[59] The Muslims won these contests. On both occasions, 'Abd al-Qadir distinguished himself by his valor. The two episodes were turning points in 'Abd al-Qadir's career. He had made his reputation. His father could now step aside and turn over to him the amirate and supervision of the jihad.

The transition of leadership went smoothly enough, helped along with a little stage-managing and manipulation. The Amir took oaths of loyalty from all the major tribes in the vicinity of Mascara and the Plain of Gharis. Delegations came to him to swear allegiance, which the Amir received under a tree, just as the Prophet had done at the Tree of Umm Ghaylan before he set off on the Hudaybiya Raid against Mecca.[60] Like so many jihad leaders in Africa (and elsewhere), 'Abd al-Qadir made a distinct effort to imitate the Prophet, to reenact precisely what Muhammad had done under similar circumstances.

Successful opposition to France could come only through some efficient sort of organization. A skillful and gifted leader, 'Abd al-Qadir chose a framework that would be acceptable to his followers; thus it was an outwardly traditional one. Having taken the title of caliph and accepted oaths from his followers, the Amir now proceeded to create what looked to the *'ulama* and the pious like an ideal Islamic common-wealth. To any onlooker, his theocracy had the air of a state like that of the Four Orthodox Caliphs. If the Amir's vision of history was a static one, and if he occasionally looked to the beginnings of Islamic history for precedents, they did not invariably guide him. He was certainly no nationalist;[61] however, his mind functioned on several planes. If he had an adherence to a remote theocratic ideal, this never prevented him from doing things that the first caliphs would have disdained, like trying to obtain aid from a Christian government (Britain). Here he differed considerably from Usuman dan Fodio. He is perhaps closest to the Muslim leaders Muhammad 'Abdallah Hasan of Somalia and the Amir 'Abd al-Karim. Like the former, 'Abd al-Qadir wanted to retain the *Shari'a* and rejected any sort of millennial thinking; like the latter, he prized efficiency and organization.

Despite the Amir's acceptance of modernity, compromises with con-servatism were inevitable. This trend was most visible in the domain of administration, less so with military matters, and very little in the attempt to create an industrial base to carry on the war. Within his state organization, the Amir used a blend of classical offices, mixed with some Ottoman forms. Thus he appointed a *wazir* (chief min-ister); a principal secretary (*bash katib*), with a number of clerical subordinates; a *hajib* (chamberlain); two supervisors of the treasury (*nazir, khaznaji*), who administered both his state and personal trea-suries; an overseer of pious foundations (*awqaf*); and a collector of taxes and tithes. In contrast, he also appointed a minister of foreign affairs.[62]

At a lower level, 'Abd al-Qadir employed a number of *khalifas* (re-gional heads), *aghas* or *'amils* (district heads), and *qadis* (judges) for all regions in Algeria under his control. By 1839, there were eight such regions, or *khalifaliks*. Sometimes these posts were confided to persons who belonged to the Qadiriya, particularly in the west; elsewhere, per-sons of the religious classes were preferred. Evidently the Amir had some prejudice against members of the *Makhzan* tribes from the days of the Ottoman regime; even capable individuals having such origins were excluded from the new government.[63] What 'Abd al-Qadir did, effectively, was to create a whole new set of *Makhzan* tribes, Berbers and Arabs, to replace the old one. It should be noted that the new *khalifaliks* did not have the same boundaries as the earlier ones. Some of the *khalifas* and local chiefs were assigned the duty of collecting taxes. Unfortunately, many of them did this by force, after the style of the Deys; for this reason, many disillusioned tribesmen eventually loosened their loyalties and ties to 'Abd al-Qadir.

The Amir also created a "Consultative Council" of leading members of the learned class, presided over by a chief *qadi*. He also brought into being numerous other *diwans* ("councils"), the functions of which are not clearly defined in the sources.[64] In a deliberate effort to win popularity, 'Abd al-Qadir abolished the former Ottoman tax structure of "fines, levies, and fees" in force before 1830. These he replaced with his own, which supposedly had a more solid basis in the *Shar'ia*. Usuman dan Fodio had made a similar move in Hausaland after his jihad, claiming that most of the taxes of the old regime were uncanonical.[65]

Because of the numbers and influences of Qadiris in western Algeria, it is surprising that the sources say so little about any formal integration of the brotherhood into the framework of 'Abd al-Qadir's new state organization. Nor is anything said about efforts to broaden, to enlarge the responsibility of the officials of the *tariqa* or employ them within the government. Because it was an all-purpose organization, it seems likely that such an attempt may have been made. The Persian Safavids of the sixteenth century did make such an attempt.[66] At any rate there was no exclusivity; being a Qadiri was no prerequisite for appointment to high office under 'Abd al-Qadir.

As his capital, the Amir chose Mascara, "to put the people of Gharis at ease," for they had been his first supporters.[67] Later, because of French pressure, he had to abandon the town – which was burnt by General Clauzel in 1835 – and withdraw to Taqdimt near Tahart. Although it was farther from French bases, Taqdimt was not immune from French attack; it, too, was attacked by Bugeaud in 1841 and partially destroyed.

The Amir's army had two major divisions: the regulars and the irregulars (or auxiliary troops). The irregulars (*mutaww'a*, "volunteers") equipped themselves with whatever they could find on the battlefield and fed themselves at their own expense, precisely the same sort of organization seen with Muhammad 'Abdallah Hasan and 'Abd al Karim at a later period. 'Abd al-Qadir's auxiliaries were largely cavalrymen armed with rifles. This was a sort of mounted infantry, which did not make costly charges like contemporary European cavalry but galloped back and forth before the enemy, shooting at whatever targets they saw. Like them, an irregular infantry was used by the Amir for guerrilla warfare, being employed for ambushes and sudden attacks when the element of surprise was on its side.

Much more information is at hand about the Amir's regular army, which was divided into three elements: infantry, artillery, and cavalry, like a European army of that time. This regular force was called the *Jund al-Ahmadi or 'Askar al-Muhammadi* – roughly, the "Muhammadan Army." 'Abd al-Qadir's chief secretary, Qaddur ibn Muhammad al-Ruwayla, wrote a descriptive treatise about it, the *Wishah al-Katib*.[68]

Here Ruwayla discusses its uniforms, weapons, commissariat, and organization, but never its effective strength; the reader is occasionally left wondering whether this is a description of an ideal or an actual military force. Here again, as with 'Abd al-Qadir's plan for a state, there is heavy emphasis on a puritanical orthodoxy and the virtues of waging a jihad. The insignia of rank, for example, bore Qur'anic quotations or pious phrases in Arabic or proverbs like "Patience is the key to victory."[69] Higher officers wore insignia of gold or silver; enlisted men wore cloth emblems.

Like guerrilla and undersupplied troops everywhere, 'Abd al-Qadir's men got much of the material and weapons they needed by picking them up on the battlefield. The French were amply equipped and well provisioned. On other occasions, the availability of weapons depended on the French policy of the moment, or sometimes on direct foreign trade in weapons. For example, when the Desmichels Convention of 1834 between 'Abd al-Qadir and the French was in force, the Amir used the ports of Rashgun and Azru (Arzew) for importing supplies and weapons from England and France. Some of the supplies from England reached him through the mediation of an Anglo-Jewish firm at Rashgun, via Gibraltar.[70] These military imports were paid for in leather, wool, wax, and wheat from the Tilimsan region. When Baron Desmichels was replaced by the hawkish Trézel, the traffic to 'Abd al-Qadir through these ports was blocked. However, the Amir was able to arrange alternative supply routes by land from Morocco and Tunis, using camel caravans. Through Morocco, for example, the caravans were organized by the Amir's agent in Fez, one al-Hajj al-Talib ibn Jallun.[71] In Tunis, the son of the British Consular Agent at Bizerta, Natale Manucci, aided the Amir very greatly.

In 1835, 'Abd al-Qadir wrote a letter to the British Consul, Drummond-Hay, at Tetuan. In the letter he declared that he wanted to be on good terms with Britain and that he was prepared to trade with English merchants from any suitable west Algerian port. An emissary who was empowered to discuss these proposals carried the proposal. A similar letter was sent to the British authorities at Gibraltar. Evidently, nothing came of these feelers. In April 1840, the Amir renewed his efforts and sent a letter to the British foreign secretary, Lord Palmerston. In it he offered the British the port of Tanas (or Tenès, between Algiers and Mustaghanim). He was prepared to reserve the place for English traders, promising them great commercial advantages. He wished to buy arms and to exchange local wheat for these or other goods from the United Kingdom. Despite the tension between France and England, Palmerston in a reply (dated 6 October 1840) refused the offer. The foreign secretary also declined to mediate between France and 'Abd al-Qadir, which the latter had requested.[72]

Although his attempts to take advantage of the hostility between France and England failed, the Amir found another source of material in Morocco. Until 1843, the Moroccan public generally and the sharifian ruler himself (when he quarreled with 'Abd al-Qadir) channeled a flow of gifts to the Algerians: weapons, supplies of all sorts, funds, clothing, and food. This reflected the solidarity of Muslim public opinion in Morocco with the Algerians, based on religious and anti-French motives.[73]

To supplement late deliveries of arms or make up for the failure of importations, the Amir created an industrial base to furnish the most crucial items and services. He erected workshops at Tilimsan, Mascara, Milyana, and Midiya, and he built an arsenal at Taqdimt. The Taqdimt arsenal manufactured muskets, bayonets, and other weapons. Similar but smaller operations as well as the manufacture of bullets and gunpowder went on in other places. During truces, the Amir obtained his chemicals – sulfur, salt, and saltpeter – through Algerian ports. At other times they arrived by caravan from Tunis or Morocco. Occasionally some sulfur was mined in the Jabal Wansharis.

Part of the technical manpower for the Amir's arms and munitions factories was supplied by French prisoners of war. The *Tuhfa* mentions Spanish technicians who helped with such difficult problems as casting cannon (which was done at Tilimsan) and weaving cloth for uniforms. The *Tuhfa* also notes a mobile workshop for weapons repairs and the presence of tailors and saddlers to do the same sort of repair work. Evidently the technical abilities of contemporary Algerians were greater than many foreign writers have conceded.[74]

Beyond what he could manufacture in his arsenals, the Amir made some surprising arms deals. Between the spring of 1837, when he signed the Treaty of Tafna, and 1840, when he came back to Algeria, the corrupt French general Bugeaud arranged privately to supply the Amir with weapons. By the terms of a secret protocol to the Treaty of Tafna (which was only revealed after Bugeaud's retirement and his elevation to a marshalship) the Amir paid him 100,000 francs, for which Bugeaud contrived to send him 3,000 muskets, via Spain. Like most of the Amir's other war materials, much of this consignment was doubtless stored at Taqdimt until it was required.[75]

Rumors of these negotiations between Bugeaud and the Amir circulated among the Algerian public. Politically, the negotiations and the ensuing rumors were very dangerous to the Amir. His enemies within the country, such as al-Hajj Musa al-Darqawi (discussed below), took advantage of them. The majority of Algerians believed that negotiations of any sort with France were dubious, either from the practical or the religious point of view. Hence 'Abd al-Qadir's emphasis on the imam's freedom of action in his questionnaires sent to foreign *'ulama* (see p. 65 below). As late as 1839, Muslim public opinion wanted no truces except for the exchange of prisoners or brief military reorganizations. Until peace prevailed, the Amir would have compromised his own position as leader by agreeing to any lengthy truce; the enemy had to be either conquered or made to leave the country.

Another piece of evidence demonstrating 'Abd al-Qadir's awareness of the political world of his time was his well-oiled espionage service. The Amir was *au courant* with what was going on in Algiers and in Paris as well. In these places he had a network of agents, often Frenchmen – well-placed persons who gave him the information he needed. Some French-speaking clerks, or a small translation bureau, made versions of French newspaper articles for the Amir. At Paris, 'Abd al-Qadir obtained the services of a well-connected, retired French general, who supplied him with useful facts.[76]

It is now known, thanks to the researches of 'Abd al-Jalil al-Tamimi, that 'Abd al-Qadir was in touch with the Ottoman Turks as well as sympathetic French quarters and the British. Until recently, documents about this issue had not been available. After being turned down in 1840 by Palmerston – who refused to get involved with Algerian ports or in arbitration with France – 'Abd al-Qadir turned to Ottoman Turkey and Sultan 'Abd al-Majid.[77]

These documents show that the Amir (who carefully addresses the Sultan as "Caliph" in one of his letters), was acting on the advice of Hamdan Khoja, a secretary of Algerian birth working at the Ottoman Embassy in Paris. One letter published by Tamimi (dated 10 December 1841) is a request for military aid. Although it is long, a paragraph will show what the Amir was after:

> If money is mentioned, you have much of it. If armies are discussed, you have an army [and] a navy. . . . Had it not been for my fears for the Muslims from the enemy . . . I would have come to you and informed you personally about the Muslims of this country. Every door is locked against them: every thread [of hope] and means of obtaining anything has been cut. For them, there is no recourse but you and God. They have grasped your strong rope and attached themselves to your cause and your tentcord.[78]

The Porte's response to 'Abd al-Qadir's appeal was negative. Tamimi was only able to find a single letter in the Ottoman archives in answer to the Algerian leader's pleas; the Turks merely commended him for resisting France and requested him to communicate with them in the future by cipher!

The grounds for such Ottoman coolness were obvious. The principal obstacle to cordial relations between the Amir and Istanbul was his rival al-Hajj Ahmad Bey of Constantine. In Algeria, Ahmad Bey was the sole political survivor of the old regime. He had fought France, winning a resounding victory over General Clauzel in 1836. Ahmad was later defeated in a second French attack on his *beylik*. By 1840, he had fled to the Sahara, where he was occupied in raising further resistance to the invaders. To support these efforts, he continued to write letters to the Porte soliciting aid, just as 'Abd al-Qadir was doing. Naturally, the Turks favored Ahmad because his loyalty to Sultan Mahmud II was quite exceptional. Although he was now politically stranded, the Porte did not realize this until too late. By 1841, Ahmad Bey was no longer worth helping.[79]

Although these years were hardly the acme of Ottoman power, the Turks did not simply submit to the French takeover in Algeria. At Algiers, they had tried to halt the hostilities between France and Hüseyin Dey. They then tried to mediate between the two sides – sending several emissaries for this purpose; they finally attempted to halt the French by force. To this end they dispatched units of the Ottoman fleet, decimated by the disaster of Navarino and badly needed as it was to support hostilities against the ambitious Egyptian pasha, Muhammad 'Ali. Even after Ahmad Bey's defeat at Constantine (late 1837), Turkish vessels appeared in Tunisian waters to add pressure to Ottoman requests to Mustafa Pasha (Bey of Tunis) to help send supplies overland to Ahmad Bey. Ultimately, these initiatives failed; likewise, simultaneous approaches to London for diplomatic support.[80]

Preoccupied in this way with Ahmad Bey and the advance of the French in eastern Algeria, the Turks were unable to aid 'Abd al-Qadir. By 1847, the Porte tacitly acknowledged that Algeria was no longer an Ottoman province. 'Abd al-Qadir's hopes for Turkish aid were not helped by his independent ways, nor by the residual distrust the Turks manifested for his family– as shown by the Bey of Oran's arrest of his father in 1825, nor by obvious doubts at Istanbul that 'Abd al-Qadir would be amenable to Ottoman political control, should he win the contest with France. So, in the end, as his rival Ahmad Bey had been, 'Abd al-Qadir was abandoned by the Porte.

At a mint (*Dar al-Sikka*) at Taqdimt, 'Abd al-Qadir minted his own silver coins. According to Shinar these were of two denominations, struck in 1256/1840–1.[81] The larger coin was called a *muhammadiya*, and the smaller coin, a half-*muhammadiya*, was called a *nisfiya*. The

Amir adjusted the exchange rate so that a Spanish *duro* (known in North
Africa as an *abu midfa'* or *abu 'umud* from its cannon or columns on
the reverse) was equal to four Algerian *riyals*. In turn, each *riyal* contained three Algerian "quarters" (*rub'*), and each quarter eight *muhammadiyas*. Thus there were twenty-four *muhammadiyas* to every
Algerian *riyal*, or ninety-six to a Spanish *duro*. For some of these coins,
the metal was obtained by melting down earlier issues of the Ottoman
Regency. The *Tuhfa* also mentions copper coins, likewise minted at
Taqdimt, but it gives few details about them. Here again, the Amir's
sophistication about economics is shown by his adjustment of his coin-
age to other coinages circulating within Algeria and outside the
country.

Aside from "notables and *'ulama,*" it is clear that 'Abd al-Qadir's
political base was centered on tribesmen from Mascara and the Plain
of Gharis, with some tribes from outlying areas. What is not so clear is
the narrowness and shakiness of this base despite the Qadiri loyalties
of certain tribesmen. Some of these tribes, such as the Banu Hashim
and the Banu 'Amir, had ties of long standing to the Amir's family,
perhaps reaching back to 1500 or thereabouts. Other tribes joined the
Amir's cause only much later. A number of them are recorded as having
sent delegations to him to pledge their loyalty at an oath-taking ceremony. There were two of these ceremonies, about three months apart,
the first on 27 November 1832, the second on 4 February 1833.[82] The
first ceremony included the core of the Amir's supporters: the Banu
Hashim; the inhabitants of the Wadi al-Hammam; some maraboutic
tribes, such as the Awlad Sidi Dahhu and Banu Sayyid Ahmad bin
'Ali; and such groups as the Sharqi, Gharbi, 'Abbasi, Khalidi, Ibrahimi,
Hasani, 'Awfi, Ja'fari, Burji, Shuqrani, with others like the Zalamita,
Maghrawa, Khalwiya, and Masharif. Many of these tribal names re-
appear in the second oath-taking also.[83]

The second oath-taking, in February 1833, was a much larger and
more comprehensive ceremony. This time 'Abd al-Qadir obtained statements of loyalty from many individuals of importance – the greater
part of the *'ulama* of Mascara and Qal'at Hawwara, many of his own
relatives, and some of his highest-ranking collaborators. Also, the range
of tribal support was much broader. It included not only tribesmen
from the center of the Gharis Plain and the Mascara region, but also
tribes from the south – from the Ya'qubiya and Ja'afira confederacies,
including the Awlad Sharif, Awlad al-Akrad (Algerian Kurds?), Sa-
dama, and Khallafa. Farther north and closer to Mascara were the
Banu Shuqran, Banu Ghadwa, and Sajrara. From the east the Sinjas,
Banu Qusayr, and 'Attaf joined the amir, as well as the *murabits* of
Majaja, the Sabihs, the Banu Khuwaydim, the 'Akirma, the Fallita and

the Mukahiliya. Notables of the Burjiya and Mahajir pledged their
aid, likewise the coastal Dawa'ir and Sumala.[84]

Some of these tribes, for instance the Dawa'ir and Sumala, had been
a part of the *makhzan* in the Turkish period. For this reason, 'Abd al-
Qadir distrusted them, and their allegiance to him was of short duration. Also, they lived close to Oran and came under French pressure.
Thus they shortly defected to the French. They may have felt that they
were so much disliked by the remaining tribes – among whom they had
gone on tax-raising expeditions – that they merely switched masters.
Later the Burjiya and the Fallita went over to the enemy, too. To keep
order and a semblance of unity among these turbulent nomads was obviously one of the amir's most difficult and persistent problems. Under
wartime conditions, when they could be sent to fight against the
French, some discipline could be achieved; when truces occurred, like
nomads everywhere, they reverted to squabbling and fighting among
themselves, no doubt because of old feuds, suspicions, dislikes, or personal hatreds. Indeed, this problem was one that might have been beyond the powers of solution of any leader, no matter how skillful.
Nevertheless, his inability to build genuine internal cohesion cost 'Abd
al-Qadir dearly.

Further, 'Abd al-Qadir's tribal political base was enclosed within a
small area. In eastern Algeria and the southern deserts (excepting the
Awlad Sidi Shaykh), the Amir had few adherents. Excluding the Sinjas
and the Banu Qusayr in the east, his supporters lived within a par-
allelogram bounded by the Mediterranean, the Moroccan frontier, the
line between the desert and the foothills to the south, and a north–
south line running through Tanas and Tahart. If the Amir had won his
war against France, he would have had to build his new state within
narrow geographical boundaries, and the limits of his new political
creation would have been vastly smaller than the confines of contemporary Algeria. What is more, such a new creation would have abutted
on the sharifian borders; there is no reason to think that the rulers of
Morocco wanted to see a powerful new Muslim state arising on their
eastern frontiers any more than they had wanted the Turks there. This
is another factor that explains the break between the Amir and the
Moroccan sultan at the start of the 1840s in spite of the earlier favor
shown 'Abd al-Qadir by Moroccan public opinion.

As to the ethnic composition of these tribes, some were Arab, some
Berber. Among the Berbers, many had been Arabic speaking for long
periods. The Amir at least managed to sink ethnic differences, if not
differences between tribes. Even so, on the grounds cited here, the
emergent commonwealth of 'Abd al-Qadir was an inherently unstable
one and not capable of long duration.

In addition to tribal instabilities and a political base that was too narrow, the Amir had many powerful enemies. Most prominent among them were the Tijanis of 'Ayn Madi. Their opposition to him was decisive. They disliked the Amir and the Qadiriya; obviously, their dislike included an element of interbrotherhood rivalry. Much more serious in Tijani eyes was the episode of 1827, when Muhammad al-Kabir al-Tijani had been abandoned on the battlefield by the treacherous Banu Hashim.[85] Alone with only 300 of his allies, the Banu 'Arba,' Muhammad al-Kabir and his friends had "hobbled themselves together as camels are hobbled" and fought to the last man against the army of the Ottoman Bey, Hasan. Captured alive, Muhammad al-Tijani was sent under guard to Algiers and there decapitated. His head was exposed on one of the city gates, and his sword was sent to Sultan Mahmud II.[86] The Tijaniya brotherhood could neither forgive nor forget this episode, and this crippled the Amir's hopes for Muslim unity even within western Algeria.

Realizing the seriousness of Tijani opposition, the Amir believed that he could defeat the Tijanis and so solve the problem. But he made a serious error by underestimating Tijani strength. In 1838–9, he besieged the fortress of 'Ayn Madi, using weapons supplied him by Bugeaud (who was quite happy to stand by and watch his enemies attack each other).[87] Although 'Abd al-Qadir took 'Ayn Madi briefly, he was unable to hold it. Thus he fell into the same trap as the Turks had earlier. On his retreat from 'Ayn Madi in 1839 without having achieved a decisive victory over Muhammad al-Saghir ("Little Muhammad," the younger brother of Muhammad al-Kabir), the Amir's prestige was heavily damaged, and his hopes for final victory over France were compromised. Indeed, the Tijanis shortly became the allies of the French, propelled into their arms by 'Abd al-Qadir's mistake.

Throughout his struggle for independence, 'Abd al-Qadir was plagued by many competitors and rivals. Many of these men were formidable personalities who hinted or claimed openly that they were mahdis or forerunners of mahdis. In the 1830s and 1840s, as readers of Suyuti's predictions well knew (see Chapter 1), they were either about forty years behind or ahead of the traditional date. Hence the timing of the traditional millennial framework would not fit, showing that such appeals were designed to appeal to the ignorant. To his credit, 'Abd al-Qadir disdained to use them. But others did; as time passed and the situation became more difficult for the average Muslim – enraged by French devastations and destruction of villages – he became more vulnerable to this kind of political ruse. 'Abd al-Qadir's prestige fell, theirs rose. By the unsophisticated, their military successes were always in-

terpreted as proofs of divine favor. Thus 'Abd al-Qadir, besides opposing the French, was convinced that he had to make war on charismatic
leaders, would-be mahdis or their advance agents, and other persons
exploiting similar political claims. They constituted real threats to his
own movement.

Nevertheless, these personages are interesting, and they reveal many
traits similar to those of Bu Dali and Muhammad ibn Sharif earlier in
the century. One of them who cultivated his apocalyptic characteristics
was an alleged *sharif*, al-Hajj Musa al-Darqawi. Although his brotherhood had been decimated by the Ottomans twenty-five years earlier,
remnants of it still existed in parts of central Algeria. Al-Hajj Musa
claimed to be the *Mawla al-Sa'a* ("Master of the Hour"), but not quite
a mahdi. He denounced 'Abd al-Qadir's making a pact with the French
as a violation of the *Shar'ia*. In doing this, he wanted to strip the Amir
of his role of champion of Islam. At the same time, he attempted to
revive the Darqawiya in the Jabal Wansharis district to the east of
'Abd al-Qadir's area. He likewise recruited in the southern deserts.[88]

According to Émerit, al-Hajj Musa was able to work the miracles –
rather like the biblical loaves and fishes – of making a small quantity of
bread into hundreds of pieces to feed his army or magically multiplying the amount of *couscous* on three or four platters so that it could
feed hundreds of people.[89] He professed to be invulnerable to cannon
balls or bullets, which allegedly turned to water within a few feet of
him or his men, as with the Maji-Maji in Tanganyika. Al-Hajj Musa's
cause was aided at this time by many politically inspired prophecies
(1834–5) announcing the advent of a *sharif* from the West who would
drive out the French. Musa sent a message to 'Abd al-Qadir to demand
that the Amir join him to fight the invaders. But the Amir evidently
believed that his own cause would be damaged by joining such an
unpredictable and ambitious associate, and he refused. Because the
Amir and al-Hajj Musa could not adjust their differences, 'Abd al-Qadir
attacked and defeated Musa in April 1835.[90]

Another millennial adventurer who created difficulties for 'Abd al-
Qadir was a certain Muhammad ibn 'Abdallah al-Baghdadi. Perhaps a
migrant from Iraq, al-Baghdadi had come to North Africa in the time
of 'Abd al-Qadir's father. As he claimed descent from the founder of
the Qadiri order, Muhyi al-Din had treated him well when he turned
up at al-Qaytana. From there, he vanished into Morocco, but he later
arrived at Fez, where he was well received by Mawla'i 'Abd al-Rahman
ibn Hashim. "When 'Abd al-Qadir was involved with the enemy," he
returned to Algeria and entered the territory of the Zanakhira and
Awlad Na'il tribes to the south of Titteri. Finding an ally in Muhammad
ibn 'Awda, chief of the Awlad Mukhtar, al-Baghdadi began to claim

that he was the "Expected Mahdi." Muhammad ibn 'Awda, described by Muhammad ibn 'Abd al-Qadir in his *Tuhfa* as one of the "biggest troublemakers" in that region, began to promote him.[91] Ibn 'Awda and al-Baghdadi took advantage of another of 'Abd al-Qadir's mistakes – the forcible collection of a supplementary tax for the holy war. Many of the tribes south of Titteri, formerly favorable to the Amir, now began to draw away from him.

When this happened, the Amir announced a forthcoming campaign, dispatching a number of written warnings and proclamations about what he intended to do once his troops reached Zanakhira and Awlad Na'il territory. This technique shook the will of the dissidents. Many of them eventually surrendered, including al-Baghdadi, who was magnanimously pardoned by the Amir and sent back to Morocco.[92]

The most important of these apocalyptic figures was a mahdi, a man whose name was Muhammad ibn 'Abdallah, as specified by the prophecies, but who is more generally known as Abu Ma'aza or Bu Ma'aza "The Man with the Goat"). Goats – but more often donkeys – have often served in Islamic history as beasts of millennial symbolism.[93] Bu Ma'aza's appearance was heralded by his partisans with rumors of a "Goat Man" who would attack and defeat the French.[94] Bu Ma'aza himself came from the Banu Khuwaydim tribe in the Shalif Valley. He profited from the troubles of another neighboring tribe, the Sinjas, who were at odds with their chief. Bu Ma'aza incited them to murder their leader and install him to his place. Out of the Dahra range on the north side of the Shalif, he began to raid the French very successfully "with an army of scoundrels," as the *Tuhfa* puts it. Like al-Hajj Musa, Bu Ma'aza claimed that neither bullets nor other weapons could touch him or his men. Bu Ma'aza won much plunder and many supplies from the French, taking some prisoners and massacring others.[95]

At Shinar suggests, it is likely that Bu Ma'aza was a member of the Tayyibiya order, a Moroccan organization whose headquarters were in the Wazzan region of northwestern Morocco. Shinar explains the late timing of Bu Ma'aza's entry into the war against France (1845) on the basis of the Tayyibiya's own calculation of the "Hour," – the correct moment for Bu Ma'aza's manifestation in his role as mahdi.[96] By 1845, 'Abd al-Qadir's jihad was in trouble. The Amir had crossed into Morocco (into the Rif) hoping, perhaps, that serious international complications, which he could turn to his own advantage, would arise between France and Morocco. Meanwhile, the Tayyibiya and Bu Ma'aza were bearing the brunt of heavy French attacks. Some of the most brutal and heartless massacres of a defeated enemy took place when the French drove the Dahra, the Banu Riyah, and the Sabih into caves in the adjoining mountains and lit fires before the entrances so

that those inside – hundreds of men, women, and children – were as-
phyxiated.[97]

Unlike the other two mahdis mentioned here, Bu Ma'aza soon abandoned his claim to a millennial role and joined – or at least cooperated
with – the Amir's troops until he was overtaken and captured by the
French near Tahart. He was taken to Paris, where he made a spec-
tacular prison escape. On his recapture, he was imprisoned a second
time at Ham Fortress, where the French kept their most important
political prisoners. In the 1850s he was released by Napoleon III.[98]

'Abd al-Qadir's Writings and Opinions

The spiritual and poetic aspects of Amir 'Abd al-Qadir's character,
which were to have fuller development during his exile in Syria in
the latter part of his life, have already been noted. Equally remarkable were his intellectual, legal, and theological abilities. For example,
he was at home with Islamic law and knew it well. Although circumstances or wishes caused him to deviate from the Maliki code at times,
he usually adhered to it, as his *'ulama* wished him to do.

Occasionally he used this knowledge in unexpected ways. On three
occasions at least, 'Abd al-Qadir sent questionnaires to foreign Muslim
authorities in Morocco and Egypt. This he did to obtain rulings from
them on legal and politico-legal points to which he already knew the
answers. Independent statements from foreign experts were useful to
show persons among his own following who might have had doubts
or second thoughts about the legality (or orthodoxy) of a given policy.

Some of these inquiries throw light on points that the Amir considered fundamental. They also demonstrated the conservative side of
his thinking. Certain of these points are further elaborated in a short
treatise he wrote entitled the *Risalat al-A'yan*. And to the theory of one
contemporary problem, 'Abd al-Qadir made a substantial contribution
– an analysis with which Usuman dan Fodio might have agreed. This
was the matter of migration (*hijra*) from enemy-controlled territory –
an issue that became of increasing importance to Muslims as the nineteenth century wore on.

During his fifteen years of rule, 'Abd al-Qadir found that not every
Algerian would automatically range himself on his side to combat the
French. Old hatreds (as in the case of the Tijanis) or self-interest (as
with Dawa'ir and Sumala, who lived near Oran) either kept some
Muslims away or made them break ties with the Amir. As usual in such
legal enquiries, 'Abd al-Qadir defines his own party as the "Muslims"
and seeks clarification about the treatment of "traitors, rebels and
apostates" and such semi-Muslims as are sunk in "unbelief" (*kufr*).

Seeking to make good his losses in money and material or to obtain forced labor for his workshops and munitions factories, the amir asked al-Tassuli (a leading learned man of Fez) and al-'Alawi (the chief *qadi* there) to furnish him with the legal justification to execute his enemies, take their property, and enslave their women and children.[99] Predictably, the answers of the *Shaykh al-Islam* (al-Tassuli) and the chief *qadi* furnished what was wanted. In general, said the advisers, the "Muslims" may attack traitors and their associates, spies and connivers, or those who shelter them. With full legal justification, "without remorse," they may be extirpated and their women and children taken, like their property. These are identical to some of the issues with which Usuman dan Fodio had dealt in his writings relating to the jihad in Hausaland (see Chapter 1).

In more detail, al-Tassuli claimed that political oaths of allegiance taken by Muslims to non-Muslim rulers were invalid. An imam (here used as a synonym for *caliph,* in Islamic political theory the political and religious head of state) is indispensable to a Muslim population of any size. He can no more abandon them than they can abandon him. Without his guidance they will inevitably commit crimes against each other and against the *Shar'ia.* Without an imam or other authoritative leader, the administration of justice must invariably suffer. Deprived of statecraft and spiritual direction, the population will diminish and fall into unbelief. Muslim duties such as the payment of canonical taxes and the performance of jihad will be in abeyance. If the imam is responsible for waging war and raising armies, his absence will cripple the community's defense.

For the relations between 'Abd al-Qadir and the French, the implications of the previous paragraphs are quite clear. 'Abd al-Qadir remained the imam of the conquered Muslim population under French colonial rule, and they owed him their taxes. If they could break out and come to him, then they had the automatic duty of carrying on the jihad. Hence their first duty was *hijra* (also stressed by Usuman dan Fodio) – a "removal" from French-controlled territory. This had first priority. It was the pivot on which all else turned. Any person, physically able to come, who refused to do so, was not only a doubtful Muslim, but probably an "unbeliever" as well.

But 'Abd al-Qadir needed no *Shaykh al-Islam* to show him the way to these conclusions. In his *Risalat al-A'yan,* the Amir wrote an even more comprehensive treatment of the *hijra* question.[100] His treatise makes a valuable contribution to a part of Islamic theory untouched by the classical writers on this subject. This is so because most of the classical Muslim thinkers about these issues composed their books at a time when the Muslim-controlled area was expanding, or remaining static, rather than contracting in size. Hence they had very little to say about Muslim populations stranded under Christian or other governments. Either this point was no immediate problem at the time, or they did not write about it because discussion of such things might have seemed unjustifiably defeatist. With 'Abd al-Qadir, the situation is reversed; it was a serious and immediate problem. He had the courage and the political and legal knowledge to work out its implications for a new era, a time of foreign imperialism and colonialism when the *Dar al-Islam* was constantly being nibbled away by aggressive foreign states with large armies.

Because the essential point is moving away from the enemy – withdrawal from hostile territory – the Amir's main theme in the *Risala* is the separation of Muslims from alien invaders and the breaking off of all contact with them.[101] Had the Amir's followers taken this point more seriously, they would have left western Algeria for the southern deserts or for some other country. Indeed, many Algerians moved into Morocco and Tunis after the Amir's surrender in 1847. Once he had settled in Damascus, a sizable Algerian colony came into being in both Syria and Palestine. As late as 1911, there was a big exodus from Tilimsan for what was thought to be a more hospitable Ottoman rule in Syria, to the dismay of the French colonial authorities.[102]

Of all the Amir's writings now available, the *Risala* is the most significant, because it deals with an issue that touched more and more Muslims as time went on. Although there is no evidence that the *Risala* was widely read, it nevertheless laid out one possible line of action for Muslim African populations and Muslims elsewhere: flight. And, as long as there was still somewhere to go, *hijra* was both canonical and practical.

CHAPTER 3

Al-Hajj 'Umar Tal and His
Jihad in Guinea, Senegal, and Mali

The career of al-Hajj 'Umar offers great contrasts (with some similarities) to that of Usuman dan Fodio. Both were mystics and intellectuals of Torodbe origin, but each man belonged to a different sufi order. Like Usuman, 'Umar drew his inspiration from the eighteenth-century sufi revival in the Middle East. Yet he was a "neosufi," a Tijani, not a Qadiri. 'Umar also became a Futa Toro leader and hero; some writers have even called him a "Tukolor imperialist." Successful in military affairs, 'Umar developed the doctrinaire side of his thinking to the point that he became a Tijani "ideologue," as Hiskett calls him. Like Amir 'Abd al-Qadir, 'Umar collided with the French. Yet unlike the Amir or Shehu dan Fodio, who survived their wars and political activities with credit, 'Umar became enmeshed in political and military entanglements, finally falling victim to a coalition of hostile Muslims whom he had provoked. 'Umar had a drastic impact on many West African Muslims and non-Muslims, particularly the Bambara. Some of his contemporaries believed that he might even be a mahdi or the agent of a mahdi. Personally, 'Umar combined self-confidence, zeal, and intellectual brilliance with other interests; his interests oscillated between spiritual commitment, mysticism, and theology on one hand, and political aspirations of major dimensions on the other. 'Umar's interests were mutually incompatible; if 'Umar was a suicide, his two conflicting roles probably contributed to it.

Usually, 'Umar's birthdate is taken to be 1794.[1] His full name, arabicized as it appears in his writings, was 'Umar ibn Sa'id ibn 'Uthman al-Futi al-Turi al-Kidiwi ("of Guédé"). He was born at Halwar near Podor, in the Gidi or Guédé district of northern Senegal. Situated on the Senegal River in Futa Toro province, Halwar and Podor are still important towns, across the stream from Mauritania and so open to influences from that country and Morocco. The seventh son of his father, 'Umar came from a Muslim clerical family. 'Umar's father Sa'id was not a man in wealthy circumstances, yet he was rich enough to support two wives.[2] By profession, Sa'id was a religious teacher.

'Umar studied Arabic and Islamic subjects under his father. A good student, he memorized the *Qur'an* and two famous books of tradition by Muslim and al-Bukhari.[3] When he was about fifteen, he left Halwar to study under various local masters, first in Futa Toro and then else-where. He was more attracted to mysticism than Islamic law, yet he read many legal texts. Having adopted his father's calling, he set off about 1814 for Satina in Futa Jallon, several hundred miles south of Halwar. Here he was fed and lodged by the townspeople in return for teaching their children the *Qur'an* and elementary religious subjects. At Satina, Karamoko 'Umar became popular. Here he stayed for about twelve years, until he was close to thirty-one, when he set off on a pilgrimage to Mecca. By this time, 'Umar evidently had a small follow-ing of his own. Yet the local people were disturbed for some reason by 'Umar's popularity, which led to differences between him and them and perhaps hastened his departure for Arabia.[4]

During his twenties, 'Umar had met representatives of a new sufi organization that was just starting to penetrate West Africa from Mauritania. Very popular because of its fresh opinions and because it was a reforming order, unlike the more conservative Qadiriya, the neosufi Tijani brotherhood had been founded only about a decade (1781) before 'Umar's birth. 'Umar's first teacher in the Tijaniya was a man from Timbo in Futa Jallon, 'Abd al-Karim ibn Ahmad al-Naqil. At the time, Timbo was the site of an important imamate, a center of Islamic proselytization in the "Far West" of Africa adjacent to Futa Toro, the "Takrur" of medieval Arab writers.[5]

'Umar soon joined the Tijaniya. The chronological distance from him to the founder of the order, Ahmad al-Tijani (d. 1815), was short. 'Umar's lineage of teachers included 'Abd al-Karim, Sidi Mawlud Fal, and Muhammad al-Hafiz wuld Mukhtar of the Mauritanian clan of the Idaw u 'Ali, a pupil of al-Tijani. Known also as "Baji," Muhammad al-Hafiz had been instructed by the order's founder to proselytize for the Tijaniya in Senegal.[6] Until his death about 1830, Baji did this with great success. After he had studied Tijani doctrine under Baji's pupil 'Abd al-Karim for "a year and some months," 'Umar convinced his teacher that they should go on the pilgrimage to the Hijaz. This was a difficult and expensive undertaking for a West African at this time; 'Umar set about raising money. It is claimed that he went to the French town of St. Louis to ask well-to-do Muslim traders there for funds; it is also possible that he obtained money from French sources.[7]

According to al-Shinqiti, 'Umar left home for the east in December 1825.[8] He was accompanied by his younger brother 'Ali (Aliyu) and a small group including fifteen slaves. The slaves were sold at intervals along the route to provide cash for the journey. 'Abd al-Karim was un-able to join the group, but he promised to do so at Masina after he had recovered from an illness. When 'Umar's slow-moving party reached Hamdallahi (the capital of Masina), 'Abd al-Karim did not appear.[9]

The pilgrims went on without him via Bobo Diulasso in Upper Volta, then to Kong in northern Ivory Coast, and from there to Sokoto in Hausaland, always on foot.[10] 'Umar regretted that 'Abd al-Karim could not accompany him; typically, 'Umar's determination and courage prevented him from turning back.

At Sokoto, 'Umar lost no time in making himself known to the Shehu's son and successor, Muhammad Bello. 'Umar claims that he did this because he wanted to halt the hostilities between Sokoto and Bornu (see Chapter 1), which were still going on in desultory fashion in 1826:

> We came to Hausaland and met with its Amir, some of his learned
> men and influential persons. . . . We discovered an ugly
> disagreement between him and the Amir of Bornu. . . . We
> were much depressed by that conflict, but could not discuss it with
> the Amir of Hausaland nor make any effort to stop it, despite
> our good opinion of him. Had we been able to talk to him, we had
> hopes that he might support us because he liked us. . . . But
> we were hesitant to try it, lest it hinder us from reaching our
> objective.[11]

Without pursuing their peacemaking efforts further, 'Umar and his friends, who had stayed in Hausaland for nearly ten months,[12] set off again for the east. On this occasion, it is doubtful that 'Umar did any proselytizing for the Tijaniya. Bello treated 'Umar well; he gave him a slave girl, Fatima, as a wife, who in turn presented him with a child.

In Sokoto the English explorer Hugh Clapperton is said to have met 'Umar. At least, he records in his *Journal* an encounter with an "intelligent man," one "Hadji Omer from Foota Torra."[13] Whether or not this identification is correct, Clapperton makes it clear why the pilgrimage route now turned north into the Fazzan and Ahir via Katsina rather than going directly east through Bornu, Baghirmi, and the eastern Sudan in the normal fashion: "there was no passing through that country, as it was now only inhabited by wandering Arabs, who plunder all that fall into their hands."[14]

When he reached Tuwaq in Ahir, 'Umar heard that Muhammad al-Ghali, the Tijani representative for the Hijaz, was staying at Mecca. "At this," says he, "I was filled with great joy, and asked God to grant me a meeting with him."[15] But 'Umar's northward journey proved unexpectedly difficult: "Between the Tubu country and a place in the Fazzan called Tajarhi . . . I was occupied with a severe illness which afflicted my brother and my slave girl. Both of them were between life and death . . . in a desert where there was nothing but sandhills."[16]

On reaching Cairo, 'Umar met an Egyptian official charged with arranging hospitality for visitors from the West; he first entertained 'Umar in his garden and then sent for learned men to check his intellectual credentials. Al-Shinqiti says 'Umar was interrogated "from morning to the noon prayers" about the "oddities of tradition, unintelligible passages in the *Qur'an,* and details of law, grammar, logic, and rhetoric."[17] When 'Umar had passed this test, the official – doubtless on a charitable basis – furnished 'Umar and his party with the necessary supplies for the journey from Egypt to Mecca via Jidda.

When 'Umar arrived at Mecca, he sought and soon found Muhammad al-Ghali:

> God answered my prayers and brought me to him that afternoon.
> . . . We talked together a little, and he made me very happy
> when he scrutinized me. He treated me sincerely and generously,
> and gave me the copy of *Jawahir al-Ma'ani* which I have today.
> . . . I stayed with him until we had finished the ceremonies of
> the pilgrimage. . . . I went with him to Madina . . . which we
> entered on the first of Muharram. That year I remained . . . with
> him in Madina. I submitted my person and my money to him,
> putting myself under his guidance. I stayed to render him service
> for three years, starting to study again under him.[18]

'Umar had chosen a fine teacher. Al-Ghali, a Moroccan, had been a close associate of Ahmad al-Tijani toward the end of the latter's life in Fez. Later, al-Tijani appointed him his deputy for the Hijaz. From al-Ghali, 'Umar, who was already familiar with higher Tijani matters, received special instruction in the rituals of the order. He was also initiated into the secrets of the brotherhood. Musa Kamara suggests that 'Umar may have become al-Ghali's doorkeeper. He seems also to have acted for him as a chamberlain and secretary.[19]

When three years had passed, 'Umar's instruction came to an end. Al-Ghali took him to Muhammad's tomb in Madina, where he gave him an *ijaza* ("license"). This confirmed him as a functionary of the order, although with what rank is not certain – probably that of *khalifa,* the same rank held by al-Ghali himself. Nor is it specified in what area al-Hajj 'Umar was to function, but perhaps this omission reflects the obscurities of West African geography as viewed from contemporary Mecca.[20]

Al-Ghali's *ijaza* stated that he considered 'Umar "his favorite in this world and the Next," and that 'Umar was authorized to give instruction in the Tijaniya to "whoever asks for it among the Muslims, young or old, obedient or rebellious, man or woman, slave or free."[21] Al-Ghali also stressed the new doctrinal basis of the order – that it was a "Muhammadan order" (*tariqa Muhammadiya*), not to be confused with older, "unreformed" organizations like the Qadiriya. It was also universal, in that it admitted slaves and women.

A passage in the *ijaza* stressed the organizational and spiritual duties of its holder:

> I have authorized him ['Umar] to nominate as a district headman
> (*muqaddam*) whoever seeks to be one, up to the number of sixteen
> men, each of whom may serve as *muqaddam* over four [others]
> according to the customary conditions. Whoever opposes this
> stipulation is deprived of his authorization. We order each
> *muqaddam* to look on his brethren with the eye of solicitude and
> magnification, to protect himself from any change in their hearts
> and to be diligent in reforming their affairs and in the execution
> of their needs, worldly and otherworldly . . . visiting them in
> health and calling upon them in illness, and [acting] sympathetically
> towards their weaknesses.[22]

Having completed his training under Muhammad al-Ghali and repeated the pilgrimage, there was no reason for 'Umar to remain in the east. Some sources claim that 'Umar spent some time in Jerusalem and Syria (where he is said to have "cured a prince of madness") before taking a ship for Egypt. From there, he intended to retrace his steps to West Africa. But before he took leave of his teacher for the last time, his teacher gave him some useful advice. Should he consort with "kings and sultans," warned al-Ghali (who had come to know his pupil well), he would no longer aid him with his prayers. He reminded 'Umar of an old sufi tradition, which 'Umar quotes in one of his books, the *Rimah:* "The best of princes are those who repair to the learned, but the worst of the learned are those who frequent princes. . . . Men of learning are trusted by God's Prophets as long as they do not mix with sultans: if they do so, they have betrayed them."[23]

Not quite truthfully, 'Umar later claimed, despite his long visits to Muhammad Bello in Sokoto, that he "had never mixed with sultans and disliked those who did so."[24] Al-Ghali's point here was that 'Umar must avoid the temptations of political power and put a brake on his ambitions. Paradoxically, another source (Muhammadu Tyam) claims that al-Ghali instructed 'Umar "to sweep the country" of unbelievers.[25]

'Umar cites an episode that occurred on his way to Egypt by sea. It suggests that he believed that he possessed divine protection:

> The wind sprang up and the ship was about to founder. All who
> were in her feared destruction. The lady Hajja Fatima al-Madina
> [sic] fell asleep and then woke up and said, "Rejoice! I have just
> seen Shaykh Tijani and Muhammad al-Ghali, who told me, 'Greet

Shaykh 'Umar and tell him . . . that we are with him and that
he should fear nothing'." The wind died down and became quiet.[26]

In Cairo again, 'Umar spent some time at the Azhar Mosque and
completed a *Qur'an* commentary.[27] After an interval (in the spring of
1830) he set off again with his books and possessions (including some
trade goods from the Holy Cities), his brother Aliyu, his wife Fatima,
and his little daughter for West Africa. Rather than going from the
Fazzan to Katsina and from there to Sokoto, 'Umar took the more difficult route to Bornu. At Tijarhi, in the southern Fazzan, Aliyu died; but
the others kept on, suffering severe hardships in the desert.[28] Finally
the survivors reached Bornu, where their reception by Muhammad al-
Amin al-Kanemi was unfriendly. Al-Kanemi's hostility might have been
understandable if 'Umar had been accompanied by a large group of
Tijanis who were trying to proselytize for their new order. Al-Kanemi
was a Qadiri of the Junaydi branch (popular at Tripoli). The Amir
might have considered 'Umar a Sokoto agent, knowing that he had
friendly links to Muhammad Bello. Another issue that 'Umar may have
been willing to use was a revival of the old Sayfawa dynasty of Bornu
(overthrown not long before by al-Kanemi), as suggested by al-
Naqar.[29]

Before he arrived in Bornu, 'Umar appears to have corresponded
with al-Kanemi. He sent him at least one letter (undated, unfortunately) that survives.[30] In it, 'Umar complained of al-Kanemi's mis-
treatment of the Tijani group in Bornu. 'Umar also mentions that al-
Kanemi had written to conservative theologians in Libya and Egypt
about the Tijani doctrine of *wilaya* (individual saintship), which the
Qadiri chief vehemently rejected. A final point in 'Umar's letter is that
he was no theological imitator (*muqallid*).

This statement is one of the first clear indications of 'Umar's theological and political position. Further, 'Umar's remark was designed to
make al-Kanemi look like a conservative diehard and 'Umar like a
liberal. A new reform current, to which 'Umar adhered, looked to a
loosening of the Sunni legal structure – particularly toward a shake-up
of sufism. At the start of the 1830s, it was slowly becoming a new orthodoxy. Clearly, these reformist views of 'Umar's had potentially dangerous aspects, which doubtless caused al-Kanemi to regard him as a
harmful political radical. For a time, this caused bad relations between
the two men, for al-Kanemi wanted no rivals in Bornu.

When their relations were at their worst, 'Umar claimed that al-
Kanemi tried to have him murdered. These alleged attempts failed,
which convinced 'Umar once more that he was under special protection. According to 'Umar, the would-be assassins were blinded, mir-

aculously stopped by high walls, or held off by "strange men with their swords drawn."[31] Soon after, 'Umar claimed that God caused al-Kanemi to have a vision in which Ahmad al-Tijani appeared to him. Then, when al-Hajj 'Umar was ready to leave Bornu, a remarkable change came over the Amir. "Despite himself, he became very gracious," 'Umar says, "and treated me very generously."[32] Traditionally, the change even extended to his giving 'Umar one of his daughters as a wife; it is more likely that she was a well-born Kanuri lady. On his part, 'Umar composed at least two poems in praise of al-Kanemi.[33] Yet, with apparent malice, 'Umar describes what happened in Bornu after he had left for Sokoto: "They starved for four years. Not a drop of rain fell from the skies. They were forced to eat carrion and the leaves of trees, donkeys, horses, and even resorted to cannibalism. Then they repented – and the rains came."[34]

At Sokoto, 'Umar renewed his acquaintanceship with Muhammad Bello, who must have heard about the clash between his Tijani friend and the Amir of Bornu. 'Umar stayed in Sokoto from 1831 approximately, until just after Bello's death in 1837. During this long visit, 'Umar concentrated on spreading the Tijaniya among the Hausa population and also among the governing elite at Sokoto. As the mutual liking of Bello and 'Umar grew, their association became closer. 'Umar came to influence Bello in religious and mystical matters. Although Bello was never converted to Tijanism, one of his books does contain quotations from a famous Tijani manual. Attributed to Bello also are some poems that praise 'Umar, in which Bello speaks as a Tijani. They may or may not be evidence in the same direction.[35]

From living at Sokoto and frequenting the court there, 'Umar became familiar with the inner workings of the Fulani caliphate. When he came to govern his own state later, such knowledge was indispensable. 'Umar now developed a great interest in military matters; according to a descendant, 'Umar claimed that he "learned how to fight" in Hausaland. Musa Kamara says, "He stayed for four years, enjoying the quiet [sic] among the Hausa population, who . . . put him at the head of their armies. Each force he commanded returned victorious, invincible, triumphant. This brought him much property, women, children and slaves."[36]

It is unclear just how much personal participation in these wars 'Umar permitted himself. Yet as Willis declares, to have allowed himself to become directly involved in a military campaign was "wholly inconsistent with his avowed role of spiritual leader and sufi *shaykh*."[37] However, the appearance of this new, activist element in 'Umar's personality is explicable if one assumes he believed that practical knowledge of war-making and other worldly concerns was essential to his

future plans. All of that had been omitted at Madina; it was abhorrent
to al-Ghali. At Sokoto, the change in 'Umar's thought must have been
radical; if he had reached the conclusion that there was no inconsis-
tency in a militant – even military – brand of Tijanism, he probably
started to concentrate on the practical details of his future jihad. In the
Sokoto setting, 'Umar could easily rationalize his own planning by
dwelling on the successful jihad of Usuman dan Fodio, taking the
Shehu's actions as an example. There is doubt that Usuman's and
Bello's influence on 'Umar was very great.[38]

That he had long planned a jihad was clear. On his return to West
Africa from Mecca, 'Umar supposedly brought with him quantities of
Qur'ans, religious literature, and Meccan specialities of value to the
pious. Various writers even claim that he sold amulets (*hujub*). During
his stay in Hausaland, according to a French author, 'Umar was already rich from the sale of such objects and by donations of slaves,
both from Bello, and al-Kanemi in Bornu.[39] If his material situation had
so improved, it seems likely that he was freed of economic worries and
could devote his time to writing, planning his war, and proselytization
for the Tijani order. Yet 'Umar's choice, implying at least a temporary
abandonment of spiritual questions and sufism, caused him many second thoughts and probably troubled the remainder of his life.

Pending the completion of his training – or retraining – at Sokoto,
'Umar may have believed that he could exercise sufficient leverage
(with some luck) over the aging Bello to come to power in Hausaland.
Prior to Bello's death, it is alleged, he gave his son-in-law 'Umar a written testament phrased so as to cancel the succession of his own son
'Atiqu in 'Umar's favor.[40] If there is any substance to this claim, 'Umar
knew that if he pressed it, his efforts to win political control might lead
to a civil war. Although he was by now married to Bello's daughter,[41]
he probably never entertained the idea of a take-over in Sokoto seriously. His quick departure from Sokoto in late 1838 with his wives and
retainers makes it seem likely that he had decided to go back to his
native region in any case, but had left early because of 'Atiqu's growing
resentment at his presence. In addition to his preaching and his participation in political and military activities in Sokoto, he had time to
write a long poem and a book of some length, his *Suyuf al-Sa'id*, later
expanded into his major work, the *Rimah*.[42] Like his years at Madina
and his second visit to Cairo, 'Umar's Sokoto period was one of the
more productive literary intervals of his life.

Before he left Sokoto, 'Umar encountered one of his future enemies,
Ahmad al-Bakka'i. This man was a grandson of Sidi al-Mukhtar al-
Kunti, who had wielded such influence on behalf of the Qadiriya in the
western Sudan at the close of the eighteenth century. It is said that al-

Bakka'i hoped to confront and discredit 'Umar; instead, al-Bakka'i was himself humiliated and left Sokoto.[43]

On his way westward, 'Umar was accompanied by his elder brother Ahmadu, who had come from Futa Toro to fetch him. 'Umar's own following, including many convinced Tijanis, his slaves, and other supporters, was now quite large. Apparently they followed the same route 'Umar had traveled in the 1820s. At Masina, where he stayed for nine months, 'Umar made many recruits for the Tijaniya. As in Bornu and, to some extent, even at Sokoto, these activities created dissension, arousing suspicion and resentment among one faction at Hamdallahi but making a good impression on others.[44]

W. A. Brown sees this dispute as a clash between elders and young people – a political generation gap. Yet the Tijani party at the capital of Masina was not a secret organization; its leader, Shaykh Yarki Talfi (Shaykh Mukhtar b. Wadi'atallah), sent congratulatory poems to 'Umar at Dingiray toward the start of the 1850s and took it on himself to write polemics against the Qadiri leader al-Bakka'i from 1848 onward.[45]

According to oral traditions, both from the Masina side and the 'Umarian side, the anti-Tijani faction at Hamdallahi (which probably included the ruler) tried to assassinate 'Umar or have him ambushed and killed after he had left Masina.[46] A number of attempts to intercept and break up the Tijani party and liquidate its chief were made as the group passed westward through this officially Qadiri region. At Jaka, Saro, and as far from Hamdallahi as Nyemina and Kangaba on the Niger, requests kept arriving from Masina to the local powers for this purpose. Like al-Kanemi and a group at Sokoto, the sons of Shaykh Ahmadu were convinced that al-Hajj 'Umar was a "seeker of Worldly Power" and "a bearer of the Flag of Might." These unfriendly comments were offset by the receptive views of others, who saw him as the "renewer" (*mujaddid*) of Islam in the region.[47]

Once 'Umar had crossed the River Niger at Nyemina, he was in even worse trouble. The pagan Bambara king of Segu, Fama Tyiflu (or Tiefolo) Sagnifiriba, took him prisoner and jailed him at Segu. That the intrigue was directed from Masina is emphasized by an Arabic source:

> At Nyemina, he found messengers from the people of Segu and from Saro, who had preceded him to the land of Segu and its king . . . Qulu Segu [Tyiflu], so that he would kill our Shaykh by treachery at their [Masina's] request. . . . Then their king sent his *wazirs* to Shaykh 'Umar at Nyemina and took him and those with him, his family, and all his possessions, to the town of Segu. . . . They put

him in a strong prison. . . . God created love for our Shaykh 'Umar
in the heart of the king's sister. She said to the king "Why don't you
release this saint before the people do mischief? The men of Masina
are persons of culture, yet they spared him. . . . Do not kill him
nor follow their example, for they are his enemies." He said to his
sister, "You speak the truth," . . . and released 'Umar from prison,
treated him well, and gave him much gold.[48]

From Segu, 'Umar went up the Niger to Kangaba (Mande-Kaba).
Here he stayed for three months. Kangaba was a famous old center of
Mande Islam. In the seventeenth and eighteenth centuries it had been
a political center and a center for the diffusion of Mande clerics into
Ivory Coast and Ghana.[49] The ruler of Kangaba came out to meet
'Umar, "playing a trick on him" with cavalry and cannon but then
treated him well, even building a "grass house" for him in his own
compound. Leaving Kangaba, 'Umar moved on to the more friendly
territory of Kankan, a town about eighty-five miles southeast of Kangaba. From Kangaba, 'Umar was accompanied by the king of Kankan,
Alfa Mahmud, who wanted to become a Tijani. At Kankan, a large
caravan town situated on the route from the upper Niger district to
Futa Jallon, 'Umar stayed for two years, "giving the tie" of the Tijaniya
to all who sought it, "slave or free." Alfa Mahmud remained one of
'Umar's most loyal supporters.[50] When 'Umar started his jihad, Mahmud dispatched a contingent to aid him.[51]

During his stay at Kankan (c. 1838-9), it is clear that 'Umar was
searching for a place to settle; a spot where he could establish a per-
manent base; a site from which he could recruit in earnest, spread
Tijani propaganda, then launch his jihad. Although Kankan was heavily
populated with Tijanis and had a cooperative ruler, it was unsuitable.
It is likely that 'Umar considered it too far from Futa Jallon and Futa
Toro, where he might expect to find recruits, and also too far from
Karta and Segu, the future objectives of his jihad. 'Umar could not
forget his bad treatment at the hands of Fama Tyiflu at Segu nor that
Futa Toro had been continually raided by Bambara from Karta who
kidnapped men, women, and children (as late as 1846). However helpful he was, Alfa Mahmud by his presence alone hindered 'Umar from
exercising full political control.[52]

About 1840, therefore, 'Umar moved on to Koumbiya (Kunbiya), in
northwestern Futa Jallon. Near the religious center of Touba and not
far from Timbo – the capital of the imam of Futa Jallon – Kunbiya was
an appropriate place to halt for a short time.[53] Yet in the end it seemed
less attractive than Jigunko or Diagunko in the Kolen district, which
was near the headwaters of the Bafing River, about a two-day journey

from Timbo, and adjoining the frontier of Futa Jallon.[54] Here 'Umar found the spot he had long sought, and he stayed at Jigunko for four years, until 1844 or 1845. At Jigunko, a traditional source claims that "the people came to him in swarms, making him their objective. He read with his students and whoever required knowledge."[55] Here too, in all probability, 'Umar finished his longest work, the *Rimah*, on 6 September 1845.[56] Significantly, this text contains material on the jihad wholly absent from its prototype, the *Suyuf al-Sa'id*. Jigunko was still a safe place for 'Umar's purposes, well out of range of Bambara raiders who still combed these parts for slaves.

With the exception of his stay at Sokoto, 'Umar's sojourn at Jigunko was his longest so far. If he were intending to lead a jihad, it could not be far in the future, as 'Umar was already over fifty. His Tijani center at Jigunko was a secure place to lodge, feed, and instruct his recruits – a place from which he could proselytize without hindrance, with appropriate accommodation for himself, his wives, and his slaves. After four years at Jigunko, having completed his *Rimah* ("The Spears of God's Party Against the Throats of the Satanic Faction"), al-Hajj 'Umar believed that he had recruited enough men locally. He could best serve his cause and the cause of the militant Tijaniya by going on an extended preaching, publicity, and recruiting tour to Futa Toro. His route led him from Jigunko via Touba to Pakao in the Casamance. At Pakao he met one Modi Muhammad Bakawi who, with his own little brotherhood of eighty men, immediately enrolled under 'Umar's banner.[57] In this vicinity, too, he is said to have passed three days talking with Ma Ba Diakhu, the leader of a Gambian Tijani rising of the 1860s.[58]

As he went toward St. Louis at the mouth of the Senegal River, the local authorities showed overt hostility to him and to his retinue, particularly in Wolof territory.[59] Apprehensively, they viewed him as a "seeker of the Political Kingdom," and tried to murder him.[60] Dodging the assassins of the angry Wolofs, 'Umar crossed into Futa Toro, aiming for his native town of Halwar and the Ile de Morfil. He had not visited his own district for nearly twenty years. Even here, the long-absent pilgrim encountered a mixed reception. He visited his family and went on to Guédé, and from there to Bakel on the Senegal River.[61]

Here he met a French officer, Hecquart, at the new military post recently garrisoned by troops from St. Louis. At first the Frenchman opposed the entry of 'Umar and his men, doubtless because of their intimidating numbers and because many of them must have been armed. At this refusal, 'Umar reportedly gave the European a Qur'anic answer and said, "Go back to your own country, accursed man: leave God's wide land to His Servants."[62] Hecquart finally relented, giving 'Umar "paper and precious textiles" perhaps paid for, as Willis suggests, by secret French funds.[63] By going upriver and then turning southeast into Futa Bondu, 'Umar visited and was received by many of the important chiefs of that region. He also met various French officers and openly discussed his future plans with them. "Preaching to the people, and obtaining many precious gifts," 'Umar ultimately returned to Jigunko via Kajuru (near Kayes), N'dyukulu, and Lumbiridi. Among others, he had talked to Imam Sa'd of Futa Bondu; he had been entertained by him under his "palaver tree."[64]

'Umar's recruiting tour was a huge success; he had been seen where he had wanted to be seen. He had had conversations with important political personalities and made them aware of his forthcoming jihad. He had added greatly to the number of his followers, most of them from Futa Toro. In addition to his oral pleadings, 'Umar had distributed "manifestos" stressing the spiritual rewards of the jihad and probably including a posthumous message from Muhammad Bello in Sokoto urging a revolution on his distant Muslim kinsmen of Futa Toro.[65]

At Jigunko, 'Umar had already benefited from the migration of Tijanis from Futa Jallon, Timbo, and elsewhere. These represented slaves and ex-slaves, the unemployed and the underemployed, the ambitious, or those who wished to fight the Bambara. A near-contemporary source says:

> Many Fulah people moved from Futa [Jallon] on account of him; and from Libbe [Labe] and from Timbo and Kakunde Maji, and from Kollade and Boji; from Timbi Tini, from Koyin, from Kebu [Kunbiya?] from Kolle; from these nine principal towns many people moved on account of him and lived with him.[66]

'Umar was able to recruit many more men in Futa Toro. As in Futa Jallon, some of his new adherents were slaves or ex-slaves, but the majority were free volunteers. Among 'Umar's emergent forces, units from Futa Toro were clearly the most significant group. During his recruiting tour, at Ha'ire (Aere), 'Umar found one of his best future generals – Alfa 'Umar Tyerno Bayla Wane. Bayla was a chief of Lawo; others were Alfa 'Umar Tyerno Mula and Alfa 'Abbas from Huri Fudi (Horéfondé) in Bossea.[67] At Jigunku, 'Umar had already been joined by Modi Muhammad Jam (Tyam), a chief from Futa Jallon. During his tour he was joined by a chief from the Casamance, Modi Muhammad Bakawi. Other adherents were Mauritanian Arabs. Although this movement of allegiance to 'Umar was no mass rising in his favor, there were good reasons for 'Umar's success in recruiting – particularly in Futa Toro.

At the close of the eighteenth century, Futa Toro had been the scene of a partially successful Islamic revolution. It brought the imam (or *almami*) 'Abd al-Qadir Kan to power about 1776.[68] The imam overthrew the local dynast in Futa Toro – the Satigi – so temporarily extinguishing the old Denyanke regime. However, the imam encountered local jealousies, which exploded while he was on campaign in Cayor in 1796. Defeated and made captive there, he was released and, later, reinstated as imam. Yet he had lost so much prestige that he was an easy target for a coalition of the deposed Satigi, a conservative Muslim faction from Futa Bondu, and the Bambara ruler of Karta. These three powers, with the occasional aid of the rulers of Khasso, sent armies into Futa Toro, raiding and enslaving the population.[69] These attacks against the weakened population of Toro occurred after 1807 (when Imam 'Abd al-Qadir was killed), from 1816–18, again in 1831, then in 1846.[70] Thus the population of Futa Toro was more than willing to aid al-Hajj 'Umar in a war of revenge against Karta, Khasso, the Bambara, and their allies generally. In Toro, a king of Nioro, Fama Musa Kurabo (known as Fulo Fobo or "Fulani Killer" to the Bambara), was recalled with particular loathing because of his sadistic exploits.[71] Later the people of Toro came to hate his successor, Mamadi Kandia, the leader of the Bambara expedition of 1846. Mamadi Kandia was later to be 'Umar's antagonist during the Tijani siege of Nioro in 1855. Those who had lost relatives to the Bambara slavers included persons from the leading lineages of Toro. Hence their zeal to join 'Umar, doubtless in the hope of finding and rescuing their captive kinsmen.

What is more, from the time of 'Umar's stay at Jigunko, it is certain that many of the people of Futa Toro began to regard him as their legitimate leader, the head of a Futa Toro "government in exile." Since 1807 and the death of 'Abd al-Qadir, Futa Toro was deprived of a dynamic imam. As 'Umar gave clear evidence of wanting to continue 'Abd al-Qadir's policies, cut off so abruptly at his demise, many Toro men were willing to join the Tijanis. Their desire for revenge on their Bambara foes was another strong motivation. Another new factor, in the 1840s and 1850s, was the appearance of the French, in force, from St. Louis downstream. Their efforts were directed against the parts of Toro along the Senegal River and the upper river basin in general. These pressures convinced many Toro Muslims to migrate – to make their own *hijra* to the east – and it also motivated large groups of them to enter 'Umar's forces.

Yet 'Umar's successful recruiting led to an important defection, that of Imam 'Umar of Futa Jallon. More than ever lukewarm about al-Hajj 'Umar and his activities (including the earlier migration of Tijanis from Timbo to Jigunko), Imam 'Umar and his council debated the issue of letting al-Hajj 'Umar pass through his territory to Jigunko from Bondu.

Eventually they decided to permit 'Umar and his swarm of new recruits to pass over. As al-Hajj 'Umar declares:

> He [Imam 'Umar of Timbo] became fearful of those whom he cal-
> culated were seeking the world and its rule. . . . He thought I was
> like that. . . . When that delusion became fixed in his mind, he
> loathed me and treated me like an enemy. . . . Because of his delu-
> sion, he sent communications to all the people of Futa Jallon . . . to
> hinder me and prevent me from reaching my centre [at Jigunku].[72]

Al-Hajj 'Umar's estrangement from the Imam of Futa Jallon was
serious because it made a further stay at Jigunku more difficult for him.
It certainly precipitated his removal to Dinghirawi (Dingiray) – his
hijra – in 1849–50, very soon after he and his recruits had returned
from Futa Toro.

Jigunku had been an unfortified center for sufi teaching – a place of
residence for 'Umar's students and a place where visitors could easily
visit al-Hajj 'Umar. Beyond Futa Jallon, east of the Bafing River and
above the marshes of the Tinkisso, Dingiray was very different. It had
the look and function of a *ribat*, a Muslim fortress on the rim of the
Islamic world, with thick walls and high towers. Willis says:

> Dinguiray served another purpose: its function was at once spiritual
> and military. . . . Shortly after his move from Dinguiray, al-Hajj
> 'Umar inaugurated the more overt . . . military phase of his *jihad*.
> . . . The geographical location of both establishments was not acci-
> dental. . . . In this respect they served one of the principal func-
> tions of a *ribat*, a place from which *Dar al-Islam* might expand into
> *Dar al-Harb*.[73]

Concurrently, underlining the new military orientation at Dingiray,
'Umar had started stockpiling arms in earnest. He was already well-
to-do, and he constantly received from admirers and well-wishers donations that he now devoted to practical military uses:

> He was perpetually trading in guns and powder with Sierra Leone
> and the business establishments of the Rio Nunez and Rio Pongo.
> The students (*talibés*) set off in caravans to meet the *dyula* [trad-
> ers]. He brought and sold gold dust from the Bouré [region], armed
> his students, filled his granaries with millet, and fortified his camps.[74]

In the theological sense, too, the theme of jihad or "holy war" was
one with which 'Umar was very familiar. If jihad seems to have had a
limited place in his writings before 1840, the second part of his *Rimah*
contains a full chapter on migration (*hijra*) and its corollary, jihad;
there are many other references throughout the book. Traditionally, the

Rimah served as a text for 'Umar's students at Jigunku and Dingiray.[75]

In this book, 'Umar drew a distinction between the major and minor jihads. The former was defined as the struggle for self-control; the latter was a military matter. In 'Umar's opinion, self-control was logically prior to military concerns. He says:

> Every person must make an effort to purify his soul. He should make a serious attempt, and genuinely strive to serve His Lord: nothing should hinder him from it. He should not be diverted by any family claim, his father or his son, his native country, a friend, his house, his clan, his money, or other things which hinder him from nearness to God . . . even if this should lead to absence from his native place, or fighting during a migration or a *jihad*.[76]

'Umar calls the jihad a "collective duty" that has spiritual value arising from its difficulties. A participant in the jihad will attain paradise. Although "every soul must taste of death," dying in the jihad is more meritorious than other ways of dying. 'Umar was capable of writing purple passages on these themes for inspirational purposes:

> O deluded one, exchange your dwelling quickly, and move on to the afterlife. Its palaces are high, its light radiant, its rivers flowing, its bunches of fruit close at hand, its towers unbroken. . . . Its buildings are of silver and gold. There is no clamor there, no illness. Even the pebbles are pearls and jewels. The rivers are of milk and honey, there the Kawthar flows. The palaces are of hollow pearl, towering seventy miles in the air, of green chrysolith of dazzling brilliance, of red ruby rising high.[77]

These exhortations had their effect: the French observers Mage and Faidherbe comment on the discipline shown by 'Umar's *talaba,* who were ready to be martyred.[78]

Just before the jihad began 'Umar renamed his headquarters at Dingiray "Daybata" ("Jalabata"), a name derived from an old Arabic name for Madina, so as to commemorate the original *hijra* from Mecca to Madina. Although he was still on bad terms with the Imam of Futa Jallon, 'Umar had carefully requested his permission to go to Dingiray. Imam 'Umar acknowledged that the place was beyond his frontiers and belonged to the Jalonke king of Tamba, Yimba. Located on the middle course of the Bafing, the town of Tamba was less than 100 miles northwest of Dingiray. Like Muhammad, who had "leased" Madina from a Jewish tribe, 'Umar agreed to pay King Yimba an annual rent for Dingiray/Daybata and its vicinity.[79]

'Umar's move to Dingiray probably took place about 1849–50. The Tijani chief and his men stayed there for two or three seasons before

the jihad started. The second of these years was called the "Year of
the Wooden Tablet," as the students wrote down 'Umar's *Qur'an* commentary on washable wooden boards so as to memorize it, in the traditional West African way.[80]

At first, 'Umar's relations with King Yimba were good. With outward
cordiality, they exchanged presents of money, horses, slave girls, and
even a few muskets. In his customary way, 'Umar "commanded the
Good and prohibited the Bad." Because of a fire in which "three houses
full of books" had burned to the ground,[81] he had recently had to dispatch a nephew to Timbuktu to have new copies made. Yet the King
of Tamba soon became anxious; 'Umar's constant acquisitions of powder, munitions, and weapons "like cannons, swords, and arrows came
to the ears of the King of Tamba . . . who sent messengers to al-Hajj
'Umar to warn him against his way of proceeding. Among them was a
herald named Jali Musa . . . who swore allegiance to 'Umar and became a Muslim."[82]

Jali Musa's actions, as recorded by a local source, are somewhat ambiguous. "Following 'Umar's instructions," he handed over his musket,
horse, and pistol to his companions when they had gone a little way
along the road to Tamba and informed them of his changed status.
When they reached home and told Yimba, the king sent word to 'Umar
that the new convert must be handed over for punishment without delay. At this juncture, 'Umar held a conference with his students:

> He told them of the question of handing Jali Musa over to the un-
> believers, or of his staying with them as a Muslim. . . . Some said,
> "We must send him back, . . ." Others said, "We cannot turn a
> Muslim over to the unbelievers. This matter touches ourselves, our
> property and our weapons." To the messengers, 'Umar said, "You
> have heard the opinion of the Community. . . ." And they went
> back to Tamba.[83]

War was inevitable after this decision, the only one 'Umar could
have made without losing his prestige and his followers at one stroke.
There is evidence, too, that 'Umar had already been working himself
into an appropriate mood for a jihad, for he later told Ahmad al-
Shinqiti:

> When the unbelievers attacked us, I had no unequivocal permission
> from God to make a *jihad* on them, but only from the Prophet and
> Shaykh Tijani. . . . When God gave me permission, it was a Sunday
> night, 12 Dhu'l-Qa'da 1268/28 August 1852. . . . A divine voice told
> me, "I give you permission to make *jihad* in the way of God." It was
> repeated three times.[84]

'Umar's conquest of Tamba proved difficult. Although they were better armed than their opponents, the Tijanis met obstacles. Situated above the River Bafing and built under the edge of an escarpment, Tamba was ringed with multiple concentric walls and had gates and towers of great strength. If he could take it, the stronghold would be of the greatest use to 'Umar. It contained Yimba's takings from the Bambuk and Bouré goldfields; according to Mage, it also contained 3,000 muskets.[85]

'Umar's capture of Tamba, after a siege of several months, was a huge stroke of publicity. Yimba had enjoyed a sinister reputation; he is said to have deliberately killed prisoners to "feed his father's vultures."[86] With the capture of the fortress and the massacre of the defenders that followed, " 'Umar's armies assumed large proportions. Adventurous persons no longer hesitated to place themselves under his orders." Mage notes that he was joined not only by "zealous Muslims" but also those "who hope to get a share in the booty, and so become rich without labor."[87] Among the "zealous" and the convinced Tijanis, there was a radical faction that opposed the contemporary Muslim establishment, the Qadiriya, as 'Umar himself did. The opinions of these militants influenced 'Umar considerably – notably as his forces approached Masina in the final phases of his conquests.

At Tamba, 'Umar not only secured an advanced base for future operations, obtained useful military stores, and acquired credit as a leader, but he also took from the fortress considerable stocks of gold. After a delay for military reorganization – the Futa Jalloni and Futa Toro contingents of his army had shown a lamentable inability to cooperate at Tamba – he moved ahead.

During the first months of 1854, 'Umar advanced from Tamba north along the Bafing River toward the Senegal River. His invasion was facilitated by minor states and towns in his way that were divided from constant internal conflict. This was true of Khasso, where the sons of Demba Sega were on bad terms with each other.[88] By the time 'Umar reached the Senegal River, resistance to his Tijanis had been negligible; at Bouré he now controlled an important source of gold, which he could exchange for war materials.[89]

Soon after the conquest of Tamba, a contemporary source reports, a strange yet significant incident occurred, which throws light on a cleavage within 'Umar's mind. This was a widening gap between his main task as he saw it – to make war with divine assistance, to spread Islam by force – and an opposing tendency to remain a sufi, to free himself from worldly things, to "avoid sultans and kings," and to halt dissension and civil conflict between Muslims. His teacher Muhammad al-

Ghali at Madina had emphasized the second tendency; 'Umar had responded (in 1829) by enshrining these principles in verse:

> Shun the man who wields authority in the land
> Who alters things forbidden to the populace
> Follow the *Sunna* and the Book
> Avoid deviation from what is right
> Except for kings, none corrupt religion more
> Than evil men of learning, by their lies.[90]

When 'Umar returned briefly to Dingiray (c. late 1853), the towns-people noted with astonishment that he was weeping. When they asked him about it, as a German missionary reports, 'Umar gave evidence of a strong internal polarization, of apparent schizoid tendencies from which he suffered:

> He said that what moved him to tears . . . was because he con-sidered how he had made war with Tamba and then attacked Gufte and was also victorious. . . . And now, as the world has made him confortable and well-to-do, he fears God may not find him in the other world, not in Heaven.[91]

Not only was 'Umar now a rich man, from the gifts and kindness of Muhammad Bello alone, but he was becoming a "worldly ruler," a sultan. He also realized clearly that his prestige as a sufi, his standing as a "good man of learning" had been compromised. Unlike Usuman dan Fodio, who had courageously dropped the role of worldly ruler once his jihad was completed to go into semiretirement and cultivate his chief interests – mysticism and theology – 'Umar could not now draw back. After Tamba, he would inevitably have to pursue the jihad to its end. His own internal tensions, pressures from his associates and adherents (many of whom had purely secular motives), and his re-stricted freedom of action may well account for 'Umar's frequent with-drawals from the society of his men, his aloofness, his use of solitary sufi retreats (*khalwa*), his long meditations, and his increasing use of incubational techniques (*istikhara*) to obtain guidance, as noted by contemporary observers.[92]

'Umar's Jihad, Views and Opinions

After the taking of Tamba, the remaining years of al-Hajj 'Umar's life (c. 1855–64) were taken up with war. The large dimensions and the surprising speed of his conquests demonstrate that he had created and equipped an efficient military organization. It was well officered and furnished with appropriate weapons. Its numbers are uncertain; Kanya-Forstner estimates the core of 'Umar's army at 12,000 men.[93] For important battles, such as the battle at Tiawal near Hamdallahi in Masina in 1862, 'Umar may have had as many as 30,000 men. And, as several clashes between Tijani troops and the French showed, the 'Umarian army proved that it was nearly as good as a European army – particularly on its own ground. It also enjoyed high morale.

'Umar's forces were divided into three parts: "students" (*talaba,* often gallicized as *talibés*); *sofas* ("grooms," slaves, and other "new Muslims"); and *tuburu,* conscripts who were often "enlisted" by force. The loyalty of the *tuburu* was often suspect, and they frequently deserted. Yet they were also ostensible converts to Islam, and their "conversion" was frequently celebrated by a head-shaving and capping ceremony. Unlike the *sofas* and the *talaba,* the *tuburu* were officially excluded from taking booty on the field.

The *sofas* fought alongside their masters (*talaba*), set up camp, did the cooking, and looked after the horses; many of the *talaba* and some *sofas* were mounted. The *talaba* were the élite of the Tijani forces, many of them being full members of the Tijani brotherhood. They could often claim some education, even if it were of a limited and doctrinaire religious kind, for these were the men who had studied under 'Umar at Jigunko and Dingiray. This element of 'Umar's forces, the military arm of the Tijani *tariqa,* could be compared to other warlike sufi organizations – the Safavid armies of sixteenth-century Iran or the troops of the Salihiya under Muhammad 'Abdallah Hasan in Somalia in the early twentieth century (Chapter 7). The fact that neither *sofas* nor *talaba* were denied the right to raid and plunder clearly made them more unified; so did their Tijani attachments and the personal desire of many of them to wreak havoc on the Bambara, particularly if they came from Futa Toro.

The ethnic origins of 'Umar's army were varied. It is likely that the largest single group was derived from Futa Toro, including contingents from Nganar, Damga, Yirlabe, Bossea, and the adjoining Futa Bondu (a frequent ally of Toro in past wars). Lesser contingents hailed from Futa Jallon, with a few Soninkes (Sarrakhole) and Wolof Muslims and some Arabs and Berbers from southern Mauritania.[94]

Like the force itself, its armament was heterogeneous. It included muskets, pistols, and perhaps a few cannon, imported with the appropriate bullets and munitions from the coast via Sierra Leone or from the French-controlled area at the mouth of the Senegal River. These arms seem to have been of European manufacture: British, French, Spanish, or Portuguese. There were many routes going inland for such goods from the Sierra Leone coast – notably via the Rio Pongo and the

Nunez, where routes from upriver points ran inland to Timbo in Futa Jallon.[95] A similar route ran inland from the Melakuri River in Guinea.[96] Considerable war material had been stockpiled by 'Umar before he began his jihad; even so, after he took the Bambuk region, he possessed quite enough gold to pay for what he wanted and perhaps used slaves for the purpose, also.[97] To keep his precious weapons in good order he recruited a corps of gunsmiths and weapons repairmen. However, it is doubtful that he was able to cast cannon – that he was able to recruit the necessary experts or that he had access to the necessary raw materials for this complex procedure. Yet only twenty years after 'Umar's death, Samory Ture was able to create a local industrial base to support his wars, and many of the same technical skills may have been available earlier. However, 'Umar's men did make gunpowder from local materials and cast musket balls.

No detailed discussion of 'Umar's wars is possible here. However, his relations with France, his conquests of the Bambara states of Karta and Segu, his conquest of the Muslim state of Masina, and his theological views deserve mention. When 'Umar moved north from Tamba in early 1854, after a military reorganization, his men overran Khasso and Bambuk. They then penetrated Karta, coming near the new French post at Bakel on the Senegal River. After a halt to rest his troops and repair ordnance, 'Umar attempted to make contact with the French, requesting from them more war material and – some sources claim – "technical assistance" in the form of a French adviser to accompany his army.[98]

Before he reached the Senegal River, 'Umar encountered some agitated Muslim traders, who wanted to know from the Tijani chief where he and his army were going. 'Umar assured them that he was not aiming at either Toro or Futa Jallon, but intended to conquer the pagan Bambara of Karta.[99] Despite these remarks to the merchants, 'Umar had two objectives in approaching eastern Futa Toro and Bondu with an army. He wished to make good his claim to the imamate of Futa Toro, backed by soldiers; he also wished to make an "arrangement" with France. In return for munitions and suitable weapons, he was prepared to tolerate the French presence and even facilitate their trade along the upper Senegal River. He also wanted to make sure that the French would not attack him in the rear while he was engaged in Karta. This had been his objective in meetings with French officials during his recruiting tour in 1847.[100]

Misled by the reception he received from such Frenchmen as Donnay, Caille, and Grammont, 'Umar believed that they might support him – at least for a time. With French weapons, he could consolidate his power in Futa Toro and, when the time was right, invade the Bambara states. The French would have to continue to pay the *coutume;*

'Umar regarded this requirement as equivalent to the Islamic usage of *jizya,* a tax paid by subordinate non-Muslim peoples. Carrère and Holle report that 'Umar declared, in an interview:

> I am the friend of the whites. I want peace and detest injustice.
> When a Christian has paid the *coutume,* he may trade with safety.
> When I become Imam of Futa [Toro], you must build me a fort.
> I shall discipline the country, and friendly relations will exist between you and me.[101]

This proposal was not taken seriously by the French. By 1854, the European colonizers were in a newly expansive, imperialistic mood, and they no longer wanted to pay "tribute" to any "inferior" Muslim ruler. Further, the French governor Protet sent an ambiguous answer to 'Umar's request for guns and ammunition.[102] This cooled relations very quickly. 'Umar retaliated by arranging minor boycotts of French goods – particularly textiles – and hindering French trade in gum arabic (still an important adhesive in the mid-nineteenth century) from the upper Senegal basin.[103]

Because of French opposition, 'Umar realized by the spring of 1855 that his subsidiary plan – to take over Futa Toro – was no longer feasible. But this did not alter his main design, which he had earlier deferred. This was the conquest of the Bambara states, starting with an attack on Karta and Segu. That he had a lingering desire to control Toro is shown by the fact that until 1859, two years after the Tijani move against the French post at Madina on the river, he believed that a military probe of French intentions and military readiness was still a useful strategem. The failure of his soldiers at Madina showed him that French military supremacy was overwhelming, that they had stepped out of their former role as mere traders, and that further contests with them might prove dangerous. Yet if 'Umar abandoned any hope of ruling Futa Toro, he did not abandon its population, to whom he tried to apply the concept of migration (*hijra*). For these reasons, although 'Umar clashed with France, the collision was largely fortuitous; the Tijani chief never intended to take over the entire length of the Senegal River, much less the city of St. Louis. His main task lay elsewhere. To have fought France would have compromised it.

Hence 'Umar's great emphasis at this time was on migration away from areas where Islam was not practiced, away from "oppressive non-Muslim rulers," African or French. This point had already been made by Usuman dan Fodio and emphasized by Amir 'Abd al-Qadir. On the theoretical side, many of 'Umar's opinions are made explicit in the *Rimah,* where an entire chapter is devoted to this subject. Here 'Umar states:

> Migration [*hijra*] is now necessary for every person living in a town
> where disobedience to God is openly practiced without any concern
> over it, where the situation cannot be altered. Migration is impera-
> tive from the land of the unbelievers. . . . *Hijra* is of two kinds, the
> greater and the lesser.[104]

He goes on to explain that the greater *hijra* is internal, personal "migration" – disassociation from worldly things and concerns – whereas the
lesser *hijra* is a military affair, "concerning bodies." Thus *hijra* runs
parallel to jihad, with its greater and lesser aspects. Ultimately 'Umar
based his arguments on two passages in the *Qur'an*. Both stress the
"breadth of God's earth" and are the identical passages employed for
similar arguments by both the Shehu and Amir 'Abd al-Qadir.[105] A corollary of migration, the question of friendly contacts with unbelievers,
is also discussed and condemned by the Tijani chief.

In practical terms, 'Umar did his utmost to enforce Islamic legalities.
In 1858, after his attack on Karta had begun, 'Umar returned for some
time to Futa Toro and Bondu. He recruited adherents there for his
campaigns, and he attempted to pressure the population in both places
to move to Karta. Many followed his advice and left, frequently from
the vicinity of French military or trading posts. In spite of some local
resistance to migration, what 'Umar intended is clear from an account
by a German missionary, writing in his own style of quaint English:

> ['Umar] said, Bundu must move away. They answered, they will
> not. He still said, move they must; if they move now, it will be better
> for them. . . . They did not mind him, they disregarded his strong
> warning. He passed to Futa Toro; when he returned, he drove away
> Bundu. He dislodged them with force, so they moved with confu-
> sion. . . . Bundu [sustained] heavy losses, their money was lost,
> their cows, their slaves, their livestock and household goods; many
> perished in the forest from hunger. . . . He directed them to Nyoro
> and gave them land there. He helped them with what they required
> to live upon; he protected and took care of all the people, lest they
> should suffer want.[106]

As he had already invaded Karta in 1855 and taken its capital, Nioro,
'Umar could leave the French to pursue their forward policy at Madina
and elsewhere along the Senegal River. He also hoped that they would
not pursue him and that some form of coexistence between him and
the French might continue; on this point his hopes were justified.

As for 'Umar's campaigns in the East, they are impressive because of
the innumerable raids, ambushes, and skirmishes carried out by the
Tijanis. Unjustifiably, perhaps, the French writer Mage claimed that it

was 'Umar's deliberate policy to spread terror among his opponents. In Bambara country at least, 'Umar's primary aim seems to have been retaliation for past Bambara misdeeds in Futa Toro; only secondarily did he strive for converts to Islam or adherents for the Tijaniya.

An Arabic source – a history of the Tijani campaigns written by 'Umar's "trusted servant and secretary," Abdallahi 'Al – makes clear the grand strategy involved.[107] 'Umar moved from Toro and Bondu into Karta, from Karta to Segu, then down the Niger from Segu toward Hamdallahi in Masina. 'Al discusses in detail a long series of military episodes; the suppression of particular groups (such as the Diawara in Karta); and slow marches by small bodies of 'Umar's soldiers (1,000 to 2,000 on average), who attacked and captured town after town as they moved eastward. 'Umar's progress toward Masina was no blitzkrieg. Like an inkblot on a flat surface, the Tijani army spread out, occasionally suffering a minor defeat or meeting desperate resistance, then engulfing a region and taking large numbers of prisoners.

'Al records an advance sometimes marked by aimless brutality, now and then enlivened by a miracle of 'Umar's. One of these occurred when his starving army crossed the Faleme River on its way to Nioro. Halted momentarily by a flood, 'Umar caused the waters to recede:

> There the river was, as if it had been dry for two years. They forded it. . . . And when they had crossed over, 'Umar asked for forty measures from his provisions. He divided it among the army of eleven hundred men, so as to fill the hand of each man twice over. Everyone who ate his portion was satisfied. This was one of his greatest miracles.[108]

When the victorious Tijanis reached Nioro, the capital of Karta, 'Umar, in an iconoclastic mood, did for the moment emphasize conversion:

> And they [Tijanis] entered and halted at the palace of Mamadi Kandia [the Bambara ruler of Nioro] when the whole region of Karta offered allegiance to him ['Umar]. Then he ordered their idols to be brought out and smashed them by his own hand with an iron mace. He ordered them to shave their heads, which they did. He ordered them to pray, to build mosques, to limit the number of their wives to four.[109]

During their attacks on Bambara towns in Karta and Segu, 'Umar's forces continually suffered considerable casualties. To make up these losses in manpower, groups of new soldiers arrived continually from Bondu and Toro, ready to go on the jihad. Their eastward traffic up the Senegal River then down the Niger was matched by long files of slaves and prisoners going under escort in the opposite direction, carrying the treasures and loot accumulated by 'Umar's men.[110] In the first phases of the jihad, these columns of prisoners with their spoil were directed to Dingiray or, later, diverted to Nioro or Segu. If the slaves and booty gathered in this way were exchanged by 'Umar for horses, guns, powder, or other war material, there is little mention of it.[111]

Once the Tijanis had overrun Karta, there was nothing to hinder 'Umar from advancing against Segu, the adjoining Bambara state. Here 'Umar (c. 1838) had been held prisoner by King Tyiflu Sagnifiriba; it must have held bitter memories for him. The capture or dismemberment of Segu also had political implications for both Karta and Masina. Segu had entertained territorial designs on Karta because of an old split separating the Bambara dynasties that ruled the two states. Further, Masina (downstream from Segu along the Niger) had made efforts to control Segu; the Sissé kings of Masina had declared themselves the heirs to Segu's territorial claims beyond its own borders, for the moment invalidated because of Segu's military weakness.[112]

Because of Segu's old claims to parts of Karta, Ahmadu III, the Sissé Muslim ruler of Masina, warned 'Umar to leave Karta in 1855, as soon as he had heard of the Tijani invasion. Ahmadu declared that Nioro itself and certain peoples living in the vicinity had already pledged allegiance to him even before the fall of the former dynasty (the Kulibalis), dislodged by 'Umar.[113] To reinforce his claims, Ahmadu III sent an army to Karta, which immediately clashed with the Tijanis. Neither side seemed to want peace; soon, the Kartan allies of Ahmadu III were crushed. 'Umar moved on toward Segu with little delay. Nevertheless, he did take the trouble to write about the origins of his quarrel with Ahmadu III. In this account, 'Umar's *Bayan,* he emphasizes Ahmadu's "erroneous" policies and castigates him for his laziness in the matter of spreading Islam.[114] Thus it has been suggested that this book was designed to be read by the Tijani faction at Masina. It included a disappointed candidate for the throne (Ba Lobbo), passed over at the time of Ahmadu III's election yet still influential in the army and at the court. In the case of open conflict, 'Umar counted on the help of this group – essentially a Tijani fifth column – at Hamdallahi.

As far as Segu was concerned, 'Umar came close to gaining control over the town without a fight soon after his capture of Nioro. The king of Segu, Turukuru Mari (d. 1856), had been ready to hand it over to the Tijanis; but he had been foiled, then killed by an anti-Tijani group that preferred to maintain good ties with Masina.[115] The leader of this coup was Fama 'Ali b. Monzon (or 'Ali Wuytala), who fled to Masina

when 'Umar occupied Segu in the spring of 1861; at Masina he became
a pensioner of the Sissé king.

Al-Hajj 'Umar regarded the capture of Segu merely as a prelude to
taking Masina, with Hamdallahi Town. Yet, for the Tijanis, the overthrow of this Muslim state – a theocratic imitation of Sokoto, also having
a Qadiri complexion – involved doctrinal as well as military problems.
Such a war would draw far less acclaim from other Muslims than a
jihad against the Bambara. Hence 'Umar's new venture required appropriate justification. Already in his *Rimah,* 'Umar had denounced excessive "love of political power" as the ailment that was "infecting the
nations" and that derived from certain "evil learned men of this age."[116]
These hostile comments were a direct attack on the conservative Qadiri
leader Ahmad al-Bakka'i and on al-Bakka'i's ally Ahmadu III. One of
'Umar's most frequently repeated accusations (designed to appeal to
militants and Muslims with few worldly goods) against Ahmadu III
was his abandonment of Masina's traditionally energetic policy of proselytization against non-Muslims.[117] Indeed, Ahmadu's father, Ahmadu II,
had been killed in 1852 while raiding the Bambara. In general, the ruling king had dropped the old policy of dynamic, militant Islam that
was favored by 'Umar himself.

Using his rhetorical bellows, 'Umar fanned these controversial points
into grounds for an attack on Masina. In his *Bayan,* he claimed that
the pagan Bambara chief Fama 'Ali of Segu had bribed Ahmadu to
give him military help against the Tijanis for "a thousand *mithqals* of
gold."[118] This sort of argument had already been used by Usuman dan
Fodio during the Fulani jihad; whosoever, claiming to be a Muslim,
makes a political alliance with a non-Muslim is himself a worthy target
of jihad. However much the unfortunate Ahmadu III tried to deflect
'Umar with men or with arguments, he lost the contest; for 'Umar was
in his element, exploiting the flaws in Ahmadu's letters to him. The
Tijani chief demonstrated an intellectual's contempt for Ahmadu's obvious ignorance of Islamic theology. In a game of hurling quotations
and counterquotations, exchanging cutting logicalities, 'Umar cut Ahmadu to pieces, as he would shortly do on the battlefield.

In a letter to 'Umar, Ahmadu had claimed that Segu and its capital
(Segu Sikoro) had already been converted to Islam, hence 'Umar had
no grounds to invade Fama 'Ali's territory. In his *Bayan,* 'Umar denies
all of these claims:

> We crossed the River [Niger]. . . . God divided them before us in
> defeat, after they had slaughtered many of our men. The unbelievers
> were overthrown and banished from their capital. With his army
> defeated, Ahmadu turned back to his own country. We entered the

capital of unbelief, Segu Sikoro, after 'Ali bin Munzu (Monzon) and his men had fled, so as to purify his land and property. . . . God . . . ordered us to move the well-known statues and idols from their great state palaces into Segu Sikoro. We assembled them there: until now we have not smashed them, so as to establish evidence against this Ahmadu [III] . . . when he falsely claimed that they had repented and broken the idols. No Muslim believing in God and the Last Day had [ever] entered that city.[119]

Al-Hajj 'Umar's progress down the Niger aroused great apprehension not only among the rulers of Segu and Masina; the Qadiri chief Ahmad al-Bakka'i was equally fearful about 'Umar's objectives. A member of the Kunta clan, which had produced such illustrious men as his father and grandfather, al-Bakka'i was heir to great religious influence and political standing. Since he succeeded his brother (c. 1846) as the leader of the Mukhtariya branch of the Qadiri order, pressures from aggressive nomads in his home district north of Timbuktu caused him to move into the town, along with other members of his clan. This move drew the Kuntas into local politics. Because Timbuktu was now menaced by both roving Tuaregs and the ambitions of the dynasts at Hamdallahi, the Kuntas now occupied themselves with propping up Timbuktu's position. To this end they worked out a triangular agreement between themselves, the Tuareg, and Masina, principally to guard the freedom of Timbuktu's trade routes, on which the prosperity of the town depended. Although the Kuntas continued to have difficulties with both Masina and the nomads, they cultivated their ties to Segu – based on their efforts to convert the Segu *famas* to Islam.[120]

Al-Bakka'i had long been aware of al-Hajj 'Umar, whom he had encountered at Sokoto in the 1830s.[121] On that occasion, tradition has it that 'Umar had worsted him in a debate. Since then, he had anxiously watched the Tijani chief's moves from Jigunku to Dingiray and from there into Karta. Increasingly, al-Bakka'i was troubled by 'Umar's advance, particularly the capture of Segu and then the seizure of Hamdallahi (captured by 'Umar in 1862). Rightly, al-Bakka'i was convinced that Timbuktu's turn would come next.

Hence al-Bakka'i began to correspond with his erstwhile enemy, Ahmadu III, against whom he had written lively polemics not long before.[122] In a letter written about 1856, after the capture of Nioro by the Tijanis, al-Bakka'i made it clear to Ahmadu III that Segu, Masina, and Timbuktu must now close ranks against a future Tijani invasion. If they did not, 'Umar would simply overrun them one by one as his army moved downriver. Al-Bakka'i was so frightened of 'Umar that he was ready to abandon the family tradition of not bearing arms (the Kuntas were a nonmilitary, *zawaya* tribe) and make an alliance with Masina; in fact, al-Bakka'i was prepared to launch a Qadiri counterjihad against 'Umar.

Although Ahmadu III did accept al-Bakka'i's advice, it was too late to form an effective coalition against 'Umar and save Hamdallahi. When the town fell to the Tijanis (spring of 1862) after a major battle at Tiawal, al-Bakka'i knew that only a short time would pass before a Tijani attack on Timbuktu. This did not happen until 1863; on that occasion, al-Bakka'i merely absented himself from the town until the raiders had withdrawn. He now concentrated on preserving Kunta influence in the region, waiting until he could rebuild the shattered Qadiri constellation. Meanwhile, he started to write letters to 'Umar, some of which have survived.

From these, it is clear that al-Bakka'i had fathomed the seriousness of 'Umar's psychological difficulties[123] – his schizoid tendencies arising from the demands of his two mutually conflicting roles: military leader versus sufi *shaykh*. Thus he addressed him as *amir*, a subtle insult emphasizing 'Umar's military rank yet denying him any spiritual standing. Further, al-Bakka'i sent complaints to 'Umar that raised large legal or doctrinal issues, insinuating that 'Umar was in the wrong and had violated elementary tenets of Islam.[124]

In one damaging passage, for example, the Qadiri *shaykh* says that he also shares 'Umar's views of the virtues of jihads. Yet, he notes, they often lead to oppressive rule or tyranny – a jab at 'Umar. Al-Bakka'i also held out to 'Umar mischievous or equivocal suggestions; although he was willing to serve as 'Umar's deputy at Timbuktu, he did not wish to meet him. Difficulties of protocol might arise: which man would swear allegiance to the other? Al-Bakka'i hinted that he would be well satisfied if 'Umar and the Tijanis would retreat upstream to Segu so that an appropriate distance would intervene between them.[125]

These attacks were infrequently answered by 'Umar, if answered at all. At this time, his preoccupations were of a military nature. Rather, he instructed the former leader of the Tijani faction at Hamdallahi, Yarki Talfi (also known as Mukhtar ibn Wadi'atallah), to reply on his behalf. The Tijani retort to al-Bakka'i appears in Talfi's book, "The Weepings of al-Bakka'i."[126] This attack struck home, for Talfi was able to borrow apposite and detrimental quotations from the writings of al-Bakka'i's father, Shaykh Muhammad al-Mukhtar. The result was a sizzling polemic, which frequently states the Tijani position on contemporary issues clearly.[127]

'Umar's own position and attitudes toward certain legal and doctrinal matters as well as his theological originality deserve mention. His views may be analyzed on several planes. In questions of day-to-day

Islamic jurisprudence, 'Umar was very much aligned with contemporary reforming neosufis, but not with the Wahhabis. His opinions ran closely parallel to those of Ahmad ibn Idris al-Fasi and Muhammad 'Ali al-Sanusi on many issues. As he had already made clear in a letter to Muhammad al-Amin al-Kanemi of Bornu about 1830, 'Umar had nothing but scorn for "pedestrian imitators" (*muqallidun*) in theology.[128] He directed severe criticism at Maliki or other scholars of Islamic law who did nothing new but merely followed the lines laid down by their predecessors.

Like Usuman dan Fodio, 'Umar was attracted by the writings of the sixteenth-century Egyptian writer al-Sha'rani; like al-Sha'rani, 'Umar had no use for the restrictions erected by the Sunni law schools among themselves, and he says so at length in his *Rimah*.[129] Further, he denied any claim of the four schools to a monopoly on legal knowledge, a position that had already been adopted by Usuman dan Fodio near the end of his life. 'Umar wished to keep open the "gate" of free interpretation (*ijtihad*); he constantly advocated legal creativity and juristic freedom.

In his *Suyuf al-Sa'id* (1837) and more fully in his *Rimah* of 1845, 'Umar reveals his opinions about many issues that were preoccupying the Muslim intellectual world of that time. Yet as a Tijani, 'Umar makes claims that go much farther than the thinking of the "free interpreters of Islamic law" (*mujtahidun*), just as he scorns the "pedestrian imitators" of their intellectual betters. Here he cites an illustration from al-Sha'rani: "If two men enter a house in the daylight and one sees all that is in it, while the other relies on information from other people about what is inside the house, not entering it himself, the first man is like an advanced sufi (*'arif*); the second is like a juridical imitator."[130] 'Umar applies this analogy to illustrate his opinion of "free interpreters" of the law. Although such persons may know a great deal through study and training, an experienced mystic – a sufi – knows far more, because he possesses inspired knowledge. Thus 'Umar makes short work of both kinds of jurists in favor of mystics, whose insights into Islamic law are deeper and better than those of any sort of legist.

'Umar was fully at home in the higher reaches of Islamic theory. Thus he could expound in detail certain Tijani doctrines (such as *wilaya*, "saintship") that set it apart from other brotherhoods.[131] In both his *Suyuf* and *Rimah*, he quotes an eighteenth-century Moroccan scholar, Ahmad ibn Mubarak, who stated that if all four legal schools were to suddenly vanish, a saint (*wali*) would be able to reconstruct the law of Islam.[132] This is so because such saints are directly open to divine influence through their relations to the Prophet Muhammad, who contemplates God. As Yves Maquet has shown, in their hierarchal order and in definition, the Tijani saints and the supreme saint particularly have an odd resemblance to the imams of Isma'ili shi'ism.[133] In the pyramidal framework of the Tijani order sketched out by al-Tijani and elaborated by 'Umar, the concept of the "Supreme Pole" (*qutb al-aqtab*) is roughly interchangeable with that of the Isma'ili imam.[134]

This component in Tijani thought may be shown by other examples too close to the heterodox original to be mere chance. Within the Tijani hierarchy of *muqaddam*s and *khalifa*s, the theme of upward movement for predesignated persons, who ascend through the hierarchy's ranks from bottom to top (guided by their superior talents and knowledge), is very prominent. Thus 'Umar, made a *muqaddam* by al-Ghali in Madina, claimed that his teacher had told him that he had been selected as one of al-Tijani's successors.[135] Later, his rank of *khalifa* in the Tijani order was "confirmed" by certain dreams that came to him or that others dreamed about him.[136] It is also significant that 'Umar, arriving in the Hijaz from West Africa with some prior training, immediately obtained "special instruction" from al-Ghali. Here again, 'Umar's period of study under a recognized master to learn the "secrets of the order" recalls Isma'ili initiatory techniques.[137]

In the case of Islamic law, too, there is more than a hint that 'Umar did not consider it the same for all Muslims. Those members of the Tijaniya who possess superior knowledge through their own mystical experience may not feel that they are required to conform to the law like other Muslims. A claim of this kind opens the way to antinomian activities. Indeed, a nineteenth-century critic of the Tijaniya accused them of being followers of a medieval antinomian group, the Malamatiya.[138] And as Yves Macquet points out, a claim to profound learning different in degree and in kind from that available to the ordinary person closely resembles the Isma'ili doctrine of the two sorts of knowledge: the one exoteric and external, the other inspired and internal.[139] Another belief held in common by the two groups is that of alternating social decay and renewal involving a mahdi or Jesus ('Isa) who would appear at the turns of Islamic millennia to rejuvenate the world; this is something like the Sunni idea of the "renewer" or *mujaddid*. Finally, Tijani thought accommodates the old sufi (Zoroastrian?) doctrine of divine light under the name of *al-Nur al-Muhammadiya* ("the light of Muhammad"), a kind of emanationism much favored by certain sufi and Shi'i groups during the early centuries of Islam.[140] None of these comparisons is intended to suggest that Tijanis are Shi'is; rather, they point out that certain Tijani views can show a long history in Islam, sometimes on the side of heterodoxy.

In spite of the *mahdi* doctrine noted above, 'Umar does not seem to have made any use of the mahdist idea. However, some of his followers evidently believed that if he were not a mahdi, he was the mahdi's *wazir* (aide, or minister). A document of obscure origin, dated about 1856, purporting to come from the Sharif of Mecca but probably written by a West African having a limited knowledge of Arabic, also connects him to another millennial figure, one Ibrahim Sharif al-Din.[141] A tradition collected by Trimingham connects 'Umar to the second caliph, 'Umar al-Khattab, and suggests that he was "revealed as the Mahdi" in Mecca or Madina.[142] It seems obvious that these characteristics were ascribed to 'Umar by enthusiastic supporters but never employed by 'Umar himself.

The final years of al-Hajj 'Umar's career – from 1862 to 1864 – show him beginning to strain his military resources, becoming overconfident, and finally extending the limits of his power too far. When he took Hamdallahi, he intended to rebuild its fortifications – perhaps to make it into the eastern capital for his state, an alternative to Nioro should the French come too close. On the other hand, there are suggestions that he intended it as an eastern base, a point of departure for further conquests such as the Mossi of Yatenga or continued military advance down the Niger toward Hausaland.[143]

At this time, 'Umar's overconfidence led him into a fatal trap; he made a false assessment of the political situation at Hamdallahi. He first overlooked and then denied the claims of his former allies – the Ba Lobbo faction in the town, the followers of an excluded candidate to the throne of Masina. By refusing to help Ahmadu III in the war against the Tijanis, they had greatly aided 'Umar.[144] Yet when 'Umar made his own son Ahmadu amir of Masina, Ba Lobbo's faction was left politically stranded. Enraged, they conspired against 'Umar. When 'Umar discovered that Ba Lobbo and his brother 'Abd al-Salam were plotting against him, he arrested and fettered both of them. Unexpectedly, both men escaped from Hamdallahi.[145]

This was the opportunity for which 'Umar's enemy al-Bakka'i had been waiting; he now aided Ba Lobbo and 'Abd al-Salam in creating a new coalition against 'Umar. Having insufficient troops of his own and having been badly crippled by the loss of two of his best generals in rapid succession, 'Umar could only shut himself up in Hamdallahi with too many mouths and too few supplies. Hamdallahi was quickly invested by the men of the coalition: Qadiris from Masina, Ba Lobbo's men, and a contingent dispatched by al-Bakka'i from Timbuktu. The siege of Hamdallahi went on from August 1863 to February 1864. All this time, Ahmadu bin 'Umar was unavoidably absent at Segu, putting down a large-scale revolt.

Knowing that his stocks of ammunition and food would last only a short time, 'Umar and a few companions made a desperate sortie through the besiegers' lines in the first week of February 1864. Elements of the investing army pursued 'Umar and his party up the Degembere escarpment adjoining Hamdallahi. Abdallahi 'Al gives the standard version of 'Umar's death, fighting against overwhelming odds:

> The enemy were frightened to follow him, but when they heard he
> had got away, they faced him and those . . . with him in the
> village of Yughuna, and attacked him and his companions, weak
> from hunger and thirst. They resisted them from dawn until sunset.
> . . . He eluded them again, and reached the village of Ghoro.
> When he reached Ghoro . . . the new moon of Ramadan had
> risen. The enemy came up, too, and surrounded the Muslims there
> for four days. When the Almighty desired, he removed him from
> this place of toil and unbroken disaster to a place of rest and
> goodness. . . . He martyred on Friday in the year *Sharaf* ("glory").
> . . . 3 Ramadan 1280/12 February 1864.[146]

A reliable oral tradition gathered at Koniakari in 1890 emphasizes suicide; a blacksmith named Kankuna who claimed to have accompanied 'Umar in his last hours claimed that he had climbed up the escarpment carrying a barrel of gunpowder. After saying his prayers for the last time, 'Umar sat on the powder barrel and removed his amulets, which he gave to Kankuna for transmission to Ahmadu bin 'Umar. The Tijani chief then fired the powder and blew himself to bits.[147]

'Umar's Tijani state, continued by his sons (who were unable to agree with each other about the succession), survived until 1893, when it was conquered by the French. In the colonial period, 'Umar was invariably drawn as a fanatic, a "marabout" implacably hostile to the French, and this view has influenced many. However, 'Umar tried to make an alliance with the French and only opposed them when they manifested hostility to him.[148]

Al-Hajj 'Umar, who has been described as an "adventurer of a new type," a "formidable conqueror," or a man who had an ambition to form a "great theocracy" with himself as its "divinely appointed ruler," was far more than that.[149] If he suffered internal conflicts over his roles as mystic and secular leader, he was a man who followed the pattern of jihad outlined by Usuman dan Fodio. He was a man of excellent education and brilliant intellect joined to remarkable organizational talents. Yet in the Actonian sense, his role of supreme leader surely sapped his judgment, and power finally spoiled him, probably making him take his own life.

CHAPTER 4

The Sanusi Brotherhood in Libya and the Sahara

Muhammad 'Ali al-Sanusi (1787–1859) and the Sanusi brotherhood continued the work of reform and of proselytization initiated by the Egyptian sufi revival at the end of the eighteenth century. Doctrinally, the Sanusiya represents a halfway house between traditional sufism and Wahhabi reform; it owes much to the neosufi views of Ahmad ibn Idris al-Fasi. Al-Sanusi himself was an original writer and thinker about the problems of Islam; he was also a prolific author. Like Usuman dan Fodio and al-Hajj 'Umar, al-Sanusi declared for juridical freedom and the opening of the "gate of *ijtihad*." He was also a historian. His biggest interest was, perhaps, conversion to Islam; this was the order's dominant goal as it moved from Libya into the Sahara and toward the interior of the African continent. During the time of al-Sanusi's son Muhammad al-Mahdi, there was also an air of subdued millennialism about the order, which was never made explicit (see pp. 116–18).

Although they had some minor differences with the Ottoman Turks, al-Sanusi and his successors got on well with them, even if Sanusi's sons did oppose the plans of Sultan 'Abd al-Hamid II to pull the order under closer Ottoman control. The Sanusi order had its constructive side; it suppressed local feuds and sectional disputes in Cyrenaica and elsewhere, when it had power. Ultimately, in a phase of Sanusi history omitted here, the order helped give birth to Libyan nationalism, which, paradoxically, brought about the order's overthrow and disappearance in 1969.

Like Italy at the time, nineteenth-century Libya was little more than a geographical expression. It was a land bridge between Egypt and such places in the nearer Maghrib as Tunis and Algiers. After the fall of the feud-ridden Qaramanlis in 1835, the Ottoman Turks reoccupied the big Libyan coastal towns and ports.[1] Yet the "second Ottoman period" in Libya witnessed interesting developments in the hinterland away from the coast.[2] One of these was steady French encroachment from Algeria eastward and southward into the Sahara; another was the emergence of the Sanusi brotherhood and its growth into a semi-independent state, centered on Cyrenaica (Barqa) in northeastern Libya.

The Sanusi order was founded by Muhammad 'Ali al-Sanusi. Known

variously as the "Great Sanusi" or "Grand Sanusi," Muhammad 'Ali al-
Sanusi was succeeded as the head of the brotherhood by his two sons,
Shaykhs Muhammad al-Mahdi and Muhammad Sharif.[3] After their
father's death, the two Muhammads were able to extend the influence
of the order far into the Sahara, to Lake Chad and the kingdom of
Waday. By enrolling new members in their order and by multiplying
the numbers of their sufi lodges (*zawiyas*) and dispersing them widely,
the Sanusis aimed to forestall any Christian conversion of the semi-
pagan peoples of the Sahara. By 1900, the Sanusis had collided with an
advancing French military expedition near Lake Chad and were driven
north again into Cyrenaica. By 1911, they were involved in a desperate
struggle with the Italian invaders of Libya, alongside the Turks. Leading determined opposition to Italy for three decades (1911–42), the
hereditary chiefs of the order emerged as kings of Libya after World
War II. In the autumn of 1969, the Sanusi dynasty of Libya was overthrown by Colonel Mu'ammar al-Qadhdhafi, and the brotherhood was
suppressed.

In its later phases, particularly after 1911, the history of the Sanusiya
is well known. Many competent scholars have dealt with aspects of
Sanusi history: Dajjani, Evans-Pritchard, Klopfer, Fu'ad Shukri, and
N. A. Ziadeh.[4] Since 1930, many of the writings of Muhammad 'Ali al-
Sanusi have been in print, so that his thought is more accessible than
before.[5] Yet the initial phases of the order's development – its theology,
its relations with the French and the Ottoman Turks, and some of its
Saharan activities – are still obscure. Moreover, the place of the Sanusis
in nineteenth-century Islam merits an investigation.

Despite the achievements of his sons, the figure of Muhammad 'Ali
al-Sanusi overshadows them. An Algerian, he was born in the village
of al-Wasita near Mustaghanim in 1787; the village was near the
Moroccan frontier. A son of a clerical family, he claimed descent from
'Ali, the son-in-law of the Prophet Muhammad. Likewise, he claimed
descent from 'Ali's son Hasan and from Sayyid Idris, founder of the
first Muslim state in Morocco. As a *sayyid,* tracing his lineage to such
distinguished ancestors, Muhammad 'Ali possessed automatic prestige.[6]
His family had a tradition of learning, too. It included both men and
women who were considered to be of the learned class, *'ulama.*[7]

In religious matters, Muhammad 'Ali followed a middle course between Wahhabism (with which he was never on hostile terms, although he differed from it) and traditional sufism. Wahhabism was the
religious radicalism of Al-Sanusi's time; like the Wahhabis, the sufi
order founded by Muhammad 'Ali al-Sanusi showed a desire for independence from foreign associates. It also demonstrated a bent for
asceticism, tempered by moral positivism and emphasis on hard work.

These features accord well with the conventional portrait of the Great Sanusi, a convinced mystic and an austere intellectual, a somewhat humorless person who took his descent from 'Ali with the utmost seriousness. Yet the British traveler James Hamilton described him as "all that an Arab saint should be – exact in the observance of religion, gay, and a capital shot: he rides a horse of the purest breed and of great value, dresses magnificently, paints his eyes with kohl and his beard with henna."[8]

The initial development of the order is inseparable from the life of its founder. Orphaned at the age of two by the death of his father (Sayyid 'Ali al-Sanusi), Muhammad ibn 'Ali was brought up by a learned aunt, Sayyida Fatima, and later by a cousin, Sharif. He received his first schooling when he lived with them. His education continued, with instruction from some of the local learned men of Mustaghanim, Mazuna, and Mascara. Here Muhammad 'Ali learned the *Qur'an,* Maliki law, traditions, and the fundamentals of sufism. These were standard subjects in a nineteenth-century Maghribi Muslim education. Al-Sanusi also spent much time practicing horsemanship and shooting – indispensable accomplishments for a North African aristocrat.[9]

When he had learned what the local Algerian *'ulama* had to teach him, the eighteen-year-old Sanusi set off, about 1805, for Fez. As Dajjani suggests, this move may have been made as much to avoid the Turks as to promote his education.[10] By the date of his departure, al-Sanusi was doubtless a member of the Darqawi brotherhood, known for its pro-Moroccan and anti-Ottoman attitudes. Later in his career, al-Sanusi altered his opinions and became more accommodating to the Turks.

At Fez, al-Sanusi studied under the best masters of the time. His teachers included the founders of the Darqawi and Tijani orders, al-'Arabi al-Darqawi and Ahmad al-Tijani. Al-Sanusi's attachment to sufism grew rapidly here, for he joined the Qadiriya, Shadhiliya, Jazuliya, Nasiriya, Habibiya, and probably other orders. Yet his mystical preoccupations were merely one side of his intellectual development; he was interested in a great range of subjects, including law and politics.[11]

In the early nineteenth century Fez was important as ever for legal, political, and historical studies. The Qarawiyyin Mosque, the institution to which al-Sanusi had attached himself, equaled or surpassed the Azhar in Cairo as an intellectual center. Here Muhammad 'Ali spent fourteen years perfecting his knowledge and getting *ijazas* ("certificates") for the books he read under the local masters, resident or itinerant. The core of his studies was Maliki law. Yet he found the time to investigate mathematics, the science of magic squares (*'ilm al-awfaq*), and general astrology. An account by Shakib Arslan contains a list of al-Sanusi's subjects and stresses his eagerness to acquire all branches of learning.[12]

Toward the end of his stay in Fez, al-Sanusi himself began to teach, giving religious and legal instruction. By the time he left the city, in 1819, he was the center of a group of students and admirers attracted by his undeniable charisma, knowledge, and sense of purpose.[13] Some of these men reappeared later among the higher *ikhwan*, the "brothers" of the Sanusi order. Even at this time, Shukri declares that al-Sanusi was erudite enough to be appointed an instructor at the Great Mosque of Fez; the French author Louis Rinn claims that his talents attracted the attention of the Moroccan ruler.[14] Whether this was because of his efficient teaching or because of his potential usefulness as a courtier is uncertain. Dajjani also hints that as a *sharif* and a descendant of 'Ali (having as noble an origin as the sharifian ruler Mawla'i Sulayman himself), he might have come under suspicion. Perhaps he might be harboring a scheme for a coup. Moreover, there were serious student riots in Fez in 1819 in which the Darqawi brotherhood was involved. Al-Sanusi may have participated in these disturbances.[15]

After he had left the Qarawiyyin, the precise sequence of al-Sanusi's movements and their chronology is cloudy. He went first to Mustaghanim, where he quarreled with some of his relatives over a piece of property.[16] From there he went to Tripoli via southeastern Algeria. Dajjani notes that he may have built a religious house in the Awlad Na'il country south of Constantine.[17] Another tradition from the same source has al-Sanusi making a journey to some unspecified region of the Western Sudan on camelback. By 1822, he had reached Tripoli, arriving at Cairo in the following year. He spent the greater part of 1824 at the Azhar. At this university-mosque, Muhammad 'Ali pursued his study of Maliki law, but he studied it this time as a mature student at the highest level.

Al-Sanusi was now thirty-seven. His individuality as an intellectual was already obvious. He had conceived a dislike of certain features of Islamic learning as it was taught at the Azhar, in an atmosphere of inflexible conservatism. Nor could he hide his reformist opinions. He began to disagree with certain doctrines considered fundamental by his fellow scholars.[18] Soon he clashed with influential men at the Azhar, who resented his independent airs. One of the points he addressed was *ijtihad*, unrestricted legal interpretation; another was its opposite, *taqlid*, blind acceptance of authority in religious and legal matters. At the urging of one of his enemies, Shaykh Hanish ("Snake" – a name that gives rise to much satirical comment in Sanusi literature), a decree for al-Sanusi's condemnation was issued by the authorities at the Azhar in 1843, long after he had left the mosque.[19] In it, al-Sanusi was specifically condemned for his insistence on the validity of *ijtihad*.[20] His short stay at the Azhar had done little to alter his convictions.

At the end of 1824, al-Sanusi went on to Mecca. He had wanted to make the pilgrimage. In Mecca, as in Fez and Cairo, he was soon in touch with important learned men, both Meccans and foreigners. One of these sojourners was a celebrated theologian and legist and the founder of a brotherhood, Ahmad ibn Idris al-Fasi. Personally and doctrinally, al-Fasi began to exercise an all-pervasive influence over al-Sanusi. Al-Fasi was the supreme sufi master whom Muhammad 'Ali had always sought but never before encountered.[21]

The personal relations between al-Fasi and Muhammad 'Ali al-Sanusi became very close. Born at Al-Ara'ish (Larache) near Fez in 1758, al-Fasi was then about sixty-five years old. By this time he was looking for a successor to guide his brotherhood, the Ahmadiya (or Idrisiya). In the Muslim sciences, law, and sufism, he was a profoundly learned man. He is generally regarded as one of the founders of "neosufism."[22] Unlike the older, conservative sufism, this theological position rejected the possibility of a mystical union with God but sought union with the Prophet Muhammad instead. Al-Fasi, like al-Tijani, claimed to have received the prayers and litanies of his order directly from the Prophet in a vision.[23] As a vigorous opponent of traditional sufism, particularly what he saw as its accretions and innovations, he came close to the reforming standpoint of the Arabian Wahhabis.

Yet al-Fasi differed from them on other issues; in general he was far less radical than they. All the same, he had a high regard for Ahmad ibn Hanbal and Ibn Taymiya, the ultimate inspirers of Wahhabism. Al-Fasi's doctrines, shared by his disciple, al-Sanusi, might be described as midway along the theological spectrum between Wahhabi radicalism and the conservative-traditional standpoint. Al-Fasi also combined great personal sanctity and an easy way in teaching his students, apparent from some of his books.[24] He espoused attractive new attitudes and expressed them in terms that Muslim moderates of the time appreciated. For these reasons al-Fasi not only recruited many followers into his own Idrisiya-Ahmadiya grouping, but he also inspired the creation of other brotherhoods. Within this cluster, the Sanusiya became the most significant. All of these new orders shared an emphasis on moral positivism and a rejection of the otherworldly trend of traditional sufism. They were far closer to Muslim orthodoxy than other contemporary brotherhoods. In other words, neosufis like al-Fasi retained the older sufi organizational framework but radically transformed its content.

Because of his outspokenly reformist views and his success in attracting followers, al-Fasi incurred the hatred of the traditional *'ulama* of
Mecca. About 1828, when jealous pressures from the hostile *'ulama*
intensified, al-Fasi (and al-Sanusi, too) left Mecca and journeyed to
Yaman, finally settling at Subya (or Sabya) in 'Asir, a coastal district
between the Yaman and the Hijaz.[25] Here al-Fasi died in 1836.
Throughout this time, the attachment of al-Sanusi to his master continued to be close. According to Sanusi sources, but denied by some
others, al-Fasi chose Muhammad 'Ali al-Sanusi to be his successor as
head of the Ahmadiya/Idrisiya some time before he died.[26] Within the
upper ranks of the brotherhood, this choice was contested. Two other
strong candidates emerged, Muhammad 'Uthman al-Mirghani and
Ibrahim al-Rashidi. Ultimately the Idrisiya order broke into three
parts.

Al-Sanusi's following was the largest of the three. He returned from
Sabya to Mecca and founded his first *zawiya* just west of the town on
Mount Abu Qubays. The hatred that had followed al-Fasi was soon
aimed at al-Sanusi by the local conservatives. It was now reinforced by
the dislike of the powerful Mirghani family and the Sharif of Mecca.[27]
At the time that al-Sanusi built his new sufi house on Jabal Abu
Qubays, he commenced his missionary preaching on behalf of his order
and started to enroll disciples in it. More than ever, these doings
attracted the malevolence of the local establishment, which thought it
could detect something of a Wahhabi odor about the Sanusi organization. Not long before this time (1813), the Wahhabis had been forcibly
turned out of Mecca by Egyptian troops. As Nallino says:

> It was natural that the *'ulama* or doctors of Mecca made violent
> opposition to the future founder of the Senussia and in the course
> of the polemic branded him with the hateful epithet "Wahhabi,"
> from which, like other historical errors, the legend arose, spread by
> European books, that Ahmad ibn Idris and his disciple were
> influenced by Wahhabism.[28]

Among al-Sanusi's following at this time were a large number from
the Maghrib. Many of these were Libyans from Tripoli and elsewhere.
Although his lone *zawiya* (al-Sanusi does not seem to have built any
others in the Hijaz during these years) functioned well, it was already
too small for the growing numbers of al-Sanusi's partisans. Moreover,
the political and religious opposition in Mecca, supported by a few of
the local Turks, accelerated al-Sanusi's departure from the Holy City.
Al-Sanusi himself wanted to leave Mecca for a better place, and most
of his adherents felt the same way. Now that al-Fasi was dead, Sanusi

was determined to promote his master's teachings – and his own – beyond the boundaries of the Hijaz.[29]

On the last day of the Muslim year 1255 (4 March 1840), al-Sanusi and a group of his close advisers, friends, and family left Mecca. He entrusted the *zawiya* at Abu Qubays to a loyal administrator and took the road for Madina and Yanbu'. At the port of Yanbu' the party divided, al-Sanusi's wives going on by sea to the port of Qabis (or Gabès) in Tunisia, a stopping place on their route to western Algeria.[30]

Al-Sanusi himself and his group went on to Egypt by land. When they reached Bulaq (now part of Cairo), they halted for some months at the house of a sympathizer, resting and obtaining provisions for the remainder of the journey.[31] On this occasion al-Sanusi doubtless avoided the Azhar. Yet if he were not visible, he continued to preach for his new order and to gather recruits. The party went from Bulaq to the Fayyum and Siwa oases, then into Libya. Although their leader and many of his companions caught fever during their slow passage through Cyrenaica, they finally reached Tripoli by the coastal road. Their wanderings among the population and the oases of the Egyptian-Libyan borderlands not only made them familiar figures to the folk of this region but also gave al-Sanusi and his friends firsthand knowledge of the geography of these provinces. Whether they deliberately passed this way looking for a future site for a brotherhood center is unclear. It seems more probable that they were intending to go directly on to Algeria, to Mustaghanim.[32]

At Tripoli, Muhammad 'Ali and his men were well treated by the Ottoman *veli*, 'Ali 'Ashqar Pasha.[33] They stayed in Tripoli for a week before going on to Qabis. Here they received bad news: to continue their intended journey into Algeria was impossible. During al-Sanusi's absence in the Hijaz, the French had invaded Algeria. It is likely that French agents had informed Paris about al-Sanusi's contacts with Algerian pilgrims. The French were convinced that al-Sanusi's return to Mustaghanim or any other Algerian town meant danger to them. Would he not raise a revolt or perhaps combine forces with Amir 'Abd al-Qadir? For these reasons, the French were determined not to allow al-Sanusi to reenter Algeria. Indeed, al-Sanusi never saw Mustaghanim again. Had he crossed into Algeria, Klopfer claims, he would have been immediately arrested and imprisoned by the French.[34] And al-Ashhab states that al-Sanusi had been sending arms and money into Algeria, entrusting these supplies to some of his students.[35] Although there is little clear evidence for this at the time of al-Sanusi's arrival in the Maghrib from Mecca, he was clearly lending a number of Algerian rebels (like Muhammad 'Abdallah al-Sharif) his moral support by

1852, as a document of that year demonstrates.[36] That he should do this was quite understandable. Hence French suspicions about the ill will of the Sanusis grew into certainties.

Although Muhammad 'Ali had wanted to establish a headquarters for his new brotherhood within Algeria, that country was now closed to him. He had to abandon his plan and look elsewhere for a base, a site from which to carry on his teaching. Tripoli was not suitable; competing brotherhoods, including the Darqawiya, were strongly established there.[37] In the 1840s, al-Sanusi was still somewhat wary of the Turks. He wished to avoid close contact with them. Later, he seems to have accepted them, although with minor reservations. Further, on al-Sanusi's return from Qabis, certain nuances in the Ottoman *veli's* conduct hinted that the Turks might be slightly less friendly to the Sanusis than they had been a few months before.[38] At that moment, the Turks were nervous about the rising of the rebel Ghuma al-Mahmudi in the Jabal Nafusa south of Tripoli.[39] Later, they captured and decapitated another rebel, 'Abd al-Jalil Sayf al-Nasr, a tribal leader from the Fazzan.[40] Yet some sources suggest that 'Ali 'Ashqar Pasha joined the Sanusi order. At length, the Sanusis were permitted to retrace their steps eastward into Cyrenaica. By this time, it was obvious that the order would have to halt and find a center somewhere between Tripoli and Egyptian territory.

By the end of 1842, al-Sanusi had arrived at Binghazi in Cyrenaica. He quickly found a suitable site for a headquarters. He built a large *zawiya* near a village called al-Bayda' ("the White"). Near the Mediterranean coast, it lay on high land between Darna and Binghazi, easily defended and difficult of access. This site, in the Jabal Khadra' (or Green Mountains), also adjoined the tomb of a famous Muslim holy man, Rafi' ibn Thabit al-Ansari; thus it had been a local place of pilgrimage. It was equally close to the lands of the Bara'asa, the 'Awaqir, and several other tribes.[41]

The situation of al-Bayda' held a number of advantages. The local tribes wanted al-Sanusi to settle there so that he could arbitrate their differences. Had he wished to assume the role of "resident saint," they would have accepted him as such. Further, al-Bayda' was conveniently within Ottoman territory yet several hundred miles from Tripoli, an appropriate distance in the unlikely chance of an altered Ottoman policy toward the brotherhood. In an east-west direction, communications were easy by land or sea to the Maghrib or to Egypt and the Hijaz. For purposes of proselytization or preaching, al-Bayda' was also well situated. It was on virgin territory, at the northern end of a strip that was lightly islamized, running southward into the deserts. As Evans-Pritchard says, "dammed to west and east, the order poured its vitality southward along the trade routes to the interior of Africa."[42] When it was founded, at least, al-Bayda' was a safe spot, not yet coveted by any European power; in addition, the port of Darna was close by. Hence, for the fifteen-year period from 1842 to 1857, al-Bayda' was the center of Sanusi activities.

If the originality and newness of the Sanusi order impressed its contemporaries, it embodied fundamental differences from other sufi groups. For many centuries in Islam, tension had existed between mystics (sufis) and the orthodox. The strain had been partially bridged over by al-Ghazali and other thinkers, but it continued to break through at intervals – often over the antinomian and latitudinarian tendencies inherent in sufism. As Fazlur Rahman says, later medieval popular sufism tended to fall into "ecstatic rites, autohypnotic visions and orgiastic rituals," into a confusion of "superstitious beliefs which degenerated ultimately into . . . charlatanism."[43]

Orthodoxy tried to recover these groups for itself, particularly in the eighteenth century. At that time external threats and a feeling of internal failure swept over Islam. There was a sense of urgency – indeed, a sense of anxiety – over the need for basic reforms. In this revival, many groups participated; the best known is the Wahhabiya. Milder, but similar attitudes may be seen among the Khalwatiya, inspired by its great figures Mustafa al-Bakri and Muhammad bin Salim al-Hifnawi (or Hifni, Shaykh of the Azhar, 1758–67), who set a great sufi renaissance in motion.[44] Another important line of reform came from India in the person of Shah Waliallah of Delhi (d. 1762).[45] Among these reformers, many were inspired by the writings of the two Ibn Taymiyas, adherents of the Hanbali School, Taqi al-Din and Majd al-Din ibn Taymiya, grandson and grandfather, who had pursued similar goals in the thirteenth and fourteenth centuries.

Above all, the orthodox tried to separate sufism from its innovations and accretions, to suppress its most obnoxious popular features, and to restore to it the sense of personal morality and responsibility that the earliest sufis had possessed. The reformers wanted sufism to move to the right, toward self-purification. The Wahhabis, under their leader Muhammad ibn 'Abd al-Wahhab (d. 1792), wanted Sunni Islam to rid itself of narrow *qiyas* (reasoning by analogy) and of *taqlid* (blind imitation and acceptance of authority) and to return to fundamentals. These fundamentals the Wahhabis wished to interpret literally and narrowly. In these moves, they had the support of moderates – to a point. And both moderates and Wahhabis wanted to retrieve the use of *ijtihad* (independent reasoning in religious matters). Although the Wahhabis were too crude to realize it, their emphasis on the "opening of the gate of *ijtihad*" was their greatest contribution to reviving

Islamic thought. The tool of *ijtihad* cut away both fundamentalism and literalism, just as it pruned the abuses of sufism. Independent reasoning gave room to a broader interpretation of text or tradition.[46] In this sense, both Wahhabism and moderate reform in the eighteenth century together paved the way for a positive reinterpretation and reconstruction of Islamic thought and, ultimately, of Islamic society.[47]

In these developments Ahmad ibn Idris al-Fasi played his role, as did his disciple al-Sanusi. Moving toward orthodoxy (for he was a jurist as well as a sufi), al-Fasi claimed that he had formed a "Muhammadan brotherhood" (*tariqa Muhammadiya*) that was inspired directly by the Prophet Muhammad. The new intellectual reorientation meant that he could lop off the latitudinarian excrescences that he abhorred, such as visits to saints' tombs to ask their intercession, the use of amulets, and other popular practices that made eighteenth-century grass-roots sufism a travesty of what Islamic mysticism had been. But al-Fasi's ideas did not make him a Wahhabi. Indeed, he and al-Sanusi were moderates who traveled in the same direction, two of many phenomena within the same reforming trend, yet another expression of that ubiquitous spirit of change that was penetrating Islam by 1800.[48]

Al-Fasi, who died in 1836, had neither the time nor the opportunity to realize his plans and ideas. Hence the significance of the new cluster of orders that grew out of the Ahmadiya/Idrisiya. These were the Mirghaniya, Rashidiya, and Sanusiya. If they employed *dhikr*s, litanies, and the older sufi organizational structure in the traditional way, they also played down ritual, stressed hard work – even toil in the fields – and promoted trading by their adherents. It was precisely these Sanusi attitudes of moral positivism that had provoked the conservative circles of the Azhar – lesser men than the great al-Hifnawi – into issuing their condemnatory decree of 1843. The success of such new ideas in practice, whether in Mecca or Cyrenaica, and their ability to garner flocks of adherents both stimulated doctrinal dislike and aroused professional jealousy.

Far from the censorious *'ulama* of the Azhar, al-Sanusi dispatched his emissaries, missionaries, and agents into every part of Barqa, to the Fazzan, and south and west throughout Libya.[49] These dedicated men insisted that the population should return to genuine Muslim thinking as defined by al-Fasi and al-Sanusi. The proselytization of the order was highly successful. What is more, by accommodating the functions of the order to tribal structures, to the local landholding systems, the Sanusiya integrated itself firmly into the lives of the people. It suited their religious and social requirements very well and was fully comprehensible to them.[50] In this way, the theocratic state that al-Sanusi had envisioned came into being, the double of the Ottoman administration in Libya. Because his order had succeeded so well and so quickly, al-Sanusi was able to leave Libyan affairs in the hands of a deputy in 1846. He set off for Mecca, where he remained until 1853.[51]

During these seven years, al-Sanusi accomplished a great deal. That he was a prolific writer has been insufficiently emphasized; he wrote more than forty books, poems, and treatises, some of them of great length. This was perhaps his chief motive in returning to Mecca. He wanted to get his own thoughts (and some of the concepts of al-Fasi) bearing on Islamic reform, revival, and renewal down on paper. He could use the excellent libraries Mecca afforded. Carlo Nallino to the contrary, al-Sanusi was much more at ease in urban places such as Mustaghanim, Cairo, or Mecca than he was in the remote Cyrenaican countryside.[52] And Mecca was a far better place from which to exercise his influence on behalf of the Sanusi order. By 1846, the malevolent hostility of the conservative Meccan *'ulama* had cooled. Meanwhile, al-Sanusi had become a highly respected person. In Mecca he could meet and have contacts with pilgrims who were attracted by his ideas and who could propagate them when they returned to their homelands.

Mecca was also a superior site from which to promote the cause of Islam, of Muslim unity. It was relatively inaccessible to the European powers, although some of them maintained consuls at Jidda, to eavesdrop on what went on there. By the late 1840s, al-Sanusi was only too well aware of the threat posed by France and some other European powers to Islam. To him, the fall of Algeria was a portent, and the future would prove him right. Therefore he wanted to set barriers, even if they were only of a religious and cultural sort, against the expansion of Europeans into areas controlled by the Sanusis or other Muslims. He also wanted to hinder European exploration in North Africa, for in his eyes explorers were merely spies. It was this attitude – less subtly expressed among his followers than by the Great Sanusi himself – of which European travelers such as Hamilton and Nachtigal complained and which Duveyrier made into an issue.[53] Personally, the Great Sanusi was a peaceful individual, an opponent of warfare and violence despite his strong political views. This feature of his character was wholly consonant with his spiritual nature. He was much more at home organizing *zawiyas* or writing books.

A great deal of information about al-Sanusi and his order is revealed by his writings. Although none of his books were printed until 1930, they appeared at intervals from Cairo publishing houses, before and during World War II and later. Their printing was largely inspired by Muhammad Idris ibn al-Mahdi al-Sanusi, later King Idris I of Libya. He had eight of them reprinted and collected in a single volume, the *Al-Majmu'at al-Mukhtara,* published at Beirut in 1968.[54] This collection represents only a small part of al-Sanusi's writings, of which al-Dajjani gives a more complete list. Many of these still exist in manuscript form in the Sanusi Archives or in the former Libyan Royal Library. They show al-Sanusi to have been a poet, a mathematician, an excellent theologian, a fine jurist, and a competent historian and genealogist. One manuscript also demonstrates the author's interest in divination (*jafr*), still intellectually respectable in nineteenth-century Islam. Unfortunately, numbers of manuscripts perished during Italian military attacks on Kufra and other Sanusi centers; the original total, according to al-Dajjani, came to forty-four.[55]

A number of major and minor themes can be identified in these writings. Most significant were al-Sanusi's preoccupation with reform, his wish to widen a narrow consensus (*ijma'*), his absolute rejection of blind adherence to authority (*taqlid*), and his total support for independent reasoning (*ijtihad*).[56]

Two of his unpublished works deal specifically with *ijtihad,* and two of the longer published pieces, the *'Iqaz al-Wasnan* and the *Book of the Ten Questions* (*Bughyat al-Maqasid*), include long sections on both *ijtihad* and *taqlid*.[57] Here al-Sanusi defines what he means by *ijtihad:* complete exploitation of all details of thought in a legal judgment by a competent jurist. The person who has reached a high enough level of legal ability to do this is defined as a *mujtahid.* A *mujtahid* ceases to be such the moment he slips into banal imitation of previous authorities; he is then an imitator (*muqallid*).[58] Constantly, al-Sanusi chides the ignorance of those who imitate and are intellectually unable to get to grips with legal fundamentals. In fact, *taqlid* is opposed to both the *Qur'an* and *Sunna,* sources of law that al-Sanusi put above human reason. In other words, he recognized that it had always been the easy way out of legal problems to fall back on the views of the Four Imams (the four founders of the Islamic juridical schools) instead of using one's own wits. He states repeatedly that such ignorance must be combatted and the principle of *ijtihad* restored. Merely because *ijtihad* had fallen out of use for such a long time did not mean that it was invalid.[59] Here al-Sanusi recognized a legal principle of self-renewal within the *Shar'ia* that he wanted to revive. Echoes of the positions taken by al-Sanusi in these two books can be seen throughout his other writings.

Testifying to al-Sanusi's deep roots in the North African learned tradition and to the conservative side of his character are his accounts of what books he studied and who his teachers were. Much of this appears in abbreviated form in his *Al-Manhal al-Rawi al-Ra'iq,* in the first sections.[60] The same theme also emerges, greatly amplified, in his *Al-Shamus al-Shariqa.* Here al-Sanusi records his commitment to

the Muslim tradition of learning, passing in a long series from master
to master down the centuries, always based on the same texts. There
are two other books on this theme, both unpublished like the *Shamus*.[61]
For a closer look at the formative educational influences operating on
al-Sanusi, all three might be worth evaluating. Henri Duveyrier, who
was so often wrong about the Sanusis, identified the *Rising Suns*
(*Al-Shamus al-Shariqa*) as the keystone of al-Sanusi's writings, "celui
qui resume toute son oeuvre."[62] Compared to the *'Iqaz* or the *Bughyat
al-Maqasid,* this can hardly be so.

Al-Sanusi took his descent from the Prophet's son-in-law, 'Ali, with
some solemnity. His attitude can be glimpsed from his historical opus,
The Resplendent Pearls about the History of the Idrisi Family (*Al-
Durar al-Saniya*). This was the first book by al-Sanusi to be printed
(1930). According to Shukri, it had been popular with the nineteenth-
century Sanusi *ikhwan* because it demonstrated to them that their
master and his sons, as descendants of 'Ali and Hasan, were members
of the Quraysh and therefore qualified as caliphs for the universal caliphate should it ever be restored.[63] Because the Ottoman ruling family
made this claim too, al-Sanusi always soft-pedaled this idea, for he
knew that it could lead to a clash with the Turks. The *Durar* is written
clearly and simply, with snippets of poetry at intervals, like other traditional Islamic histories. As a sideline to history, al-Sanusi also wrote
some genealogical works. One of these, the *Shudhur al-Dhahab,* may
have served as a model for parts of the 186-page *Durar*.[64]

A number of other studies explore such matters as tradition and
traditionists, commentators on the *Qur'an,* and sufism. A book on
sufism, the *Al-Salsabil al-mu'in fi'l-tara'iq al-arba'in,* is the only one of
al-Sanusi's works to excite controversy over its originality.[65] This
work is an analysis of forty or more sufi brotherhoods (similar in content to the second part of the *Manhal al-Ra'iq*). The author discusses
their origins, their founders, their prayers, and their peculiarities. At
the beginning of the book, he admits that he has summarized it from
the *Risala* of Hasan 'Ali al-'Ujaymi (d. 1702), but he says nothing
about borrowing a section of a work by Abu Sa'id al-Qadiri (d. 1686)
on the Hallajiya order.[66] Yet unacknowledged use of other authors'
books was still no crime in the nineteenth-century Muslim world.

To complete the list, al-Sanusi composed a mathematical work on
planes and sines[67]; a *Great Key to Divination*[68]; and what, from its
title, appears to be a book on astrology, *Al-Mawahib al-Sirriya fi
muntaqa al-awda' al-harfiya*.[69] It is apparent from the range of al-
Sanusi's interests and the profundity of his legal and theological
thinking that he can be classified among the more outstanding intel-
lects of the Maghrib and of Islam in the nineteenth century. In this

sense, he compares with Usuman dan Fodio, his teacher al-Fasi, or Jamal al-Din al-Afghani. Perhaps overawed by their father's genius and his many productions, al-Sanusi's sons appear to have written nothing, but the family tradition of writing was resumed again by his grandson, Sayyid Ahmad al-Sharif, who wrote at least four books, two of which have been printed.[70]

To return to al-Sanusi in Mecca, it is paradoxical that during his stay there, which ended in 1853, although he attempted to obtain still more adherents for the order in the two Holy Cities and other large towns of Arabia, he always had better success among country people and nomads. Despite his efforts to build *zawiyas* in the cities of Egypt and the Hijaz, for example, he found few recruits. This might well have been the result of the competition of other orders. But the real secret of al-Sanusi's success was his recruitment among pilgrims and among social groups despised by conventional religious leaders.[71] Carlo Nallino has pointed out that al-Sanusi did not disdain to send his agents out among the notorious Banu Harb tribe – a group living between Mecca and Madina in the Hijaz, whose main profession was brigandage. For a time, they nearly stopped caravan traffic between the two places. Yet the Banu Harb responded to al-Sanusi's efforts. He made them recite their prayers, with a few Sanusi formulas, and convinced many of them that they should settle and practice agriculture, which until then they had despised as unmanly.[72] Further, according to Sadiq Mu'ayyad al-Azm, they refused to attack any caravan if they knew that there were Sanusis accompanying it.[73] For their work with the Banu Harb the Sanusis obtained great credit, and al-Sanusi's settlement scheme prefigures the agricultural colonies of the Qadiriya and Salihiya in Somalia. It also resembles certain settlements on the land promoted in the 1920s by Ibn Su'ud in Najd.[74]

Much as the Meccan *'ulama* may have been scandalized by these doings, their opposition was muted by the growth and successes of the Sanusiya. Further, such residual pro-Wahhabi influence as still existed within Arabia in the mid-nineteenth century was far from hostile to the Sanusis. The similarity and common goals of the two movements were widely recognized by their sympathizers.

By 1853, al-Sanusi realized that he could stay no longer in the Hijaz. Among his Libyan supporters, there was much murmuring and grumbling about his overlong sojourn abroad. Why did he not return to Cyrenaica? At the end of 1853, therefore, he traveled overland through Egypt to the Green Mountains.[75] The Egyptian ruler, 'Abbas Pasha, tried to befriend him in Cairo, but al-Sanusi rebuffed him.[76] Undoubtedly he believed in the old sufi maxim that only dubious men of religion and uncertain mystics enjoyed the company of sovereigns.

Soon after his return to Libya, al-Sanusi dispatched a team of his collaborators and advisers to seek a new site for the headquarters of the order. They chose a place named Jaghbub several hundred miles southeast of al-Bayda'. Jaghbub was still within Libya but closer to the Egyptian border and the Oasis of Siwa; it was at the crossing point of two inland trade routes. Reputedly, it had been a center for thieves and robbers before al-Sanusi went there.[77] Louis Rinn and some other European writers have suggested that al-Sanusi transferred his center here because of the growing enmity of the *'ulama* of Mecca and Istanbul. Or they suggest that the Ottoman Turks were more than ever anxious about the Sanusiya's increasing prestige and numbers.[78]

It is more likely that al-Sanusi was becoming increasingly convinced that the best hopes of the Sanusiya lay in southward expansion. Hence, after al-Sanusi's return to the Maghrib, the order placed less emphasis than before on the recruitment of pilgrims or the regeneration of Arabian robber tribes; it turned instead to sending agents and missioners toward Lake Chad, to Waday and Darfur.[79] These moves were supported by the construction of a tight network of *zawiyas*. Moreover, prestige was derived from austerity, from hard desert surroundings. Many Muslims could appreciate the order's policy of protecting itself from the subtle influences of corrupt or degenerate neighbors, including other sufi orders with less severe ideals.[80] Then too, al-Sanusi may have had at the back of his mind the idea of a *hijra*, the "migration" of himself and the order from undesirable surroundings. Margoliouth mentions this idea in an article, although it is hard to find explicit discussion of it in al-Sanusi's writings – at least the published ones.[81] The successive moves of the brotherhood after the Great Sanusi's death – to Kufra in extreme southeastern Libya in 1895 and to Qiru in Borku (now in Chad Republic) in 1899 – were almost certainly dictated by these same considerations.

Another factor, that of al-Sanusi's prophetic intuitions, is worth pointing out. It is revealed in a trustworthy oral tradition cited by both Shukri and al-Dajjani.[82] In conversation with a certain Shaykh Darnawi, the Great Sanusi made some startling predictions in the mid-1850s. He foretold the impending capture of Alexandria by the British, the seizure of Tripoli by the "Neapolitans," and an invasion by Europeans of Tunis and the "coasts of the Maghrib."[83] Al-Sanusi, very much a man of his time who adhered to the old Islamic world view (as shown by his interest in divination and astrology), interpreted these coming events as signs, portents of the coming of a mahdi. It is also likely that the defeats of the Ottoman Turks at Russian hands in the Crimean War were regarded by him in the same apocalyptic light. For all these reasons, Jaghbub was a better center for the Sanusiya than al-Bayda'.

Soon Jaghbub became an important religious and intellectual center, more significant than al-Bayda' in its time. Evans-Pritchard describes it as a sort of Saharan Oxford, the seat of an Islamic university "second only in Africa to the Azhar." He notes that it was a "university society" with a library of 8,000 volumes.[84] Here the Great Sanusi had his intimate circle; here he trained his disciples and planned his missionary efforts. These men were not necessarily selected from the local Libyans of Jaghbub. They were tested members of the *ikhwan* drawn from all parts of the Islamic world. Hence, as Evans-Pritchard declares, al-Sanusi was able to build a unified missionary group within a tribal society, yet an organization that could not be identified with any single tribe.[85]

From Jaghbub, al-Sanusi continued to have good relations with the Turks. In his younger days, he had always kept in mind the example of his teacher, Ibn al-Qanduz, hanged as a dissident by the Turks at Mascara in 1829.[86] But that episode did not hinder him from cementing good relations with the Ottomans when there was a real need for it. Even in view of the fact that Jaghbub and al-Bayda' were far from Tripoli, it is worth noting that the independence of the Sanusis within interior Libya created no friction. This had been true from the start, when 'Ali 'Ashqar Pasha had furnished hospitality to al-Sanusi and his party in 1841. It can also be demonstrated by examples of friendly correspondence between the Sanusis and Ottoman officials.[87] Further, al-Sanusi would hardly have left al-Bayda' and gone off to Mecca for such an extended period had he been apprehensive about the attitude of the Porte and its Libyan representatives. The same attitudes continued when his sons were in power, although Sultan 'Abd al-Hamid II was anxious about the Sanusis on at least two occasions, when he sent his aide-de-camp to see what was going on at Jaghbub.[88] The purpose of these missions was consistently misinterpreted by European observers, who wanted to believe that beneath the friendly surface of Sanusi-Ottoman relations an underlying layer of mutual mistrust existed.[89]

After spending the final productive years of his life at Jaghbub, al-Sanusi died there in September 1859.[90] Later, a magnificent domed tomb, visible for many miles, was erected over his remains.[91] Thanks to its founder's preparations, the order weathered the crisis without much difficulty. Until al-Sanusi's sons came of age, the direction of the order was assumed by a "regency council" composed of al-Sanusi's oldest friends, colleagues, and missioners.[92] On his father's death, his eldest son, al-Mahdi, was between fifteen and sixteen years old; his younger son Muhammad al-Sharif was about thirteen. Both sons had accompanied their father to Mecca in 1846 to continue their educations.[93] Both of them received substantial amounts of instruction from him. By temperament as well as by training, the two half-brothers were well fitted to guide the order along the lines foreseen by their father. By mid-1859, both of them had returned to Libya from the Hijaz, for their father's health had already begun to deteriorate.[94]

In all essentials, the education of the two Muhammads was identical to that of al-Sanusi himself. Muhammad al-Mahdi was the more active, and he possessed a more tangible spiritual nature than his less imaginative brother. As al-Sanusi said, "Al-Mahdi holds the sword, al-Sharif the pen."[95] Together they worked in harmony, an excellent team; during the thirty-six years that they remained in Jaghbub (1859–95), the Sanusiya attained its greatest prestige and enjoyed its widest expansion.

After he had reached his majority, al-Mahdi retained his father's council, including the most experienced figures within the Sanusiya. It met at least once a year and sometimes more often, presided over by Muhammad al-Sharif. According to their knowledge or expertise, the various members of the council dealt with finances, the reception of guests, missionary matters, the construction of new *zawiyas*, and so forth.[96] Trimingham gives a good description of the plan and functions of such Sanusi lodges during the time of Muhammad al-Mahdi:

> Each local *zawiya*, a cell of Islamic culture set in a nomadic or animistic environment, was the means by which adherents were organised and through which expansion was effected. Each formed a complex of buildings constructed around an inner courtyard, with a well. . . . These embraced the residence of the *muqaddam*, representative of the Sanusi, his family, slaves, pupils, and a mosque, school, rooms for students, rooms for keeping vigils, and a guest block for the use of passing travellers and caravans. The whole interrelated construction was surrounded by a wall and could be defended if need arose. Around it were lands cultivated by the *ikhwan*. The *zawiya* was no alien settlement, but was regarded as belonging to the tribe in whose region it was situated from whose members many of the *ikhwan* were drawn. Thus it was a centre for tribal unity and this gave it strength to survive.[97]

During the years that al-Mahdi was head of the Sanusiya, the number of its *zawiyas* were multiplied by a factor of four. Linked together by an efficient system of couriers who traveled over existing routes or built new ones, the *zawiyas* spread all over the Libyan desert and beyond toward the southern fringes of the Sahara.[98] There is also a hint here and there that both al-Mahdi and his father thought of the lines of *zawiyas* extending southward in terms of the medieval *ribats* of the Maghrib, strong points laid out on the periphery of Islam.[99] These boundaries enclosed a safe territory, a region that would serve as a refuge for Muslims under pressure, an area to which they might move if a real *hijra* were imperative.

In spite of dogged efforts to convert the peoples of the Sahara to a more perfect Islam, the most significant factor in the spread of the order in the time of al-Mahdi lay in the name of the leader himself. As Duveyrier rightly said, "Le surnom seul de Sidi Mohammed el-Mahedi renferme tout un programme politique."[100]

After the death of al-Sanusi in 1859, there is convincing evidence that a majority of the brothers of the order really believed that Muhammad al-Mahdi was indeed the expected mahdi. This idea filled the minds and conversations of the simpler *ikhwan,* who transferred their latent mahdist expectations to their leader. In a manuscript history of the Sanusiya written by Ahmad al-Sharif, al-Mahdi's nephew,[101] some pertinent couplets are quoted, written by a certain Shaykh Husayn, about 1845, which run as follows:

> The Almighty has announced to us
> The good news of a glorious *Imam*
> Saying that he is a *mahdi*
> Being in his cradle (*mahd*)
> An *Imam* related to the Prophetic House
> For these two reasons, there's no doubt
> That he's in fact the *Mahdi.*

Why did his father give him this name? Drawing again on Ahmad al-Sharif's manuscript, al-Dajjani supplies some answers to this enigma. During an alleged argument at Sabya or Mecca between al-Sanusi and his rival al-Mirghani about the coming of the mahdi, the disputants referred the matter to Ahmad al-Fasi.[102] Al-Fasi dismissed al-Mirghani's suggestion that he, al-Fasi, was the mahdi. However, he made the mysterious pronouncement that the "secret of the Mahdi" lay with al-Sanusi. And when one of his four wives asked al-Sanusi why he had given his little boy that name, al-Sanusi answered that he had hoped his son al-Mahdi might receive all sorts of divine guidance (*hidaya*). Then he supposedly said, "We hope that God will make him a leader, (*hadi*) who will be rightly guided (*mahdi*)."[103]

Another story from the same source claims that the Great Sanusi often expressed the wish that his eldest son might be the Expected Mahdi. With the passage of time, his hopes and beliefs seem to have become convictions. Yet if a hostile critic could suggest that making his son into the mahdi was a sure way to secure the gains of the

Sanusiya after his death, al-Dajjani claims that Muhammad 'Ali al-Sanusi had very serious and valid reasons for what he did:

> The main reason which induced al-Sanusi to believe in the
> mahdiship of his son were the evil circumstances of Islamic society
> and the threatening power which menaced it from the West. The
> Ottoman sultanate had grown weak and was paralysed from the
> breakdown of security in remote places, bureaucratic corruption,
> and the decay of the state. . . . On the other hand loomed the
> Western European power, its efforts to acquire political control
> over Egypt, its occupation of Algeria, and its threat to the
> homeland of Islam. Al-Sanusi thought long and hard over these
> matters, groping for a way to put a stop to them. . . . [His best
> means] for mobilizing the minds of the people was the expectation
> of a savior, a *mahdi*.[104]

Al-Sanusi was aware that the Islamic world was more than usually predisposed to this line of argument because of the approach of the Muslim year 1300/1882–3. Although the year 1200/1785 had come and gone without the mahdi, matters might be different by 1300. Expectations like this were only too common among his contemporaries. To demonstrate their omnipresence, one need only look at the example of the Sudanese mahdi, who made public his mahdiship just before 1300.[105] In the *Muqaddima*, Ibn Khaldun had stressed the longing of the Muslim masses for a savior at the end of time and pointed out that the fulfillment of millennial prophecies was perpetually anticipated by them.[106] Although Muhammad al-Mahdi al-Sanusi repeatedly denied that he was a mahdi, the effect of his frequent public repudiations of the claim helped to keep it alive, much as the denials of American presidential hopefuls keep alive their campaigns.

The political utility of the mahdiship issue to the Sanusi cause is illuminated by the actions of Muhammad al-Mahdi in the same Muslim year, 1300/1881–2, when an emissary of the Mahdi of Khartum brought him a letter.[107] If Muhammad al-Mahdi would only acknowledge the leadership of Muhammad Ahmad ibn 'Abdallah, the letter ran, he would be welcome in Khartum to take up the role of the third caliph – 'Uthman – following the scenario of the original events of the seventh century.[108] This the Sanusi refused to do; he compelled the messenger to return to the Sudan with all speed. Apart from doctrinal reasons, Muhammad al-Mahdi's refusal was obviously based on fear of what might happen among his own following if he were to support a claim by another mahdi. His claim to the support of his somewhat credulous *ikhwan* – so far unspoken but potentially useful – would have instantly

vanished. It also seems that Muhammad al-Mahdi some time in the
later 1880s gave instructions to the rulers of Baghirmi and Waday –
over whom he exercised great influence – to oppose and hinder the
spread of the Khartum movement within their territories.[109]

The remarkable increase in the number of Sanusi *zawiyas* and in
Sanusi influence into the Sahara in al-Mahdi's time was merely the
continuation of a policy initiated by the Great Sanusi after his return
from Mecca. Perhaps the idea had been suggested to him by his encounter with al-Hajj Muhammad Sharif, Sultan of Waday, in Mecca
during the 1830s. Waday's connection with the Sanusiya was maintained by his son, Yusuf.[110] The capital of Waday, Abeshr, saw frequent Sanusi visitors or delegations. Duveyrier claims that Muhammad
'Ali strengthened his influence there by purchasing slaves from Waday
from a passing caravan and freeing them after a period of training in
a Sanusi *zawiya*. He then sent them back to Waday to proselytize for
the order.[111]

The policy of southward expansion initiated by the Great Sanusi is
worth consideration in some detail. Although it brought successes at
first, it also contained political implications. Through it, the Sanusiya
became embroiled with the French and had ultimately to withdraw
from the Sahara and those parts of the western Sudan where they had
won influence. The southward movement of the order may be broken
down into a series of phases, starting with the founding of the first
Sanusi headquarters at al-Bayda' in 1843.

From al-Bayda', al-Sanusi naturally concentrated on building other
zawiyas in Cyrenaica. According to Duveyrier, there existed thirty-
eight of these in 1833. More reliable figures derived by Klopfer from
Sanusi sources only mention twenty-four functioning by 1859, the year
of al-Sanusi's death.[112] From Cyrenaica, the order spread into the
western desert of Egypt. By 1852, *zawiyas* were operating in the Siwa
Oasis; they were operating in the Bahariya and Farafara oases by 1860.
The order then moved westward into Tripolitania and southern
Tunisia. There was almost certainly a *zawiya* in Tunis itself by 1860;
some sources even claim a *zawiya* near Mustaghanim in Algeria
around 1855. From Mizda and al-Tabaqa in west-central Tripolitania,
the Sanusi penetrated the Fazzan. Here a number of centers were built
by the end of the 1850s, for example, Zawila, Waw al-Kabir, and
Zalla.[113]

The 1860s saw continued Sanusi expansion into the southwestern
fringes of the Fazzan and into the Libyan-Algerian borderlands. On his
journey to Ghat in 1861, Duveyrier saw a Sanusi *zawiya;* once there,
the Frenchman was the object of some local pressure for a hasty departure, for which he blamed the Sanusis.[114] He enumerated further

Sanusi lodges built in this period at 'Ayn Salih (In Salah) and Tuwat in the far south of Algeria. This he reckoned as a part of the contemporary Sanusi thrust to the southwest.[115] Although his account of his journey and his lectures about his explorations were doubtless noted in Paris, the French government in the 1860s did not worry much about the advance of the Sanusi order.

During the period of Muhammad al-Mahdi's minority, when the order was controlled by a council of *shaykhs*, a shift in the direction of expansion was noticeable. Many of the influential Sanusi figures on the council wanted to turn the main thrust of activities directly southward from Cyrenaica. This can be explained by their sensitivity to a growing French "presence" in southern Algeria, a direct result of intensified military activity there. Hence the Sanusiya began to turn toward Kawar (Enneri Tuge), to Borku, to the Tibesti region. By 1870, Shimmedru in the Kawar Oasis had a *zawiya*, observed by the German explorer Nachtigal on his southward journey.[116] Nachtigal also saw Sanusis in Kanem in 1871, when he was camping there as the guest of the Awlad Sulayman tribe.[117] And, according to Duveyrier, the Teda-Daza clans near Tu in the Tibesti massif were coming under much Sanusi influence by 1873.[118] Further, *zawiyas* for immediate future construction were projected for Barday, west and north of Borku.

By 1871, there was a functioning *zawiya* at Ngurma in Borku. In the years 1871 and 1872, representatives of the Sanusiya had reached Wanyanga (or Wajanga) on the road from Ennedi to Darfur, although *zawiyas* were not actually built there until later.[119] By the end of the 1870s, one of the most distant outposts of the Sanusi order was situated at 'Ayn Kalaka (or Galaka) in Waday. From here perhaps the Sanusiya foresaw a future thrust toward Bornu and Chad or into the northern Cameroons. At least they reached Kano in the mid-1890s. It is claimed that by 1902 they were in touch with the ruler of Gulfei in the northern Cameroons.[120]

During the 1870s and 1880s, another trend was visible. In places where only one or two Sanusi centers existed and where a large Sanusi following lived, the order constructed supplementary *zawiyas*. New ones were constructed at Ghat and Ghadamis and here and there in the western desert of Egypt.[121] All the same, the main thrust of the Sanusiya was directed southward. By the end of the nineteenth century, it was perfectly apparent that the main axis of Sanusi development ran in a straight line from Jaghbub to the Kufra Oasis, where Muhammad al-Mahdi moved in 1895, and then on to Qiru (or Ghuru) in Chad, where al-Mahdi transferred his headquarters for a second time in 1899.[122]

The successful thrust of the Sanusiya could not be indefinitely prolonged without a collision with the ambitious colonial plans of the European powers. This was already clear by the late 1880s. In addition to Turkey, four powers were interested in Libya: England, Italy, Germany, and France. Britain had been concerned with the Libyan slave trade since the 1830s. She had placed consuls like Gagliuffi in the Fazzan and Warrington at Tripoli to hasten its abolition. Toward the end of the century, however, British interests in Libya declined as her interests in Egypt became more important. France and Italy now moved in. In the mid-nineteenth century, certain Italian states, such as Sardinia, Tuscany, and Naples, maintained their traditional commercial interests at Tripoli. After Italy was unified in 1870, these interests continued to exist and laid the groundwork for the Italian take-over of Libya in 1911.

Libya and its hinterlands were known to the Germans, too. A number of Prussian and German explorers such as Vogel, von Maltzan, Nachtigal, and Rohlfs had passed through Libya. During the Franco-Prussian War, Rohlfs had led a political mission to Libya. His chief aim was to make trouble for the French; unsuccessfully, he had attempted to make contact with Muhammad al-Mahdi.[123] Although Rohlfs failed, his doings again aroused the attention to Paris to events in Libya. Once more, French bureaucrats focused on the Sanusis, who had been somewhat lost to view in Paris since the time of the Algerian conquest and the rising of 'Abd al-Qadir.

During the Crimean War in the 1850s, Franco-Ottoman and Franco-Libyan relations had improved briefly.[124] Yet the harsh repression of Muslim revolts in Algeria by France and the large body of resident Algerian refugees within Libya generated a hostile attitude toward France.[125] During the war between France and Prussia in 1870, the Turkish grand vizier 'Ali Pasha founded and promoted a "Turkish-Algerian Friendship Society," which certainly included some anti-French political activities in Libya.[126] 'Ali Pasha died too soon for the organization to do much, but its support for the revolt of the Muqranis and the Rahmaniya brotherhood at Constantine and in the Awras Mountains has now been substantiated.

Any conciliatory feelings on the part of Libyans toward France were extinguished by the declaration of a French protectorate over Tunis in 1881. Most Libyans – Ottomans, Arabs, or Berbers – now hardened their attitudes to France. They were apprehensive about a French attack on Tripoli from Tunis.[127] Further south, on the Libyan-Tunisian-Algerian border, French officials frequently blamed the Sanusis for any Muslim uprisings on their side of the frontier. Indeed, since 1871 many French politicians had been paranoid enough to see the Sanusis as partners in a conspiracy with the Turks (with occasional aid from the

Germans or Italians) directed at them. Their attitudes were reinforced by the occasional deaths of European travelers or explorers in the Sahara, invariably laid to the "machinations" of the Sanusis.[128]

In the domain of Franco-Sanusi relations, the most influential Frenchman was the publicist and geographer Henri Duveyrier. Duveyrier's father, Charles, had been a leading Saint-Simonian, holding a belief in a sort of rudimentary socialism, complemented by a well-intentioned desire to "uplift" such foreigners as Arabs or Africans. Henri, brought up on these thoughts and nourished by some knowledge of Arabic, soon became a leading expert on North Africa. Often he was consulted by the French government about matters within his purview.[129] In the early 1860s, he had visited Ghat and other places in western Libya, making the personal acquaintance of numerous chiefs of the Tuareg. At that time, he was already unfavorably impressed by the Sanusis. In a book published in Paris in 1864,[130] he condemned the Sanusis, claiming that the brotherhood was opposed in every way to the introduction of "Western civilization."

In another study published twenty years later (*La Confrérie Musulmane de Sidi Mohammed ben 'Ali es-Senoussi et sa domaine géographique*), Duveyrier repeated and broadened his attack on the Sanusiya. Despite his hostility, Duveyrier was a good observer; occasionally his books provide useful bits of information. Yet, blinded by his hatred for the Sanusis, he misinterpreted what he knew and erected a superstructure of erroneous conclusions about the order. One of Duveyrier's greatest disservices – which contributed heavily to a malicious myth about the Sanusiya in Europe – was his emphasis on the order's hostility to all foreign Christians, of whatever nationality. Another claim he made was of alleged mutual scorn of Sanusis and Turks, a claim that has since misled many writers.

It is significant that Duveyrier was a close friend of such French politicians as de Freycinet and Jauriguiberry, men attracted by the mirage of an Eldorado in the Chad Basin, one day to be a French possession.[131] Crossed by railways and "opened up" to French commerce, this region would, in the near future, justify the francs and the French lives used to secure it. Duveyrier was also a leading member of the Paris Société de Géographie, a popular imperialistic organization that supported any colonial acquisition on principle, and under whose auspices Duveyrier's second book was printed. His theories had wide influence and were enthusiastically taken up. The kind of expansionist thinking initiated by Duveyrier clearly supported a French drive for new territories in North Africa between 1884 and the start of World War I. Finally, the alleged hostility of the Sanusis to France helped to justify an attack on them.

Having suppressed a number of Muslim disturbances in Algeria by 1890, the French military in Algeria felt well enough established to extend their Saharan influence. In these plans, they were supported by a coordinated policy from Paris in West and Central Africa. French strategists saw the subjection of the Sahara as a three-pronged operation. One prong would move eastward from the upper Senegal area toward the Chad Basin, while another would strike north from the Congo toward Chad. A third, coming south and east from Algeria, would unite with the others. An Anglo-French convention of 1890 opened the way to actual operations in the field. By its terms, England left to France all Saharan territories north of a line from Say on the Niger to Barroua just east of Lake Chad. Of these three French thrusts, the Algerian one would injure the Sanusis the most.[132]

As allies of the Sanusis, the Ottoman Turks had long been aware of French aims in this area. The Turkish occupation of Ghat and Ghadamis in 1875 had doubtless been staged with these thoughts in mind. Mustafa 'Asim Pasha, the *Veli* of Tripoli, was known for his advocacy of a more active Turkish role in the Sahara. In this he was aided by Mustafa Fa'iq Pasha, *Müteserrif* of the Fazzan. Before this, the Turks had been corresponding with or sending small missions to the Amir of Zinder and the Mai of Bornu to demonstrate their interest and power in the far south. Even by the end of the 1860s, there had been obvious pan-Islamic overtones to these activities.[133]

Ottoman policy for southern Libya and its hinterland was ambivalent.[134] In 1881, Mustafa Fa'iq Pasha was deposed by the new *Veli* of Tripoli, Ahmad Rasim Pasha. Ahmad Rasim's grounds for dismissing his *müteserrif* were his dispensing state funds "without reason" to "promote his fantastic plans of subjugating the whole Sudan, through stipends to chiefs."[135] Nevertheless, other elements in the Ottoman government persisted in their forward policy, trying to foster trade and surveying for railways. The project of a Turkish General Staff colonel, Ömer Subhi, submitted to Sultan 'Abd al-Hamid II in 1888, is a case in point.[136] In a mood of protest at the activities of the French (and British) in the Sahara, a forward policy faction at Istanbul caused a circular note to the powers to be drawn up in November 1890. In it, the Ottoman government defined its own claims in the Sahara and beyond; it claimed Kawar, Bornu, Borku, Kanem, Waday, the Tibesti massif, parts of Baghirmi and northern Nigeria, a bit of the Cameroonian "Duck's Bill," with a slice of the northeastern Congo.[137]

In the absence of any effective Ottoman occupation of these enormous areas, the French military simply shoved aside any small Turkish units they found in their way. Hence the efforts of the two Mustafa Pashas to activate an Ottoman "presence" in southern Libya counted for little. Likewise, their schemes of planting small garrisons at strategic wells, oases, or commercial towns. Then too, several unfortunately timed frontier incidents on the Algerian-Tripolitanian-Tunisian border furnished precisely the justification required by certain French politicians for a forward policy of their own. One of these episodes was the assassination of an adventurer, the Marquis de Morès, and the massacre of his party in 1896.[138]

Just two years later, in 1898, the Foureau-Lamy Column followed the western side of the Tripolitanian frontier past Ghadamis and Ghat, occupied Janet, and pushed on to Lake Chad. The expedition was the first move in the encirclement of Tripolitania from the rear. It marked the start of a more active trend in French Saharan conquests. The French believed that they must halt a dangerous Sanusi influence from radiating any farther into the deserts. Very soon, there was news of armed clashes between the Sanusis and the French forces.

Simply because they were a genuinely mystical but not a military organization, the poorly armed and weak Sanusis could not hope to sustain effective resistance to advancing bodies of French Saharan troops armed with artillery.[139] These weapons were employed with disastrous effect on several Sanusi *zawiyas*, causing heavy casualties. These included such important Sanusi personalities as Sayyid Muhammad al-Barrani, one of the most active Sanusi proselytizers and builders of sufi lodges.[140] Kanem – where the Sanusis had achieved great influence among elements of the Awlad Sulayman tribe between 1895 and 1899 – had to be evacuated under French pressure. The Sanusis also withdrew from the more exposed parts of Borku and the Tibesti. This was done on Ottoman advice, for French activities were making the Sanusi order rely more and more on the Turks. Finally, in 1902, an attack by a large French force on the *zawiya* of Bi'r 'Alali in Kanem forced the Sanusis to realize that they would have no chance to return to these regions again. Six months later, Sayyid al-Mahdi al-Sanusi died, perhaps as a result of his grief over the course of events in the south. His younger brother Muhammad al-Sharif had died six years before at Jaghbub. With the deaths of these two men, the heroic period of the Sanusi order came to a close.[141]

Under the third successor of Muhammad 'Ali al-Sanusi, Ahmad Sharif, the decline of the order continued. Although Ahmad Sharif did his best to protect the southernmost *zawiyas* against the French and to organize armed opposition, his efforts were largely unsuccessful; this was so even though he had intermittent support from Istanbul in the form of small detachments of Ottoman troops. Successful French operations had exposed the weakness of the order, which many Europeans had hitherto believed invincible. It is significant that Italian staff officers, agents, and planners who prepared the attack on the Ottomans in Libya in 1911 felt that they could now cope militarily with the Sanusis. Both the French and Italians succeeded in diminishing the spiritual strength of the order, ultimately forcing it to remold itself into an instrument of emergent Libyan nationalism as well as a means of Islamic opposition.[142] Paradoxically, by World War I the Sanusiya had almost become what its enemies claimed it was. Although the mystical side of the Sanusiya was not rejected by Ahmad al-Sharif, he subordinated these concerns to its struggle for existence. It battled the Italians and then the British, and once again the Italians after the end of World War I. It has been suggested with good reason that the order might have disintegrated after 1919 had it not been for the threat of Italian colonization in Libya, which once more brought it into the foreground as the one local organization capable of sustained opposition to foreign imperialistic activities.

CHAPTER 5

Ma' al-'Aynayn al-Qalqami, Mauritanian Mystic and Politician

Muhammad Mustafa "Ma' al-'Aynayn" (or Ma' al-'Aynin)[1] al-Qalqami was born near Walata in the Hawd of southeastern Mauritania in 1831. He died at Tiznit in southern Morocco in 1910. Half-Mauritanian, half-Moroccan, and a traditional religious figure, he was also a mystic and a prolific writer. Of great political shrewdness, he made a personal alliance with the sharifian dynasty of Morocco. Ma' al-'Aynayn was then drawn into armed resistance to France, in which several of his sons later perished, and which shortened his own life. Ma' al-'Aynayn was a sufi of the Qadiri persuasion, of a nineteenth-century Mauritanian branch. This suborder was known in his father's time as the Fadiliya, but later it was known as the 'Ayniya after Ma' al-'Aynayn. Among Ma' al-'Aynayn's main interests were magic and the acquisition of cosmic secrets. Even politically, this preoccupation was of some use to him, for it attracted disciples. Ma' al-'Aynayn was also renowned as a peerless camel rider, a digger of wells, and an energetic builder of sufi lodges (*zawiyas*). If Ma' al-'Aynayn accelerated the coming of nationalism in both Morocco and Mauritania, he was unfortunately unable to cope with foreign military technology or diplomatic pressures, being without the resources to thwart the maneuverings of the colonial states of his time. Although both Morocco and Mauritania would like to claim him as one of their national leaders, he clearly belongs to the era before mass nationalism in the Maghrib.

Although the outlines of Ma' al-'Aynayn's career are well known, the sources for information about his life are limited. With a few exceptions the bulk of his writings remain in manuscript, unpublished. One of his sons, Murabbih Rabbuh, wrote a long hagiography of his father (the *Qurrat al-'Aynayn*), which is amplified by a few articles in Spanish, French, and English, with an occasional page by a historian in Arabic.[2] No full assessment of him can be made until his own work becomes more accessible. Meanwhile, this chapter is intended as a provisional account of his life with a short analysis of certain of his ideas.

Murabbih Rabbuh states that Ma' al-'Aynayn was precisely thirty-five lunar years younger than his father, Muhammad Fadil wuld Mamin.[3] Muhammad Fadil was himself a mystic, and Ma' al-'Aynayn was the

125

twelfth of his forty-eight sons. In southeastern Mauritania, Muhammad Fadil was a local Qadiri leader of repute. According to Murabbih Rabbuh, Ma' al-'Aynayn:

> was brought up by his father, among his brothers. He studied under his father, pledged him his loyalty, obtaining an education from him. He made great efforts at reading and in all religious observances, excluding himself from all but his father. He had attracted his attention because he was not fond of mixing [with his half-brothers]. . . . He paid attention to God and the orders of his *Shaykh*.[4]

According to Norris, Ma' al-'Aynayn's mother was Manna bint al-Ma'lum, of the Ijayjba clan, but there is little information about her. Whether or not she claimed sharifian ancestry is uncertain.[5]

Her husband Muhammad Fadil certainly did, and this point continues to generate controversy; many Mauritanians are still unconvinced of Muhammad Fadil's claim. In the nineteenth century, such ancestry was still a significant issue. Indeed, a claim of sharifian descent was indispensable for a successful religious or clerical career at the highest level, as the careers of other North Africans such as Amir 'Abd al-Qadir and Muhammad 'Ali al-Sanusi show (Chapters 2 and 4). The Spanish officer Domenech Lafuente claims that Muhammad Fadil was descended from the Lamtuna Berbers of the Hawd. Yet Ma' al-'Aynayn's clan, the Ahl Talib Mukhtar, say that they derive from a seventeenth-century migrant from southern Morocco who lived at that time in the Hawd.[6] A more remote ancestor, Yahya al-Qalqami, who hailed from Qasaba Tadala in central Morocco, lived in the fifteenth century and gave his name to the clan.[7] From this man, the Ahl Talib Mukhtar trace their line to the 'Alid *sharif* Idris, the apex of most sharifian genealogies in the Maghrib. Essentially, this was a claim to belong to the appropriate clerical élite in the land.

Underlying what seemed to be a sterile dispute – over who was descended from the Prophet Muhammad or was not – was a serious doctrinal and political controversy. As a boy, Muhammad Fadil (c. 1797–1870) had studied under the great Qadiri master of the western Sudan, Sidi al-Mukhtar al-Kunti (d. 1811). This man had exercised much influence over the Qadiri states and revolutions in West Africa, as well as the career of Usuman dan Fodio in Hausaland. Later, Muhammad Fadil became a determined rival of the Kuntas, and he finally broke with them. He and they diverged over theology, sufi practices, and politics. The Kuntas appear to have scorned Muhammad Fadil's interest in certain forms of magic as intellectually unworthy. This interest was bequeathed by Fadil to Ma' al-'Aynayn. In spite of these divergences, both the Fadiliya and the Kunta branches (*Mukh-tariya*) remained within the framework of the Qadiri order.

Yet the Fadiliya's success in recruiting members was such that it aroused the irritation of the Kuntas, who picked flaws in Muhammad Fadil's genealogy. They also criticized his organization because of its loose requirements for membership and because Fadil maintained ties to three other orders, including the Tijaniya, although he never favored al-Hajj 'Umar.[8] The noisy and popular religious aspects of the Fadiliya also repelled the austere Kuntas.[9] Roughly speaking, the Fadiliya represented a left wing to the contemporary religio-political spectrum in the western Sahara and the northern fringes of the Sahil. The conventional sufi techniques and attitudes espoused by Muhammad Fadil were well tested. Thus they were adopted en bloc, by Ma' al'Aynayn, who knew that their use would guarantee him popularity and success among the local nomads.

"At the age of twenty-eight, when he had become thoroughly proficient in the sciences, internal and external," declares Murabbih Rabbuh, "Ma' al-'Aynayn emerged from his isolation and set off on the pilgrimage."[10] Ma' al-'Aynayn's route (spring 1858) took him to the Wadi Nun in Morocco, then to al-Sawira or Mogador. On his way north he passed through Marrakish, where he visited the heir to the sharifian throne, Muhammad ibn 'Abd al-Rahman. Nor did he neglect to pay his respects to the reigning sultan, 'Abd al-Rahman, at Miknas (Meknes), before going on to the east. In conversations with both men, Ma' al-'Aynayn gave evidence of his intelligence and orthodox opinions. He also gave Sultan 'Abd al-Rahman news of his father's doings and current Mauritanian politics. 'Abd al-Rahman reciprocated by showering Ma' al-'Aynayn with gifts and hospitality before sending him off to his resident agent in Tangier. This man put him on a steamer for Egypt and perhaps paid his fare.[11] This visit marked the start of a friendly understanding between Ma' al-'Aynayn and a succession of Moroccan sultans, based on mutual interest. As Ma' al-'Aynayn was the son of a prominent religious leader in a region where Morocco wanted to maintain or to extend her political influence, the sultans treated him well. Mauritanian personalities who might support Morocco in a war were welcome; there were already unmistakable signs of heightened European interest in North Africa. Of this, the recent war between France and Morocco (1844) was the latest example. From Ma' al-'Aynayn's standpoint, it was useful to have powerful backers, even if they were not Mauritanians.

What is surprising about Ma' al-'Aynayn's pilgrimage is how slight an effect it had on him. He stayed only for three weeks in Mecca and

Madina, compared to al-Hajj 'Umar's three years.[12] If he frequented the learned men, the *'ulama* of the city, his hagiographer says little about it. Yet the Moroccan writer al-Susi records his meetings with a "great sufi *shaykh*," one 'Abd al-Rahman Efendi.[13] From his own account, Ma' al-'Aynayn was much surprised by the unawaited cordiality and kindness of 'Abd al-Rahman Efendi. It turned out that this man – who had experienced visions of Muhammad Fadil for some years – was really searching for the "Secret of the Letter H" (*hā'*), which Ma' al-'Aynayn was presumably able to give him.[14] This curious incident highlights one of Ma' al-'Aynayn's perpetual interests: magic. This included the acquisition of awesome secrets affecting the cosmos or weather, of magic working on human beings in strange ways, and the writing of charms and amulets for medical purposes.

After his brief trip to Mecca, Ma' al-'Aynayn visited Madina for a few days before returning to Egypt. At Alexandria, he fell ill with smallpox. He convalesced in the city, then waited for five months before he could find a ship for Morocco. How he passed his time on this occasion is unclear.

Ma' al-'Aynayn disembarked at Tangier in March 1859, about six months before the death of the old sultan, 'Abd al-Rahman ibn Hisham.[15] He retraced his steps homeward via Miknas, where he admired Mawla'i Isma'il's unfinished capital, and Marrakish. In both towns, he enjoyed a sharifian welcome, which may well have included gifts of money. Then he went along to the Saqiyat al-Hamra' ("Red River Valley") and the Adrar in Mauritania via the Wadi Nun and Tinduf (now in far western Algeria). His sea voyages and pilgrimage to Arabia had taken him only about a year. As did his visit to the two Holy Cities, Ma' al-'Aynayn's contacts with the Moroccan royal family heightened his reputation and lent him real distinction among his countrymen. From this time onward, his loyalty to the sharifian dynasty never wavered.[16]

If he had not stopped to study in the East, perhaps because of a lack of time and money as well as because of illness, Ma' al-'Aynayn did halt for some months at Tinduf. Here two famous learned men, a grammarian named Muhammad Mawlud and a Qadiri leader named Muhammad al-Jakani had settled, the latter about 1852. He and his colleague attracted a number of students; Ma' al-'Aynayn is said to have studied for a time in al-Jakani's library before quitting Tinduf in early 1861. It seems unlikely that he had a quarrel with al-Jakani, as some sources report; but it does seem likely that his stay at Tinduf was supported by aid from the Moroccan dynasty. On his return to Mauritania, perhaps in mid-1861, his father, Muhammad Fadil, bestowed on him a turban and the title of *shaykh*.[17]

Ma' al-'Aynayn now tried to lengthen the radius of his religious and political influence. Showing at first some hesitation about the place best suited to his teaching and preaching, Ma' al-'Aynayn left his ancestral Hawd for northern Mauritania and the southern Moroccan borderlands. In time, his influence spread, covering the Saqiyat al-Hamra', the northern Adrar, and the Shinqit region.[18] By moving north, Ma' al-'Aynayn avoided conflict with those of his half brothers, who shared in their father's religious inheritance. Three of them who sought to succeed Muhammad Fadil in the leadership of the Fadiliya order were Sa'd Bu, Sidi al-Khayr, and al-Hadrami wuld Muhammad. Sa'd Bu chose to settle in the southern Adrar and the Trarza district; Sidi al-Khayr stayed at Walata; and al-Hadrami stayed in the Hawd. Some years before his death in February 1870, Muhammad Fadil – doubtless for reasons of old age and illness – withdrew from active leadership of the Fadiliya and of his clan, the Ahl Talib Mukhtar. He relinquished responsibility for these matters to his four most prominent sons. Of these, Ma' al-'Aynayn had been a favorite, and he was now emerging as the leader.[19]

Like the Hapsburgs, Ma' al-'Aynayn extended his growing influence through marriages. Al-Susi claims that the total of Ma' al-'Aynayn's marital ventures came to 116, and he makes the following comments:

> It was the custom of Shaykh Ma al-'Aynayn to marry frequently. Whenever he took a wife, he assigned her a tent and money for maintenance. If he did not sleep with her, he divorced her. Hence he had many children. . . . Frequent marrying and divorcing among the Saharans is not disapproved, it does not offend their sense of honor: it is the standard practice.[20]

Al-Susi's remarks are confirmed by the observations of Camille Douls, a French traveler who was taken before Ma' al-'Aynayn in 1887 by his captors, the Awlad Dalim. Douls says specifically that he limited his wives to the canonical number of four.[21] The children of these marriages were numerous; Marty mentions twenty-one sons and some thirty daughters. Despite the flexible and quite temporary terms of these marriages, his alliances with women of different clans and groups had political significance, for they reinforced ties that Ma' al-'Aynayn wished to foster or maintain.[22]

Ma' al-'Aynayn's removal to the Saqiyat al-Hamra' (just before 1870) and his installation there as resident saint also meant the spread of relative order and stability. He was able to find effective means for settling personal and sectional disputes among the nomads, reduce the scale of disastrous interclan feuds, and generally lessen social anarchy.[23] Thus, by the time of Douls' arrival in northern Mauritania in

1887, Ma' al-'Aynayn's prestige was already well established. This is demonstrated in Douls' account; he notes that when his captors were unable to decide what to do with him, they referred the matter to Ma' al-'Aynayn, whom Douls called the "Chief of the Saharan nomads."[24] Once Ma' al-'Aynayn had made a decision about Douls, it was no longer seriously questioned. This was a tribute to the skill and success by which Ma' al-'Aynayn had cemented his political authority in northern Mauritania over the preceding two decades. Apparently, his nearest rivals were the hereditary *qa'ids* of the Bayruk family of Gulimim (or Goulimine) in the Wadi Nun, about a ten-day camel-journey north of the Saqiyat al-Hamra'.[25]

One of the few European eyewitness descriptions of Ma' al-'Aynayn was written by Douls. Pretending to be a Muslim to facilitate his explorations, and going under the name of 'Abd al-Malik, Douls aroused the suspicions of the Awlad Dalim clan, who buried him in the sand up to the neck with his hands tied behind him, leaving him to succumb in the sun's heat. When he mumbled a few prayers in Arabic, they took pity on him and led him to Ma' al-'Aynayn, whom he describes:

> The *Shaykh* was seated on a fine Moroccan carpet, surrounded by his students. Mel-Aynin looked like an Indian *poussah* [*sic*] with his face veiled and his head crowned by a turban. . . . He was hidden beneath the folds of a light blue robe. All that could be seen of his massive person were his two brilliant eyes, and his hands, resting on his knees.[26]

This description has echoes of audiences given to visitors by Muhammad al-Amin al-Kanemi of Bornu, another nineteenth-century ruler, who wore a face veil as he sat on a boxlike throne. Norris suggests that the use of a face veil was a part of the Lamtuna tradition for important religious leaders.[27] Or did it cover a face ravaged by smallpox?

As Douls reports it, Ma' al-'Aynayn's conversation with his French visitor was revealing:

> He told me to sit next to him. . . . He held out his hand to me, which I kissed, as I had seen the nomads do. Then in low, but benevolent tones, he asked me several questions. . . . Telling him I was French, I spoke to him of Algeria as my country, but said . . . that I was Muslim. "Do you know the *Fatiha?*" [first *sura* of the *Qur'an*], the Shaykh asked me? . . . When I had finished, he asked me if I could write in Arabic. "Without being a literary person or student," said I, "I know enough Arabic to do my trading." He asked me to write my name in Arabic in the sand with a piece of wood. . . . When I had answered all of his questions in a satisfactory way,

he spoke to the Moors who were anxiously awaiting his judgment.
. . . "This man is a true Muslim. . . . Take off his irons and welcome him into your tribe like a brother."[28]

These observations by a foreigner throw some light on Ma' al-
'Aynayn's roles of religious and political leader, expert on the Muslim
world beyond Mauritania, and omnicompetent intellectual with an answer for every problem. This may account for some of Ma' al-'Aynayn's
numerous writings (see pp. 145–50), which come to more than a hundred.

The Spanish anthropologist Caro Baroja offers some useful suggestions about the details of Ma' al-'Aynayn's political objectives after his
settlement in the Saqiyat al-Hamra'. The jihad of al-Hajj 'Umar (Chapter 3) created much dislocation and disturbance on both sides of the
Senegal River. When a French-enforced peace temporarily halted
Mauritanian raids (by the Brakna and Trarza) at the end of the 1850s,
the new situation brought a reorientation of European trade on an
east-west axis along the river. Traditional commerce going north and
south – in slaves, grain, cattle, and precious metals – declined, creating
economic hardship in Mauritania. Hence, Caro Baroja claims:

> It is not surprising that in the areas as yet uninfluenced by the mili-
> tary activities of the French in the Adrar, Tagant, and Sahil, the
> Sharq and the Tell – a [public] opinion should form – hostile to
> them. We find Shaykh Ma' al-'Aynayn as one of the leaders of that
> opinion. . . . For the first time since the Portuguese period, Chris-
> tians had set foot in Muslim territory, but could not be treated as
> slaves. For the first time since the 17th century, the southern ports
> were closed. Both religious ideals and economic interests were
> threatened. Under these circumstances, Ma' al-'Aynayn saw his op
> portunity.[29]

It is apparent that increasingly, during the 1860s, Ma' al-'Aynayn
saw one of his roles as rouser, molder, and leader of local Muslim
opinion against foreign incursions. His best policy, it seemed, lay in
closer relations with the sharifian rulers to the north. Very quickly
(certainly before 1880) Ma' al-'Aynayn and the sharifian sultans attempted to implement their common purpose, the creation of a bul-
wark against inevitable European encroachments along the exposed
Atlantic coast of Morocco and Mauritania. In a sense they were trying
to create a joint Moroccan-Mauritanian *makhzan,* a defense designed
to repel foreign incursions wherever they might take place.

The first such European incursion had a strange, even ironical basis.
About 1874, Donald MacKenzie, an eccentric Scottish entrepreneur
with utopian ideas, became convinced that he could build a "water-
highway" into the western Sahara from the Atlantic:

since there exist in those regions vast depressions covered with salt.
. . . Some of these depressions were supposed to be under the level
of the sea . . . I felt they could once more be covered by the navi-
gable waters of the Atlantic. . . . A water-highway would be
opened to the interior of Africa . . . of great commercial importance.[30]

In 1878, MacKenzie personally visited Cape Juby (Tarfaya), which
he deemed suitable as an advance post for his project. After some
"friendly intercourse with the natives," MacKenzie bought Cape Juby,
its harbor, and a small strip of land adjoining from an "aged chieftain,"
none other than Sharif Muhammad wuld Bayruk, Ma' al-'Aynayn's
leading rival and head of a little "maraboutic state" near Tazarwalt in
the Wadi Nun.[31]

MacKenzie's "purchase" triggered a whole series of events that realized some of the nightmares of Ma' al-'Aynayn and the sharifian sultan.
Spanish interest in the Mauritanian coast revived; an expedition under
Emilio Bonelli was dispatched to Mauritania to find a place for a future Spanish colony.[32] Sultan Hasan I decided to send an army immediately to the Sus and Wadi Nun to forestall any further concessions
to foreigners.[33] Arriving at the head of his men from Marrakish in
1882, Hasan I pressured the reluctant Muhammad wuld Bayruk into
becoming an official of the *makhzan*. During a second expedition
(1886), Hasan I corresponded regularly with Ma' al-'Aynayn, as he
doubtless had done earlier.[34] To both men, collaboration over the political problems of the Sus, Tazarwalt, and regions farther south was
important; the contemporary Moroccan historian al-Salawi speaks of
Hasan I moving to expel the "Christians," to "excise the root of this
evil."[35] In 1887, Douls observed:

> Jealous of his conquest, Muley el-Hasan wished to remove it from
> the greed of Europeans, whose entry he carefully barred. He placed
> garrisons at the inhabited points on the coasts. Rigid orders were
> sent to governors, who even today are under orders to imprison any
> Europeans of whose presence they become aware.[36]

Yet al-Hasan's solution was costly. Moroccan troops descended on
Cape Juby – the sultan having ordered MacKenzie previously to leave –
in 1888. They killed his English manager and plundered his trading
post.[37] The issue ended only in 1895, when Sultan 'Abd al-'Aziz bought
Tarfaya back from the British for £50,000.[38] In the same year, 'Abd
al-'Aziz established a permanent garrison at Tarfaya to show a Moroccan presence there.[39] A yearly or semiannual steamer from Mogador
supplied this garrison. Hence the collaboration between Ma' al-'Aynayn

and the sharifian rulers assumed practical form from at least 1886 and doubtless prior to that. These developments can be linked not only to doings of the French in the south, but also to Ma' al-'Aynayn's visits to Fez and Marrakish in the 1870s or before. Officially, al-Hasan I entrusted responsibility of the southern frontiers from Villa Cisncros (al-Dākhila) to Cape Juby "and what lay between them" to Ma' al-'Aynayn in 1892–3. This was a long stretch, several hundred miles of open coastline, difficult to watch over.

When he was not visiting the Moroccan rulers in Marrakish or Fez, a custom observed with some frequency by Ma' al-'Aynayn from the beginning of the 1870s, he moved about in the desert, along the coast or inland, with his people and adherents, following his animals, which sought areas with good pasturage. For a time (about 1868) he had stayed at Shum and Aseffal in the Adrar, then at Tiris nearer the Atlantic shore. By the start of the 1870s, Ma' al-'Aynayn moved to the region where the Wadi Tigsert joins the Saqiyat al-Hamra'. Here in 1871–2, Ma' al-'Aynayn commenced building the first of two permanent headquarters, his "Red House" (Dar al-Hamra'). This was a fixed *zawiya*, or sufi center – a single building of mud and stone with a courtyard, space for storing grain, and rooms for guards and servants. Here, according to Domenech Lafuente, Ma' al-'Aynayn "passed some years," leading the "free, simple, and enjoyable life of a nomad."[40]

Ma' al-'Aynayn's placid nomadizing was to be of short duration; despite al-Hasan I's prohibitions against landings on the Mauritanian shores, Europeans were still entering the country deliberately or inadvertently. There was a long history of shipwrecks, of the sufferings and captivities of castaways on this treacherous and barren coast, with its eccentric currents and strong winds, stretching from Morocco to the Senegal River.[41] Starting with the MacKenzie Affair, Spain began to take an interest in Mauritania and exploited maritime disasters involving Spanish vessels for occasional intervention and as a pretext to spy out the country and choose a permanent base for colonization. After 1884, Spanish activities radiated from such a new site seized by them; this was Villa Cisneros. Several of these expeditions tried to penetrate the Adrar, making "treaties" with certain of the nomad groups they encountered (much in the style of Karl Peters in Tanganyika). The intruders quickly felt Ma' al-'Aynayn's opposition and disapproval; petulantly, one of them wrote:

> Emissaries arrived from Negshir, sent by Me-Lainin [sic], a religious head of great influence, who put about false rumors . . . inciting the Arabs to hinder our march through the Sahara, and prejudicial to our persons. This was a region which . . . we would sully by our

impious plans, attracting to the Faithful the anger of the Prophet and the curse of God.[42]

About 1890, both Ma' al-'Aynayn and Sultan al-Hasan realized that they were powerless to take on two European adversaries at once.[43] It was simpler to appease the weaker one; circumstances might then arise where they could embroil France with Spain to their own advantage. Thus the sources cite increasingly frequent reports of Spanish sailors and traders repatriated via Morocco.[44] In 1893, a Spanish lieutenant was able to sign an agreement with a nephew of Ma' al-'Aynayn, Muhammad al-Amin, regulating the treatment of such castaways. This arrangement grew out of the capture of five Canary Islanders in 1892 (the Ycod Affair), which was finally settled amicably. The Sociedad Geografica de Madrid even sent a gilt dagger to Ma' al-'Aynayn, as a reward for his help in rescuing the crew.[45] Nevertheless, the Spanish government continued to justify its new base at Villa Cisneros by claiming that its retention was indispensable to hinder future incidents of this sort.

When Sultan al-Hasan I died in 1894, good relations between Ma' al-'Aynayn and his successor, 'Abd al-'Aziz, were quickly established. Murabbih Rabbuh describes his father's triumphal entry into Marrakish in 1896–7:

> The day of his entry into Marrakish was a memorable occasion. The Sultan ordered all the great men of the state, leading persons among his subjects, all the military, and notables, and commoners to attend with drums and guns, so as to greet him [Ma' al-'Aynayn] at about two miles' distance from the *madina*. . . . 'Abd al-'Aziz showered him with gifts: great men competed with each other to give him presents and do kind actions to him.[46]

During this visit, Murabbih Rabbuh claims that Ma' al-'Aynayn received a total of a million silver dirhams from 'Abd al-'Aziz. Further, the new ruler joined the 'Ayniya brotherhood, Ma' al-'Aynayn giving him personal instruction in the practices of the order. Al-Susi claims that the sultan joined it at the suggestion of Ba Ahmad ibn Musa, the Grand *Wazir*, himself a Saharan and member of the 'Ayniya.[47] Perhaps at the *wazir*'s suggestion also, 'Abd al-'Aziz provided Ma' al-'Aynayn with a site for a new 'Ayniya sufi center at Marrakish and made it a pious foundation (*habs*) to be controlled in perpetuity by Ma' al-'Aynayn or members of his family.[48] Ma' al-'Aynayn already owned other pieces of property in Marrakish – farms, houses, and gardens. Not long after, the 'Ayniya opened a new house (*zawiya*) at Fez, and then at Salé (Salā) adjoining Rabat; yet most of the followers of the order seem to have lived on the Plain of Marrakish and among the nearby Dukkala. The building of all three structures had the enthusiastic moral (and financial) backing of 'Abd al-'Aziz.[49]

These tangible rewards from the sharifian house were the results of Ma' al-'Aynayn's close ties to it ever since the time of Sultan 'Abd al-Rahman ibn Hisham forty years before. The Mauritanian leader had visited each sultan in turn, being closest to al-Hasan I. Other factors that cemented the relations between the dynasts of Marrakish and Ma' al-'Aynayn were Ma' al-'Aynayn's age and prestige, his knowledge, his political success among the nomads to the south, and his miracle-working powers. One source claims that a minister of Muhammad IV, Muhammad wuld Bulla, was completely cured of leprosy by Ma' al-'Aynayn, who wrote an amulet that he tied around the *wazir*'s neck.[50] Similar reports concern Ba Ahmad (Ahmad b. Musa al-Marrakishi, 1841–1900), the chief minister of al-Hasan I. At this time the sharifian court – according to Domenech – accepted Ma' al-'Aynayn as its "wizard, wise man, sorcerer, distributors of amulets, and diviner." At one time Ba Ahmad had studied under Ma' al-'Aynayn in the south, along with Idris ibn Ya'ish, chief of the Court Service. Another writer declares that whenever Ba Ahmad had trouble in getting al-Hasan to accept his advice, or if his numerous enemies slandered him to the sultan, the minister employed an intermediary to obtain "spiritual assistance" from Ma' al-'Aynayn, in whom he possessed "total confidence."[51]

Despite the unbroken alliance between him and his Moroccan hosts, Ma' al-'Aynayn could speak to them in a forceful, even an arrogant way. Murabbih Rabbuh one day observed his father and Ba Ahmad talking in a garden at Marrakish. When the *wazir* became abusive to him, Ma' al-'Aynayn said: "Know that God has put your state into my hands. If I wish, I shall raise it up: if I want, I shall let it fall. . . . After Mawla'i al-Hasan will come a sultan whose state will be controlled by a man who veils himself – namely me."[52] Murabbih Rabbuh also credited his father with power to control others by directing elemental powers of nature. Once, he claims, al-Hasan I and Ba Ahmad went out to attend a festival. The *wazir* rode behind on a mule, the sultan in front on a horse. Then a lightning bolt struck directly between them, killing some of al-Hasan's retainers walking behind him, "and then they knew that this was something which he [Ma' al-'Aynayn] had conceived within his mind."[53]

Having 'Abd al-'Aziz and the *wazir* Ba Ahmad in his pocket, Ma' al-'Aynayn now had as much money as he could want. Moroccan government steamers usually carried him and his men back and forth from Cape Juby to Mogador (al-Sawira), whence he led them to

Marrakish or Fez, on one occasion curing many victims of a plague whom he met along his route.[54] By 1898–9, Ma' al-'Aynayn had acquired enough sharifian money to launch a startling new venture. This was a combined headquarters, political capital, and religious center, like the "Red House" of the 1870s but on a vast scale. It included some large permanent masonry structures along a small *wadi*, the Wayn Silwan, at a place called Simara or Smara (the "grassy place" or "reedbed" in Hassaniya Arabic). Simara adjoined the meeting point of the Wayn Silwan and the Saqiyat al-Hamra'. Norris speculates that this vast and hugely expensive complex (five years in the building, from 1898 to 1903) was constructed to "impress the nomads" with the power and resources of its builder.[55] It may well have been inspired by accounts of the colossal size and architectural magnificence of Jaghbub in Cyrenaica, built by Muhammad 'Ali al-Sanusi for the members of his brotherhood.

Simara was in a remote place, about three or four days by camel-back from the port of Tarfaya (Cape Juby). The construction costs were truly immense. M. A. Ba notes that the building expenses were helped along by the *wazir* Ba Ahmad:

> Ba Hemade, a Saharan of humble origins who had reached the rank
> of vizier at the Sharifian Court, and the Caid Hameida professed
> a limitless admiration for Shaykh Ma el-Ainin. Hence they worked
> without pause to satisfy the demands which the holy marabout con-
> ceived. From Tarfaya, whole caravans brought goods of every sort
> which ships unloaded. . . . A widespread opinion in the Mauri-
> tanian sahil thought these gifts emptied the *Bit el-Mal* or treasury
> of Moulaye 'Abd el-Aziz.[56]

It is said that the site of Simara was shown to Ma' al-'Aynayn by his followers in 1898; it was a place where there was abundant water from a spring and good stone for building. The site was near a caravan track linking the Wadi Nun in the north to the Adrar and Tiris. In the light of his *zawiya*-building activities and his earlier effort to settle and make a center for the 'Ayniya, the idea of a new headquarters appealed strongly to Ma' al-'Aynayn. He went ahead with his plans, despite the fears expressed by the Ruqaybat (a local tribe) that such construction might attract European attack or some form of political control. With his abundant funds and aided by the enthusiasm of his sons, visitors, and guests, Ma' al-'Aynayn set to work in haste. Although he was nearly seventy, he channeled all of his still considerable energies into his new enterprise.[57]

A comprehensive description of these remarkable buildings may be found in Caro Baroja's "Santon Sahariano."[58] Baroja first surveyed and then described a huge walled compound, 200 feet on a side, having a multistoried, domed structure in its center. This served as Ma' al-'Aynayn's reception room and living quarters. The front of the compound wall was decorated with a magnificent gate through which loaded camels could be driven. The gate looked south to the dry bed of the Wayn Silwan, and the corners of this facade had watchtowers. Within the compound were houses for each of Ma' al-'Aynayn's four wives and another structure, perhaps for his concubines. Though Caro Baroja complains that the compound, facades, and dome are built in a "bastardized Hispano-Moorish style," its mere dimensions make it impressive.[59] Adjoining the front of this desert palace (in some ways like the hunting palaces of the Umayyads in the Syrian desert) were lesser enclosures, inhabited by Ma' al-'Aynayn's sons. Directly behind the main enclosure and laid out at an angle to its central axis was a large mosque with a *mihrab* or niche, at its rear, facing Mecca.

Close to the principal compound but behind it were quarters for students, a walled area for slaves, dwellings for carpenters and masons, a guest house, and a small round building – no doubt a *khalwa,* or house for sufi retreats.[60] Simara also had food warehouses and cisterns. Close at hand were extensive palm groves laid out by Ma' al-'Aynayn; also present were many new wells, whose number Ba estimates at about fifty. At the time of its construction and occupation by Ma' al-'Aynayn, according to a contemporary writer, Simara supported 10,000 adherents of the 'Ayniya order as well as many destitute persons.[61] At that time, the masonry structures must have looked like an island in a sea of tents. Ba writes:

> The first Moors who saw "Dar Samara" extolled the solidity and beauty of its buildings throughout the land. The nomads used to go there in hundreds, some out of curiosity, others drawn by the liberality which the holy marabout was able to dispense to his visitors. Thus the fame of the *Kasbah* soon spread.[62]

Simara was occupied by the *shaykh* soon after it was finished, by 1902 or 1903. Yet it was only used until the end of 1909. Simara was not a fortress and was wholly indefensible. When Ma' al-'Aynayn moved to the Sus under French pressure, he abandoned it, although it was occupied for short periods after that by his sons. In March 1913, Simara was overrun by a French column whose commander, Colonel Mouret, took pains to blow up part of the domed structure and to burn the sections of Ma' al-'Aynayn's library that he had left behind.[63]

In many respects, Ma' al-'Aynayn's visits to Fez and Marrakish and his construction of Simara were the apogee of his career. After 1900, Ma' al-'Aynayn's ambitions became gradually muted, his hopes blunted. This was not because of Spanish colonial ambitions, which remained relatively static, but because of long-range French designs to take over Morocco. These plans were first given expression at a conference on Morocco held at Madrid in 1880. Although the question of Mauritania was only another aspect to this problem, many observers in Morocco and Mauritania did not grasp the implications – as seen from Paris – of the simultaneous penetration of both counties by the French. To many Mauritanians, the French advance into their land from the south after 1900 seemed merely a resumption of Faidherbe's attacks on the Trarza and Brakna in 1858.

Behind France's new forward policy was a man of Corsican origin, Xavier Coppolani (1866–1905).[64] A member of the Algerian colon class, his father had migrated to North Africa while Xavier was still a boy. Coppolani acquired fluency in Algerian Arabic and came to know local Muslims well. He understood their strengths and weaknesses, and he took time to study sufism and Islamic magic. Coppolani's attitudes toward Muslims and his interests ran parallel with the opinions of the French Algerian military and bureaucracy of that time. Coppolani was well known in the Bureaux Indigènes and the Intelligence Department. In 1899, Coppolani was sent to southern Mauritania as director of a "Mission to the Soudan and Southern Sahel." Disguised as an official inquiry, the mission's real objective was to make contact with Mauritanians and investigate them, looking toward their eventual submission.[65]

From St. Louis in Senegal, Coppolani in 1899 conducted a personal reconnaissance into the Hawd. Like Ma' al-'Aynayn – of enormous physical size and having the "face and serenity of a Roman emperor," as one of his admirers has described him – Coppolani busied himself with learning Mauritanian geography and making the acquaintance of local leaders.[66] Many of them were impressed by his knowledge of Arabic and seeming sympathy toward Islam; some even believed he might be a lapsed Muslim. Within a short time, Coppolani had no trouble in identifying certain political powers in the region: Ma' al-'Aynayn, his brother Sa'd Bu, and Shaykh Sidya Baba, among others.

Under Coppolani's influence, the Ministry of Colonies in Paris adopted a proposal he had elaborated for the future organization of the new territory when it came under French control. It was to be known as "West Mauritania," running along a line drawn from the north bank of the River Senegal, bounded by the Atlantic on the west, and bounded on the east and north by a line drawn from the vicinity of Kayes to Cape Juby. This ministerial decision to create a new territory was predicated on Coppolani's confidential reports, which foresaw a new administration in the near future, after a quick "peaceful penetration" – an easy military conquest with a loss of few French lives. Once Mauritania was overrun, pressure could be exerted on Morocco from the south; thus the French had a useful political and strategic lever for use at the appropriate moment.[67]

Although some voices in Paris opposed his plan, Coppolani neutralized them through the support of the powerful *président du conseil*, Waldeck-Rousseau. In Senegal, also, Coppolani generally had his way, although he was opposed by some St. Louis merchant families that wished to continue selling arms to the nomads. Certain bureaucrats also opposed Coppolani because of his ties to French military interests. From earlier African campaigns, these interests were well aware that such operations often brought promotion, yielding good publicity for their commanders.[68] Coppolani also had time to create a Bureau d'Études Maures, of which he became the director. By the autumn of 1904, Coppolani had become the first *commissaire général* of the future civil territory of Mauritania.[69] By the phrase "peaceful penetration," Coppolani meant the exploitation of divisions and rivalries among clans and tribes, among sufi brotherhoods or sections of brotherhoods, and between clerical groupings and warriors. In his reports, he stressed that such a procedure was the best and cheapest way of making a conquest. He realized that such emphasis would please the parsimonious bureaucrats at Paris and St. Louis.

Coppolani's designs for Mauritania were aided by the incorrigible political confusion in its southern districts, which spilled over into Senegal. In 1900, nomads from the north were still occasionally raiding their traditional targets – the blacks along the river – for slaves, cattle, or foodstuffs. In his reports, Coppolani took care to exaggerate the scale and damage of these periodic descents on Podor, Matam, Madina, and other riverside towns. He won a useful opening in 1902, when the Trarza Arabs revolted against their amir, Ahmad Sallum. Ahmad was a French protégé, whereas his rival, Wuld Sidi Muhammad Fal, was anti-French. Coppolani intervened in this dispute with troops who settled the affair in Ahmad's favor. Coppolani then turned north into the Adrar. He recognized that the low Adrar Plateau was the strategic pivot of Mauritania. Once they occupied it, the French could turn west against the coastal inhabitants or north toward the Saqiyat al-Hamra' and Morocco.

By the spring of 1905, Coppolani had penetrated far into Mauritania, pushing aside all opposition. At Tijikja in the southern Adrar, he set up camp among the palm groves, inviting local personalities to visit him. Many complied. But an important clan, the Idaw u Aysh, rejected his invitations. Earlier, they had sent a delegation to Ma' al-'Aynayn asking him to enlist the aid of the sharifian sultan on their behalf.

By this time, Ma' al-'Aynayn had an effective agent in the Adrar, his son Hassana, who functioned as regent in the Adrar sultanate and advised the child-amir Ahmad wuld Ahmad.[70]

In the tense atmosphere of the French advance, Ma' al-'Aynayn was able to create a working alliance among the nomads – the men of Adrar, Idaw u Aysh, Ruqaybat, and Awlad Ghaylan. This despite a crippling attack by the French, which had killed the amir of the Idaw u Aysh. By this time, too, Ma' al-'Aynayn had created a rudimentary intelligence network. The French discovered the identity of one of his agents, a trader from Shinqit Town who made frequent journeys to St. Louis. And, perhaps at Ma' al-'Aynayn's suggestion, Sultan 'Abd al-'Aziz had sent letters to certain prominent Senegalese Muslims, hoping to foment trouble for the French. Some of these missives fell into Coppolani's hands, so that he obtained a good idea of his enemies' intentions.[71]

The farther the French penetrated the Adrar, the stiffer resistance became. By 1905, it was difficult to speak any longer of "peaceful penetration." Coppolani was beginning to lose numbers of men in ambushes and unexpected attacks; the assailants melted away into the Sahara. He and his associates began to worry about the emergence of a solid Muslim coalition under Ma' al-'Aynayn's leadership. Whether or not this coalition was conceived by Ma' al-'Aynayn as a jihad against France is not certain, although he did announce such a jihad by 1908. It was at this point that Xavier Coppolani was waylaid and assassinated in his camp at Tijikja on 12 May 1905. His assailants were a band of twenty men led by Sidi al-Saghir wuld Mawla'i Zayn. This man was a local leader (*muqaddam*) of a small sufi order called the Qudhfiya, an offshoot of the Qadiriya. Sidi al-Saghir also met death in the attack.[72]

Coppolani's death was a clear turning point in the course of the French conquest. What had first seemed an uncomplicated military advance into hostile territory was turning into a serious problem, if not a major one. For the sake of prestige and "honor" it had to be solved quickly. Universally, French soldiers and administrators discerned the hand of Ma' al-'Aynayn in the killing.[73] Yet the Qudhfiya was an aberrant order; its founder, Muhammad al-Aqdhaf, was a contemporary of Ma' al-'Aynayn's father, but the group had developed in a radical way, having little in common with Ma' al-'Aynayn and his mystical ideas.[74]

In St. Louis and Paris, those interested in laying the blame for Coppolani's assassination evolved a complicated, *cui bono* reasoning. They held Ma' al-'Aynayn responsible for planning the act. They reasoned that he had recruited members of the Qudhfiya to do it for him so that he could shift the blame from himself; but their evidence for this was purely circumstantial. The hated Coppolani was an obvious target for such an attack without prompting from Ma' al-'Aynayn. In any case, the lighthearted French military excursion was over. The invaders were determined to take over Mauritania and to pursue their designated archvillain, Ma' al-'Aynayn, until they caught or killed him.

Ma' al-'Aynayn was soon aware of the changed French mood. After an interval, their advance resumed. Delegations from threatened areas in the south came to him with greater frequency to ask that he use his influence with the sultan to procure them arms and that he find appropriate Moroccan military leadership. This was already happening before 1900, as al-Susi points out:

> They began to ask for arms from . . . 'Abd al-'Aziz while the [*wazir*] Ahmad b. Musa was still alive. The sultan intended to send the weapons to the tribesmen. But the French warned that if the arms were used against them, they would treat it as a declaration of war against France. . . . When Ahmad . . . saw this disaster looming before him, he began to temporize with the Saharans, in spite of the urgent appeal the *Shaykh* made to him.[75]

After the *wazir*'s death, there was a slight shift in Moroccan policy. In discussions with the French consul in Fez, the foreign minister ('Abd al-Karim b. Sulayman) touched on the matter of arms for Mauritania. The Frenchman declared that Morocco had no claim to Mauritania, because its frontier lay directly south of the Wadi Nun. On instructions from the sultan, 'Abd al-Karim did his best to mislead Gaillard about continuing weapons shipments to Mauritanian Muslims.[76] At the same time, Ma' al-'Aynayn now claimed that all Saharan tribes in his area, as far south as the other side of Shinqit Town, would pledge allegiance to Morocco. The time had come, he declared, for the sultan to send a *khalifa*, or district governor, for the Sahara.[77]

Ma' al-'Aynayn's suggestion was accepted at Marrakish. In 1906, Idris b. 'Abd al-Rahman, a cousin of Sultan 'Abd al-'Aziz, arrived in the Saqiyat al-Hamra'. With him was a staff of three men and a number of blank sharifian decrees in which the names of tribal leaders could be inserted, identifying them as appointees of the Moroccan government. Idris also brought 500 rifles for distribution to those who would resist. He also requested that local chiefs pay their *zakat* tax to him; payments of this kind were a usual attribute of Islamic sovereignty. Yet Idris achieved very little, for French pressure from the south was too intense. Although he did carry out a short siege of a French outpost at Taghanit, the French were quickly relieved by another force.

Idris stayed on in the vicinity of the Saqiyat al-Hamra' until the "last days of Sultan 'Abd al-Hafiz" (c. 1912); but lack of weapons and supplies along with perpetual Mauritanian anarchy and growing internal troubles in Morocco crippled his attempts to aid Ma' al-'Aynayn and his son Hassana in creating a viable tribal coalition to resist the French.[78] At least, he can be credited with delaying their advance.

In 1907 and 1908, Ma' al-'Aynayn spent considerable time in Morocco trying to mend the increasingly fragmented internal situation there. The hopeless inefficiency of 'Abd al-'Aziz was now causing considerable popular discontent. Ma' al-'Aynayn ceased to back his former benefactor and switched his allegiance to his brother, 'Abd al-Hafiz. The *shaykh's* support for the Hafiziya movement (as the backers of 'Abd al-Hafiz were called) indicated that Ma' al-'Aynayn broadly agreed with and championed a cause upheld by many among the Moroccan learned class, even though many of his fellow clericals had modernist (Salafi) convictions that he did not share.[79] Indeed, the first public announcement of the deposition of 'Abd al-'Aziz and a provisional oath-taking to his brother was made by Ma' al-'Aynayn at Marrakish in August 1907. A later proclamation of the same group (January 1908) indicates more fully the opinions of the Moroccan *'ulama* at the time. Ma' al-'Aynayn, associated with these men, would also have applauded its Pan-Islamic tone; as part of a new political program, the religious elite demanded "unity, and mutual aid for our Muslim brothers, such as the Ottoman Turks and other independent Islamic states."[80]

If 'Abd al-Hafiz and the learned class (abetted by Ma' al-'Aynayn) wanted friendly contacts with the Turks, they were unable to banish hostile foreigners from the country entirely. Thus, French diplomats or correspondents who visited Marrakish occasionally observed Ma' al-'Aynayn and his 'Ayniya. One such visitor noted that Ma' al-'Aynayn's men wore long, shirtlike gowns (*jallabiyas*) of coarse *khant* (blue cotton cloth from West Africa) and turbans of the same stuff.[81] These "Blue Men," he alleged, were both turbulent and venal, from what he could observe at Marrakish. They had arms and used them to control "first the quarter where their *zawiya* was, then the whole city." He accused them of stealing merchandise and "pillaging mosques." He then complained that they entered private Muslim houses, where they demanded "tea and women." Finally, says al-Moutabassir, the exasperated population forced the Pasha of Marrakish to disarm them.[82]

The French reporter adds further details; en route from the port of Mogador (al-Sawira) to Marrakish, the Mauritanian visitors accepted the offerings that the population made to them in their roles as "warriors for the faith" (*mujahidun*). Then, he states, rather than keeping the guns they bought with these gifts, they sold them and kept the cash. On their return journey, when the 'Ayniya left by ship for Cape Juby in September 1906, the same source states that a "universal sigh of relief" rose from both Europeans and Moroccans "cruelly maltreated" by the Mauritanians.

Worst of all, says al-Moutabassir, special temporary levies were raised by the Moroccan government while the 'Ayniya stayed in Marrakish – *hadya* and *ziyara* taxes along with a daily levy to pay for the bread, fat, oil, porridge, tea, and chocolate that the 'Ayniya's adherents consumed, as well as heavy deliveries of arms. To this, the correspondent adds a description of Ma' al-'Aynayn himself, perhaps based on a glimpse of him from a hidden window above the narrow lanes of Marrakish:

> Ma' al-'Aynayn wears a huge hat of white wool, shaped like a sugarloaf, which completely covers his head. It makes him invisible, it seems, thanks to an amulet of which no one knows the content but the Sheikh. When he goes out in the town, or even on the road, he is surrounded by a compact mass of his servants and followers, who unceasingly chant, "There is no god but God and Muhammad is his Prophet." This odd way of reciting the ritual [*dhikr*] of the 'Ayniya . . . and the overheated fervor of the Mauritanians, who, as Berbers, profess a real cult for their master, and . . . his own self-importance have caused a rumor to spread among the people that Ma' al-'Aynayn is not content to be a wizard, but thinks he is God himself. . . . He has such a reputation for holiness among the learned class that they have given him the title of "Supreme Pole" [Qutb].[83]

Another French writer, Paul Marty, claims that in September 1906 the 'Ayniya plundered Casablancan merchants and that in the summer of 1907 they returned to the town again, triggering the "Casablanca massacres," which brought a French occupation of that port at the end of July.[84] Marty also pins the responsibility for various "armed assaults" and the assassination of two Frenchmen – Lasallas and Dr. Mauchamp – at Marrakish in March 1907 on Ma' al-'Aynayn. But as Marty admits, the latter affair was a handy pretext for French intervention in Morocco, for he states that the assassinations of Lasallas and Mauchamp could "certainly be attributed to Ma' al-'Aynayn and his gangs of followers and students."[85]

Whatever the truth of these claims, Ma' al-'Aynayn, under French pressure, found a new base for himself and the 'Ayniya, this time within Morocco. The new center was at Tiznit in the Sus, a town slightly inland between Sidi Ifni and Agadir. If Ma' al-'Aynayn continued at Tiznit as a sharifian representative and had some hopes of damping the independence of the local Samlali *sharifs* at Tazarwalt and the Awlad Bayruk in the Wadi Nun, he was apprehensive, for the French were coming closer:

> In that year, 1327/1909–10, the Christians entered the Adrar. When they approached, our Shaykh made up his mind . . . to make a migration (*hijra*) in the Path of God, so he went to Tiznit because it was far from the Christians at that time, and because of money from his supporters there. The money given him by Sultan 'Abd al-'Aziz had run out before then . . . so he made all who were with him, family, children and students, weak or strong, leave in Dhu'l-Qa'da of that year [November–December 1909]. He took the coastal road and reached Tiznit at the start of Rabi' I 1328/end of March 1910.[86]

Ma' al-'Aynayn's removal could have been foreseen; he realized that Simara would not be defended if the French appeared in strength. From Tiznit, for about seven months, the *shaykh* tried to direct the increasingly hopeless war in the south. Muslims who wanted to go on the jihad there could still obtain arms from him and were directed to one of his sons in Mauritania or perhaps to Idris ibn 'Abd al-Rahman. Caro Baroja credits one of his sons, Hassana, with brilliant resistance against the invaders at Akjujt and Taghanit.[87] Ma' al-'Aynayn could now do little more. Under General Gouraud, the French were still moving northward. Their difficulty was less local resistance now than getting their supplies to the proper destinations. By the summer of 1909, Gouraud had won most of his objectives – wells and cultivated areas – but Ma' al-'Aynayn was still beyond his reach to the north.

Ma' al-'Aynayn was now seventy-nine (or eighty-two if the calculation is made in Muslim lunar years). After making an effort to place 'Abd al-Hafiz on the Moroccan throne, Ma' al-'Aynayn lost faith in him, just as he had lost faith in his brother. As Norris declares, "perhaps Shaykh Ma' al-'Aynayn foresaw that it was his destiny to be the champion of the faith in this critical hour."[88] If he was a *sharif*, then his claim to the throne was as good as that of the incumbents.

Thus it is widely believed that in May 1910, Ma' al-'Aynayn announced his claim to the Moroccan throne; Marty commented that Ma' al-'Aynayn "wanted to begin over again the Almoravid epic of the 11th century, or the Filali one of the 16th."[89] He made a final effort to rally his followers and to rally the Moroccan population. He entered Marrakish then moved toward Fez. Ma' al-'Aynayn's gamble led him to a trap that the French – already in Morocco in force – had foreseen. About 6,000 of the 'Ayniya and their leader were confronted then dispersed by General Moinier at Qasaba Tadala (midway between Marrakish and Fez) on 23 June 1910.

Many of Ma' al-'Aynayn's followers now abandoned him. In defeat, the *shaykh* turned southward into the mountains. Shorn of much of his earlier prestige, Ma' al-'Aynayn was repeatedly robbed. It is said that he was forced to sell what remained of his books, his possessions, his draft animals. In September 1910, the elderly *shaykh*, now ill and broken, reached his *zawiya* at Tiznit. He and his party had just survived several ambushes and plunderings in the frozen passes of the High Atlas. Ma' al-'Aynayn lived on for a month then died at Tiznit on 29 Shawwal 1328/28 October 1910.[90]

Ma' al-'Aynayn's Writings

Ma' al-'Aynayn had been rightly described as a prolific writer; Caro Baroja credited him with 314 books, although a list in Murabbih Rabbuh's *Qurrat al'Aynayn* lists only about 140.[91] The majority of these "books" remain in manuscript, and many of them are probably only a few pages long. All the same, that critical French correspondent, al-Moutabassir, had to admit that Ma' al-'Aynayn's was "no vulgar mind, and that his abundant writings dealt with the most varied matters (law, theology, sufism, astronomy, astrology, philology, etc.)."[92]

From various accounts of Ma' al-'Aynayn's writings (published or unpublished) it is possible to extract some information and then to combine it with facts from certain available texts so as to identify some of his interests and preoccupations. It is hoped that this may serve to encourage future investigations into Ma' al-'Aynayn's many-sided personality.[93]

Murabbih Rabbuh divides his list of Ma' al-'Aynayn's writings into six categories: 1) law and religious fundamentals; 2) theology, traditions, and "good breeding"; 3) grammar, rhetoric, and metrics; 4) sufism; 5) the "science of reckoning"; and 6) "prayers and secrets." Many of these loose divisions overlap.[94]

Of least significance and represented by the fewest items on the list are the third and fifth categories – grammar and its subdisciplines and the "science of reckoning." In the third category (thirteen items) Ma' al-'Aynayn wrote several poems on grammar, versification, Arabic verbs, the technical details of metrics in that language, and the "tricks of the Arab tongue." Representative of these are his "Grammatical Gift for Beginners" and "A Clarification of Obscurities in the Metrical Arts."[95] The fifth category (four items) concerns weather forecasting, the meaning of zodiacal signs and phases of the moon, and lucky and unlucky days and dates. These writings are sometimes assembled in

almanac form, as in Ma' al-'Aynayn's *Daw' al-Duhur*.[96] Most of this
information appears in rhyme.

The second category contains twenty-one items, on "good breeding,"
manners, traditions, and theology. Here Murabbih Rabbuh notes
several works about women; in his *Fatiq al-Ratq* (a commentary on
a poem punningly entitled the *Ratiq al-Fatq*), Ma' al-'Aynayn shows
that he is aware of women's problems. Although he does not put them
on the same level as men, he insists that they must have better treatment from them. The work throws an interesting sidelight on one
aspect of the male-oriented Mauritanian society of the 1870s:

> As for the husband [his wife] has rights over him. He should keep
> company with her, and tolerate her even if she is insolent to him.
> He must pardon her lapses, and be kind and patient with her in
> private. If she is weak or speaks foolishly, he must instruct her
> about the principles of ritual cleanliness, prayer, menstruation, and
> similar matters, about which she may not know. He must see that
> she eats ritually proper food. He must not be oppressive to her over
> her rights . . . nor expect too much from her. . . . He must not
> obstruct her from visiting her parents or going to the mosque . . .
> nor be harsh with her when she is tired.[97]

Talking about animals in his *Ratiq al-Fatq*, Ma' al-'Aynayn shows
his kindly and humanitarian opinions: "An owner should water his
livestock during a drought. Milking is not permitted, if it might injure
the animal during a shortage of food. If the animal requires milking,
then he should do that. . . . Bees should have some honey left to
them in their hives."[98]

Elsewhere, he recommends good treatment of and happy relations
with one's neighbors, who must be treated with kindness and patience.
Here was one of the secrets of Ma' al-'Aynayn's success with the
nomads of the Saqiyat al-Hamra', such as the rough Awlad Dalim.
Beggars and orphans should be treated in the same fashion. Slaves
have rights as well:

> A slave has the right to share in his master's food, to be clothed by
> him. He should not be regarded with the eye of disdain or superi-
> ority . . . nor be entrusted with matters beyond his ability. If he
> asks to be sold, sell him. . . . He must be instructed in important
> religious matters.[99]

In another passage in the *Fatiq al-Ratq*, Ma' al-'Aynayn touches on
the important issue of the relationship between the "learned" classes
and kings and sultans. Because learned men are the "heirs of the
prophets," their place is morally higher than that of rulers. Ma' al-

'Aynayn quotes al-Sha'rani's *Kashf al-Ghumma* to suggest that on that basis alone, the *'ulama* deserve respect and veneration. But sultans and their governors also deserve respect and deference: are they not "the shadows of God on earth?" Whoever treats them with respect, God will also respect. Ma' al-'Aynayn then advances a tradition of a tendentiously conservative kind to justify his argument: "The just and humble sultan is sheltered and treated with mercy by God; and every day, God raises up the just and humble governor."[100] Thus Ma' al-'Aynayn – unless he altered his views at the end of his life – appears to have taken a highly traditional, even a reactionary view of government.

Ma' al-'Aynayn wrote a number of books about sufism (the fourth category); this is the second largest single group of his writings and includes thirty items. One of his books, the *Na't al-bidayat*, printed once at Fez and twice in Cairo, shows many of his attitudes about sufism. In content, it is quite conventional, showing few departures in Ma' al-'Aynayn's 'Ayniya from his father's Fadiliya. Significantly, he lays heavy emphasis on the idea of the brotherhood among all Muslims and sufi organizations, declaring that brotherhood between Muslims transcends mere genetic brotherhood.[101] It is easy to see how he could continue – as Muhammad Fadil had done before him – to distribute the ties of four sufi organizations: the Shadhiliya, Nasiriya, Tijaniya, and Qadiriya. Here Ma' al-'Aynayn speaks of "God's favor, which we possess." He then claims that God's grace is "larger and broader" than any single sufi organization.[102]

This conclusion (also expressed in a poem, "That I am a brother to all sufi brotherhoods") has certain manifest political implications.[103] If all sufi brotherhoods exhibit only minor divergences among themselves, and no one of them is better than any other, then they can easily unite. Once united, they can be directed for political purposes. It is possible that Sultan al-Hasan I wished to unite all Moroccan brotherhoods behind him for the sake of national unity in the face of foreign political encroachments. Perhaps he wished to enlist Ma' al-'Aynayn's aid in this. In the 1820s Al-Hasan's ancestor, Sultan Sulayman, had tried to manipulate the Tijaniya against the others; his descendant may have hoped to do something similar with the 'Ayniya.[104]

That such an idea was applied by Ma' al-'Aynayn not only on a national plane but also on a supranational plane is shown by some comments in another of his printed books, the *Mubsir al-Mutashawwif*, written about 1895. It may well be that Ma' al-'Aynayn, at first apparently indifferent to international Islamic politics, altered his ideas about 1880 after creating close ties to Sultan al-Hasan I. As the sharifian Sultan and his advisers had to cope with intensified foreign pressure, they could not but look with sympathy on the Ottoman Turkish regime, subjected to similar pressures. Thus Ma' al-'Aynayn can draw a comparison between God's purposes in creating a series of prophets, the best of whom was Muhammad; the best of revealed books, the *Qur'an;* the best of states, the nation (*umma*) of Muhammad; and the best of contemporary governments:

> Hence the [divine] intention was [best fulfilled] among past rulers
> and former sultans by the Ottoman kings. For they are the cream
> of kings and their state is the cream of states: there will be no state
> after them until the appearance of Jesus and the Mahdi. . . . They
> will fight corrupt unbelievers like the English and French. They
> possess the best organization, the longest hand, the mightiest state
> in the Seven Climes. . . . None of that was granted to any state
> before theirs.[105]

In this passage, Ma' al-'Aynayn sounds as if he had become a convinced supporter of the Pan-Islamic idea. These views were compatible with those of al-Hasan I, who, after the Madrid Conference on Morocco in 1880, sent an emissary to Istanbul to establish diplomatic relations.[106] The Moroccan ruler sought the services of Ottoman experts – doubtless military officers. In 1877, through his Shaykh al-Islam, Sultan 'Abd al-Hamid II had communicated with the Moroccan *wazir* Musa b. Ahmad.[107] And again in 1886, the Ottoman foreign minister, Mehmet Sa'id Pasha, had proposed the creation of a Turkish embassy at Tangier. Nothing came of these efforts, and it may be that they were foiled by France.[108]

In the *Mubsir al-Mutashawwif* Ma' al-'Aynayn also devotes some pages to the Last Judgment and the coming of the Mahdi – subjects of the greatest popular interest in Morocco and Mauritania and elsewhere in the Islamic world at the end of the nineteenth century. The following passage may echo one of the books of Abu'l-Faraj ibn al-Jawzi:

> At that time a person will appear called the Mahdi. He will be
> recognized from a mark on his right cheek and a mark between his
> shoulder blades. The people will gather around him. . . . Jews and
> Christians will be united with the Nation of Muhammad, and justice
> will come to all people, on land and sea. . . . Jesus ('Isa) will make
> the pilgrimage to Mecca and visit Muhammad. Then he will fall
> ill and die there and be buried beside Muhammad. . . . After the
> death of 'Isa, the Mahdi will take all the noble *sayyids* and go to
> Kufa, where he will die. And God will send a pleasant wind to

take the spirit of every Believer on the face of the earth, but the
evil among mankind shall remain behind. For them, the Hour will
be close at hand.[109]

In Murabbih Rabbuh's list, the largest category (the sixth) of Ma'
al-'Aynayn's writings (forty-six items) is concerned with "prayers and
secrets." Nearly all contemporary observers speak of Ma' al-'Aynayn's
fascination with this subject and remark on his competence in it. This
is a reflection of the widespread, if not almost universal, belief in and
use of magic in nineteenth-century Mauritania and much of Morocco
as well. If some Europeans regarded him as an "ignorant common
sorcerer," he was simultaneously the "author of numerous books having
a great reputation" among his contemporaries.[110]

The magic favored by Ma' al-'Aynayn was of a learned type with a
long history in medieval Islam. It concentrated on protective formulas,
medical spells, and charms that might induce certain states of mind
in one's self or others. It is hard to see much difference between what
Ma' al-'Aynayn used and items noted in the texts of either a thirteenth-
century Algerian writer on magic, Ahmad b. 'Ali al-Buni (d. 622/1225)
or his fellow-countryman, Ibn al-Hajj al-Tilimsani (d. 1337).

In a small book that first appeared at Cairo in 1962 and that has
had four printings since then, Ma' al-'Aynayn's *Madhhab al-makhuf
ala da'wat al-huruf*, the author lists twenty-nine prayers to be recited
on the first and eighth hours of certain weekdays.[111] For example, the
first such prayer is based on the first letter of the Arabic alphabet. It
contains scraps of quotations from the *Qur'an*, pious phrases, references
to the intention of the person who prays, and references to God. When
used during the first hour on a Sunday, it is said to "bring tranquility,"
to "envelop a person in grace." If recited either 11 or 111 times, it
grants special protection from evil and guards the person using it from
misadventure.[112] Similar prayers can be found throughout the book,
sometimes with an accompanying magic square using either letters,
numbers, or a combination of both. This is clearly what Ma' al-
'Aynayn's clientele believed in and wanted, and what he supplied to
them.

Certainly one of Ma' al-'Aynayn's most attractive sides, one that
brought him great fame and many followers, was his alleged ability to
work miracles. Few of the *shaykh*'s Mauritanian contemporaries would
have agreed with David Hume that miracles are impossible. Thus
Murabbih Rabbuh's *Qurrat al-'Aynayn* contains at least 100 miraculous
episodes, woven carefully into the text and compared with analogous
miracles of the Prophet drawn from classical Arab writers.

For example, Ma' al-'Aynayn was making a voyage in a ship on

one occasion. On that day, "High waves caused three hundred ships
to sink." The mast on Ma' al-'Aynayn's own vessel snapped off, its
planking broke, and it began to go down. Those on board were in
mortal terror, except for Ma' al-'Aynayn himself, who at that instant
was rapt in a mystical ecstasy. When asked to save the crew and
passengers, he prayed calmly, a formula his father had given him,
"useful at any time or place." Hardly had he finished his prayer when
the sinking ship righted itself, a favorable wind sprang up, and *shaykh*,
passengers, and crew were saved.[113]

The final category of Ma' al-'Aynayn's writings (the first) concerns
law and religious fundamentals. Here there are only twenty items listed
in Murabbih Rabbuh's compilation. One of these books, the *Dalil
al-rifaq*, a compendium of Maliki law with a commentary, is very
long – about 1,000 pages in three volumes. Also noteworthy here is a
book entitled *Ahkam al-Taqlid (Principles of Juridical Imitation)*.
There are no less than seven titles under Section VI ("Prayers and
Secrets"), which includes the word *tawassul* (intercession through
saints).[114] If Ma' al-'Aynayn depended on juridical imitation and on
the intercession of saints, these were old-fashioned attitudes even in
his day and hint at a highly conservative position in law and theology
without much originality in juridical questions. Obviously, without
access to the books in question, this can be no more than an informed
guess. Yet such attitudes are consistent with reports that Ma' al-'Aynayn
was not an adherent of the Salafi movement (a reforming current
then popular in North Africa), that he was essentially a moderate, and,
above all, that he opposed political takeovers by foreign powers.[115]

Thus Ma' al-'Aynayn can be provisionally described as a flexible conservative, an intelligent and sympathetic man, and a son who followed
his father (Muhammad Fadil) in many things. Well taught by him
in the traditional ways, he was probably his favorite. He was much
more aware of the world beyond Mauritania than any of his brothers.
Yet his pilgrimage did not alter his basic conservatism. His opportuni-
ties raised him above his origins. Having become a leading figure in
northern Mauritania, he became the confidant, friend, and adviser of
several sharifian rulers. If his powers of spiritual healing brought him an
entrée to the court, his legal knowledge and popular prestige cemented
his position there. His writings, his personality, and the growing repute
of the 'Ayniya order helped to make him one of the most prominent
personalities in late-nineteenth-century Morocco. In his homeland of
Mauritania, his reputation is hardly less.

Ma' al-'Aynayn still remains an enigmatic figure. There is much about
him – particularly his spiritual power – that remains unexplained. This
strange quality was described by Odette du Puigaudeau when she

visted his tomb at the 'Ayniya *zawiya* at Tiznit, "a short, square tower, with crenels, rises above the buildings of stone and mud like a lighthouse. . . . Behind its high walls, the noises of the town ceased. I found again that mysterious, penetrating feeling left by the students, disciples, and pilgrims; historical reminders which can be sensed in all of the interiors of *zawiya*s."[116]

CHAPTER 6

The Qadiri and Shadhili
Brotherhoods in East Africa, 1880–1910[1]

In 1880, two separate Muslim brotherhoods were making progress in
East Africa. The smaller of these was a Shadhili organization from
Grand Comoro led by the social reformer and preacher Muhammad
Ma'ruf. The larger and more influential was the Uwaysi branch of the
Qadiri order named for its Somali leader, Shaykh Uways bin Muhammad al-Barawi. Between them, they accounted for a considerable
expansion of Islam in Tanganyika, southern Somalia, eastern Zaire,
parts of Mocambique and Malawi, the Comoro Islands, and northwest
Madagascar. In East Africa, the Qadiriya was the more active of the
two. Although neither group offered any persistent opposition to the
encroachments of the colonial powers in East Africa, they were nonetheless involved in politics. Two episodes, one involving Sayyid
Barghash of Zanzibar (1887) and the other known as the "Mecca
Letter Affair" of 1908, touched the Qadiriya. Through their leaders,
both Shadhilis and Qadiris had contacts with the Ottoman Turks, but
Istanbul seems only to have had a peripheral interest in East Africa
at this time. Finally, there are indications of millennialism – even
mahdism – among the Qadiriya, although it found only limited expression.

On the Comoro Islands, the chief of the Shadhili movement was
Shaykh Muhammad Ma'ruf bin Shaykh Ahmad ibn Abi Bakr (1853–
1905). These islands, situated in the Mocambique Channel between
the northern tip of Madagascar and the East African coast, were cul-
turally and religiously united with Zanzibar, but they were under
French political control. Mayotte, the island closest to Madagascar, became a French colony in 1841; the remaining three islands of the
archipelago (Moheli, Anjouan, and Grand Comoro or Ngazija) were
not taken over by France until 1886.

Muhammad Ma'ruf was a *sharif*, claiming noble descent from the
Prophet Muhammad through his membership in the Abu Bakr bin
Salim clan.[2] He was of South Arabian origin, from the Hadramawt. Yet
rather than adhering to the 'Alawiya brotherhood, the traditional sufi
organization of his forebears, Shaykh Ma'ruf generated much enthusiasm and won many adherents by first joining and then promoting a
branch of a major mystical order, the Shadhiliya. He was the first

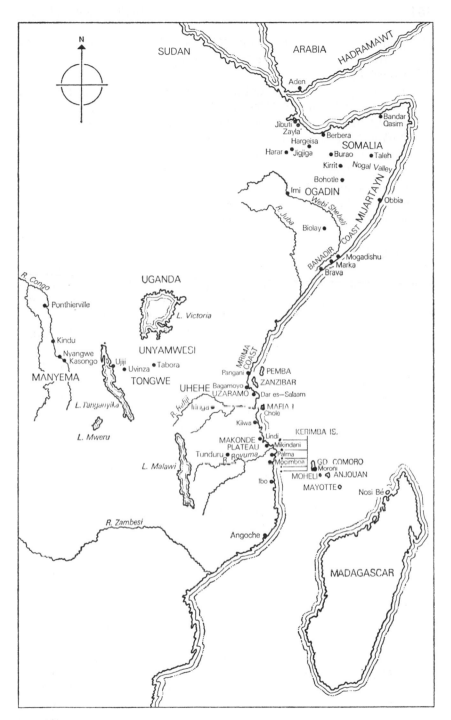

East Africa

sharif on Grand Comoro to join it.[3] This branch, the Yashrutiya, had its headquarters in Palestine; like its parent organization, it was of North African origin.

A hagiography of Ma'ruf, written by one of his relatives, states that he was born at Moroni in 1853.[4] In this small port on Grand Comoro, Ma'ruf obtained a conventional schooling, starting his education with the *Qur'an*. He concluded his training in Zanzibar, where he obtained instruction from a migrant uncle, 'Ali I'tibari. 'Ali was a son of the sultan of Bambao on Grand Comoro, a district including Moroni and the western slopes of Kartala Volcano.[5]

On completing his studies, Ma'ruf went on the pilgrimage with his mother and sister. In Mecca, he came into contact with an important Shadhili teacher, yet he did not accept membership in the brotherhood. On his way back from Jidda to the Comoros, Ma'ruf's ship stopped at Zanzibar. Here Ma'ruf was briefly attracted by Shaykh Uways, but his short meeting with the Somali Qadiri leader made no lasting impression.[6] Shortly after, Ma'ruf accepted the tie of the Shadhili order from a fellow islander, 'Abdallah Darwish. Earlier, on his own pilgrimage, Darwish had visited Palestine, joined the order, and became a student of 'Ali Nur al-Din al-Yashruti. A Tunisian from Bizerta, Yashruti had established his branch of the Shadhiliya (from the Madaniya suborder) at 'Akka (Acre) in northern Palestine.[7]

Guided by 'Abdallah Darwish, his aristocratic recruit set about winning members for the Shadhiliya on Grand Comoro, Anjouan, and the coast of northwestern Madagascar. This process did not always go smoothly; on one occasion, the Shafi'i *qadi* of Anjouan and the leading author and intellectual of that island, Shaykh Fadil b. 'Ali Mbangwa, denounced Ma'ruf and all his works before the ruler of Anjouan.[8] To escape the royal irritation, Ma'ruf had to flee for a time to the island of Nossi Bé off the Madagascar coast. Later he returned to Anjouan, where he was reconciled to the offended sultan. After the death of the hostile *qadi* (c. 1884), Ma'ruf continued to make converts on all four islands of the Comoro group as well as on Madagascar and Mocambique. Although Ma'ruf was himself a *sharif*, well-off, and able to circulate with the ruling élite of Grand Comoro, he had differences of opinion with them over social issues and deliberately avoided close association with the hereditary order of conservative *sharifs*, the 'Alawiya brotherhood.

On hearing that his cousin by marriage, Sultan 'Ali bin 'Umar of Grand Comoro, was unready or unwilling to do his "Muslim duty" by suppressing "obnoxious customs" and "things hateful to God and his Prophet," Ma'ruf began to oppose him in public. Specifically, Ma'ruf attacked his sale of many acres of fertile land on the island to French *colons.*[9] When Ma'ruf failed to mention 'Ali's name in the Friday prayers, Sultan 'Ali sent French troops to arrest him. 'Ali was then becoming deeply involved with the French (and the Germans), for both powers wanted to take over the remaining three independent islands of the Comoros. 'Ali seems to have been anxious about a possible coup aimed at him by Ma'ruf and his associates. When French troops landed from Mayotte and began to comb the island for Shaykh Ma'ruf, he eluded them and escaped by boarding a ship for Zanzibar. He stayed there for many years, living among the local Comorian community and employing his enforced absence to spread the Yashrutiya there and on Pemba and Mafia, as he had done on Madagascar during his first exile.[10] Meanwhile, the French, attracted by the possibilities of coaling stations, *ylang-ylang* plantations for their perfume industry, vanilla, cloves, and other local products, had taken control of Grand Comoro, Anjouan, and Moheli.[11]

Until he fled Grand Comoro (c. 1886) Ma'ruf's preaching was buoyed up by a wave of religious enthusiasm, of Islamic revivalism. "For the great majority of Comorians," claims Sultan Chouzour, "confronted with the hard realities of daily life, who had no chance to learn Arabic, the liturgical language of religion . . . the Shadhiliya was the object of devotion and of naive fervor."[12]

Before his death in 1905, Shaykh Ma'ruf was permitted by the French to return to Grand Comoro. He built a sufi center, a *zawiya*, in the Bajanani quarter of the town, just up the hill from the harbor and close to his own birthplace.[13] When he died, Shaykh Ma'ruf was interred in this Shadhili *zawiya*. Built of the local coral limestone, the building is whitewashed with white coral lime. Its five-story minaret dominates Moroni, and Ma'ruf's tomb has since become a place of pilgrimage for the Shadhilis of East Africa.

Ma'ruf had nominated a number of deputies (*khalifas*) for Moroni and elsewhere on Grand Comoro, and others for Anjouan. Since 1905, these khalifaships[14] have continued to be filled in the archipelago, in Madagascar, and elsewhere. The ties of the Comorian branch of the Yashrutiya to the parent house in 'Akka have been maintained (even after the first Arab-Israeli War of 1948, when the Yashruti family transferred their headquarters to Beirut).[15]

Like other classical sufi orders, which regard themselves as branches from a single trunk, the Yashrutiya can trace its origins far into the past. The personal affiliation of Shaykh Ma'ruf runs through 'Abdallah Darwish to 'Ali al-Yashruti (d. 1898). It continues through Yashruti's Shadhili teacher, Muhammad ibn Hamza Zafir al-Madani (originally from Misurata in Libya). Al-Madani was taught in his turn by al-'Arabi al-Darqawi, founder of the Darqawiya order. Ultimately his spiritual genealogy goes back to Abu'l-Hasan al-Shadhili (d. 1258), and to the Prophet.[16]

Yashruti's teacher, Muhammad al-Madani, had a son of the same name who was very close to Sultan 'Abd al-Hamid II and the Pan-Islamic movement. Indeed, most experts agree that the Madaniya was one of two brotherhoods (the other being the Rifa'iya under Abu'l-Huda al-Sayyadi) that were entirely dominated by this Ottoman sultan. Although the Palestinian Yashrutiya had many Turkish members ('Akka was a Turkish garrison town in the late nineteenth century) and al-Yashruti had access to the Sublime Porte in Istanbul, the East Africa branch had little visible Ottoman influence about it.[17]

Al-Yashruti's daughter, Fatima al-Yashrutiya, claims that the order was very successful in East Africa, on "Zanzibar and its coasts, the Comoro Islands, Madagascar, Kenya, New Guinea, Tanganyika, and elsewhere in all the towns of the region and on the islands and shores, where numerous *zawiyas* were erected by the sons of our noble brotherhood, and friends in God, in those remote parts."[18]

If the mention of New Guinea seems out of place in this passage, it may be that the Yashruti order penetrated the western end of this island, where Islam first appeared "in the 16th century, and then revived in the 19th," brought by missionaries – perhaps Arabs from East Africa or the Comoros.[19]

By the year of its leader's death (1905), the Yashrutiya was widely diffused along the East African coastline and the islands offshore. Ma'ruf's activities had taken it precisely to these places. On the mainland, it is less easy to follow the way in which it spread. However, in the time of Shaykh 'Ali Wafa', a son of Ma'ruf (d. 1954), a major effort was made to gain converts there, either non-Muslims or Muslims without affiliations to brotherhoods. In this work, 'Ali Wafa' was aided by Shaykh Husayn bin Mahmud, who founded a *zawiya* on the coast just south of Kilwa in Tanganyika.[20]

If the Shadhiliya spread to Madagascar and Mocambique, Zanzibar and Pemba, Mauritius and Mafia Island, the precise details of its diffusion there remain obscure. For instance, in the case of Mocambique, a Comorian author does record a migration of "learned men" from Grand Comoro. Among them were Shaykh 'Amir bin Jimba of Moroni and his fellow townsman, Ahmad Mruzi. Mruzi settled in Angoche (Nguji, Angoxa) to teach Arabic and Islamic law, while Shaykh 'Amir recruited elsewhere for the Shadhiliya.[21] It seems obvious that Comorian Muslim teachers should sail to Angoche, which enjoyed new prosperity after 1845 under Sultan Hasan b. Yusuf and his successors. Angoche had old commercial links to the Comoros, doubtless from the slave trade of the early nineteenth century or before.[22]

A Portuguese account of 1905 noted heavy Muslim concentrations (known locally as *monhés*) along the coasts of the northern provinces of Mocambique.[23] These *monhés* were found at Lurio, Pemba [*sic*], Quissanga (or Kisanga), Ibo, Mocimbao, and Tungue. They practiced a strict Islam, abstained from wine and certain foods, and attended mosques assiduously. Such enthusiasm, strictness, and other puritanical manifestations might have been generated by the appearance of a new brotherhood, although the author does not suggest this.[24]

Further inland, many Muslims lived in the Tungue district, as far as the Mocimboa River. Most of the Yao and Makua in these chiefdoms (*regulos*) were Muslim, although many of the nearby southern Makonde were not. In Ibo district and the Karimba Islands, there were many Muslims at Changane (Shangani) under their chief, Hajji Musa; likewise at Ulumboa. In the Mogabo chiefdom, an important chief of the Mazeze named Sa'id 'Ali (or Sayyid 'Ali) had a large following of *monhés*. By 1906, Islam had also spread as far as the eastern shores of Lake Malawi (Nyasa), within Mocambique.[25]

From this account, the impression that emerges is of a dense Muslim population along the Mocambique coast between the Lurio and Ruvuma rivers, becoming thinner and more patchy and diminishing in proportion to its remoteness from the shoreline. Among other tribes, the Yao seems to have accepted Islam readily, between 1870 and 1910. Whether or not this development had anything to do with the presence of Shadhili teachers from the Comoros is uncertain, but several pieces of evidence suggest that such a link was very likely. Traditionally, Comorian traders[26] had been seen in numbers in the coastal towns of Mocambique, and the Shadhili *zawiya* of Shaykh Husayn bin Mahmud (reputedly 120 years old in 1974!) was probably functioning by 1900. It is also certain that Qadiris and Shadhilis were competing in this region, for the Comorian writer Burhan b. Muhammad Mkelle noted the zeal of Shaykh 'Isa b. Ahmad al-Msujini (from Tsujini on the west coast of Grand Comoro), who "led many among African polytheists to Islam, who accepted it at his hands." Shaykh 'Isa (see pp. 159, 174) was a Qadiri and one of the *khalifas* of Shaykh Uways.[27]

In this regard, a pertinent quotation is cited by E. A. Alpers from an unpublished manuscript by Canon Lamburn. The men in question here, working among the Yao of southern Tanganyika, may well have had attachments to one brotherhood or the other:

About 1885 . . . two men came from the coast where they had become Muslims, to tell the Yaos [at Tunduru] about the faith of Islam. . . . None of these men administered the "baptism," that is the initiation of an uncircumcised man in Islam, but those who having heard of the preaching, wished to become Muslims, went down to the coast towns to become initiated. Later, Muslim teachers from the coast came upcountry to Yaoland, and there "baptised converts."[28]

In the Yao country (both north and south of the Rovuma), the efforts of such wandering preachers as these were supplemented by the presence of Muslim traders and *mwalimus* (teachers). It is here that the representatives of brotherhoods played their parts. In addition, many Yao and other chiefs employed secretaries literate in Arabic who dealt in commercial transactions, wrote other tribal communications, and were in touch with other peoples and rulers generally by the medium of the Arabic language.[29]

The Qadiriya

In contrast to the Shadhiliya, the spread of the Qadiriya is better known, for it has received far more publicity. In late July 1908, the German colonial administration in Tanganyika began to receive alarming telegrams from Lindi, a town on the Lukuledi Estuary in the south of the protectorate, suggesting that an important Muslim movement was under way. These telegraphic reports, from a district officer at Lindi, mentioned a "letter from Mecca" that was being spread amongst the Muslim population there. It had millennial overtones that were causing much excitement. The telegrams spoke of "fanatical preaching" against foreigners, of "aggressive plans" aimed against "Europeans" and "Christian missions." The local district officer feared attempts would shortly be made to subvert German authority by turning their Sudanese Muslim *askaris* against them, and he reported the diffusion of a dangerous "grossislamitischer Tendenz" into the Makonde Plateau, inland from Lindi Port.[30]

When these reports reached Dar es-Salaam, the capital of the German East African protectorate, they were taken with the utmost seriousness by the German governor, Albrecht von Rechenberg, and his subordinates. It was little more than a year after the final suppression of the Maji Maji rising, a very bloody affair that had cost thousands of African lives. Almost immediately, an officer of the Protectorate Defense Force (*Schutztruppe*), Major von Schleinitz, was dispatched to Lindi on the steamer Reichstag, accompanied by an 'Umani Arab, Sulayman bin Nasir al-Lamki, formerly the *liwali* of Dar es-Salaam in the German service. An ex-*akida* (lieutenant) named Muhammad bin 'Abd al-Rahman went along too. Very quickly, they pressured the population into silence. The "agitation" and "fanatical preaching" mentioned in the German reports stopped. Matters went back to normal. Throughout the protectorate, German planters and officials felt relieved to know that there would be no "second round" to the Maji Maji, of which they had been very apprehensive. At Lindi and in the neighboring towns of Mroweka and Mikindani, the Germans arrested a number of persons. An official investigation was begun by them to discover what persons and what organizations, if any, were behind the spreading of the "Mecca Letter" amongst local Muslims.[31]

Copies of the letter had meanwhile fallen into German hands. In Arabic, the letter spoke of the dream of a certain Shaykh Ahmad, described as the "Servant of the Prophet's Tomb." In the letter, the Prophet warned Shaykh Ahmad to tell his fellow Muslims of God's exasperation at their backsliding and bad habits. He cited their abandonment of prayer, their wine-drinking, their fornication, and their slanderous talk. The end of the world was not far distant. Those who read the letter and did not pass it on were warned that the Prophet would be their "opponent" on the Day of Judgment. The letter had also been read in mosques and commented upon by the local *shaykhs* and *mwalimus* in many of the mosques of the district and by certain clerical personalities. These included the chief of the Qadiri *tariqa* (formerly in Mocambique but now in the Lindi district), a *khalifa* of the brotherhood named Shaykh 'Isa bin Ahmad al-Ngaziji al-Barawi, who hailed from Tsujini on Grand Comoro but normally lived at Zanzibar. Earlier he had resided at Brava on the Somali coast. At the time, the Qadiriya was gaining many adherents in Lindi District.[32]

By late August 1908, copies of the Mecca Letter had been intercepted and impounded by the Germans at such places as Bagamoyo, Tabora, Iringa, Morogoro, Mpapwa, Mohoro, Kilwa, Mafia Island, the Ndonde country, and the Sasawara border post on the frontier between German East Africa and Mocambique. The Qadiri *khalifa*, Shaykh 'Isa bin Ahmad, had fled Lindi for his local base at Palma or Ibo in northern Mocambique when he knew that the Germans were on his trail. Further investigations by them revealed that the letter had originated in Zanzibar. There, it had been composed by or written for the family of Muhammad bin Khalfan bin Khamis al-Barwani, better known as "Rumaliza," a member of the Qadiriya and a famous slave trader and ivory merchant. Rumaliza had been active in the 1880s and early 1890s in inner Tanganyika, and many of his relatives of the Barwani clan lived in the vicinity of Lindi and Mikindani.[33]

By now the Germans were well aware that the letter had been designed and distributed with the hope of causing a maximum of political disturbance within the protectorate. They also knew that Rumaliza belonged to an élite – a group of interrelated Zanzibar Arabs, some of whom had lived at Lindi for a long time and whose commercial and political interests had been badly damaged or ruined by the creation of a German protectorate in 1891.[34] The Barwani clan was of considerable political weight in Zanzibar, where they had lived since about 1800 or before and where one of them, Salim bin 'Isa al-Barwani, had been for a long time the head of an Arab political faction (the Hinawis or Hina'is). They had close and friendly ties to the Harithi clan, too (also Hinawis), one of whose most famous members had been the resister Bushiri (Bashir bin Salim al-Harithi), hanged at Pangani by von Wissmann in 1889.[35] In addition, the membership in or close ties to the Qadiri brotherhood on the part of some of the Barwanis is quite clear. Politically close to them was the young sultan of Zanzibar, 'Ali bin Hamud, like his father and some of his predecessors chafing under British tutelage.

At this point it is worth having a look at the origins of the new Qadiri brotherhood in East Africa. At this time, it was led by Shaykh Uways bin Muhammad al-Barawi.[36] Shaykh Uways (the Somali pronunciation is "Awis," hence the common Swahili version of it, "Shehe Awesu") bin Muhammad al-Barawi was born at Brava (or al-Barawa) on the southern Somali coast in April 1847. Uways and his family were members of the Tunni tribe, which lived in and around Brava. His father was al-Hajj Muhammad ibn Bashir al-Barawi; his mother was Fatima bint Bahro. Little is known of his first years, but he was sent as a small child to a *Qur'an* school in Brava kept by a certain Shaykh Muhammad Tayini (or Zayini) al-Shashi (locally pronounced "Shanshi"), where he learned "useful sciences," including *tafsir* (*Qur'an* interpretation), grammar and syntax, the principles of Shafi'i law, and sufism.[37] It was Muhammad Tayini who gave him his first links to the Qadiriya brotherhood and urged him to go to Baghdad, the headquarters of the order, for further instruction and advanced study.[38] This Uways did, but not before living for a time in an old minaret near Brava, whence his hagiographer claims that he "expelled many *jinns*." Uways left Brava by ship for Masqat and Basra about 1870. In 1290 H./1873, Uways was at Madina for the first of a series of pilgrimages. From there he went back to Baghdad for more training by his Qadiri *shaykh* there, Sayyid Mustafa ibn al-Sayyid Salman al-Jaylani.[39]

Eventually, Uways became a full-fledged sufi, receiving the "absolute authorization" of the order and the body of secret spiritual knowledge transmitted from the founder of the order, 'Abd al-Qadir al-Jaylani (or Gilani), to all Qadiri *khalifas*. The head of the order, Sayyid Mustafa ibn Salman, now sent Uways from the mother house of the Qadiriya back to his homeland. Uways traveled to the Banadir coast of southern Somalia by way of the Hijaz, Yaman, and Aden, visiting the tombs of important saints and *shaykhs* as he went along in order to obtain their blessing. About 1880, Shaykh Uways arrived in Brava after completing his training, making a short halt at Qolonqol (or Kulunkul) in north central Somaliland near the tomb of the recently deceased Shaykh 'Abd al-Rahman al-Zayla'i, an important Qadiri saint. At Brava, Uways was now the undisputed chief of the local Qadiris. Very quickly, the Bravanese branch acquired the name of the Uwaysiya.[40]

At Brava, Uways had his admirers and his detractors. Among the latter were members of a rival brotherhood, the Salihiya. In Somalia, the Salihiya were led by the so-called "Mad Mullah," Shaykh Muhammad 'Abdallah Hasan. A deadly rivalry existed between the two orders. To some extent this reflected tribal and regional differences (south vs. north), but it also arose from profound doctrinal disagreements. Doctrinally, the Salihiya was descended from the Ahmadiya brotherhood, founded by the reformer Shaykh Ahmad ibn Idris al-Fasi (1758–1836).[41] Like the Sanusis, the Ahmadiya were representatives of a somewhat puritanical tendency and rejected, for example, the practice of visiting the tombs of saints to ask intercession (*tawassul*). The Ahmadiya transmitted its puritanical opinions to its daughter order, the Salihiya. Moreover, these two orders shared some of the views of the Wahhabis of Arabia. If the Wahhabis were in political eclipse at the end of the nineteenth century, their views were widely shared by certain Somalis and were quite familiar throughout the country.

After a time, the doctrinal, ethnic, and political differences between the two orders led them into controversy. The Salihis did not believe that a deceased saint should serve as an intermediary between Muslims and God. The Qadiris took the opposite view. Thus the Qadiris came in for bitter criticism from their enemies for their custom of mediation through saints. The Salihiya claimed that visits to tombs were an invalid and improper form of religious activity. Very soon, Uways attacked Shaykh Muhammad 'Abdallah Hasan and his followers with murderous polemics, criticizing them as a "satanic faction" or worse, as shown in the verses below:[42]

> Blessed are Muhammad and his family
>   Turn to them in every evil calamity
> The person guided by Muhammad's law
>   Will not follow the faction of Satan
> Who deem it lawful to spill the blood of the learned
>   Who take cash and women, too: they are anarchists
> They hinder the study of sciences
>   Like law and grammar. They are the Karramiya[43]
> To every dead *Shaykh* like al-Gilani

They deny access to God, like the Janahiya[44]
Don't follow those men with big shocks of hair
   Their characteristic mark is
A coiffure like the Wahhabiya!
   Publicly, they sell Paradise for cash
In our land, they are a sect of dogs
   Having permission, they dally with women
Even their own mothers, which is nothing but incest
   They follow their own subjective opinions.
And no book of ours!
   Their light is from the Devil
They deny god at their *dhikr*
   In word and action they are unbelievers
Like their game of saying "God?"
   "Lodge a complaint with Him!"
How they are glorified by the Northerners
   Great clamor they make, a moaning and groaning!
A noise like the barking of curs
   In divorce cases they augment the oaths
But they abridge the religious ceremonies
   They've gone astray and make others deviate on earth
By land and sea amongst the Somalis
   Have they no reason or understanding?
Be not deceived by them
   But flee as from a disaster
From their infamy and unbelief.

After some time, these verbal hostilities, exemplified by the verses above, become actual ones. Shaykh Uways was assassinated by a band of Salihi raiders on 14 April 1909, when he was about sixty-two. The murder took place at Biolay (an agricultural settlement that Uways founded, situated 150 miles north of Brava) after he had been compelled to leave the town by the "envious" (this word, used in his hagiography indicates a number of Salihis, without doubt). Shaykh Uways' tomb at Biolay is still visited in an annual pilgrimage by many thousands of Somali and other Qadiris, who see in him the reviver and refounder of their brotherhood in southern Somalia and one of the order's greatest leaders, together with Shaykh 'Abd al-Rahman al-Zayla'i.[45]

Prior to writing his unrestrained polemics, before his assassination, Uways was concerned to spread his branch of the Qadiriya. The "Lord of the White Turban," the "Master of the Time" (*sahib al-waqt*),[46] and the "Standard Bearer of the Qadiri Army" – titles his hagiographer records – concentrated on spreading the brotherhood in areas away from the southern Somali coast, already heavily islamized and partially penetrated by the Salihiya. Uways had good success among the Rahanwayn tribes of the upper Juba Valley. Here his excellent organizing capacity, leadership, and spiritual gifts won him many supporters.[47] Uways was also one of the first to use the Arabic script for writing Somali and its dialects, and he circulated a number of his Somali poems in this way.[48] When he was not roaming around the country – in the fashion of a typical itinerant Somali learned man of his day, accompanied by his disciples – he was training many of his adherents for missionary activities. He himself created hundreds of deputies (*khalifas*) in the Qadiri order. It is notable that these men came not only from Brava and southern Somalia, but also from Zanzibar, the Comoros, and other coastal regions of East Africa. To a lesser extent they came from the islamized tribes of the interior. In the 1880s, the newness and the rapid growth of the Uwaysiya made it fashionable to join the order. According to the *Al-Jawhar al-Nafis* (*The Precious Jewel Concerning the Characteristics of Shaykh Uways*) the "Possessor of Three Excellences" created no fewer than 520 *khalifas*, some of whom are listed in this hagiography and whose names give clues as to their ethnic origin.[49]

In the 1880s and 1890s Uways seems to have traveled extensively, both to make Qadiri converts and to stay out of the way of the Salihiya. According to the *Jawhar:*

> He made every effort towards the spiritual guidance of the servants of God, both men and women, along the Straight Path. . . . For that reason he used to journey to distant places on the coasts of East Africa, its settled regions and its ports, and the Banadir Coast likewise, its towns, villages, and country districts. . . . When he went on a journey a large group would accompany him, men, women, and children, slave and free, for the sake of aiding devotion with prayer and with the *dhikr,* and to nourish the unfortunate. Uways was generous and a free giver. No food or *dirhams* or *dinars* came into his hands but he soon gave them away for charitable reasons.[50]

Both the *Jawhar al-Nafis* and the *Jala' al-'Aynayn* (another hagiography of Uways) contain collections of his "miracles" and his "wonders." By sifting the miraculous element from the biographical and combining it with written and oral evidence, the main features of Uways' career in East Africa can be brought out. Thus it is clear that in the 1880s and later, Uways made Zanzibar his principal religious center outside of Somalia. Until the time of his death in 1909, Uways regularly visited Zanzibar from Brava or, toward the end of his life, from Bilad al-Amin, a Qadiri agricultural colony that he had founded.

These visits to Zanzibar took place in the time of Sayyid Barghash bin Sa'id (to 1888) and in the days of his successor, Khalifa bin Sa'id (1888–90). Uways also went to Zanzibar during the reign of Hamid bin Thuwayni bin Sa'id (1893–6) and certainly after that, although the hagiographies are imprecise as to dates.[51]

Shaykh Uways was not a sufi who believed in avoiding the "great men of the world." He had no objection to official support and was on good terms with the Bu Sa'idi rulers of Zanzibar. His contacts with Europeans were similar; his contacts with the Germans cannot be traced, but when the Italians appeared in southern Somalia, he seems to have accommodated himself to them – at least superficially. This reinforced the Salihiya's dislike of him. Yet it is likely that Shaykh Uways shared in the general Muslim abhorrence of European colonizers but channeled his sympathies to the rulers of Zanzibar. At this time their situation was difficult because of the losses of Zanzibar territory to the British and Germans. Uways, for political or pious reasons, visited Zanzibar in 1883–4 with his followers and pupils; his hagiographer, 'Abd al-Rahman bin 'Umar, records: "every day, it was the custom of the Sultan of the land [Barghash] to send him trays of food to eat."[52] In the same year, the *Jala' al-'Aynayn* mentions that the popular Zanzibari preacher, Shaykh 'Umar ibn al-Qullatayn al-Nadiri, a Bravanese living there, accepted a *khalifa*ship from Uways.[53] The same book claims that another man of distant Bravanese origin – the historian, chief *qadi*, and principal adviser of Barghash and other rulers, Shaykh 'Abd al-Aziz al-Amawi of Lamu (1832–96) – also became one of Uways' *khalifa*s. This is possible, but it is also known that 'Abd al-'Aziz also founded his own branch of the Qadiriya – the Nuraniya – and that this development created some competition between him and Uways.[54] There may also have been other, older branches of the order on Zanzibar, about which little is known.[55] At any rate, there is no doubt that Uways and his branch were highly popular and that "many of the learned men and the noble among the *shaykh*s entered the ranks of the Qadiriya in those regions, and were illuminated by its light."[56]

On his second pilgrimage to Mecca and Madina, during the short reign of Sayyid Khalifa bin Sa'id (1888–90), Uways was given a grant of 2,500 rupees when he passed through Zanzibar; in the days of Hamid bin Thuwayni (1893–6), Uways was presented with a large house in Zanzibar Town for his own use and the use of his students, and he received food and fruit every day from the royal kitchens.[57] On his return to Brava on this occasion, Uways received from Sayyid Hamid a donation of 20,000 rupees "and other gifts of money and princely clothing."[58] Most remarkable of all, the *Jawhar* lists both Sayyids Barghash and Hamid bin Thuwayni as *khalifa*s in the Qadiri brotherhood.[59] As both men were nominally Ibadis, of 'Umani descent – Barghash being rather strict about this matter – there can have been only some extraordinary reason for them to "join" a Sunni brotherhood or, more likely, to give it close support. The most convincing explanation is that they adhered to it for political reasons. This point will be taken up again below.

From Zanzibar Island, it is clear that the Qadiriya spread to the mainland opposite – to Dar es-Salaam – helped along by personal visits by Shaykh Uways; to Bagamoyo and Pangani on the Mrima coast; to the area behind Dar es-Salaam (Uzaramo); and to Lindi and Mikindani in the south.[60] It spread to the Rufiji delta and to the Yao country along the Mocambique border as well. Further inland in Tanganyika, the Qadiriya made converts and contributed to the islamization of Uhehe, Unyamwesi, and Ujiji, including Tabora and Ujiji Town. Farther west, the Qadiriya penetrated deep into the Manyema country on the far side of Lake Tanganyika, following the trade route down the Lualaba River; they proceeded along the river downstream to Kasongo, Nyangwe, Kindu, and Ponthierville – still a major Qadiri center.[61]

In the coastal areas the Qadiriya competed with the Comorian Shadhiliya (directed by Muhammad Ma'ruf from Moroni on Grand Comoro) and doubtless with the Rifa'iya order also.[62] Yet wherever they went, the Uwaysiya branch of the order won many adherents through the dynamic preaching and recruiting of its *khalifas*, of whom there were far more than in the other, competing orders.

German diplomatic sources give indications of some of the stages of the Qadiri movement. Penetration of some of the mainland ports and the coastal districts opposite Zanzibar began in the late 1880s. In the following decade progress was slower, but in 1901 and 1902 and again in 1908 the Qadiriya was making special efforts to enlarge its membership. These missionary activities were fairly obvious, even to the Germans, because the Qadiri *dhikrs* (or *zikri* in Swahili) were loud and prolonged, frequently ending with the Arabic phrase *La ilaha illa'llah* ("There is no god but God") chanted by an enthusiastic circle of Qadiris sitting in a mosque and swaying together to the beat of a drum or chantng the poetry of Shaykh Uways.[63]

By the end of the 1870s the European powers participating in the scramble for colonies in East Africa put increasing pressure on Sayyid Barghash and his successors. Once the question of who was to control the interior was resolved in favor of the Europeans, the Arabs of Zanzibar were forced to leave inner Tanganyika. The arabized coastal strip came under pressure as well, and it is certain that the Arabs and other Muslims were determined to resist, wherever and however they could. Huge areas were in dispute – from northern Zambia to Lake Tangan-

yika and its adjacent territory; Rwanda and Burundi; and Manyema-
land and the approaches to Uganda from the south and east. In this
unequal contest, Barghash and the Arabs were at a great disadvantage.

Barghash was, nevertheless, not a weak person. His strength was
shown in 1856 by his coup d'état against his half brother, Sayyid
Majid.[64] Although Barghash was on the losing side at the Battle of
Machui in 1859, Majid pardoned him on his return from a short exile
in Bombay. Barghash finally gained the throne in 1870.[65] The battle at
Machui was significant, because it revealed an underlying polarization in Zanzibari politics. This was the lingering tribal factionalism between the Hinawis and the Ghafiris, which had been going on since
about 1722 in 'Uman and had been imported into East Africa by the
Mazru'is (Ghafiris) and Bu Sa'idis (Hinawis).[66] Barghash was supported by the Hinawis, a large and turbulent party, many of whom fled
Zanzibar in 1856 for Tabora in Unyamwesi to escape the vengeance of
Sayyid Majid. The Hinawi party included such clans as the Harithis
(pl. Hurth), the Barwanis, the family of the Banu Lamk (or Lamki),
the Sumris, the Marhubis, the Bahris, and many other smaller groups.
The al-Jabri al-Barawi clan, Ibadis from 'Uman with ties at Brava, also
supported Barghash. The opposing Ghafiri faction included the Mu-
ghayris, the Maskiris, the Riyami family, and some others.[67]

During the lifetime of Barghash, the Hinawis were his main political
support, although his relations with them were not exclusively cordial;
he had some Ghafiri adherents as well.[68] It is noteworthy that the faction of the Ibadi Arabs from 'Uman (the "Wamanga" of the Swahilis) that was most active on the African mainland and thus hardest
hit by the incursions of the Europeans in the 1880s and 1890s were the
Hinawis. They included Tippu Tib (the husband of a Barwani lady
who was the first cousin of Rumaliza), Bushiri, and Rumaliza or
Muhammad bin Khalfan al-Barwani.[69] What is more, the Bravanese
community on Zanzibar (and a Bravanese faction at court) had fairly
friendly ties to the Hinawi party. Further, the Qadiri brotherhood,
which had at least two branches on Zanzibar, had two Bravanese leaders – Shaykh Uways and Shaykh 'Abd al-'Aziz al-Amawi, the chiefs of
the Uwaysiya and Nuraniya branches of the order.[70]

In his "Some Factors in the British Occupation of East Africa, 1884–
94,"[71] written in 1951, and his *The Missionary Factor in East Africa*
(1952),[72] Roland Oliver traced and amply documented a sudden reversal of the hitherto friendly attitude of the Arabs of central Africa
and Zanzibar toward Europeans. "Between 1884 and 1888," he writes:

> the policy of the Arabs changed radically all over Central Africa.
> What were the connecting threads in this movement, and in par-

ticular what part was played in it by Sultan Barghash bin Said at
Zanzibar will probably never exactly be known. The fact that the
same thing happened at so many difference places, must I think, be
taken as proof of central planning, and since there was no direct
communication, say between the Arabs of Nyasa and those of Tanganyika, the planning must have taken place at the coast. . . . The
Arabs were now aiming at political power, and they were seeking to
drive out the Europeans.[73]

Two of Oliver's "threads" in this reversal of attitudes may now be
discerned. One of them was the strong support of Barghash by the
Hinawi group among the 'Umanis. Another was the Qadiri *tariqa,*
which obtained most of its members from Sunnis, particularly from
Shafi'is – a majority among the "Old Arabs" of the coast, a group to
which many Ibadis from 'Uman had converted.

For example, during the Muslim coup in Uganda in 1888, which terminated in the deposition of the Kabaka Mwanga, a leading role was
played by a trader who was both an emissary and a close personal
friend of Sayyid Barghash – Sulayman bin Zahir al-Jabri al-Barawi.[74]
At this time a leading member of the Qadiriya in Buganda, Sulayman
had begun his mercantile career as a trader from Tabora, a town where
the Arab majority were of the Hinawi faction. Sulayman opposed the
European Christian missionaries at the Kabaka's court with some success in 1887 and 1888. On his return to Zanzibar in 1888, Sulayman was
heavily fined by Barghash for "his part in the Buganda disturbances."
Oliver notes that "this fact need not show that he or for that matter
Barghash himself, were not heavily involved in the affair."[75] Because
Barghash bin Sa'id, and after him Khalifa bin Sa'id and Hamid bin
Thuwayni, had such close and cordial ties to the Qadiriya – both
Barghash and Hamid being named as *khalifas* of it in the *al-Jawhar
ul-Nafis* – it may be assumed that their real reason for supporting was
a political one. Nor is the description of *"khalifa"* to be taken too lit-
erally. What it signifies is some species of honorary attachment, for
Barghash in particular was a strict Ibadi.[76]

Barghash and his successors were in an increasingly weak position
in regard to the British on Zanzibar, to say nothing of the Germans
on the mainland. Hence any political group that might be of use –
such as the turbulent, slave-dealing Harithis or a Sunni brotherhood
that was gaining adherents – was pressed into use. These two groups
were the instruments that might stave off political disaster; they might
rally old friends and supporters to the ruler when nothing else existed.

At the end of the nineteenth century the weak position of the Sayyids
of Zanzibar (beginning with Barghash) drove them to expedients and

intrigues that they would never have countenanced earlier. Thus they
had to play a double game with the Germans and the British – "a deceptive strategem," as Oliver says, that allowed them to collaborate
with the colonial power (or seem to do so in public). Covertly, they
gave as much aid as they could to those Muslims who attempted to
resist.[77] Khalifa bin Sa'id, Barghash's successor, did his utmost to aid
Bushiri at Pangani in 1888 and 1889. Before Bushiri was hanged by
the Germans, he admitted this fact to them; it was confirmed by the
finding of papers and letters belonging to him which, as the German
commander von Wissman remarked, contained "certain treasonable
matter."[78]

The community of interest – the loose alliance – that had functioned
in the interest of Sayyid Barghash and that had included the Qadiriya,
the Hinawi party, and their auxiliaries, lingered on for at least another
two decades after the Pangani Rising of 1888–9. This is clear from both
Arabic and German sources for the Mecca Letter episode.

By 12 August 1908, official German investigations at Lindi and Dar
es-Salaam had progressed far enough to enable the governor to pre-
pare a preliminary report for the Reichskolonialamt in Berlin. According to von Rechenberg, the main culprit was Rumaliza, whom he
describes as follows:

> Mohammed bin Khalfan al-Barwani . . . was formerly associated
> with Hamed bin Mohammed and Mohammed b. Said [Bwana Nzige]
> in a company that was largely concerned with slave trading and
> possessed political power, particularly in the Congo State. With the
> introduction of German administration, its ancestral region was cut
> off from its area of power in the Congo State. That Rumaliza, who
> had shown himself for decades to be a bold, tenacious, and cunning
> adversary should not have been friendly to German rule – at least in
> its earlier years – is not surprising. At that time, because of an insult
> to the German flag, he was made to pay a heavy fine. . . . His in-
> timate friend and dearest companion Kassim was even hanged at
> Tabora. What is more, Rumaliza's people were among the defenders
> of Iringa [in 1894] against Governor von Schele. . . . This was for-
> given him. His commercial connections with Hamed bin Mohammed
> broke up and a long and tedious court case ensued, when the courts
> here [i.e., Dar es-Salaam] made over to him all the property of the
> company within the protectorate. His existence today depends on
> this. One would think that he had every reason to abandon his old
> ill-will. He gives the impression of having reconciled himself to cir-
> cumstances, and was in Dar es-Salaam only a short time ago, when
> he introduced himself to me.[79]

In his short account of Rumaliza's career, von Rechenberg omits saying or perhaps did not know that Rumaliza had been born at Lindi about 1855, that he went to Zanzibar for schooling during the reign of Majid bin Sa'id (1856–70), and that his clan was a leading one among the Hinawis of Zanzibar. His was a widespread family, as powerful and numerous in Lindi District as on Zanzibar, and it had been established in both places for some time. In Zanzibar, it is likely that the founders of the clan were two brothers, 'Abdallah bin Jum'a al-Barwani, *wali* of Zanzibar for Sayyid Sa'id about 1815, and his brother Muhammad bin Jum'a, a general who expelled Madagascan invaders (Sakalava) from the ports of the Mrima coast about 1816.[80]

According to oral history collected at Lindi, the ties of the Barwanis to Lindi date from an incident that occurred about 1800 or earlier. Some Arabs cruising in a dhow kidnapped a young girl from a local tribe, the Mwera, as she played on the beach. She was taken to Zanzibar and sold, eventually becoming the concubine of 'Isa bin 'Ali al-Barwani. In the course of time she had four children by him, who came back to their mother's homeland, Ng'ando ya Lindi, provided with a letter from their mother to an Mwera chief and one of her lip plugs (*ndonya*) as proof of their claim. Eventually, they were acknowledged by their mother's kinsmen and began to trade from Lindi in iron and salt. Later their activities expanded to include slaving, the Mwera and others selling their children as slaves for the Zanzibar market or sometimes even selling themselves during periods of famine.[81]

Eventually the Barwanis of Lindi made so much money from the slave and legitimate trade that they were able to divide Lindi Town into four quarters, each the possession of one of the sons of 'Isa bin 'Ali. They hired a Muslim teacher to instruct their children and others in religion.[82] After these commercial successes, some of the clan returned to Zanzibar, but one of those who remained, 'Abdallah bin 'Amir al-Barwani, left at his death a large estate at Lindi with 1,500 slaves – even larger than the Kitundu estate of his relative 'Isa bin 'Ali on Zanzibar. He had possessed great influence throughout Lindi District.

Other Barwanis from Zanzibar came to settle at Lindi, attracted by the success of the sons of 'Isa. Two of them, Muhammad and Nasr (or Nāsir), built a fort at Lindi.[83] This structure was presumably erected to guard the seaward end of a trade route in which the Barwanis were interested. The route ran from Lindi through the Mwera, Makonde, and Ndonde countries to Lake Malawi (from whence branches ran to the southern end of Lake Tanganyika) and as far west as Lake Mweru. Another member of the Barwani family, 'Abdallah bin Salim (a grandson of 'Isa bin 'Ali and the grandfather of Tippu Tib's wife, Bint Salim bin 'Abdallah), was a rich merchant and shipowner. He had at least two sailing vessels, one of which was appropriately named the Hari-thiya.[84] No doubt these vessels served to transport slaves from Lindi to the Zanzibar market. In any case, Rumaliza had suffered directly from the actions of the Germans at Lindi, for most of the Barwani properties had been confiscated by them at the beginning of the 1890s.[85]

With his background, it was quite natural that Rumaliza should become a professional slave trader and ivory collector. By 1879, the date of one of the first notices of him and his activities by a European, Muhammad bin Khalfan al-Barwani was settled at Ujiji on Lake Tanganyika.[86] In the early 1880s, he was raiding for slaves first in Uvinza and then in Rwanda. He spent some time in the company of Tippu Tib at this time in his life, at Tabora. His name, Rumaliza, dates from these years, as there is said to be an outlying village or a part of Tabora Town known as Rumaliza (or Lumaliza). After 1884, Rumaliza was helping to conquer the region around Lake Tanganyika for Sayyid Barghash and at the same time hunting slaves and gathering ivory. Occasionally, European missionaries, explorers, or travelers met him on the east side of Lake Tanganyika, sometimes on the west.[87]

As Oliver notes, the relations of the Arabs with the Europeans after the middle 1880s and the 1890s were different and much less pleasant than they had been.[88] Rumaliza was no exception; he made war on the Belgians who were moving into his areas of influence from the west by approaching Lake Tanganyika from the Congo "Free State." Rumaliza also displayed renewed hostility toward the Germans, not only because of the Lindi confiscations but also because they were poised at the start of the 1890s to move inland from their bases on the coast.[89] Nor did Rumaliza's friends admire the Germans. One of these was Muhammad bin Qasim (Rechenberg's "Kassim"), who was hanged at Tabora in 1890 by the protectorate authorities for his murder of a German ivory trader, Giesecke, four years previously.[90] Muhammad bin Qasim was also an associate of Bwana Heri, the Wali of Sadani. For a time, Bwana Heri had been the ally of Bushiri in the Pangani Rising, even though the two men ultimately quarreled because their political objectives were incompatible.[91]

The episode mentioned by Rechenberg, Rumaliza's "insult to the German flag," took place in Ujiji in 1893.[92] The exasperated Rumaliza had threatened the Germans approaching Lake Tanganyika from the coast with war when they invaded his slaving and trading preserves and established military posts within his zone of influence. When a German officer appeared at Ujiji in the summer of 1893 to build a post there, Rumaliza tore down the flag. Knowing that he could hold out no longer, he fled Ujiji and crossed the lake, only to find the Belgians advancing toward his camp from the northwest via the Manyema country.[93] After his defeat by the Belgians at Ogella near Kabambare (now in North Kivu Province, Zaire) in January 1894, Rumaliza made his way back to Ujiji.[94] There he was repudiated by an Arab collaborator – Misbah bin Najm al-Shahini – one of his former friends, who had been appointed *liwali* of Ujiji by the Germans. After some weeks, Rumaliza made his way through the difficult Tongwe country to the land of the Hehe in central Tanganyika.[95] The Hehe chief, Mkwawa, was then the focus of resistance to the Germans in the interior of the country. Rumaliza took the Wahehe oath of blood brotherhood with Mkwawa, and then he helped him to rebuild his earth citadel at Kalenga near Iringa in stone so as to offer a better defense against an impending German attack.[96] When the Germans, under Governor von Schele, stormed the fort, Rumaliza and Mkwawa were both inside it. Rumaliza escaped and returned to Zanzibar in a fishing boat, successfully evading the inquisitive Germans all the way to the coast.[97] Later he returned to Dar es-Salaam to participate in the court case Rechenberg mentions. He won considerable money from Tippu Tib when the case was terminated in 1902.

Because of his slaving and trading in regions where the Germans wanted to halt slaving and to monopolize trade themselves; because of his membership in the Qadiri brotherhood (he was probably one of those Barwanis who had converted to the Sunni majority[98]); and because of his membership in the Hinawi faction, Rumaliza had every possible reason to dislike and to hinder the progress of European imperialists, whether Belgian or German.

For these reasons, doubtless pushed along by his ambitious sons, Rumaliza, in 1908, was willing to undertake a political initiative with religious overtones. With its millennial terminology and its attacks on whatever was not orthodox, the Mecca Letter had a lot in common with certain manifestos distributed by the Sudanese Mahdi Muhammad Ahmad,[99] although the letter does not mention the coming of a mahdi. In Algeria in the 1830s and 1840s, some of the rivals and competitors of Amir 'Abd al-Qadir had employed similar phrases in their propaganda; the Algerian Darqawis did this just after 1800 (see Chapter 2).

Had a successful uprising taken place on a suitable scale, Rumaliza might have come to Lindi from Zanzibar to lead it. But as it failed, he stayed in Zanzibar to observe the course of events from a safe distance. Nevertheless, the way in which the Mecca Letter was composed betrayed familiarity with the habits of thought of the semi-islamized population in and near Lindi. The author knew very well how to play on their fears and millenarian beliefs. Ultimately, the incipient rising failed, because Rumaliza and his sons and allies underestimated German strength and determination to hold onto their colony after the Maji Maji crisis.

On his side, Governor von Rechenberg seems to have grasped some of Rumaliza's objectives. In his dispatch he continued:

> Even if no dangers have arisen from this movement, it would be wrong to ignore certain questionable phenomena. The Muslim coastal population has made no effort since the Bushiri Rising to oppose the new order of things. At that time the religious tolerance of Europeans was unknown, and the Muslims feared a government which would act along the lines of the saying *cuius regio eius religio,* in the Islamic manner. But in the last twenty years, they have become convinced that German rule does not signify any limitation of Islamic belief. . . . However, the contrivers and propagators of the letter have obviously taken as their point of departure the idea of exciting the Muslims against the regime and assuring them of pagan support. . . . The idea of playing off the Bush Negroes under Muslim leadership against the Europeans is based on the realization that the Rising of 1905 failed over two things: 1) the lack of communications, organization, and leadership among the mutinous tribes, and 2) because of the loyalty of the colored troops. . . . Through the participation of the Muslim population in such a movement, the fidelity of the largely Muslim *'askaris* could be shaken. The events at Lindi point directly at such an intention.[100]

In this dispatch and in others, von Rechenberg saw advantages for Germany in the deeply divided Muslim community of Tanganyika. Hence his distinction between "genuinely pious Muslims" and "Islamic agitators." This was not the only division. The Muslim community of the time was split religiously, ethically, socially, and politically. Many of these divisions are still visible.[101] The Sunnis were divided into a number of groupings. There were also Shi'is (Isma'ilis) and Ibadi Arabs of 'Umani origin. Among the Sunnis, there were Hadrami Arabs from South Arabia, many of whom had been imported by Sayyid Sa'id to do menial tasks at the end of his reign[102] and others who came in 1881 (and for a few years thereafter) – the followers of an ousted Naqib of Mukalla.[103] Then there were Zanzibar and mainland Swahilis, Comoro Islanders, Bravanese, and Baluchis.[104]

Politically, there had existed a difference between "resisters" and "collaborators" since 1889. As in other African colonial political situations, it was the rich and well-to-do – those who had the most to lose – who compromised and accepted the new situation. Some of the Isma'ili community, for example, accepted German rule without demur. Certain 'Umani Arabs who had been higher civil servants in Zanzibar or on the mainland, such as Sulayman bin Nasir al-Lamki, transferred to the German administration and continued to function as *liwalis* or *akidas* for the new colonial overlords.

Yet since the days of Bushiri and the Pangani Affair, those Muslims who felt less easy under the Germans, including the former holders of power, were now politically displaced persons. This group included Rumaliza himself; broadly speaking, the Hinawi faction; and those *jumbes* or *akidas* or sultans who were suspect to the Germans or refused to accept German supervision. These persons also had their privileges and incomes abridged or abolished by the Germans. The leaders of the Kilwa Rising of 1894, Hasan bin 'Umar (Hasani bin Omari) and his lieutenant Akida Akran, are examples. The poorer classes and semi-islamized tribesmen, who were now regularly taxed by the Germans, included the Swahili, the Washihri, the Bravanese, certain Comorian migrants, the Wamanyema, and the other socially disturbed and decimated tribes of western and southern Tanganyika. All of these people can be put in the anti-German camp. They had one regret in common: they looked back with sorrow to the days before the arrival of the German colonizers. It was from this group that the Qadiriya made its converts (and the Shadhiliya too), for it was the most rootless and least secure of any. Joining the brotherhood and accepting Islam could furnish its members new hope through a revised value system or new social contacts to take the place of the stable tribal existence that many of them had enjoyed in the past. Hence, in Tanganyika at this period, the impact of the Germans and the spread of Islam went hand in hand.

Was Governor von Rechenberg justified in suspecting some organized resistance, some serious anti-German plotting, in the Mecca Letter affair? The answer is affirmative. The Germans were opposed by a Muslim alliance that included Rumaliza, his sons and relatives, a number of Comorians and Bravanese, and some Swahilis – most of whom shared membership in the Qadiriya brotherhood and many of whom had ties to the Hinawi group. The Sultan of Zanzibar may have supported Rumaliza's activities also, out of feelings of Islamic solidarity. 'Ali bin Hamud's sympathies for Pan-Islam and the Turks are well known and contributed largely to his abdication in 1911.

The investigations initiated by von Rechenberg brought to light part of the network that was distributing the Mecca Letter. At Bagamoyo, on 2 August 1908, the governor was informed by his district officer that a prominent local learned man, Abu Bakr bin Taha al-Jabri al-Barawi (a distant relative of the Sulayman al-Jabri al-Barawi mentioned above in connection with the Muslim disturbances in Uganda), was disseminating copies of the Mecca Letter in and around Bagamoyo.[105] Abu

Bakr was a *khalifa* of the Qadiriya and operated a *Qur'an* school there. His school was attended by the sons of wealthy local Arabs and Muslim Indians and by Arab children from Tabora and Ujiji and elsewhere whose parents had sent them to Bagamoyo for schooling. Abu Bakr's brother 'Umari had lived for a long time at Ujiji, where he was on friendly terms with Rumaliza. Another brother, Yasin bin Taha, was a leading resident of Chole Town on Mafia Island.[106] Abu Bakr's nephew, Zahir bin Muhammad al-Jabri al-Barawi, was a Qadiri *khalifa* at Tabora, and both he and his uncle maintained friendly ties with Rumaliza during their occasional visits to Zanzibar.[107] When the Germans uncovered this last bit of information, it led to the immediate expulsion of Zahir bin Muhammad from the German protectorate in December 1908, followed by "discreet surveillance" of his uncle Abu Bakr and a forced public disavowal by him of the Mecca Letter in a mosque at Bagamoyo.[108] At the southern end of the same network, the Qadiri *khalifa* 'Isa bin Ahmad al-Ngaziji al-Barawi had already fled German territory for Palma in northern Moçambique; he then returned to his usual post as a *khatib* ("reader") in a mosque in the Ng'ambo Mwiafui quarter of Zanzibar Town and to his role as an organizer of Qadiri *dhikrs*.[109]

With the expulsion of Zahir bin Muhammad from German East Africa, the measures planned by von Rechenberg and his helpers to halt and punish the spreaders of the Mecca Letter were almost concluded. It merely remained to try Rumaliza's brother, Nasir bin Khalfan al-Barwani, and Rumaliza's son Hemedi. Nasir had been caught with copies of the letter, and Hemedi had been snatched by the German police from a mail steamer in Lindi Harbor. In October 1910, after more than two years in jail awaiting trial, Nasir was sentenced to a prison term of five years. Hemedi was acquitted. Although the Germans were aware of the part he had played in the affair, they were unable to prove it. Another person received a four-year sentence, but two of the other defendants on Zanzibar were beyond the reach of the Germans.[110]

An interesting issue hovering over the Mecca Letter affair is the question of involvement in it by the British and participation in it by the ruler of Zanzibar. It is possible that British officials on the island, seeing the increasing tension between Britain and Germany just before World War I, might have supported activities designed to embarrass the Germans in East Africa. Much more likely is the suggestion that Sayyid 'Ali bin Hamud (reigning 1905–11) knew about it and silently supported the affair. Like Barghash, Khalifa, 'Ali bin Sa'id, and Hamid bin Thuwayni – but unlike his father, Hamud bin Muhammad – 'Ali tacitly and passively resisted the British. Although he had been sent to a British public school (Harrow) and was much westernized in the process, he was bitter and disillusioned about the manipulation of Zanzibar politics and finances by the colonial power.[111] He set out to place obstructions in its way and to force a return to the situation before the Anglo-Zanzibar Agreement of 1890, by which the internal affairs of Zanzibar had been removed from local control.[112] The constant "reforms" pressed by the British, usually over the slavery issue, had alienated 'Ali as they had many of the slaveholding élite on Zanzibar and Pemba. Some of those affected by the British regulations fled to German territory, where slavery was still permitted. Further, Sayyid 'Ali had a great admiration for Barghash and his independent policies. He wanted to imitate the strong line that Barghash had taken with the British (at least at the outset of his reign, in 1870). Like Barghash, who suffered from elephantiasis, 'Ali, too, had bouts of bad health that made it difficult for him to maintain any chosen policy.

'Ali was much interested in German activities on the mainland. In order to irritate the British and gain political leverage, 'Ali flirted with the Germans whenever possible; he paid a visit to Berlin in 1907.[113] More significant, 'Ali cultivated close relations with the Ottoman Turks and was friendly with Sultan 'Abd al-Hamid II. On his journey to Europe and the Middle East in 1907, 'Ali stopped at Istanbul, where he was warmly greeted and entertained by 'Abd al-Hamid II, who was always looking for recruits for his Pan-Islamic plans. In the same year 'Ali gave practical proof of his sympathies; he conceived the idea of acting as a mediator between the Ottoman ruler and some rebels in Yaman. His ostensible motive here was to pull together the parts of a warring Islamic commonwealth and halt a conflict between Muslims.[114]

Thus, the known anti-British attitudes of 'Ali bin Hamud, his strong sympathies for the Pan-Islamic movement, and his friendship for the sultan of Turkey might well have overcome his slight sympathies for the Germans – to the extent that he would uphold Rumaliza's schemes for an uprising in former Zanzibar mainland territory. Another significant point that would argue for the popularity of the Pan-Islamic idea among Zanzibar Muslims was the naming of 'Abd al-Hamid II as "caliph" in the Friday bidding prayer on Zanzibar and on the mainland, even after it was under German control. This prayer (*khutba*) mentioned the sultan of Turkey as the supreme head of Islam; it was even used on the mainland for a time after the area was under German rule.[115] Then too, Zanzibar had a Pan-Islamic newspaper in Arabic, *Al-Najāh*, with a good number of subscribers.[116] 'Ali bin Hamud was on good terms with a leading *qadi* and intellectual named Ahmad bin Sumayt. In the 1880s, Ahmad bin Sumayt had spent a year in Istanbul in the milieu of the Yildiz Palace, had been decorated by 'Abd al-

Hamid, and had been an associate of Jamal al-Din al-Afghani and Sayyid Fadl, of Zufar. These three men were working under Sultan 'Abd al-Hamid II, planning and promoting Pan-Islamic projects in Africa and elsewhere.[117] These bits of evidence suggest that many among the Muslim population had strong feelings favoring Islamic unity.

The actions of 'Ali bin Hamud under altered circumstances are quite similar to the actions of his predecessors. They are of a piece with the doings of Sayyid Barghash, who favored the *mutawwi'un* of 'Uman and Zanzibar (an antiforeign and anti-Western movement led by Barghash's relative, 'Azzan bin Qays al-Bu Sa'idi) in the early 1870s. At one point, Barghash was even considering flight to 'Uman to escape the British.[118]

After Barghash's death, Khalifa bin Sa'id had aided the resisters of Pangani, and his successor, 'Ali bin Sa'id, had cooperated with the British only with great reluctance. In 1896 Khalid bin Barghash enlisted many of the alienated and disaffected Muslims of Zanzibar Town in a mutiny against the British. This episode terminated in the shelling of the Zanzibar waterfront by British warships, killing and wounding many people. When Hamid bin Thuwayni was installed instead of Khalid in 1893, the British believed that he would be wholly pliable; this turned out to be a wrong estimate. He intrigued in Masqat, and when Lloyd Matthews and Hardinge – two leading British officials – left Zanzibar to crush Mubarak bin Rashid on the Kenya coast in 1895, Hamid used the occasion to attack the followers of the British administration.[119] Hardinge also tricked Hamid out of part of the Kenya coastal strip when the Imperial British East Africa Company took over that region in 1894. Hamid's bitterness and disillusionment over his diminished status doubtless accelerated his early death in 1896.[120]

In its spread from Brava to Zanzibar to the mainland of Tanganyika and then westward into the Congo, the Uwaysiya Qadiriya became a major Muslim movement in East Africa. Though it began as early as 1883, Qadiri proselytization is still continuing. In a region where adherence to a *tariqa* is synonymous with conversion to Islam, such a movement assumed more than ordinary significance.[121]

CHAPTER 7

Sayyid Muhammad 'Abdallah Hasan of Somalia

Contemporary Somalia is a large country composed of two former colonies, Italian Somalia and the ex-British Somaliland Protectorate. Populated chiefly by nomads, it has settled inhabitants as well, who live in the scattered ports, villages, and towns along the few rivers, the Juba and the Webi Shebelli. Away from the coast, in the arid landscapes of acacias, aloes, and thornbushes, are the domains of such large pastoral groups as the Isaq, the Dir, and others who roam with their herds of cattle and camels over these plains and also along the low ranges running parallel to the south shore of the Gulf of Aden. In the "Horn of Africa" proper live the Darod. Further south are the Digil, Rahanwayn, and Hawiya, along with isolated elements of other clans. Like the nomads of Arabia, the majority of Somalis are concerned with their animals – furnishing them with appropriate water and pasturage. Like the Arabs, too, the hardy Somalis raided each other until very recently, fighting over grazing lands and water rights at their infrequent wells and water holes.

The attachment of the Somalis to Islam is of long standing, for they embraced Sunni Islam in medieval times. They were converted by Arabs from the north, arrivals in Somalia from across the Red Sea, Aden, Yaman, or the Hadramawt.[1] These Arabs were later reinforced by Persians, who came in numbers to the Somali shores.[2] Both of these groups of foreign Muslims built trading towns on the northern Somali coast facing Arabia and along the long straight Indian Ocean coast running to the south. In age, the northern Somali ports such as Bandar Qasim, Mayt, or Zayla' rival the southern coastal towns such as Mogadishu, Marka, and Brava. Later, when trade drew Muslims inland to found such amirates as Adal and Ifat, these little states were among the earliest Islamic governments in East Africa. These outposts of the larger Islamic world were soon in touch with the peoples of the interior, the Zinj (or Zanj) of the old Arab writers. Later, they had contacts with the migrant Galla and finally with the latest comers, the pastoral Samale (or Somalis). From medieval times onward, the inhabitants of the horn became more intensely Muslim, a trend that was perpetuated by their frequent wars with their old enemy, Christian Ethiopia. Certainly after the conflicts of the sixteenth century – the campaigns of Ahmad Gran – the Somalis were almost wholly islamized.

Before the nineteenth century, few Europeans had contacts with Somalis. At intervals, various maritime states had occasionally tried to rescue their shipwrecked sailors from these inhospitable coasts. After 1840, however, a number of European powers began to regard the Horn of Africa as an area where they might establish their political influence. Deliberately, they overlooked an older Ottoman claim to parts of the Somali coasts.[3] As European attention – French, British, and ultimately Italian – was beginning to focus on the Somali lands, a new Islamic consciousness was perceptible there. In a process of mutual reinforcement, Islamic revival kept pace with European penetration, playing back and forth over the country.

In the nineteenth century, one of the initial episodes in the rise of the new Islamic consciousness is connected with Shaykh Ibrahim Hasan Jabaro, the leader of a reforming movement that grew powerful along the Juba River in the south about 1820.[4] About 1836, a group of militant Somalis took and briefly held the important town of Brava.[5] Yet by 1880, the Qadiri order of sufis was the most important in the land. It had two centers, one at Brava and one farther to the north in the Hawd ("red earth region") at Kolonkol (or Qulunqul) in the Ogadin, not far from the Ethiopian border.[6] Their leader, the great *widad* (or "saint") of the northern Somali Qadiris, was Shaykh 'Abd al-Rahman al-Zayla'i (d. 1299/1882). According to his hagiography, he was a wonder-working figure who could raise men from the dead or halt an epidemic of smallpox with a wave of his hand.[7] In the south, the local Qadiris were much attached to the charismatic Shaykh Uways bin Muhammad al-Barawi (1847–1909; see Chapter 6).[8]

By the end of the nineteenth century, northern and southern Qadiris were well rooted. The two Qadiri nuclei followed a traditional pattern of conservative sufism. Yet their many adherents added some distinctly original features, founding large collective agricultural settlements. Here members of the order could practice their rites, raise crops, and herd sizable flocks of sheep, goats, and camels.

The renaissance of Somali Islam brought adherents not only to the Qadiriya of the south. Other brotherhoods competed for the religious loyalties of the Muslims of the horn. Some of the smaller orders were the Dandarawiya,[9] the Ahmadiya, and the Rifa'iya.[10] Among the emergent orders the most significant was the Salihiya, which soon became the greatest rival of the Qadiriya. At the beginning the 1890s, the Salihiya was not only a new order, but a representative of a radically different neosufi tradition, a tradition of reform utterly opposed to the Qadiris in doctrine. Here was the germ of a serious conflict.

The Salihiya took its name from its leading *shaykh*, Muhammad ibn

Salih al-Rashidi (c. 1854–1917 or 1919). Muhammad ibn Salih al-Rashidi was a Sudanese of the Maliki school who lived in Mecca. He was the nephew and religious heir of Ibrahim ibn Rashid al-Duwayhi (d. 1291/1874), who hailed from Dongola on the Nile.[11] In turn Ibrahim ibn Rashid had been the pupil and close friend of Ahmad ibn Idris al-Fasi (1758–1836) and had studied with him in Mecca and at Sabya in Yaman.[12] Ibrahim ibn Rashid was well acquainted with his two fellow pupils, also founders of orders, Muhammad 'Uthman al-Mirghani and Muhammad 'Ali al-Sanusi. This cluster of ninteenth-century sufi orders – the Salihiya, Rashidiya, Ahmadiya, Sanusiya, and Mirghaniya – followed the doctrines of Ahmad ibn Idris al-Fasi and accepted his outlook on many issues. Al-Fasi was wholly in favor of reform and rejected traditional sufism; he was decidedly closer to the reforming Wahhabis than to the Qadiriya.[13]

Accounts differ as to the founding of the Salihiya and the circumstances of its breaking away from its parent order, the Rashidiya. The problem is complicated by the lack of printed documents or manuscript material about the order. Chances are that it emerged at Mecca between 1887 and 1890.[14] It became popular there and began to spread throughout southwestern Arabia, then across the Red Sea into Somalia. Here it had been preceded by its ancestor, the Ahmadiya, and perhaps by the Rashidiya as well. On the African shore the Salihiya was very successful in gaining adherents. One of its first *khalifas* (initiators, recruiting *shaykhs*) was Muhammad Qulid (or Guled) al-Rashidi. This man founded several agricultural settlements, like settlements founded by the Qadiriya, along the upper valley of the Webi Shebelli ("Leopard River").[15] Another Somali *shaykh* who aided in the drive for recruits was Isma'il ibn Ishaq al Urwayni. A third Salihi recruiter was Shaykh 'Ali Nairobi, whose real name was 'Ali ibn Muhammad al-Adali.[16] He took his nickname from his proselytizing activities on the Kenya borderlands and in the extreme south of the Somali-speaking area. At Mecca, all three had been initiated as *khalifas* in the order by Shaykh Muhammad Salih.

The most famous *khalifa* initiated by Shaykh Muhammad ibn Salih was easily Sayyid (or Ina) Muhammad 'Abdalla Hasan. The Sayyid is best known as the "Mad Mullah" of Somaliland.[17] Yet he was neither insane nor a mullah (in this context an Anglo-Indian term reserved for Muslim clerics) but an important Somali intellectual and religious leader. Sayyid Muhammad led resistance to the British and Italians in his country for more than two decades (1899–1920). An Islamic leader of a recognizable type, he resembled in certain ways the Moroccan chief 'Abd al-Karim and the Algerian amir, 'Abd al-Qadir. Although he has been compared to the Sudanese Mahdi, he himself never claimed to be a mahdi.[18] He tried to preserve Somali Islam and Somali pastoral values, using the Salihiya brotherhood as an organizational support. He now ranks as the Somali national hero, defined by some as a "proto-nationalist." If he was the "father of his country," he was never a secular nationalist, and to define him as such is to misconstrue his objectives and misunderstand his achievements.

Sayyid Muhammad 'Abdallah Hasan was born in April 1864 near Bohotle in north central Somalia.[19] Here his grandfather, Shaykh Hasan Nur (a member of the Bah Geri fraction of the Ogadin clan) had settled and married a woman of the Dulbahante, the local clan at Bohotle. Little is known of Sayyid Muhammad's father, 'Abdallah; but he was at least interested in his son's education and sent him to a *Qur'an* school.[20] Aged fifteen, the precocious Muhammad had become a religious teacher; at nineteen he was given the title *shaykh* in recognition of his knowledge. Some accounts say that he traveled to Harar in Ethiopia and to Mogadishu to study.[21] Aged about twenty-five, he married. About 1885, he set off for Arabia.[22] In 1893, he visited Madina and made the pilgrimage to Mecca. The Sayyid remained in Mecca and Madina or in Yaman for five or six years to study, returning to Somalia at intervals; but few definite details of his life in this period are available.[23] At Mecca, he encountered Shaykh Muhammad ibn Salih al-Rashidi, joined his new order, and became a *khalifa* in it. Judging from his writings in Arabic – in prose and verse – Sayyid Muhammad had been very well trained by Muhammad ibn Salih in the Islamic sciences. He had a good knowledge of Shafi'i law, of the *Qur'an,* and of traditions in particular. His poetry shows that he was no stranger to Arabic metrics, and by the time he returned to Somalia he was bilingual in Somali and Arabic.

In 1895 Sayyid Muhammad came back from Mecca, via Aden, to Somalia.[24] Landing at Berbera, he stopped for a time to preach the reforming doctrines of the Salihiya to those of the townspeople who would listen. He attacked the use of tobacco, intoxicating drinks, tea, and coffee, and he castigated persons who chewed *qat* – a mild narcotic still popular in Aden and the Horn of Africa.[25] He was also perturbed by the presence of Catholic missionaries in Berbera; some of them were raising Somali orphans as Christians. But the sharpest comments of Sayyid Muhammad were reserved for the practice of *tawassul* – intercession of saints for believers with God. Intercession of this sort, particularly by deceased saints, was fully accepted by the Berbera Qadiris, who encouraged pilgrimages to tombs in the neighborhoods for the purpose. Sayyid Muhammad frequently reminded the townspeople that such doings were *bid'a* ("undesirable innovations").[26]

Yet they rejected his charges; he made few converts to the Salihiya.

A majority of them remained Qadiris; many of them were making money out of the export trade in sheep and cattle to Aden. They had no wish to alter the favorable status quo. Within a year or two, sharp hostility arose between Sayyid Muhammad and certain circles in the town. Although his teaching of religious subjects in schools or private houses was not objectionable to them, his radical preaching and his promotion of a new brotherhood made him enemies. His fulminations against *qat,* which many Qadiris used to keep awake at their *dhikrs,* led to a confrontation between Sayyid Muhammad and certain of the religious leaders of the town in 1897. In spite of the cautioning he received from these *'ulama,* including a former teacher of his, Sayyid Muhammad refused to compromise or to shift his attitudes.[27]

Relations between the Sayyid and the British at Berbera were not much better. During his stay in Aden, the Sayyid had had an encounter with a British officer; he had tossed him over a parapet, breaking his leg.[28] On his arrival in Berbera from the Aden steamer, Sayyid Muhammad was angered by a British customs employee, who instructed him not to move his baggage without first paying customs dues. The Sayyid answered, "Did you pay customs dues when you landed here? Who gave you permission to enter our country?" After the Somali interpreter had translated the Sayyid's remarks, he added for the Englishman's benefit that Sayyid Muhammad was known as the "Crazy Shaykh" (*al-Shaykh al-majnun*). Although this story may be apocryphal, it contributed to the legend of the "Mad Mullah."[29] Another similar story is told of a British governor or consul at Berbera who found the call to prayer from a mosque adjoining his house very annoying when he wanted to take his siesta. He forbade the call to prayer and sent some soldiers to arrest anyone who might disturb his slumbers. A prayer caller nevertheless eluded the guards, mounted the minaret, and awakened the colonial official. At this the latter took up a rifle and shot the man dead.[30] This alleged episode is said to have had a profound effect on Sayyid Muhammad, intensifying his latent antiforeign and anticolonial attitudes. Moreover, his sojourn in Mecca and Madina and in Yaman in these years must have put him in touch with the strong Pan-Islamic currents of the time and reinforced his anti-European opinions.

Oppressed by the colonial atmosphere of Berbera and irritated by the local Qadiris, Sayyid Muhammad made a personal *hijra* from what he saw as a "place of corruption" to the free air of the Ogadin Plains, to Bohotle or Kirrit. This move was accomplished in 1897.[31] Here he stayed for about two years, in the vicinity of his mother's clan, the Dulbahante. He also journeyed to the Nogal Valley, his father's home district, where some of his uncles and brothers still lived. At this time, Sayyid Muhammad seems to have begun thinking about armed resistance to the foreign intruders. He started to collect arms and welcomed men who wanted to follow him; then he began to preach publicly against the presence of unbelieving foreigners in Somalia. He made it known that donations for his cause were welcome in the form of weapons or livestock. Every ten she-camels could be exchanged for a rifle. At the start, most of the guns that came into the Sayyid's hands were old Le Gras or Lebel rifles, doubtless diverted from the French arms trade into Ethiopia or smuggled across the Red Sea from Aden.[32] As yet, the Sayyid made no military moves.

One of the speeches of Sayyid Muhammad from this time survives. Typical of his prose, laced with traditions of the Prophet and Qur'anic quotations, it is harsh. It stresses obedience to God and the Muslim duty of struggle against unbelievers. Although they are powerful, there is hope for their expulsion:

> Unbelieving men of religion have assaulted our country from their remote homelands. They wish to corrupt our religion, to force us to accept Christianity, supported by the armed force of their governments, their weapons, their numbers. You have only your faith in God, your arms and your determination. Do not be frightened by their soldiers or armies: God is mightier than they. . . . Be patient and steadfast in hardship. . . . If you see persons who aid the Unbelievers by serving them as guides to water holes or along paths, they are their spies and agents; attack them. They are no Muslims, for the Prophet said, "Whoever bears arms against us is not one of us." Our aim is to cleanse the land of Unbelievers.[33]

An unforeseen episode in March 1899 allowed Sayyid Muhammad to begin the jihad that he had been planning. A Somali policeman named Hirsi fled to the Sayyid from Berbera, carrying his rifle. Whether the Sayyid bought it from him or not is uncertain. Hearing of this, the British consul-general at Berbera, Cordeaux, wrote a note to the Sayyid demanding the return of the rifle. The Sayyid sent his reply on the back of the consul's letter; it read, "Man, I have stolen nothing from you nor anyone else. Get what you want from whoever has stolen it. Serve whatever [god] you have chosen to serve. Farewell."[34] At this, the consul declared Sayyid Muhammad a "rebel." This definition automatically made any assistance to him or communication with him an offense. Yet, as Lewis points out, it is doubtful that the Sayyid was really a resident of the British zone.[35] An immediate punitive expedition, contemplated by the British at Berbera, was out of the question, because they had few troops available and much British energy at the time was being taken up by the Boer War. A few months later, the Sayyid appeared, with several thousand men, threatening Burao, an

English inland outpost; he then raided a Qadiri settlement at Shaykh, on the road from Berbera to Burao.

In spite of this move by the English, the first real military clash of Sayyid Muhammad's jihad was an attack by his "dervishes" on the advancing Ethiopians at Jigjiga. For some years the Ethiopians had been sending irregular units into the Hawd and Ogadin regions. In a circular letter to the powers in 1891, Emperor Menilik had claimed Jigjiga.[36] The Ethiopian occupation of the town was intermittent until the beginning of 1900, when the invaders reoccupied the town, building or rebuilding a small fort (*zariba*) there. In March 1900, Sayyid Muhammad led a raid on this fort with several thousand dervish horsemen. They were beaten off with heavy casualties; some of the raiders were Dulbahante and some were of the Habar Tol Ja'lo and Habar Yunus clans.[37] The fact that two of these clans of the Isaq participated in the raid, although they were hereditary enemies, is striking and testifies to the powers of Sayyid Muhammad in mediation and conciliation, to say nothing of his ability to create enthusiasm for the jihad. He was forging new political links and trying to make a united front of Somali clans, membership in the Salihiya being one of the stronger bonds tying together men of different origins.

The Jigjiga affair did nothing to lessen the standing of the Sayyid amongst the clans. As for the British, who had been occupied with a campaign against the Muhammad Zubayr clan of the Ogadin in Jubaland (a reprisal for the murder of an overzealous official named Jenner), they now realized that they would have to deal seriously with Sayyid Muhammad and that he might prove to be a difficult and elusive enemy.[38]

It would be repetitious to recapitulate the details of the British, Ethiopian, and Italian campaigns against Sayyid Muhammad. This has already been done very ably by Hess and Lewis.[39] From the standpoint of his enemies, the problem was how to destroy the Sayyid's forces and to capture or neutralize him. The British – first alone and later in combination with the Italians and Ethiopians – joined together to pursue the Sayyid into remote regions and try to corner him, deny him water, take his food supplies away, and cut off his shipments of guns and ammunition coming from Jibuti, Ethiopia, or Arabia.

Here the British and their allies faced difficult problems. To their cost they learned that a mere "punitive expedition" would not suffice, for the Sayyid was no insignificant foe like the Muhammad Zubayr. By 1903, he probably had about 6,000 men, with 1,000 or 2,000 auxiliaries. Of these, fewer than half were armed with rifles. In difficult terrain, much of it covered with low scrub and thorn trees, the dervishes had the advantages of good mobility and, generally, of surprise. No matter where they went, except in the territory of certain coastal sultans, most Somali Muslims, even if they were not Salihis, naturally sided with their own countrymen against the foreigners. Hence the Sayyid's men had relatively few supply difficulties, save the provision of imported arms and munitions.[40]

In contrast, the slow-moving British units were fighting in a country almost unknown to them, in great heat, with poor knowledge of watering points, with their operations limited to a period of less than half the year (January to May). They were encumbered by elaborate baggage trains of indispensable but heavy war material. All of this had to be brought up from the coasts by imported Indian camels, as the Somali variety are inferior for big loads. Their coordination with their Italian and Ethiopian allies was poor. The Somali "guides" and mercenaries whom they hired frequently deserted, taking their weapons along. In addition, the English brought to Somalia Sikh troops, Baluchis, Yaos, South Africans, and Englishmen; consequently, there were often problems in communication, to say nothing of the inevitable friction. Each ethnic group also required large amounts of food of many different varieties – a further complication to the already complex supply problem. At the start of hostilities, therefore, and until the Illig Convention of 1905, the contest between the Sayyid and the English can be compared to a struggle between a wasp and an elephant.

Like so many guerrilla leaders, Sayyid Muhammad's difficulties in the strictly military sense – with the exception of the matter of European arms – were less serious than questions of organization, discipline, and loyalty. Only if he avoided big pitched battles and continued to harass his foes by ingenious guerilla warfare and ambush could he hope to succeed. He wanted to create his version of a theocratic Muslim state and to maintain his alliances with other clans by marriages and by exchanges of arms, livestock, and gifts. Essentially, the Sayyid's political appeal was made to moderate Muslim opinion among his followers and other Somalis; he was always able to exploit their justifiable resentment at the takeover of their lands by armed and uninvited aliens. This was another link binding his forces together.

The Sayyid's forces were supplied with the simplest of "uniforms" – a white cotton outer garment (worn by most Somali men of the time anyway), a white turban, a *tasbih* (or rosary), and a rifle.[41] Many of the dervishes also had small horses or ponies of their own and already possessed firearms. Often these were of French origin – Lebels or Le Gras rifles (model 1874) and Martini-Henrys – with an occasional captured Lee-Metford or American Remington or Winchester. Other weapons, such as swords, muzzle-loaders, oryx-hide shields, and flat or barbed spears, they furnished themselves. The majority of Sayyid

Muhammad's followers were mounted, but on occasion they fought on foot.[42] Grandiloquently, the Somali historian Jama' 'Umar 'Isa notes that they "preferred death to life under the shadow of imperialism and tyranny" but that they were also men "who resembled their pious ancestors in the strength of their faith, their ability to fight, and their confidence in God."[43] These judgments are confirmed by contemporary British and Italian observers.

From the time of the first three British expeditions against the Sayyid, in 1901, 1902, and 1903, the advantages of military weight and effective firepower on one side were equally matched by determination and mobility on the other. One example of this was the breaking by the dervishes of a reconnaisance column of the King's African Rifles under Colonel A. W. V. Plunkett at Gumburu Hill. In this engagement, 9 British officers and 187 men were killed and 29 wounded – Englishmen, Sikhs, Yaos, and Somali auxiliaries. Such a defeat as this had not been administered to a British force by African "natives" since the days of the Sudanese mahdi, whose men had frequently routed British "squares" in the 1880s.[44]

An eyewitness account from the dervish side at the Battle of Gumburu Hill illustrates the savagery of these encounters, in which no prisoners were taken:

> When the enemy force approached, the Sayyid had divided his army into four, placing each section in a separate area. After a short interval the English army came over a little mountain and the two sides met face to face at 7 a.m. on 17 April 1903. The fighting started and it was said that the English commander had shackled the feet of his men and lashed some to others to prevent them from fleeing and to make them fight. It was the custom of the Dervishes not to halt their assaults until they had penetrated among the enemy . . . for they believed whoever died . . . would ultimately reach the Garden of Felicity after death. The battle went on until four in the afternoon. Victory flew to the Dervish side and innumerable amounts of booty – property and war material – were obtained. The British army was horribly defeated. On that day, their [Dervishes] biggest capture was ten Maxim guns. The number of British slain could not be counted. The bodies of the dead lay in heaps and blood flowed downhill like a brook. Only about six [British] officers and men escaped, but many of the Dervishes died there as well.[45]

To commemorate occasions like these, the Sayyid often composed poetry in Arabic or Somali. Here are a few lines from one of his Arabic poems as cited by 'Isa:

Salutations to the Brothers
  Who have barred the Gate!
They have built the foundations of religion
  By striking downward blows on necks!
From years of plundering, by raids on horseback,
  Events in the land are
Like a raging torrent!
  The expectations of the enemy are ground down
By the number of widows, their rewards,
  By the heaping-up of griefs which
Desolate their youthful state.[46]

For Sayyid Muhammad, the clashes at Gumburu Hill, Daratoleh, and other points inland from Obbia (Hubya), where the British had landed with Italian cooperation, had turned out very well. The British expedition of 1903 – the object of which was to trap the Sayyid in open country without water in the dry season – was a failure. The English force finally had to withdraw into British Somaliland. Another expedition under a new general, Egerton, followed in 1904. This was a second attempt to carry out the earlier strategy, and it also failed when the Sayyid and his men slipped through the British lines. This time, too, another costly and difficult expedition had been a fiasco. Although a naval landing force had taken Illig, an important port on the Indian Ocean coast that the Sayyid had fortified, success for the British looked as far away as ever.[47]

Despite his victories, the Sayyid also had suffered heavy losses and needed time to recuperate, recruit more followers, obtain further supplies, and make plans for the immediate future. Hence the end of the 1904 campaign marks a turning point in the activities of the Sayyid as well as the British. He now sought to take advantage of the presence of the Italians in the neighborhood of Mogadishu and the south (the Banadir coast) in order to make peace both with them and with the English. The Sayyid also wished to improve his relations with Yusuf 'Ali Kenadid, the sultan of Obbia, and Boqor 'Uthman, the ruler of the Mijartayn sultanate, which had been intermittently hostile. The territories of Boqor 'Uthman represented a valuable avenue for the importation of arms.[48]

Fortunately for the Sayyid, the Italian side had an able negotiator, fluent in Arabic: Giulio Pestalozza. Pestalozza won the Sayyid's confidence. After protracted negotiations with his own government and the British at Aden, Pestalozza and the Sayyid signed a convention at Illig in March 1905. Two of the provisions of this accord were that the arms and slave trade in the area controlled by the Sayyid was to cease

and that fighting between the Sayyid and his British and Ethiopian
foes was to halt. Nor would there be any hostilities between the
Italians and the Sayyid. A triangular piece of territory, with its point up
the Nogal Valley and one of its sides parallel to the Indian Ocean
shore, was allotted to the Sayyid. This was, in fact, within the area
that the Italians were claiming as their "sphere of influence." Like a
wedge, it was sandwiched between the Mijartayn state to the north
(in the Horn proper) and the Obbia sultanate to the south. The port
of Illig was to be the Sayyid's capital and trading harbor. This arrangement was cemented by exchanges of dowried women (*erko*) for
eligible men in both the Obbia and Mijartayn sultanates.[49]

For British and Italian politicians, the Illig Convention raised hopes
that the Sayyid would remain fixed in his new area, under Italian
protection. They wanted a modus vivendi that would make future
military campaigns unnecessary. Then, too, like the Sayyid, the
Italians and the British could gain time. Yet all parties regarded each
other with such suspicion that the continuing validity of the convention was at stake. Both Yusuf 'Ali Kenadid of Obbia and Boqor
'Uthman were understandably irritated at having had a solution im-
posed on them by the Italians. The Sayyid was now their immediate
neighbor. Further, each sultan had wanted to control the coastal area
around Illig and for some distance inland. Matters were made worse
by both British and Italian criticism of the results of the convention,
which were seen as both impermanent and disadvantageous; it was
said that the Sayyid was merely gaining time and winning prestige. In
fact, the Sayyid was now in a fairly favorable position. He had obtained
something akin to recognition from both the British and the Italians.
And, by an exchange of notes, both powers had regulated their positions in regard to Ethiopia, which had also given tacit assent to the
new arrangements.[50]

Nor was Muhammad 'Abdallah Hasan entirely happy with the outcome of the Illig Convention. He could not look on it as permanent,
because it excluded him from certain areas, such as the Dulbahante
clan region near Bohotle, which he wished to control. He was even
farther away from the Ogadin, inhabited by the Bah Geri – another
clan that had supported him loyally; and his southern "frontiers" were
still some way from Mogadishu, which he wished to include in his
state along with a majority of Somali-speaking areas. About a decade
later, he defined the borders of his state as "the sea and the Mijartayn
clans on the east, the confines of Ethiopia on the west, the Warsangheli
clans and the sea to the north, and Mogadishu to the south."[51] He had
still not succeeded in ridding Somali territories of Europeans and
other "unbelievers"; this was an important objective. Even by negoti-

ating with the enemy, he was risking self-compromise in his followers'
eyes. To agree with them and then to remain quiescent for any period
would have compromised him still further – a political risk he would
have been reluctant to take. Nevertheless, this movement was still
intact. His prestige had never been higher; he was also gaining new
adherents.

Among these were the Bimal clan, who lived between the port of
Marka and the Webi Shebelli. The Bimal had long resisted the Italians,
largely because the Italians had abolished slavery in their district. The
Bimal used many slaves to cultivate their lands along the Webi
Shebelli.[52] Another point of conflict was continuing Italian penetration,
which the Bimal had opposed since 1896. They had also besieged an
Italian garrison at Marka in 1904 and had ambushed and attacked their
enemies repeatedly. From 1903 on, there was contact between the
Sayyid and the Bimal; moreover, the Salihiya had a sufi center (*zawiya*)
in Bimal territory headed by a *shaykh,* 'Abdi Gafle, who could "throw
the evil eye, transform men into animals, or change bullets into water."[53]
The Sayyid sent advice and guidance to the Bimal, and probably
weapons as well. Even so, the clan was finally overcome by the Italians
in 1908, when a number of Bimal chiefs had to go to Mogadishu to
make their submission to the Italian governor. The guidance sent by
the Sayyid was the *Risalat al-Bimal* (*A Message to the Bimal*), which
is a statement of the Sayyid's ideas on the jihad, relations with the
unbelievers, and other points, which will be discussed below.[54] The
timing and the content of the *Risala* also show very clearly that the
Sayyid saw the Illig Convention as a tactical maneuver. Later, he
would take up and lead the jihad again. His advice to the Bimal on
the necessity and significance of the jihad follows these lines.

Within a year of the signing of the convention, its arrangements –
unstable at best – began to crumble. Interclan hostility and mutual
raiding recommenced. The cessation of the arms trade became a dead
letter. It revived, largely through Ethiopia, where independent and
unscrupulous frontier post commanders alternately raided the Somalis
and sold them arms at a good profit. Their objective was to push the
Ethiopian frontier eastward as far as possible. By the spring of 1908,
the three-year truce had largely eroded. The Sayyid and his enemies
faced each other once more. Mutual recriminations and altered aims
made a truce irrecoverable.[55]

Before resuming military operations, the British and Italians jointly
made an ingenious move to undercut the Sayyid's prestige. Although
the exact arrangements – carried out by English and Italian diplomats
in Aden – are still not clear, they successfully suborned the head of
the Salihiya brotherhood, who disavowed the Sayyid. One of the

persons whom they used to approach Muhammad ibn Salih was a former agent of Muhammad 'Abdallah Hasan at Aden, 'Abdallah Sheheri (or Shihri). A member of the Habar Tol Ja'lo clan, he was disillusioned with the Sayyid because one of his wives and some of his relations had been detained by him. He led a group to Muhammad ibn Salih in Mecca, and there he obtained from him a letter reading the Sayyid out of the Salihiya *tariqa*.[56] The letter was full of damaging criticism, and it ended with Muhammad ibn Salih's promise to have no more communication with the Sayyid and his declaration that Muhammad 'Abdallah Hasan was no longer a Muslim.[57]

With this letter, the Italians and British scored a very heavy hit on the Sayyid: they effectively split the Salihiya brotherhood in two – into pro-Sayyid and anti-Sayyid factions.[58] When the letter reached the headquarters of Muhammad 'Abdallah Hasan in March 1909, some waverers immediately deserted him, including his brother-in-law with a large troop of horsemen. Others, who dared to uphold Muhammad Salih's viewpoint (including the *Qadi* of Illig, 'Abdallah Koryo), were personally cut down and killed by him.[59] Nevertheless, the Sayyid made an attempt to excuse himself to the chief of the brotherhood, and a part of a manifesto addressed to him, entitled *Qam' al-Mu'anidin* (*Suppression of the Rebellious*) is extant.[60] Naturally, this communication is largely self-exculpatory and self-justificatory and rejects the points made by Muhammad ibn Salih.

A further effort was made by the English in 1910, with a mission to the Sayyid. It was composed of two "old Sudan hands," Rudolf Slatin Pasha and Sir Reginald Wingate, who was at the time governor-general of the Sudan. With the joint prestige of these two men and their knowledge of dervishes – at least those of the Sudanese Mahdi – the government in London was convinced that they would somehow succeed in getting the Sayyid to make peace, to come to terms. This oversimple approach failed completely; the report of the two experts still remains unpublished.[61]

On the failure of the Slatin-Wingate mission, and after some months of deliberation, the British government came to the conclusion that the lives and expense that would be required for further military expeditions in Somalia would not be justified by the results. Hence, London adopted a policy of "coastal concentration." In practical terms, this meant the abandonment to the Sayyid of the interior of the area claimed by the British, who now took over such towns as Hargeisa and Burao along with most of the military outposts and minor fortifications of the interior. Another, less fortunate, aspect of this policy was to allow such tribes as had had good relations with the British to arm themselves or to be furnished with arms for self-protection by the withdrawing English. The actual consequences were perhaps less related to self-defense than had been imagined; Caroselli describes the distribution of weapons as a "capital error." It led, he says, to an "awakening of the spirit of vendetta, and the taste for violence and rapine . . . the levelling of old scores and blood feuds. . . . The sport of the *razzia* became a daily affair . . . resulting in bloody anarchy."[62]

Another observer, G. H. Thesiger, writing in 1912, commented on certain consequences of the "coastal concentration" policy at Berbera: "Berbera is now full of starving refugees, who are literally eating any filth they can pick up, and the unfortunate [Commissioner H. A.] Byatt cannot feed them, because, if he did, thousands more would flock in and it would be literally impossible to supply the country."[63]

In the same year, the British reversed their policy of abandoning the inland areas in favor of a limited holding operation. This meant the dispatch of more Indian troops to Somalia and the reemployment of a small number of Somali mercenaries. This was a significant change of policy, and although the British were unable to move back into the areas claimed by them until after World War I, it was clear that London was contemplating further and perhaps decisive moves against the Sayyid.[64]

For his part, the Sayyid had moved away from the Italian-occupied area into the region claimed by the British – into Dulbahante territory. Here, after importing some Arab masons from Yaman, he built a number of forts. The largest of these was at Talih (or Taleh) and served as his headquarters until 1920.[65] Other forts were erected at Jid 'Ali and Madishe, north of Taleh. The construction of Taleh Fort, with its enclosed wells and food storage facilities, suggests that it was destined by the Sayyid to be the permanent capital of his emergent Muslim state.

In addition to concentrating Indian and Somali troops at Berbera, the British created a camel constabulary, the Somaliland Camel Corps. It was assembled to guard the town and the adjacent areas. The corps was also recruited to assist the "friendlies," such as the Isaq clans, whose encampments and animals were so often the target of dervish raids. This was frequently done without the Sayyid's knowledge or permission. The commander of the force was Captain Richard Corfield, a professional officer who had grown tired of monotonous policing operations.

He longed to strike at the dervishes. In August 1913, after a heavy raid by the Sayyid's men, he could no longer restrain himself and led his men after the retreating raiders.

Daringly, the injudicious Corfield placed himself and his camelmen across the dervish line of retreat. He was immediately attacked by them, and he and many of his men were casualties. At the start of the battle, his Dulbahante auxiliaries had also deserted him. This episode at Dulmadobe ("Black Hill") was a serious blow to rising British prestige. It was also the occasion of one of the Sayyid's finest Somali poems, which begins:

> O Corfield, you are a traveller who
>   Will not stay long here below
> You will follow the Path where there is no rest
>   You who are among the Denizens of Hell
> You will journey to the Next World.[66]

The results of the clash at Dulmadobe were felt quickly; in 1914 the Sayyid and his men raided Berbera and its outskirts with little opposition.

Meanwhile, the British, hard-pressed by the Central Powers at so many points, were unable to do much in Somalia except undertake token activities, such as the attack on the Shimber Berris forts in 1915.[67] All the same, the long lull had its effects on both sides. By inactivity, by the building of masonry forts, the Sayyid's situation altered drastically. Stone forts are fixed, immobile, and the Sayyid himself had become overconfident. The roles of attackers and defenders were reversed; the British could go over to the offensive whenever they wished. The Sayyid and the dervishes were now the targets – defending their flocks, forts, wells, and encampments. This was a style of warfare that did not suit them at all. When they abandoned their older, basic strategy of guerrilla warfare, their hopes for ultimate success evaporated.

For a time, this new but unfavorable situation was masked by another success for the Sayyid. He made an alliance with the new Ethiopian emperor, Lij Yasu. Lij Yasu was both pro-Muslim and in favor of the Central Powers. He was in touch with the Sayyid, one of whose daughters he hoped to marry. But Lij Yasu's Islamic inclinations alarmed and alienated many of his Christian Amhara subjects. With his deposition in 1916, the nightmare of Allied politicians – a hostile Muslim state in the Horn of Africa – receded. Yet during his period of friendly contact with the Sayyid, the new emperor had sent a German technician (Emil Kirsch) to Taleh. Muhammad 'Abdallah Hasan used this man to repair and recondition rifles, machine guns, and other pieces of ordnance. Badly mistreated by the Sayyid, Kirsch escaped from Taleh only to die of thirst as he tried to reach the coast.[68]

The Sayyid was also in contact with the Germans and Turks in South Arabia. He employed an emissary named Ahmad Shirwa' bin

Mahmud, who visited the Turkish commander at Lahj near Aden in 1916 and 1917. The commander, 'Ali Sa'id Pasha, agreed to recognize the Sayyid on condition that he acknowledge the overlordship of the Ottoman Sultan-caliph, Mehmet V Rashad. This agreement may have been dictated by the Sayyid's Pan-Islamic sympathies, but he wanted also to be on the winning side in case the Turks and Germans were victorious. Indeed, as Caroselli suggests, it is not certain that the Sayyid ever saw the document outlining this agreement; it was intercepted by the Italians before it reached him. However, a Turkish adviser, Mehmet 'Ali, did reach Taleh, where he was ultimately captured by the British.[69]

One of the literary byproducts of the Sayyid's contacts with the Turks of Lahj was a long panegyric in Arabic addressed to the Ottoman ruler. Conventional in form but fresh in imagery and in conception, parts of it deserve translation:

> I send you my greetings from Duha
>> Increased by seven and by seven
> Black as the night may be, and gloomy
>> The Sun of Noon comes near
> And day intensifies in strength, burning with light
>> Suddenly a mirage flickers
> Heat sears the face
>> The breeze brings a pleasant odor
> A wind sweeps above the ground
>> Branches bend and sway
> As rainclouds shake and rumble
>> Lightning flashes, striking a cloud
> Water pours down in a flood
>> Falling on the lowlands
> The scent of it drifts with the wind
>> At sunrise a cock cries
> And chants into the morning
>> A file of camels walks with even step
> While horses march in the dawn
>> Yet the rider has reined in
> Borne down by the weight of his burden
>> Crushed by the unbelievers . . .
> And he turns to his Dear Friend
>> Taking refuge with that Pillar of Religion
> Girded by glory and most firm in dignity
>> A broad spreading tree of munificence
> The distributor of God's benefits
>> Unique, he shows himself towering

> Above others, unattainable
>> Looking down over those who praise him
> Sultan of every Victory
>> Twister of Tyrants
> Who strikes out the Eye of Unbelief
>> Who lashes unbelievers
> Breaks their power
>> And treads on their necks
> The great among them he cuts down
>> What they bind up, he tears apart
> He strikes blows from every side
>> He slits their tongues like young camels
> Whatever they have, he conquers
>> Whatever they possess, he strikes down
> See the rabble, struck silent
>> Poisoned to the heart, they run to their burrows
> Opinion over this is unanimous
>> His position is most exalted
> How many times he strikes at them
>> Disdainfully, with a spear![70]

Once the war was over, in 1918, the British could deal with their colonial "problems" at leisure. In their eyes, the dervish movement, with its leader, was one of the oldest and most troublesome. The successes of Muhammad 'Abdallah Hasan had embarrassed the London government more than once; the British were anxious to come to a conclusion with him. New weapons and new military techniques, such as aircraft, promised them final success. Accordingly, in the first months of 1920, the English assembled their men and launched a "combined operation." It included infantry and camel troops, supported by De Havilland DH 9 bombers. They counted on the factors of surprise and fright as well as on the ability of the pilots to pursue the dervishes from the air, bombing and machine-gunning with little fear of retaliation. The combined strategy also called for the encirclement of Taleh and its adjoining forts, together with the sealing of any escape routes that the Sayyid might attempt to use, either southward toward the region of his Bah Geri allies or east into the Mijartayn district.[71]

These methods, particularly bombing, were very successful. The Sayyid and his dwindling number of dervishes were forced to abandon their ill-conceived fortifications and flee westward into Ethiopia. Constantly harried from the air, they were easy targets in the daytime, visible from the columns of dust they raised in flight. On several occasions, the Sayyid narrowly escaped death. But once over the frontier in the Ogadin, where the British could no longer pursue him, he tried to rebuild his army from new recruits. His foes sent him several messages to surrender, but to these he gave no clear answer. One of these offers would have permitted the Sayyid to move to the West Aden Protectorate (now South Yaman Republic) and live there free from interference as the chief of a Salihi settlement. This message was carried to the Sayyid by a delegation of *'ulama'* both from his own brotherhood and from the Ahmadiya and Qadiriya.[72] When they came before him, he humiliated them repeatedly, and he finally refused the offer they bore.

To underline his disdain for the British and their friends, he followed the departure of the delegation with a big dervish raid on some of the Isaq clans. The raid brought heavy losses to the dervishes, who were pursued a long distance by the outraged clansmen. The Isaq also asked the British in Berbera for permission to make a raid in force on the Sayyid, and their request was unhesitatingly granted.[73] Meanwhile Muhammad 'Abdallah Hasan had reached the headwaters of the Webi Shebelli at Gwano Imi. Here, still committed to his disastrous concept of static defense, he constructed a number of forts; all of these were well beyond British-occupied territory. Not long after, in December 1920, at the age of about fifty-six, Sayyid Muhammad 'Abdallah Hasan died, possibly of influenza. With him died the hopes of his followers for an independent Somali Muslim state on the traditional model.

An extract from one of the Sayyid's last poems, cited by 'Isa, shows his forebodings about the future of the Somalis under colonial rule:[74]

> Somalis, arise from sleep!
>   Catastrophe has fallen on the land
> The Unbelievers have deceived you
>   Since you failed to continue the jihad!
> Do not be dazzled by their gifts
>   They carry a lethal poison
> They'll wrest your weapons from you
>   You'll be like defenseless women!
> They'll take away your livestock, putting their brand on it
>   They'll live on them alone
> They'll snatch your money and your land
>   They'll run off with it in front of you, like racehorses!
> I left them behind at Imi and Adar on the plateau
>   By banishing [myself]
> Brothers, what sort of country can it be
>   Where people fall into slavery to them
> On every side?

Muhammad 'Abdallah Hasan's Writings

Until recently, the writings of Muhammad 'Abdallah Hasan seemed limited to poetry in Somali. "Writings" is not an accurate definition, as the poems were recited by the Sayyid to men in his entourage who memorized them. Others did the same in turn, and they spread throughout the country by word of mouth. In this way, the Sayyid created an effective kind of propaganda. Although it was known that the Sayyid composed poetry in Arabic, his Arabic prose works were largely unknown, even though Andrzejewski and Lewis stated that a number of "Arabic manuscript works on religious themes" existed.[75] Until now the content of these "religious writings" have remained a mystery. Since 1965, two of these have become known. They yield sufficient information about Muhammad 'Abdallah Hasan's political and religious opinions to classify him quite clearly as a follower of Ibn Taymiya, as a man to some extent influenced by the Arabian Wahhabis, and as a champion of reforming Islam in general. Until more of these texts can be recovered, perhaps from the relatives and descendants of the Sayyid at Mogadishu or elsewhere, many of the details of his thinking will remain unknown. Obviously, the conclusions offered here are tentative and will have to be modified in the light of whatever may turn up.

The two texts that are now known are the *Risalat al-Bimal* (*Message to the Bimal*) and the *Qam' al-Mu'anidin* (*Suppression of the Rebellious*).[76] Taken together, they clarify many points of the Sayyid's ideology. They show what great intellectual resources the Sayyid possessed and how significant he was as a religious and political leader.

Unfortunately, no more than a quarter of the *Qam'* is accessible. It is a long apology to Shaykh Muhammad Salih written in 1909 as an answer to the Shaykh's letter of disavowal. In its first lines the author describes it as a *wathiqa* (manifesto) with two purposes. The first is to greet Muhammad Salih. The second is 1) to discuss whether his own beliefs are such that he can still be called a Muslim, 2) to comment on the condition of the Somalis, 3) to define the enemy and those who have relations with them, 4) to refute a denunciation of himself by one Mahmud bin Yusuf al-Warsanghali, and 5) to justify his own actions and exculpate himself from Muhammad Salih's accusations.[77]

This fragment only includes a part of the first section, which breaks off in the midst of a discussion of the ability of prophets to communicate whatever they wish to mankind.[78] Among other arguments tending to prove his orthodoxy, Muhammad 'Abdallah Hasan makes a number of political observations. One of these illustrates the conventionality of his opinions about politics. He speaks of the "order of the world" (*nizam al-'alam*) maintained by "governors, *walis*, and sultans."[79] Defining his own attachments, he claims that he is of Hashimi descent; a member of the Salihi brotherhood; a Shafi'i in his legal views; and theologically, an adherent of al-'Ash'ari.[80] He omits to mention that he is an admirer of the eighteenth-century theologian Muhammad ibn 'Abd al-Wahhab and a student of the fourteenth-century neo-Hanbali thinker Ibn Taymiya.

The *Risala* reveals far more about the Sayyid's doctrines and beliefs.[81] As he did in the *Qam'*, the Sayyid states at the outset that he had two aims in writing it. One was to praise the Bimal for their energetic resistance to the Italians. The second was to clarify some doctrinal points and answer criticisms made by those who opposed the "holy war" (jihad).[82] Here the Sayyid proceeds systematically, discussing twelve points in turn. Of these, the first four concern the jihad. According to the Sayyid, it is an inescapable duty for all Muslims. It is an individual obligation (*fard 'ayni*), particularly now (the *Risala* was written about 1905) that "unbelievers have invaded Muslim lands." The jihad is a perpetual obligation, not a duty that has ended in the past. At all times, it is one of the most excellent things any Muslim can do.[83] As for those who claim that the rituals of a brotherhood, the *wird* or the *dhikr*, are acceptable substitutes for the jihad, this is false.[84] In any case, the jihad is a pillar of the faith. This discussion ends with comments on the various sorts of jihads – the little jihad, which is equivalent to the jihad against unbelievers; the great jihad against the self; and the *jihad al-nafus*, which is left undefined.[85]

Muhammad 'Abdallah Hasan now attacks the Christian invaders. Some Somalis, he says, praise the Christians and attribute the well-being of the people and the prosperity of the land to them, likewise the increase in the population.[86] All of this is lies and falsehood; any person who so praises the unbelievers is himself suspect of unbelief. The growth of the population or an improvement in its welfare cannot emanate from the Christians. This is so because of their fundamental hostility to Muslims. Nor can justice (*'adala*) derive from any Christian source, nor from other unbelievers. Justice, the Sayyid explains, can only arise from God's Book and the *Sunna*. Hence, any Muslim who calls the Christians just is making God an unbeliever. Those who have to do with the Christians, the Sayyid warns, led on by their wishes for worldly gain, are already in serious trouble. This argument is supported by long quotations from a book by 'Abdallah al-Ahdal, *Al-Sayf al-Battar 'ala man yuwali al-kuffar* (*The Trenchant Sword against Those Who Befriend Unbelievers*).[87]

The Sayyid emphasizes the danger of consorting with Christians. Any Muslim who goes to a Christian country and lives there exposes his faith – to say nothing of his way of life – to eventual contamination and degeneration.[88] He goes on to quote Ibn Hajar's *Al-Fatawi al-haditha,* in which it is written that Muslims ought not to have their cooking fires nor their houses near those of Christians.[89] Indeed, the idea of withdrawal (*hijra*) from the proximity of Christians is more than commendable.[90] The less a believer has to do with Christians, the better. Over this point, so often ventilated by Muslim leaders of the nineteenth century, Muhammad 'Abdallah Hasan is aligned with the majority.

Nor should Muslims consort with "outsiders" or the "hangers-on" of the Christians. They are already condemned in the *Qur'an* (III, 118): "O you who believe, do not take the hangers-on as friends."[91] In the eyes of the Sayyid, such persons are dubious Muslims and can only cause trouble. He warns against the familiars and associates of the Christians; these may be clerks, doormen, mercenaries, or clan heads who have attached themselves to foreigners. All of them are undesirables. The Sayyid makes much of another Qur'anic quotation (IV, 140): "If you persist in keeping company with unbelievers, you will become like them."[92]

Other things condemned by Muhammad 'Abdallah Hasan are wearing "infidel clothing," sporting foreign hair styles, "walking" like an unbeliever, or exhibiting outlandish manners of any sort. Studying the books of the unbelievers or participating in their gatherings or festivals is illicit; it can be confused too easily with love for them.[93] Here the Sayyid quotes with relish a saying of the Prophet: "Whoever resembles a certain people, then he is one of them." This tradition is followed by a quotation from Ibn Taymiya concerning persons who attend the celebrations or the festivals of foreigners.[94] The Sayyid's close ties to the doctrines of Ibn Taymiya will be discussed further below.

To justify his attacks on other Muslims, Muhammad 'Abdallah Hasan states that such hostilities can be warranted when the others aid or keep company with unbelievers. On this basis, interference with them is praiseworthy, for "we believe that they are unbelievers pure and simple."[95] Incorrect beliefs or actions might also be grounds for stigmatizing a person as an unbeliever. Examples of such unbelief are individuals who refuse to say the profession of faith, do not appear at Friday prayers, or abandon the Muslim community. These arguments are developed at length.[96]

The Sayyid then turns to a point that occupied as much of his thinking as the jihad problem. This is the matter of *tawassul* – intercession for individuals by the Prophet or his companions. The Sayyid expressly excludes the validity of such intercession by a deceased saint. As a corollary, visits to the tombs or graves of deceased holy men are forbidden.[97] This issue is crucial in comprehending Muhammad 'Abdallah Hasan's theological views and is the central doctrine of the *Risala*. The argument over *tawassul* explains why the Sayyid and his Qadiri enemies adopted such mutually hostile and irreconcilable positions. To Muhammad 'Abdallah Hasan, intercession through the Prophet or his companions was wholly acceptable, whereas intercession by way of local saints and traditional holy men was not. The latter position was espoused without restriction by the Qadiriya. The Sayyid had already encountered these opinions during his stay in Berbera in the 1890s.

The key dogma of intercession – defined loosely by the Qadiriya but strictly by the Sayyid – is not only the central point of the conflict between these opposing attitudes; it also epitomizes the struggle within Islam between traditional and reforming sufism that had been going on since the time of Ibn Taymiya (1262–1328) or before. In the continuing battle, the traditional sufis were ranged against the neo-Hanbalis – Ibn Taymiya, his pupil Ibn Qayyim al-Jawziya, Ibn Hajar, and other hanbalizing members of the Shafi'i school.[98] Later representatives of the same trend were the Arabian reformer Muhammad ibn 'Abd al-Wahhab and Ahmad ibn Idris al-Fasi, the immediate intellectual ancestor of the Salihiya. The locus classicus of the criticism of loose intercession is Ibn Taymiya's book, *Qa'ida Jalila fi'l-tawassul wa'l-wasila*.[99]

The adherents of the reforming tradition attacked what they saw as dangerous tendencies gaining ground in Islam. Simultaneously, they stressed a definition of God that emphasized God's remoteness and transcendance. On the other hand, traditional sufis had emphasized the immanence of God in nature and His closeness; they were inclined to pantheism. These underlying, opposing attitudes found expression in clashes over *tawassul*.

The warfare between these two orders, Salihiya and Qadiriya, over these points had a great deal in common with the struggles of the Arabian Wahhabis and their traditional sufi opponents at the close of the eighteenth and the start of the nineteenth centuries. In these disputes, often very bloody, loose *tawassul* was a fundamental issue.[100] It had been attacked with vigor by Muhammad ibn 'Abd al-Wahhab in his *Kitab al-Tawhid*. The scene of these schisms was only a few hundred miles from Somalia, on the other side of the Red Sea. Had this sort of reforming Islam not found a vehicle in the Salihiya brotherhood, it might have entered Somalia in some other guise. Without the presence of the French, British, and Italians, the dispute might have created a large-scale religious split, even warfare, among the Somalis. The presence of the encroaching colonialists doubtless decelerated or hindered the spread of such a quarrel.

Although the quantity of material from the Salihi side is very sparse, a number of pro-Qadiri writers were very active in Somalia. Their polemic writings, prose or poetry in Arabic, often throw the doctrines of the Salihiya into relief. In addition to southern Somalis such as Shaykh Uways bin Muhammad and Shaykh Qasim al-Barawi[101] – who wrote relatively little – there was also the important northern Somali polemicist Shaykh 'Abdallah ibn Mu'allim Yusuf al-Qutbi of Kolonkol. IIis collection of polemics, *Al-Majmu'at al-mubaraka* (*The Blessed Collection*) was published in Cairo in 1338/1919–20.[102] All five pieces in the collection are written to confute the Salihis; this is illustrated by the uncompromising title of one of them, "The Sacrificial Knife for Barking Dogs."[103] Another is called the "Victory of the Believers over the Rebellious Heretics."[104] In al-Qutbi's vocabulary, "barking dogs" and "rebellious heretics" are mild epithets. He applies them indiscriminately to the Salihiya, the Wahhabis, and also to Ibn Taymiya, by name.[105]

In the "Victory of the Believers," al-Qutbi's arguments are frequently repeated in various forms and they are easily summarized. First, the Salihiya is to him a doctrinally eclectic group that has adopted its "vicious and damaging" doctrines from all quarters: the Kharijites, the Shi'is, the Mu'tazila, and the Murji'a, among others.[106] From the Kharijites, he says, they have adopted the stand that an attack on the lives or the possessions of other Muslims who do not adhere to their views is lawful. From the Shi'is they have adopted their dubious distinction between dead and live saints. From the Murji'a they have taken the opinion that although an individual's sins may be "as numerous as the waves of the sea," they are forgiven by the mere repetition of the profession of faith, the *shahada*. From the Wahhabis they have adopted the position of hindering pilgrimages and visits to the tomb of the Prophet, because they abhor any sort of *tawassul*.[107] Yet certain arguments, he declares, may be made for this practice. Al-Qutbi also says flatly that the Salihiya is fundamentally anti-intellectual and wishes to hinder the reading of devotional books and the law texts of the various schools. To this Shaykh 'Abdallah adds the standard accusations of "unbelief" and of "undesirable innovation." The Salihiya will not pray behind a man who has hair on his head. Finally, states Qutbi, a comprehensive refutation of the Salihis may be found in

books such as Ahmad ibn Zayni Dahlan's *Al-Durar al-Saniya*. To all
practical purposes Salihis and Wahhabis are doctrinally interchangeable.[108]

Shaykh al-Qutbi then turns his polemical skills to the problem of
intercession. He claims that there is no difference between *tawassul*
to the Prophet himself and *tawassul* through subordinate intermediaries
for the same purpose. In fact the Salihis have already committed unbelief because they want to interfere with a principal Muslim duty,
the pilgrimage. Further, the deceased saint in his tomb is in the "inter-
mediate state" – he has a special sort of existence between death and
life that leaves his spiritual powers unimpaired. Hence there is no
difference between a dead saint or a live one, as the Salihiya, the
Wahhabis, or their master Ibn Taymiya pretend.[109]

Nor can Shaykh Muhammad Salih be the "spiritual pole" of the
age, much less the "Great Intermediary." He is merely a Meccan
shaykh, not even a member of the "House of the Prophet." Moreover,
well-regarded "men of religion" do not speak favorably of him.[110]
Neither he nor Sayyid Muhammad 'Abdallah Hasan can properly
claim to be independent interpreters of the law (*mujtahids*). Shaykh
al-Qutbi agrees with the Arab writer al-Suyuti (d. 1504) that the gate
of "independent legal decision" had been closed about 500 years
previously. Hence, any person claiming to be a *mujtahid* is automatically suspect.[111] Although Shaykh Muhammad Salih may have
achieved some popularity, he is nevertheless worthy of condemnation.
He is in error and misleads others. Thus, his brotherhood, in al-Qutbi's
eyes, is a "deceptive, Pharaonic, and Satanic" organization. Al-Qutbi's
criticism is by no means restrained; wielding his verbal knife, he says
openly that the murder of a Salihi is as meritorious in God's sight as
the slaying of "a hundred hostile unbelievers."[112] As Cerulli points
out, such inflammatory prose "provoked bitter polemics with the
Salihiya on its appearance in Somalia."[113]

Toward the end of his epistle, al-Qutbi defends tobacco smoking,
coffee drinking, the use of the narcotic *qat*, and certain eating and
slaughtering practices offensive to the Salihiya.[114] If tobacco is on the
fringe of acceptability, coffee is the "fruit of the saints," despite the
condemnation of some writers. As for *qat*, it is admittedly controversial but not actually forbidden.[115] Dancing by sufis, like drumming
and dancing at weddings and other festivities, is acceptable.[116]

Significantly, the "Victory of the Believers" contains no attack on
Muhammad 'Abdallah Hasan for claiming to be a mahdi. This issue
has been brought up repeatedly by various writers, most recently by
the Egyptian Muhammad al-Mu'tasim Sayyid in his *Mahdi al-Sumal*

(Cairo, 1963). But the claim was not advanced by the Sayyid himself, often as it was alleged by others.

However, the mutually hostile attitudes of the Qadiriya and Salihiya and the smoke of sectarian polemic cannot obscure the real achievements of Sayyid Muhammad 'Abdallah Hasan. He had remarkable gifts as a leader of men, a politician, and a religious personality. His abilities were many-sided. He brought into being a theocratic Muslim state, which he conceived along the lines of reforming Islam as laid down by Ibn Taymiya and Ahmad al-Idris al-Fasi. (As his enemies realized, he may have been influenced somewhat by the Wahhabis, too.) With the Salihiya as an organizational underpinning for his movement, he founded an ideology and built a framework that allowed him to mount a military movement that was both long sustained and successful, perhaps more so than any other movement led by an African Muslim leader of the nineteenth or early twentieth century. For more than twenty years he held off repeated British and Italian attempts to crush him. Above all, he hindered the two powers from carrying out their plans of exploitation to the fullest. He tied their hands and made them spend huge sums and many lives on purely military operations. In this way, he maintained and defended the traditional Somali Muslim values and ways of life.

Notes

Introduction

1 J. S. Trimingham, *The Sufi Orders in Islam,* Oxford, 1971, p. 14. See also A. M. M. Mackeen, "The Rise of al-Shadhili," *JAOS,* 91, 1971, pp. 477–86.

2 W. S. Haas, "The Zikr of the Rahmaniya Order in Algeria: A Psychological Analysis," *MW,* 33, 1943, pp. 16–28. Some researchers have suggested that these techniques may be of ancient Jewish, Christian, or Indian origin, but wherever they started, they have been known and used for a long time.

3 B. G. Martin, "A Short History of the Khalwati Order of Dervishes," in N. Keddie (ed.), *Scholars, Saints, and Sufis,* Berkeley 1972, pp. 276–305.

4 A phrase coined by T. O. Ranger.

5 Fazlur Rahman, *Islam,* N.Y. 1968, Chapter XII.

6 For this Islamic revival, credit is customarily given to a number of Indian and Arab thinkers, including Ahmad Sirhindi, Shah Waliallah of Delhi, Murtada al-Zabidi, Mustafa al-Bakri al-Nabulusi, and Shaykh Khalid of Shahrazur. A parallel movement, which rejected sufism, is the Wahhabi one, led by Muhammad ibn 'Abd al-Wahhab. Here a neo-Hanbali strain entered Islam, which influenced Muhammad 'Abdallah Hasan (see Chapter 7), mediated by Ahmad ibn Idris al-Fasi, a Moroccan sufi. Other contributors to this broad trend were Muhammad al-Hifnawi (Shaykh of the Azhar, d. 1768) and Mahmud al-Kurdi, who influenced the Tijanis, the Rahmaniya, and the Sammaniya. Via his teacher, Jibril ibn 'Umar, Usuman dan Fodio was influenced by the Khalwatiya, and the Amir 'Abd al-Qadir through the Naqshbandis, in all probability. In the chapters below, these lines of intellectual descent will be followed in more detail.

7 The idea of political succession to the Prophet in Islam.

8 See A. J. Toynbee, *Survey of International Affairs,* I, Oxford 1927, pp. 25–32.

9 Albert Hourani, *Arabic Thought in the Liberal Age, 1798–1939,* Oxford 1967; Bernard Lewis, *The Middle East and the West,* London 1968, *passim.*

10 B. G. Martin, "Five Letters from the Tripoli Archives," *JHSN,* 2, 1964, pp. 365–6.

11 Anthony Reid, *The Contest for North Sumatra: Acheh, the Netherlands and Britain, 1858–98,* Oxford 1969, *passim.* See also A. Reid, "Nineteenth-Century Pan-Islam in Indonesia and Malaysia," *Journal of Asian Studies,* 26, 1967, pp. 267–283; "Habib Abdur-Rahman az-Zahir," *Indonesia,* 13, 1972, pp. 37–59.

12 See F.O. 800/32 and 800/33, Miscellaneous correspondence regarding Turkey, 1889–94 and 1895–1911.

13 'Alawi b. Tahir al-Haddad, *'Uqud al-Almas bi-manaqib . . . Ahmad b. Hasan al-'Attas,* 2nd ed., II, Cairo 1388/1968, pp. 102–103.

14 Abu'l-Huda, *Da'i al-Rashad li-sabil al-ittihad wa'l-inqiyad,* Istanbul n.d., p. 6.

15 Muhammad Zafir al-Madani, *Nur al-sati' wa Burhan al-Qati'*, Istanbul 1301/ 1883–4, p. 58.
16 C. Snouck Hurgronje, "Eenige Arabische Strijdschriften besproken," *Verspreide Geschriften*, 3, 1962, pp. 151–88.
17 Hourani, *Arabic Thought*, p. 110.
18 David Pocock, *Social Anthropology*, London 1971, p. 111.
19 D. S. Margoliouth, "On Mahdism and Mahdis," *Proceedings of the British Academy*, 7, 1916, p. 258.
20 B. G. Martin, "A Mahdist Document from Futa Jallon," *BIFAN*, 25, 1963, p. 62.
21 Anthony F. C. Wallace, *Religion, An Anthropological View*, N.Y. 1966, p. 158 ff.
22 'Abd al-Jalil al-Tamimi, *Buhuth wa watha'iq fi'l-ta'rikh al-Maghribi, 1816–1871*, Tunis 1972, pp. 103–130.
23 See Muhammad al-Mu'tasim Sayyid, *Mahdi al-Sumal*, Cairo 1963.
24 Martin, "A Mahdist Document," p. 53.
25 See M. Barkun, *Disaster and the Millenium*, New Haven 1974.

Chapter 1

1 For a list of Usuman dan Fodio's writings, see D. M. Last, *The Sokoto Caliphate*, London 1968, pp. 237–40.
2 Adolph Brass, "Eine neue Quelle zur Geschichte des Fulreiches Sokoto," *Der Islam*, 10, 1920, p. 2.
3 D. A. Olderogge, "Osman dan Fodios Aufstand und seine Bedeutung," *Akten des XXIV. Orientalistenkongresses*, 26, 1957, p. 735.
4 Abdallahi (H. F. C.) Smith, "The Islamic Revolutions of the 19th Century," *JHSN*, 2, 1961, p. 2.
5 Mervyn Hiskett, "Material Relating to the State of Learning among the Fulani before Their *Jihad*," *BSOAS*, 19, 1957, pp. 550–78.
6 Abdallahi dan Fodio, *Tazyin al-Waraqat*, ed. Mervyn Hiskett, Ibadan 1963, p. 58.
7 See Last, *Caliphate*, p. 73; J. R. Willis (ed.), *The Cultivators of Islam*, London, forthcoming, pp. 54–67; J. A. Ajayi and M. Crowder, *History of West Africa*, I, London 1971, pp. 461–3; and L. Tauxier, *Moeurs et Histoire des Peuls*, Paris 1937, pp. 142–50.
8 Muhammad Bello, *Infaq al-Maysur fi ta'rikh bilad al-Takrur*, Cairo 1383/ 1964, pp. 226–7.
9 For Muhammad al-Kashinawi, see A. D. H. Bivar and Mervyn Hiskett, "The Arabic Literature of Nigeria to 1804: A Provisional Account," *BSOAS*, 25, 1962, pp. 104–148, esp. pp. 135–7. Al-Kashinawi wrote a number of books on magic, the most famous of which is *Al-Durr al-Manzum wa khulasat al-sirr al-maktum fi'l-sihr wa'l-tilasim wa'l-nujum*, Cairo 1381/1961; it contains much material on contemporary magic and poisons. For Muhammad al-Tahir b. Ibrahim al-Fallati, see Bivar and Hiskett, "The Arabic Literature of Nigeria," pp. 135–8. This author composed a long *qasida* on the theological differences between al-Maturidi and al-'Ashari, quoted by the Shehu, part of which is translated below.
10 Last, *Caliphate*, pp. 79–80.
11 Smith, "Revolutions," p. 172.
12 D. M. Last and Muhammad al-Hajj, "Attempts at Defining a Muslim in

19th Century Hausaland and Bornu," *JHSN*, 2, 1965, pp. 231–40.

13   Fathi Hasan al-Masri, "A Critical Edition of Dan Fodio's *Bayan wujub al-Hijra 'ala'l-'ibad*," unpublished Ph.D. thesis, Ibadan 1968, Introduction.

14   Smith, "Revolutions," p. 176.

15   See Usuman Dan Fodio, *Nasa'ih al-ummat al-Muhammadiya*, Section III.

16   Muhammad Bello, *Infaq al-Maysur*, p. 55.

17   *Ibid.*, pp. 207–8.

18   Abdallahi dan Fodio, *Tazuin al-Waraqat*, p. 26. An English translation of the entire poem may be found in Mervyn Hiskett, *The Sword of Truth*, N.Y. 1973, p. 33.

19   F. H. al-Masri, *"Bayan,"* Introduction, p. 15.

20   Abdallahi dan Fodio, *Tazyin al-Waraqat*, p. 27.

21   Mervyn Hiskett, "The Origin, Sources, and Form of Hausa Islamic Verse," *Spectrum*, 3, 1973, pp. 128–9.

22   Mervyn Hiskett, "The Song of the Shehu's Miracles, A Hausa Hagiography from Sokoto," *African Language Studies*, 12, 1971, pp. 89–91.

23   As suggested earlier, the greater part of Usuman's writings in Arabic are now known and available for analysis. His poetry in the Fulani language (Fulfulde) occasionally survives in oral versions or Hausa translations. It may be from such literature that detailed information about certain obscure phases of the Shehu's career will be recovered.

24   Usuman dan Fodio, *Majmu' thalatha kutub* (*Litattafai uku a habe*), Zaria 1962, p. 1.

25   *Ibid.*, pp. 2–3.

26   F. H. al-Masri, "The Life of Shehu Usuman dan Fodio before the *Jihad*," *JHSN*, 2, 1962, p. 445.

27   *Qur'an*, Sura IV, verse 98.

28   Abdallahi dan Fodio, *Tazyin al-Waraqat*; Muhammad Bello, *Infaq al-Maysur, passim.*

29   Abdallahi dan Fodio, *Tazyin al-Waraqat*, pp. 57–8.

30   *Ibid.*, p. 58

31   Usuman dan Fodio, *Bayan wujub al-Hijra 'ala'l-'ibad*, ms. no. 193, Shahuci Judicial School, Kano, from microfilm in the possession of Mervyn Hiskett, fol. 50.

32   See Muhammad Bello, *Infaq al-Maysur*, pp. 155–98, for the correspondence between Bornu and Sokoto.

33   See B. G. Martin, "A Short History of the Khalwati Order of Dervishes," in N. Keddie (ed.), *Scholars, Saints, and Sufis*, Berkeley 1972, pp. 275–305. See also J. O. Hunwick's analysis of Abdallahi dan Fodio's *Bayan al-arkan wa'l-shurut li'l-tariqat al-sufiya was talqin al-asma' al-sab'a 'ala tariqat al-Sadat al-Khalwatiya, CADRB*, 1, 1965, p. 48.

34   Martin, "Short History," p. 300.

35   Mervyn Hiskett, "The Nineteenth Century Jihads in West Africa," in the *Cambridge History of Africa*, V, Cambridge, forthcoming, Chapter 6. An uncatalogued Arabic *qasida* in the 'Umar Falke Collection at Northwestern University Library c. 1790 supports Jibril's position and speaks of "the gross sins amongst the people/There are twenty kinds, each with a recognizable symptom, they say/" This poem may be evidence for an abortive jihad, or at least a major theological controversy of that time.

36   See Usuman Dan Fodio, *Ihya' al-Sunna*, Cairo edition 1382/1962, pp. 126–8. Here Usuman deals with burials, funeral customs, and tombs. The discus-

sion by the Shehu in this connection about permissible *tawassul* (intercession by a deceased person) shows just how far Usuman stood from the Wahhabis, who would not admit any sort of *tawassul*.

37 D. S. Margoliouth, "On Mahdis and Mahdism," *Proceedings of the British Academy*, 7, 1916, pp. 213–33, esp. p. 231.

38 For the idea of the *mujaddid*, see I. Goldziher, "Zur Charakteristik Gelal el Din us-Sujuti's und seiner literarischen Thaetigkeit," *Sitzungsbericht, Wiener Akademie der Wissenschaften*, 69, 1871, pp. 7–28.

39 Adamu 'Abdallah Iluri, *Al-Islam fi Nijiriya wa 'Uthman ibn Fudi*, Cairo 1368/1948, p. 29.

40 Iluri (see previous note) gives the date of Umm Hani's death as 860 H., p. 28. The text of the prophecy appears in Muhammad Bello, *Infaq al-Maysur*, p. 57.

41 See al-Suyuti, *Al-Kashf 'an mujawaza hadhihi'l-ummat al-alf*, ms. Loth 1031/Bijapur 85, India Office Library, London, an appendix to 'Ali Husam al-Din al-Hindi, *Al-Burhan fi 'alamat Mahdi akhir al-zaman*. On folio 67a of this manuscript, al-Suyuti says, "Na'im also stated on the authority of Abu Qubayl . . . that people expect the Mahdi in the year 1204." See also M. al-Hajj, "The 13th Century in Muslim Eschatology: Mahdist Expectations in the Sokoto Caliphate," *CADRB*, 3, 1967, pp. 100–16.

42 Al-Hajj, "Expectations," p. 114.

43 See Paul Lovejoy and Stephen Baier, "The Desert-Side Economy of the Central Sudan," *IJAHS*, 8, 1975, forthcoming.

44 In Thomas Hodgkin's unpublished paper, "Usuman dan Fodio," on p. 4, he says "Much of his [Usuman's] support came from the *talakawa*, the Hausa peasantry. Their economic and social grievances and experience of oppression under the existing dynasties stimulated millenarian hopes and led them to identify him [Usuman] with the Mahdi, whose appearance was associated with the end of the 12th century Hijra (A. D. 1786) an identification which he explicitly rejected, though sharing and indeed encouraging their expectations."

45 See F. H. al-Masri, R. A. Adeleye, J. O. Hunwick, and I. A. Mukoshy, "Sifofin Shehu, An Autobiography and Character Study of 'Uthman b. Fudi in Verse," *CADRB*, 2, 1966, p. 11.

46 Hiskett, *The Sword of Truth*, p. 125.

47 B. G. Martin, "A Muslim Political Tract from Northern Nigeria, Muhammad Bello's *Usul al-Siyasa*," *Boston University Papers on Africa*, 5, 1971, pp. 64–5.

48 Usuman dan Fodio, *Nur al-Albab*. For an Arabic text of this work and a French translation by Isma'il Hamet, see *RA*, 42, 1898, pp. 59–60.

49 Usuman dan Fodio, *Wathiqat al-ikhwan*, Zaria n.d., p. 15.

50 Usuman dan Fodio, *Shifa' al-Ghalil fima ashkala min kalam Shaykh shuyukhina Jibril*, ms. belonging to Imam Nasir Kabara of Kano. I would like to thank him and also Mallam 'Abd al-Qadir Datti for obtaining a Xerox of it for me. A full translation by Bivar and Hiskett of the same poem appears in their "Arabic Literature," pp. 140–3.

51 Hodgkin, "Usuman dan Fodio," pp. 9–10.

52 Hiskett, "Nineteenth Century Jihads," Chapter 6.

53 Usuman's pamphlet, the *Siraj al-Ikhwan*, 1811, shows the extent of the Shehu's intellectual attachment to al-Maghili. It is largely drawn from the Algerian author's *Misbah al-Arwah*. In his *Ta'lim al-ikhwan*, ed., trans. B. G.

Martin, *Middle Eastern Studies*, 4, 1967, pp. 50–97, the Shehu even lists a short bibliography of al-Maghili's writings that he knows of or has read.

54 'Abd al-'Aziz Batran, "An Introductory Note on the Impact of Sidi al-Mukhtar al-Kunti (1729–1811) on West African Islam in the 18th and 19th Centuries," unpublished paper, 1972. By the same author, see "The Kunta, Sidi al-Mukhtar al-Kunti, and the Office of Shaykh al-Tariqa al-Qadiriya," in Willis (ed.), *Cultivators.*

55 *Ibid.,* pp. 297–308.

56 Muhammad Bello, *Infaq al-Maysur*, p. 221. Apparently Sharif was the name of one of Sidi al-Mukhtar's emissaries.

57 *Ibid.,* p. 222.

58 Usuman dan Fodio, *Ihya' al-Sunna, passim.*

59 Books by al-Sha'rani frequently quoted by the Shehu are: *Bahr al-Mawrud fi'l-mawathiq wa'l-'uhud, Yawaqit al-Jawahir, Al-Kibrit al-Ahmar,* and *Kashf al-Ghumma.*

60 Usuman dan Fodio, *Bayan wujub al-Hijra*, fol. 11.

61 *Ibid.,* fols. 8–19.

62 For an illuminating discussion of this matter, see A. Kasembeg, "De l'*Ijtihad* et de Ses Différents Degrés," *Journal Asiatique*, 15, 1850, pp. 178–214.

63 Usuman dan Fodio, *Hisn al-Afham*, ms. from 'Umar Falke Collection, Northwestern University Library, fol. 31. See note 9 for the author, al-Fallati.

64 Usuman dan Fodio, *Hidayat at-Tullab*, Zaria n.d., pp. 1–2.

65 Fathi Hasan al-Masri, "*Bayan,*" Introduction, p. 96.

66 Usuman discusses the matter of sin and apostasy at some length in his *Nasa'ih al-ummat al-Muhammadiya*, as well as the *Shifa' al-Ghalil*. In the third section of the former book, he attacks the radicalism of Jibril and his followers.

67 Hiskett, "Nineteenth Century Jihads," Chapter 6, draft.

68 Muhammad Bello, *Infaq al-Maysur*, pp. 94–5.

69 *Ibid.,* p. 67.

70 *Ibid.,* p. 66.

Chapter 2

1 A town in northern Iraq.

2 See Peter von Sivers, "The Realm of Justice: Apocalyptic Revolts in Algeria (1849–1879)," in *Humaniora Islamica*, I, The Hague 1973. The career of one of the last resisters, Bu 'Imama, is recorded by Abu'l-Qasim Sa'dallah, *Watha'iq jadida 'an thawrat al-Amir 'Abd al-Malik al-Jaza'iri bi'l-Maghrib (New Documents about the Rising of Amir 'Abd al-Malik in Morocco), RHM*, 1, 1973, pp. 52–69.

3 A good general book on this subject is C. -A. Julien, *Histoire de l'Algérie Contemporaine . . . 1827–1871*, Paris 1964, including full bibliographies on pp. 507–588.

4 See also Chapter III in P. M. Holt *et al., Cambridge History of Islam*, II, Cambridge 1970, pp. 266–98.

5 *Ibid.,* pp. 284–5.

6 Julien, *Histoire*, Chapters I and II.

7 See Note 2 above.

8   See P. Shinar, "Note on the Socio-economic and Cultural Role of Sufi Brotherhoods and Marabutism in the Modern Maghrib," *Proceedings of the First International Congress of Africanists, Accra 1962,* 1964, pp. 272–85.

9   J. M. Abun-Nasr, *A History of the Maghrib,* Cambridge 1971, Chapter VIII.

10   P. Boyer, "Contribution á l'Etude de la Politique Religieuse des Turcs dans la Régence d'Alger," *Revue de l'Occident Musulman et de la Meditérranée,* 1, 1966, pp. 11–50.

11   *Ibid.,* pp. 16–34.

12   Muhammad ibn 'Abd al-Qadir al-Jaza'iri, *Tuhfat al-za'ir fi ta'rikh al-Jaza'ir wa'l-Amir 'Abd al-Qadir,* Beirut 1384/1964, p. 929.

13   Muhammad ibn 'Abd al-Qadir al-Jaza'iri, *Tuhfa,* pp. 146–47; see also Lucette Valensi, *Le Maghreb avant la Prise d'Alger, 1790–1830,* Paris 1970, Chapter V.

14   According to J. Wilson Stevens, *An Historical and Geographical Account of Algiers, Comprehending Novel and Interesting Details of Events Relative to the American Captives,* Philadelphia 1797, p. 142, "Such is the despotism of the Turkish soldiers that they will not only turn others out of the way on the streets, but will go to the farm houses in the country for twenty days altogether, living on free quarters and making use of everything, not excepting the women. . . . Though their numbers are small, yet they tyrannize over the native Moors in throughout the whole country." These statements are confirmed by the Tunisian historian Ibn Abi Diyaf, *Ithaf ahl al-zaman,* III, Tunis 1963, p. 167, who speaks of how the "people of Algiers and the nomads there, who formed the majority, were irritated by the cockiness of the Turkish troops. The affair came to a head [about 1830]. They were disliked heartily in the country for that, or their narrow-mindedness and for abominable acts of oppression, sometimes leading to violations of the *Shar'ia.*"

15   Stevens, *Account,* p. 189, states that Oran had "lately" been ruined by an earthquake. According to Valensi, *Le Maghreb,* pp. 21–25, returning pilgrims introduced the plague from Alexandria to Algiers in 1784. It returned again in 1787, when Stevens, *Account,* p. 210, described it as "a most malignant plague . . . which carried off immense numbers of the inhabitants: the disease was so virulent that the streets were full of dead bodies and the mortality so great that sufficient number of persons could scarcely be procured to bury them." It returned to Algiers in 1788, and visited Mascara in 1789. It was noted in Tilimsan in 1790 and 1791. Tunisia and Morocco were not spared either. Famines sometimes accompanied the plague, which revisited Algeria at intervals until 1822. At other times, cholera, smallpox, locusts, and great storms came, which made many ill or killed them and spoiled the harvests. These disasters were compounded by urban disorders and migrations of starving people.

16   Boyer, "Contribution," p. 45, note 70.

17   *Ibid.,* pp. 42–4.

18   Muhammad ibn 'Abd al-Qadir al-Jaza'iri, *Tuhfa,* pp. 117–18.

19   *Ibid.,* p. 117.

20   A. Berbrugger, "Un Chef Kabyle en 1804," *RA,* 3, 1859, pp. 209–14, suggests that Ibn al-Ahrash called himself *Sahib al-Waqt* ("Master of the Time") – a claim that he was a forerunner of a mahdi. See also E. Vaysettes, "Histoire des Derniers Beys de Constantine depuis 1793," *RA,* 3, pp. 259–64; L. C. Féraud, "Histoire des Villes de la Province de Constantine," in

Recueil des Notices et Mémoires de la Société Archaéologique de la Province de Constantine, IV, Paris 1870, pp. 1–29, esp. p. 18 for Ibn al-Ahrash.

21   Muhammad ibn 'Abd al-Qadir al-Jaza'iri, *Tuhfa,* p. 115–6.

22   Abu'l-Qasim Ahmad al-Zayyani, *Al-Tarjuman al-mu'rib 'an duwal al-Mashriq wa'l-maghrib,* events of 1220/1805–6, in O. V. Houdas (tr.), *Le Maroc de 1631–1812 par Ezzeiani,* Paris 1886, pp. 100–2.

23   Muhammad ibn 'Abd al-Qadir al Jaza'iri, *Tuhfa,* pp. 115–6.

24   Boyer, "Contribution," p. 44.

25   Ahmad al-Nasiri al-Salawi, *Kitab al-Istiqsa' li-akhbar duwal al-Maghrib al-Aqsa',* VIII, Casablanca 1956, pp. 109–11.

26   A. Cour. *L'Établissement des Dynasties des Chérifs au Maroc,* Paris 1904, *passim.*

27   For the Tijaniya, see J. M. Abun-Nasr, *The Tijaniyya, a Sufi Order of the Modern World,* Oxford 1965, esp. Chapter IV.

28   Abun-Nasr, *Tijaniyya,* pp. 60–61.

29   Muhammad ibn 'Abd al-Qadir al-Jaza'iri, *Tuhfa,* p. 125.

30   Abun-Nasr, *Tijaniyya,* pp. 64–65.

31   A. Raymond in Holt *et al., Cambridge History of Islam,* p. 284.

32   J. Deny, "Les Registres de la Solde des Janissaires Conservés à la Bibliotheque Nationale d'Alger," *RA,* 61, 1920, pp. 19–46, 212–260, says nothing about the effects of the suppression of the Anatolian janissaries on Algeria. The last recruiting expedition mentioned by Deny took place in 1826. It seems doubtful that there were any further expeditions after that date.

33   A. Raymond in Holt *et al., Cambridge of Islam,* p. 284.

34   Marcel Emerit, "Un Problème de Distance Morale: la Résistance Algérienne à l'Époque d'Abd-el-Kader," *Information Historique,* July–October 1952, pp. 127–31, esp. p. 128.

35   Valensi, *Le Maghreb,* pp. 64–69 and the graph of captures on p. 65 makes this point with great clarity.

36   Muhammad ibn 'Abd al Qadir al-Jaza-iri, *Tuhfa,* p. 932.

37   Most of the geographical information here has been taken from Michelin, *Algérie-Tunisie,* Paris n.d. (c. 1968), map 172.

38   Tafarsit is about forty kilometers southwest of Ajdir and the Bay of Al-hucemas. For 'Abd al-Qawi, see *Tuhfa,* pp. 926–7.

39   Muhammad ibn 'Abd al Qadir al-Jaza'iri, *Tuhfa,* pp. 929–30.

40   *Ibid.*

41   *Ibid.,* p. 930.

42   *Ibid.*

43   *Ibid.,* p. 931.

44   Albert Hourani, "Shaykh Khalid and the Naqshbandi Order," in S. M. Stern (ed.), *Festschrift Richard Walzer,* Oxford 1974, p. 78.

45   *Ibid.,* p. 81.

46   E. Allworth (ed.), *Central Asia, A Century of Russian Rule,* N.Y. 1967, pp. 167–9.

47   Muhammad ibn 'Abd al-Qadir al-Jaza'iri, *Tuhfa,* p. 932.

48   *Ibid.,* p. 932.

49   Cour, *L'Etablissement,* p. 13. Cour claims that in general, the Qadiris took the side of the Turks in the western Algerian struggle between the Turks and Moroccans, whereas the Shadhilis and their suborders supported the

sharifian sultans. The decisive turning of the Qadiris of al-Qaytana against the Ottomans probably dates from the imprisonment of Muhyi al-Din at Oran at the end of the 1820s. 'Abd al-Razzaq Al-Baytar's *Hilyat al-Bashar*, III, Damascus 1961–3, pp. 1489–92, includes a biography of Muhyi al-Din and a "miracle" with some anti-Turkish overtones to it.

50 Julien, *Histoire*, pp. 89–90.
51 M. Emerit, "L'Exploitation des Os des Musulmans pour le Raffinage du Sucre," *RHM*, 1, 1974, pp. 11–3.
52 Julien, *Histoire*, pp. 90–2.
53 Muhammad ibn 'Abd al-Qadir al-Jaza'iri, *Tuhfa*, pp. 146–7.
54 Julien, *Histoire*, pp. 61, 66–8.
55 Muhammad ibn 'Abd al-Qadir al-Jaza'iri, *Tuhfa*, pp. 146–7.
56 Al-Nasiri al-Salawi, *Istiqsa'*, IX, p. 153.
57 Muhammad ibn 'Abd al-Qadir al-Jaza'iri, *Tuhfa*, p. 147.
58 Julien, *Histoire*, p. 83.
59 According to H. Pérès, "Les Poésies d'Abd al-Kader Composées en Algérie et en France," in *Cinquantenaire de la Faculté des Lettres d'Alger*, Algiers 1932, pp. 357–412, esp. p. 360, note 2, Khanq al-Nitah is now "Karguenta," a section of downtown Oran, whereas Burj Ra's al'Ayn is known as the "Ravin du Chateau-Neuf" or "Ravin de Ras el-Ain." See the map facing p. 134 in *Algeria*, II, Naval Intelligence Handbooks, London 1944.
60 Muhammad ibn 'Abd al-Qadir al-Jaza'iri, *Tuhfa*, p. 156.
61 Attempts had been made to transform 'Abd al-Qadir into a nationalist. This is misleading. See the comments of D. C. Gordon, *The Passing of French Algeria*, Oxford 1966, pp. 185–7.
62 Muhammad ibn 'Abd al-Qadir al-Jaza'iri, *Tuhfa*, p. 166.
63 *Makhzan* tribes were employed by the Ottoman regency and by the sharifian government in Morocco to collect taxes and for other purposes. Sent out as semimilitary units (*mahallas*), they compelled "subject" (*ra'iya*) tribes to pay the levies assigned them. In return the *makhzan* tribes either received a reduction in their own taxes or paid none at all. In this sense, the word means "government" rather than "treasury," its literal meaning.
64 Muhammad ibn 'Abd al-Qadir al-Jaza'iri, *Tuhfa*, p. 166.
65 See Chapter 1 above.
66 R. M. Savory, "The Principal Offices of the Safavid State during the Reign of Shah Isma'il," *BSOAS*, 33, 1960, pp. 91–105, esp. p. 92.
67 Muhammad ibn 'Abd al-Qadir al-Jaza'iri, *Tuhfa*, p. 166.
68 The text of this treatise (of which the full title is *Wishah al-Katib wa zinat al-'askar al-Muhammadi al-ghalib*) is printed in the *Tuhfa*, pp. 192–208.
69 Muhammad ibn 'Abd al-Qadir al-Jaza'iri, *Tuhfa*, p. 194.
70 Julien, *Histoire*, p. 104.
71 *Ibid.*, p. 186.
72 'Abd al-Jalil al-Tamimi, *Buhuth wa watha'iq fi'l-ta'rikh al-Maghribi, 1816–1871*, Tunis 1972, p. 199ff. I owe this reference to Peter von Sivers. The correspondence is preserved in the Public Record Office, London, 3/43 file.
73 Julien, *Histoire*, p. 186.
74 *Ibid.*, pp. 184–5; *Tuhfa* pp. 313–5. In the latter source, p. 314, Muhammad ibn 'Abd al-Qadir claims that he had seen, during a visit to Paris, three cannon captured by the French from the Amir's forces. On one of them, an

inscription in Arabic read: "Made at Tilimsan in the time of the amirate of Nasir al-Din, al-Sayyid 'Abd al-Qadir ibn Muhyi al-Din in the year 1255/ 1839–40."

75   Julien, *Histoire*, p. 138.
76   *Ibid.*, pp. 185–6.
77   Tamimi, *Buhuth*, pp. 225–6.
78   *Ibid.*, pp. 225–6.
79   Ercümend Kuran, *Cezayirin Fransizlar tarafından işgali karşişinda Osmanli siyaseti, 1827–1847*, Istanbul 1957, *passim;* also in Arabic as *Al-Siyasat al-'Uthmaniya tujah al-ihtilal al-Faransi li'l—Jaza'ir, 1827–47*, trans. 'Abd al-Jalil al-Tamimi, 2nd ed., Tunis 1974. An article by Kuran, "Cezayiri garb mudafü, Kostantine Beyi Ahmad Bey," in *V. Türk Tarih Kongresi, Ankara 1956 . . . Kongreye sunulan tebliğler*, Ankara 1960, pp. 681–9, is printed as an appendix to Tamimi's translation, pp. 78–85, also in Arabic.
80   Tamimi, *Al-Siyasat al-'Uthmaniya*, p. 78.
81   P. Shinar, " 'Abd al-Qadir and 'Abd al Krim, in *Asian and African Studies*, I, Jerusalem 1965, pp. 146–7; *Tuhfa*, p. 197 for the fixing of exchange rates, and pp. 313–4 for other details.
82   Equivalent to 3 Rajab and 13 Ramadan, respectively. Written texts of some of these oaths, recorded by the amir's secretaries, can be found in *Tuhfa*, pp. 157–62 and 163–5.
83   Muhammad ibn 'Abd al-Qadir al-Jaza'iri, *Tuhfa*, p. 158.
84   *Ibid.*, p. 165.
85   Abun-Nasr, *Tijaniyya*, pp. 58–101.
86   Muhammad ibn 'Abd al-Qadir al-Jaza'iri, *Tuhfa*, p. 125.
87   *Ibid.*
88   Emerit, "L'Époque," pp. 201, 208–10.
89   *Ibid.*, p. 208.
90   Julien, *Histoire*, pp. 125, 150.
91   Muhammad ibn 'Abd al-Qadir al-Jaza'iri, *Tuhfa*, p. 288.
92   *Ibid.*, pp. 289–91.
93   For a predecessor of Bu Ma'aza, Abu Yazid b. Kaydad, the "Man on the Donkey," see C. -A. Julien, *Histoire de l'Afrique du Nord*, II, Paris 1961, pp. 62–4. Another "donkey man," Bu Himara, appeared in the Moroccan Rif c. 1900. The use of donkeys may have been adopted from Christian symbolic vocabularies: Christ rode on a donkey.
94   Muhammad ibn 'Abd al-Qadir al-Jaza'iri, *Tuhfa*, p. 457.
95   *Ibid.*
96   Shinar, " 'Abd al-Qadir," p. 148.
97   Julien, *Histoire d'Algérie*, p. 320. See this same source, pp. 315–22, for a clear account of French techniques of raiding and methodical devastation of parts of Algeria.
98   Muhammad ibn 'Abd al-Qadir al-Jaza'iri, *Tuhfa*, p. 481. See also M. A. Martel, "La Politique Saharienne et Ottoman," in *Le Sahara, Rapports et Contacts Humains, 7ième Colloque d'Histoire . . . Aix en Provence*, Aix 1967, pp. 89–144, esp. p. 113. Bu Ma'aza later turned up as a Muslim volunteer fighting alongside the Turks in the Crimean War. In the 1860s and 1870s, he continued to support Muslim causes. In 1878, he visited the Amir 'Abd al-Qadir in exile at Damascus. Near the end of his life, he was living at Batum on the Black Sea, and at the start of the 1880s, he went briefly to Tunisia to start a jihad against France at the behest of 'Abd

al-Hamid II. When this jihad failed, he returned to Batum, where he died.

99 Muhammad ibn 'Abd al-Qadir al-Jaza'iri, *Tuhfa*, pp. 316–331, for 'Abd al-Qadir's questions and the responses of al-Tassuli; for the responses of the chief *qadi* of Fez, see pp. 384–9. The Amir's questionnaire is dated Dhu'l-Hijja 1252/March 1837. Despite the claim of Abdallah Laroui, in his excellent *Histoire du Maghreb*, Paris 1971, p. 279, note 12, that the Arabic phrase *watan al-Jaza'ir* in this document means "patrie algérienne," it can as easily be translated the "land of Algeria." Thus 'Abd al-Qadir cannot be made out as a nationalist merely because he employs this phrase.

100 For the text of the *Risala*, see *Tuhfa*, pp. 411–22.

101 Likewise a favorite theme with Usuman dan Fodio.

102 See C. -R. Ageron, *Les Algériens Musulmans et la France*, II, Paris 1968, Chapter 39, pp. 1079–92 on the migration of Algerian Muslims and the affair of 1911.

Chapter 3

1 M. Aliou Tyam, *La Vie d'el Hadj Omar, Qacida en Poular*, Paris 1935, p. 202, claims that 'Umar was seventy (lunar) years old in 1864; but Muhammad al-Hafiz al-Tijani, *al-Hajj 'Umar al-Futi, Sultan al-Dawlat al-Tijaniya*, Cairo 1382/1963, p. 20 makes 'Umar's birth date 1212/1797–8.

2 Ibrahim-Mamadou Ouane, *Pérégrinations Soudanaises*, Lyon n.d., p. 179, makes 'Umar the seventh son in a family of twelve children.

3 Jules Salenc, "La Vie d'el Hadj Omar," *BCEHSAOF*, 1, 1918, p. 409.

4 J. R. Willis, "Al-Hajj 'Umar b. Sa'id al-Futi al-Turi (c. 1794–1864) and the Doctrinal Basis of His Islamic Reform Movement in the Western Sudan," unpublished Ph.D. thesis, London University 1971, p. 48. I would like to thank Dr. Willis for his kindness in letting me use his study and many documents about al-Hajj 'Umar, likewise Dr. David Robinson of Yale University.

5 Al-Hajj 'Umar Tal, *Rimah hizb al-rahim 'ala nuhur hizb al-rajim*, Cairo 1382/1926–3, I, p. 180. 'Umar's *Rimah* (*The Lances of God's Party against the Throats of the Satanic Faction*) is printed on the margin of 'Ali Harzihum (or Harazim) ibn al-'Arabi al-Fasi, *Jawahir al-ma'ani wa bulugh al-amani fi fayd Sidi Abu'l-'Abbas al-Tijani*.

6 Al-Hajj 'Umar Tal, *Rimah*, I, p. 180; Christiane Seydou, "Trois Poémes Mystiques Peuls du Futa Jalon," *REI*, 40, 1972, pp. 141–85.

7 David Robinson, "Abdul Qadir and Shaykh Umar: A Continuing Tradition of Islamic Leadership in Futa Toro," *IJAHS*, 4, 1973, p. 298, note 33.

8 Ibn al-Hibat al-Shinqiti, *Manaqib al-Shaykh 'Umar*, fol. 1.

9 See W. A. Brown, "The Caliphate of Hamdallahi, A Study in African History and Tradition," unpublished Ph.D. thesis, University of Wisconsin, Madison, 1969, "Overview."

10 That 'Umar passed through Bobo-Diulasso is confirmed by the discovery of Ivor Wilks that he stopped for a time to study under Ibrahim b. Muhammad Saghanughu (d. 1825–6) and is said to have helped build the Saghanughu Mosque there, named for this famous clan of local men of learning. See Ivor Wilks, "The Saghanughu and the Spread of Maliki Law," *CADRB*, 2, 1966, p. 16.

11 Al-Hajj 'Umar Tal, *Tadhkirat al-Ghafilin 'an qabh ikhtilaf al-mu'minin* (*Manzuma fi Islah dhat al-bayn*), ms. no. 5609, Bibliothèque Nationale,

Paris, fols. 20a–b, Xerox lent me by Dr. J. R. Willis. This *rajaz* poem of about 200 verses, broken at intervals by 'Umar's commentary, was composed as he crossed the desert from Katsina to Egypt (c. 1828); it was later written down and corrected, perhaps in Cairo or Madina.

12   Tyam, *Vie*, p. 6.
13   Hugh Clapperton, *Journal of a Second Expedition into the Interior of Africa*, Philadelphia 1829, p. 249.
14   *Ibid.*, p. 250.
15   Al-Hajj 'Umar Tal, *Rimah*, I, p. 181.
16   Al-Hajj 'Umar Tal, *Tadhkirat al-Ghafilin*, fols. 20b–21a.
17   Ibn al-Hibat, *Manaqib al-Shaykh 'Umar*, fols. 1–2.
18   Al-Hajj 'Umar Tal, *Rimah*, I, p. 181. This date probably corresponds with 14 July 1828: see 'Umar al-Naqar, *The Pilgrimage Tradition in West Africa*, Khartoum 1972, p. 71.
19   Shaykh Musa Kamara, *Ta'rikh al-Hajj 'Umar*, fol. 96.
20   Al-Hajj 'Umar Tal, *Rimah*, I, pp. 185–5.
21   *Ibid.*, p. 183.
22   *Ibid.*
23   *Ibid.*, p. 185.
24   *Ibid.*
25   Tyam, *Vie*, p. 16.
26   Al-Hajj 'Umar Tal, *Rimah*, I, p. 189.
27   Naqar, *Pilgrimage*, p. 72.
28   Tyam, *Vie*, p. 16.
29   Naqar, *Pilgrimage*, p. 74.
30   Al-Hajj 'Umar Tal, ms. no. 5693, Bibliothèque Nationale, Paris.
31   Al-Hajj 'Umar Tal, *Rimah*, I, pp. 189–90.
32   *Ibid.*, p. 190.
33   See these poems, ms. Bornu 32 and 33a at the Library of Ahmadu Bello University, Zaria, or ms. no. 33, Bornu Native Authority Library, Maidugari. An analysis of one of them is given in Naqar, *Pilgrimage*, p. 73.
34   Al-Hajj 'Umar Tal, *Rimah*, I, p. 190.
35   See Murray Last, *The Sokoto Caliphate*, London 1968, pp. 216–9 for this controversy. See also Muhammad Bello's *Raf' al-ishtibah* for quotations from Harzihum's *Jawahir al-Ma'ani*, cf. note 5 above.
36   Musa Kamara, *Ta'rikh*, fol. 95.
37   Willis, "Al-Hajj 'Umar," p. 74.
38   This even extended to 'Umar's imitating the Shehu's Arabic prose style.
39   E. Mage, *Voyage dans le Soudan Occidentale (Sénégambie-Niger)*, Paris 1868, p. 233.
40   A. H. Ba and J. Daget, *L'Empire Peul du Macina*, Paris 1962, p. 245.
41   Al-Hajj 'Umar Tal, *Rimah*, I, p. 190 says that Bello's daughter Maryam died at Sokoto in February 1838.
42   'Umar composed his *Maqasid al-Saniya* at Sokoto, likewise his *Suyuf*, which he later expanded into the *Rimah*. A detailed comparison of these two latter texts would show much about the evolution of 'Umar's thought.
43   Ba and Daget, *Empire*, pp. 242–6.
44   Brown, "Caliphate," p. 149.
45   *Ibid.*, pp. 149–50.
46   *Ibid.*, p. 150.

47 Several versions and many manuscripts of an anonymous chronicle of al-Hajj 'Umar in Arabic are available, the precise interrelationships and origins of which are not yet clear. Probably written in the vicinity of Segu c. 1895, this chronicle may represent oral traditions that were eventually written down. The account's titles vary: *Rihlat Shaykhina al-Hajj 'Umar* (Sayyid Nuru Tal Library, Dakar); *Kitab al-'Aja'ib al-qadriya* (Dakar, Fonds Curtin 5); or *Kayfiyat al-Hajj 'Umar* ('Umar Falke Collection, Northwestern University Library, Evanston, Illinois). Many of the identical details appear in M. Delafosse (trans.), Histoire d'el-Hadj Omar," in *Renseignements Coloniaux*, 23, 1913, pp. 355–63. Here I have used the *'Aja'ib al-Qadriya* (kindly lent me by Professor Curtin), with occasional additions from the *Rihla* and *Kayfiya*, where there are marked differences. See *'Aja'ib*, fols. 7a–8a.

48 *'Aja'ib*, fols. 8a–9a.

49 Ivor Wilks, "The Transmission of Islamic Learning in the Western Sudan," in J. Goody (ed.), *Literacy in Traditional Societies*, Cambridge 1968, p. 174.

50 *'Aja'ib*, fol. 9b.

51 Yves Person, *Samori, Une Révolution Dyula*, I, Dakar 1968, p. 157.

52 *'Aja'ib*, fol. 9b.

53 *Ibid.*, fols. 9a–10a; *Rihla*, fol. 3. Touba had been founded by the famous Kunta-educated Qadiri Al-Hajj Salim Jabi Ghassama (Karamoko Ba), c. 1823. Salim had died in 1836. From Koumbia, 'Umar doubtless thought he might attract some students from Salim's undistinguished successors, who would join the Tijaniya. See J. Suret-Canale, "Touba in Guinea – Holy Place of Islam," in C. Allen and R. W. Johnson (eds.), *African Perspectives*, Cambridge 1970, pp. 57–82.

54 Tyam, *Vie*, p. 23, note 126.

55 *'Aja'ib*, fol. 10a.

56 Al-Hajj 'Umar Tal, *Rimah*, II, p. 283, where the date is given as 3 Ramadan 1261 but there is no mention of where the work was finished.

57 *'Aja'ib*, fol. 10b.

58 Tamsir Ousman Ba, "Essai Historique sur le Rip," *BIFAN*, 19, 1957, p. 572.

59 En route to St. Louis in 1847, 'Umar composed most of his poem The *Safinat al-Sa'ada* (*Ship of Happiness*), a metrical amplification of al-Fazazi's *'Ishriniyat*.

60 *'Aja'ib*, fols. 10b–11a.

61 *Ibid.*, fol. 14a.

62 An echo of Sura IV, verse 97.

63 Willis, "Al-Hajj 'Umar," p. 121.

64 *'Aja'ib*, fol. 14a.

65 Willis, "Al-Hajj 'Umar," pp. 123–5.

66 C. A. L. Reichardt, *A Grammar of the Fulde Language*, London 1876, p. 290.

67 Musa Kamara, *Ta'rikh*, fol. 82.

68 David Robinson, "Legitimacy, Constituency, and Failure in the Torodbe Movement of Futa Toro," unpublished paper, New Haven, Conn. 1972, p. 5.

69 David Robinson, "Abdul Qadir," p. 291ff.

70 David Robinson, personal communication, 8 February 1975.

71 M. Guilhem and S. Toé, *Precis d'Histoire du Mali*, Paris n.d., p. 119.
72 Al-Hajj 'Umar Tal, *Safinat al-Sa'ada*, fols. 4–5, from the copy in the Nuru Tal Library, Dakar, kindly lent me in xerox form by J. R. Willis.
73 Willis, "Al-Hajj 'Umar," pp. 88–9.
74 Mage, *Voyage*, p. 233.
75 See Al-Hajj 'Umar Tal, *Rimah*, II, Chapter 51, pp. 209–236; Willis, "Al-Hajj 'Umar," p. 101.
76 Al-Hajj 'Umar Tal, *Rimah*, II, p. 209.
77 *Ibid.*, pp. 233–4.
78 Mage, *Voyage*, pp. 508–514; L. Faidherbe, *Le Sénégal*, Paris 1889, p. 216.
79 *'Aja'ib*, fol. 15a.
80 Here the chronicler refers to the wooden boards (*lawh*) used by students in the Western Sudan. After a text had been copied on the board and memorized, the ink could be washed off for the next day's lesson. This information is from 'Abdallahi 'Al, *Dhikr ibtida' jihad Shaykhina Amir al-Mu'minin 'Umar b. Sa'id*, a manuscript from the Nuru Tal Library in Dakar, kindly lent me in Xerox by Dr. J. R. Willis. The text was translated into French by Mamadon Sissoko in *Bulletin de l'Enseignement de l'AOF*, 1936–7, n. 95, pp. 242–55; no. 96, pp. 6–22; no. 97, pp. 127–48. This translation has been heavily used by B. O. Oloruntimehin, *The Segu Tokolor Empire*, London 1972.
81 Reichardt, *Grammar*, p. 290.
82 *'Aja'ib*, fols. 15a–16a. See another version of the story of Jali Musa Diabate in Ousman Socé, *Contes et légendes d'Afrique noire*, Paris 1962, p. 63.
83 *'Aja'ib*, fols. 17a–18b.
84 Ahmad al-'Ayyashi Sukayrij, *Kashf al-hijab 'an man talaqa ma' al-Shaykh al-Tijani min al-ashab*, Fes 1332/1913–4, pp. 335–6. A slightly different date is given in Jules Saleuc, "Vie," p. 412 (21 Dhu'l-Qa'da 1268/6 September 1852.)
85 Mage, *Voyage*, p. 238.
86 *Ibid.*, p. 237.
87 *Ibid.*, p. 238.
88 Oloruntimehin, *Segu Empire*, p. 18.
89 Mage, *Voyage*, p. 238.
90 Al-Hajj 'Umar Tal, *Tadhkirat al-Mustarshidin wa falah al-Talibin*, lines 173–6. This poem was completed by 'Umar at Madina in April 1829, according to its colophon.
91 Reichardt, *Grammar*, p. 306.
92 *'Aja'ib*, fol. 20a.
93 A. S. Kanya-Forstner, in M. Crowder (ed.), *West African Resistance*, London 1971, p. 57.
94 Mage, *Voyage*, p. 427.
95 *Ibid.*, p. 235.
96 Lord Stanley, "Narrative of Mr. W. C. Thompson's Journey from Sierra Leone to Timbo, Capital of Futah Jallo in Western Africa," *JRGS*, 16, 1846, pp. 106–138.
97 'Abdallahi Smith, review of Trimingham's *History of Islam in West Africa*, *Ibadan Magazine*, March 1963, p. 33.
98 Willis, "Al-Hajj 'Umar," p. 157.
99 Mage, *Voyage*, p. 239.

100 Y. -J. St. Martin, *L'Empire Toucouleur et la France, Un Demi-Siècle de Relations Diplomatiques* (*1846–1893*), Dakar 1967, p. 76.
101 F. Carrère and P. Holle, *De la Sénégambie Française,* Paris 1855, p. 138.
102 St. Martin, *Empire,* pp. 81–2 for the text of this letter.
103 *Ibid.,* pp. 79–80.
104 Al-Hajj 'Umar Tal, *Rimah,* II, p. 209.
105 Sura IV, verse 97 and Sura XXIX, verse 56.
106 Reichardt, *Grammar,* pp. 309–10.
107 'Al, *Dhikr,* fol. 8. See note 80 above.
108 *Ibid.,* fol. 7.
109 *Ibid.,* fol. 12.
110 See the engraving in Mage, *Voyage,* p. 108.
111 Ibid., pp. 297–8; p. 415 mentions a quantity of forty-two kilograms of locally made gunpowder. However, see St. Martin, *Empire,* Chapter V, pp. 52–62, which suggests that 'Umar in fact may have obtained some arms from the French, despite outward appearances.
112 L. Kesteloot *et al., Da Monzon de Segou, Épopée Bambara,* I–IV, Paris 1972; see especially I, Introduction.
113 *Ibid.,* I, Introduction.
114 Al-Hajj 'Umar Tal, *Bayan ma waqa'a bayni wa bayn Amir Masina Ahmad bin Ahmad, ms.* BNP 5605, Bibliothèque Nationale, Paris.
115 Mage, *Voyage,* p. 246.
116 Al-Hajj 'Umar Tal, *Rimah,* I, p. 26.
117 Al-Hajj 'Umar Tal, *Bayan,* fol. 5.
118 *Ibid.,* fols. 5–6.
119 *Ibid.,* fol. 6.
120 Abdelkader Zebadia, "The Career of Ahmed al-Bakkay in the Oral Evidences and Recorded Documents," *RHM,* 3, 1975, pp. 75–83, esp. p. 75.
121 Ba and Daget, *Empire,* pp. 242–6.
122 Al-Hajj 'Umar Tal, *Bayan,* fol. 8, includes an undated, polemical letter from al-Bakka'i to Ahmadu III.
123 Ms. BNP 5716, Bibliothèque Nationale, Paris, fol. 184.
124 Willis, "Al-Hajj 'Umar," pp. 268ff.
125 *Ibid.,* pp. 268–9.
126 Yarki Talfi, *Tabakkiyat al-Bakka'i, ms.* BNP 5697, Bibliothèque Nationale Paris.
127 Ms. BNP 5259, Bibliothèque Nationale, Paris, fols. 66–8, cited by Willis, p. 269.
128 See p. 73.
129 Al-Hajj 'Umar Tal, *Rimah,* I, pp. 61–86.
130 Al-Hajj 'Umar Tal, *Suyuf al-Sa'id, ms.* BNP 5401, Bibliothèque Nationale, Paris, fol. 6 and *Rimah,* I, pp. 89–90 both quote this same example from al-Sha'rani.
131 This is the central theme of his *Suyuf al-Sa'id.*
132 Al-Hajj 'Umar Tal, *Suyuf,* fol. 6; *Rimah,* I, p. 88.
133 Y. Marquet, "Des Ikhwan al-Safa' à al-Hajj 'Umar," in *Arabica,* XV, 1968, pp. 6–47.
134 *Ibid.,* p. 20ff.
135 Al-Hajj 'Umar Tal, *Rimah,* I, p. 184.
136 *Ibid.,* pp. 185–6.

137 *Ibid.*, p. 184.
138 This was 'Abdallah al-Kansusi (d. 1877), in his *Al-Jawab al-Muskit*, Algiers 1913, p. 14, cited by J. M. Abun Nasr, *The Tijaniyya, A Sufi Order in the Modern World*, Oxford 1965, p. 49.
139 Maquet, "Ikhwan," p. 34.
140 *Ibid.*, p. 34ff.
141 B. G. Martin, "A Mahdist Document from Futa Jallon," *BIFAN*, 25, 1963, pp. 47–65.
142 J. S. Trimingham, *Islam in West Africa*, Oxford 1961, p. 229.
143 Tyam, *Vie*, p. 185.
144 Willis, "Al-Hajj 'Umar," p. 312ff.
145 Tyam, *Vic*, pp. 189–90.
146 'Al, *Dhikr*, fol. 44.
147 St. Martin, *Empire*, p. 75, quoting Lartigue's *Notices Historiques et Géographiques du Sahel*, Senegal Archives, IG 156, p. 4.
148 For the post-Umarian Tijani state, see Oloruntimehin, *Segu Empire*.
149 J. S. Trimingham, *A History of Islam in West Africa*, Oxford 1962, pp. 149, 163, 184.

Chapter 4

1 For the history of the Qaramanlis, see Rodolfo Miccacchi, *La Tripolitania Sotto il Dominio dei Caramanli*. Rome 1936, or an expanded Arabic translation of this book with documents, translated by Taha Fawzi, Hasan Mahmud, and Kamal al-Din Kharbutli: *Tarabulus Gharb taht hukm usrat al-Qaramanli*, Cairo 1961. Another standard source on the later Qaramanlis is 'Umar 'Ali b. Isma'il, *Inhiyar hukm al-Qaramanliya fi Libya, 1795–1835*, Tripoli 1966.
2 See A. J. Cachia, *Libya under the Second Ottoman Occupation, 1835–1911*, Tripoli 1945, or the more easily available Arabic translation by Yusuf al-'Asali, *Libya fi'l-'ahd al-'Uthmani al-Thani*, Tripoli 1946.
3 Nicola A. Ziadeh, *Sanusiyah, A Study of a Revivalist Movement in Islam*, Leiden 1958, p. 35, note 1, gives the date of al-Sanusi's birth as 12 Rabi' I 1202/22 December 1787. This is confirmed by ex-King Idris of Libya in his unsigned introduction to a collection of Muhammad 'Ali al-Sanusi's works, *Al-Majmu'at al-Mukhtara*, Beirut 1388/1962, p. 7.
4 Ahmad Sidqi al-Dajjani, *Al-Harakat al-Sanusiya, nashatiha wa namuwwuha fi'-l-qarn al-tasi' 'ashar*, Cairo 1967, is perhaps the best and most comprehensive study of the Sanusiya to date. It is based in part on family records and documents made accessible to the author by ex-King Idris I of Libya. Al-Dajjani supplemented his written material by many conversations with the king about the Sanusi family, the history of the order, and other points. See also E. E. Evans-Pritchard, *The Sanusi of Cyrenaica*, Oxford 1949; Helmut Klopfer, *Aspekte der Bewegung des Muhammad ben 'Ali al-Sanusi*, Wiesbaden 1967; Muhammad Fu'ad Shukri, *Al-Sanusiya, din wa dawla*, Cairo 1948. Another useful study is Muhammad al-Tayyib al-Ashab, *Barqa al-Arabiya ams wa'l-yawn*, Cairo 1366/1947. For N. A. Ziadeh, see note 3 above. A very useful article is Carlo Nallino, "Le Dottrine del Fondatore della Confraternita Senussita," in *Raccolta di Scritti Editi ed Inediti*, II, Rome 1940, pp. 395–410. See further, Shehbenderzade Felbeli Ahmet Hilmi, *Senusiler we önücüncü asrin büyük mütefekkir-i-Islamisi Sayyid Mu-*

hammad al-Senusi, Istanbul 1325/1907–8. This book also includes, in its second part, *Abdülhamit ve Sayyid Mahdi al-Senusi ve asr-i-Hamidide Alem-i-Islam ve Senusiler* (pp. 58–124).

5 King Idris I of Libya (ed.), *Al-Majmu'at al-mukhtara,* Beirut 1388/1962.
6 In the introduction to his *Durar al-Saniya fi akhbar al-sulalat al-Idrisiya* (a work included in the *Majmu'a* – see note 5 above), Muhammad 'Ali al-Sanusi gives a lengthy exposition of his family's descent.
7 See the comments by Sayyid Ahmad al-Sharif in the notes to the Arabic version by Amir Shakib Arslan of Lothrop Stoddard, *Hadir al-'alam al-Islami,* II, Cairo 1352/1934, p. 399, note 2.
8 James Hamilton, *Wanderings in North Africa,* London 1856, p. 268.
9 Shakib Arslan, *Hadir,* II, p. 399, note 2.
10 Dajjani, *Haraka,* p. 46.
11 Dajjani, *Haraka,* pp. 47–50.
12 Shakib Arslan, *Hadir,* II, p. 401.
13 Dajjani, *Haraka,* pp. 54–5.
14 Shukri, *Sanusiya,* p. 14; Louis Rinn, *Marabouts et Khouan,* Algiers 1884, pp. 483–4; Ziadeh, *Sanusiyah,* pp. 36–7.
15 Dajjani, *Haraka,* pp. 55–6.
16 Ziadeh, *Sanusiyah,* p. 36, note 7; Dajjani, *Haraka,* p. 58.
17 Dajjani, *Haraka,* p. 58. In a conversation with King Idris, Dajjani was told that no such house was built.
18 Dajjani, *Haraka,* pp. 60–4.
19 The Arabic text of this *fatwa* ("decree") may be found in Muhammad 'Ulaysh, *Fath al-Malik fi fatawa ibn Malik,* I, Cairo 1327/1909, p. 77, with an English translation in Ziadeh, *Sanusiyah,* pp. 40–4.
20 Al-Sanusi devotes much discussion to *ijtihad* in his *Iqaz al-Wasnan fi'l-'amal bi'l-hadith wa'l-Qur'an* and his *Bughyat al-maqasid.* Both texts are included in King Idris I, *Majmu'a.*
21 Dajjani, *Haraka,* p. 61.
22 The life of al-Fasi is an enigma. Some material is included in Amin al-Rihani, *Muluk al-'Arab,* I, Beirut 1951, Chapter VI, pp. 278–293. There is hagiographical material in Yusuf al-Nabhani, *Jami' karamat al-Awliya',* I, Cairo 1957, pp. 566–79. Further information can be found in a compilation by an anonymous follower of al-Fasi's, *Al-'Iqd al-nafis fi nazm jawahir al-tadris,* Cairo 1372/1953, pp. 3–6, and in *Majmu'at al-ahzab wa awrad wa rasa'il,* Cairo 1359/1940, pp. 201–5. See also Muhammad Amin al-Hasani, *Al-Lu'lu' al-nafis al-mustakhraj min bahr Sidi Ahmad b. Idris,* Cairo n.d.
23 Al-Fasi is quoted about this vision in *Al-'Iqd al-nafis,* pp. 56–7. The idea of the *Muhammadiya tariqa* goes back at least to the eighteenth-century Moroccan sufi 'Abd al-Aziz al-Dabbagh and probably earlier (see Nallino, "Dottrine," p. 405). An account of the idea and a definition of it is given by al-Sanusi in his *Manhal* (included in the *Majmu'at Mukhtara*), pp. 49–50.
24 *Al-'Iqd al-nafis, passim.*
25 This date is disputed; it is 1835, according to Ziadeh, *Sanusiyah,* p. 45; in J. S. Trimingham, *The Sufi Orders in Islam,* Oxford 1971, p. 115, the date is given as 1827, whereas Nallino, "Dottrine," p. 397, suggests 1828 or 1829.
26 Dajjani, *Haraka,* pp. 79–80.

27   *Ibid.,* pp. 80–2.

28   Nallino, "Dottrine," p. 401.

29   Dajjani, *Haraka,* pp. 73–4.

30   *Ibid.,* p. 75.

31   *Ibid.,* p. 76.

32   Nallino, "Dottrine," p. 397, suggests that al-Sanusi might have been plan-
      ning to stay in Libya from 1822 or 1823, and that even on his journey to
      Cairo at that time he stayed at Yizliten (Zliten) near Tripoli, where he
      "made friends with learned and pious persons, who were useful to him a
      few years later for the realization of his large-scale plans."

33   Dajjani, *Haraka,* pp. 78, 80; Shukri, *Sanusiya,* p. 30. For the career of
      'Ashqar 'Ali Pasha, see al-Tahir Ahmad al-Zawi, *Wulat tarabulus min
      bidayat al-fath al-'Arabi ila nihayat al'ahd al-Turki,* Tripoli 1390/1970, pp.
      244–6; Mehmet Behij al-Din, *Tarih-i-Ibn Ghalbun,* Istanbul 1284/1867,
      pp. 132–7.

34   Klopfer, *Aspekte,* p. 35. Klopfer's source here is a *Festschrift* written by the
      staff of the Sanusi University (Benghazi?) on the occasion of the hundredth
      anniversary of al-Sanusi's death; it was published at Tripoli in 1376/1956.

35   Dajjani, *Haraka,* pp. 78–80, quoting al-Ashhab, *Al-Sanusi al-Kabir,* Cairo
      1952 (?), p. 103.

36   The document in question is in the *Dar al-Mahfuzat al-Ta'rikhiya,* no.
      196/3/501, Tripoli, and is reproduced in Dajjani, *Haraka,* pp. 295–6. From
      Muhammad bin 'Abdallah in southern Algeria to the Ottoman *mudir* of
      Ghadamis, al-Hajj Musa Agha, dated 6 Jumada II 1268/28 March 1852,
      the letter refers to the "blessing" of al-Sanusi for one of Muhammad b.
      'Abdallah al-Sharif's enterprises against the French. See also Peter von
      Sivers, "The Disease of the Infidel: Crisis of Authority in 19th-Century
      Muslim Algeria," unpublished paper, Los Angeles, 1970, pp. 19–21.

37   Dajjani, *Haraka,* p. 82, mentions clashes between the adherents of the
      Sanusiya and the Darqawis in Tripoli at this time.

38   Dajjani, *Haraka,* p. 81.

39   For the fantastic career of Ghuma al-Mahmudi, see A. Streicker, *Govern-
      ment and Revolt in Tripoli Regency, 1795–1855,* unpublished M.A. thesis,
      Northwestern University, 1970; 'Ali Mustafa al-Misurati, *Ghuma, faris al-
      Sahra',* Tripoli 1968.

40   See E. Subtil, "Histoire d'Abd el-Gelil Sultan du Fezzan," *Revue de
      l'Orient,* 1844.

41   Klopfer, *Aspekte,* p. 36.

42   Evans-Pritchard, *Sanusi,* pp. 15–6.

43   Fazlur Rahman, *Islam,* N.Y. 1968, p. 240.

44   B. G. Martin, "A Short History of the Khalwati Order of Dervishes," in
      N. Keddie (ed.), *Scholars, Saints, and Sufis,* Berkeley 1972, pp. 297–8.
      For the Wahhabis, see Fazlur Rahman, *Islam,* pp. 240–7.

45   Fazlur Rahman, *Islam,* pp. 247–50.

46   Fazlur Rahman, *Islam,* Chapter XII, *passim.*

47   Fazlur Rahman, *Islam,* pp. 242–5. For another interesting reformer, Mu-
      hammad b. 'Abdallah al-Shawkani (1758–1834) of San'a' in Yaman, see
      'Abd al-Muta'al al-Sa'idi, *Al-Mujaddidun fi'l-Islam, min al-qarn al-awwal
      ila'l-rabi' 'ashar,* Cairo n.d., pp. 472–5. Al-Shawkani was a prolific author,
      a critic of *taqlid,* and an advocate of *ijtihad.*

48   Nallino, "Dottrine," p. 401.

49 Dajjani, *Haraka*, pp. 85–8.
50 Evans-Pritchard, *Sanusi*, Chapter III, pp. 62–89.
51 Ziadeh, *Sanusiyah*, pp. 46–7.
52 Nallino, "Dottrine," pp. 409–10.
53 See the comments by Hamilton, *Wanderings*, pp. 96–7, about a hostile *zawiya* chief near "Grennah" in Cyrenaica; G. Nachtigal, *Sahara and Sudan*, ed. A. G. B. and H. J. Fisher, IV, London 1971, pp. 43–4; Henri Duveyrier, *La Confrérie Musulmane, passim*.
54 Dar al-Kitab al-Lubnani, Beirut.
55 Dajjani, *Haraka*, pp. 132–6.
56 Another issue was his rejection of loose analogical reasoning. This was another procedure rejected by the Hanbalis and the two Ibn Taymiyas. According to Nallino, "Dottrine," p. 400, al-Sanusi used to quote Imam Ja'far al-Sadiq (d. 765), who attacked the founder of the Hanafi school of law: "O, al-Nu'man, I have heard that you interpret knowledge ['ilm] on the basis of analogical reasoning [*qiyas*]. . . . Don't do it: the first to make comparisons in that way was Iblis [the Devil]."
57 Dajjani, *Haraka*, p. 136, includes two unpublished writings entitled *Bughyat al-sul fi'l-ijtihad wa'l-'amal bi-ahadith al-Rasul* and *Fahm al-akbad fi mawadd al-ijtihad*.
58 *Bughyat al-Maqasid*, in King Idris I, *Majmu'a*, pp. 93–4.
59 See Section IV of *Bughyat al-Maqasid* in King Idris I, *Majmu'a*, 83ff., on the types of *ijtihad* and the various kinds of *mujtahids*.
60 In King Idris I, *Majmu'a*, pp. 5–47.
61 Dajjani, *Haraka*, p. 134, lists: *Al-Shamus al-Shariqa fi asanid shuyukhina al-Maghariba wa'l-Mashariqa, al-Budur al-Safira fi 'awali al-Asanid al-Fakhira*, and *al-Kawakib al-Durriya fi awa'il al- al-kutub al-athariya*.
62 Duveyrier, *Confrérie*, p. 6.
63 Shukri, *Sanusiya*, p. 42; Dajjani, *Haraka*, p. 141.
64 *Shudhur al-dhahab fi mahd muhaqqaq al-nasab*, Dajjani, *Haraka*, p. 135.
65 See King Idris I, *Majmu'a*, which includes this work also.
66 This point was noted by the anonymous author of the article "al-Sanusi," in *EI*[1].
67 *Rayhanat al-Hubub fi 'amal al-sutub wa'l-juyub*, Dajjani, *Haraka*, p. 136.
68 *Miftah al-jafr al-kabir*, Dajjani, *Haraka*, p. 136.
69 Dajjani, *Haraka*, p. 136.
70 Ahmad al-Sharif's books are difficult to find. One of them is *Al-Durrat al-fardiya fi bayan mabni'l-tariqat al-Sanusiya*, Bombay n.d.; another, better known, is *Al-Anwar al-Qudsiya fi muqaddimat al-tariqat al-Sanusiya*, Istanbul 1339–1342/1920–4. Two manuscripts, the *Kawakib al-zahir* and the *Durr al-farid*, are listed in Dajjani, *Haraka*, p. 304.
71 Dajjani, *Haraka*, p. 89.
72 Nallino, "Dottrine," pp. 408–9.
73 Dajjani, *Haraka*, pp. 89–90, quoting Sadiq al-Mu'ayyad al-'Azm, *Afrika Sahra-yi kebirinde seyahat*, Istanbul 1314/1896–7.
74 See also Nallino, "La Dottrine del Fondatore della Confraternita Senussita," in *Raccolta*, I, pp. 111–7.
75 Dajjani, *Haraka*, pp. 96–7.
76 See the story of 'Abbas Pasha, his mother, and the gold purse, narrated by Dajjani, *Haraka*, pp. 97–8. According to the King of Libya, his ancestor "disliked having anything to do with rulers and avoided them."

77   Ziadeh, *Sanusiyah,* pp. 47–8; Shukri, *Sanusiya,* pp. 36–7.
78   Rinn, *Marabouts,* p. 492.
79   Shukri, *Sanusiya,* p. 39; Dajjani, *Haraka,* p. 115ff.
80   Ziadeh, *Sanusiyah,* p. 98.
81   D. Margoliouth, "Sanusi," in J. Hastings (ed.), *Encyclopedia of Religion and Ethics,* XI, p. 195.
82   Dajjani, *Haraka,* pp. 99–101; Shukri, *Sanusiya,* p. 34.
83   Dajjani, *Haraka,* pp. 100–1.
84   Evans-Pritchard, *Sanusi,* p. 14.
85   *Ibid.,* p. 18.
86   Klopfer, *Aspekte,* p. 26.
87   See Dajjani, *Haraka,* pp. 71–2, 103–7. Although 'Ashqar 'Ali had been suspicious of al-Sanusi at the start, al-Sanusi soon won the pasha's confidence and appreciation. The subsequent course of friendly relations may be illustrated by the documents exchanged between al-Sanusi and the Ottoman government in Libya. Dajjani (pp. 103–4) includes a long extract from one of these documents, and others are included in the appendices to his book. Other similar documents, showing the identical good relations between al-Sanusi and the Turks, and al-Mahdi al-Sanusi and the Ottoman authorities may be seen in Klopfer, *Aspekte,* pp. 70–90, with German translations. Thus the weight of the evidence is clearly against the line taken by Rinn and Duveyrier that there was unrelenting mutual hostility between the Sanusis and Ottomans.
88   Sadiq Bey al-Mu'ayyad was one of the famous 'Azm clan of Damascus, and he served as the sultan's chamberlain, or aide-de-camp. He went to Jaghbub on one occasion (1891) and to Kufra on another (about 1895). Rashid Pasha, the *veli,* or *müteserrif,* of Cyrenaica, was another visitor about 1890. See Ziadeh, *Sanusiyah,* pp. 62–4; Shakib Arslan, *Hadir,* II, pp. 142, 144. See note 73 for the title of Sadiq Bey's book, unfortunately not accessible to me.
89   See Dajjani, *Haraka,* pp. 103–7 for a lengthy discussion of this point.
90   Al-Sanusi died on 9 Safar 1276/7 September 1859, according to Klopfer, *Aspekte,* p. 24.
91   Evans-Pritchard, *Sanusi,* p. 18.
92   Muhammad al-Ashab, *Barqat al-'Arabiya, ams wa'l-yawm,* Cairo 1366/1947, pp. 142–160, contains a long list of the companions of al-Sanusi, with short biographies of each. Many of these served on the council – 'Imran bin Baraka and Ahmad al-Rifi, for example.
93   Dajjani, *Haraka,* pp. 174–5.
94   Shukri, *Sanusiya,* p. 38.
95   Dajjani, *Haraka,* p. 180.
96   *Ibid.,* p. 179.
97   J. S. Trimingham, *The Sufi Orders in Islam,* Oxford 1971, p. 120.
98   Dajjani, *Haraka,* p. 181.
99   *Ibid.,* p. 272.
100   Duveyrier, *Confrérie,* p. 22.
101   Dajjani, *Haraka,* p. 182.
102   *Ibid.,* p. 182.
103   *Ibid.*
104   *Ibid.,* p. 183.
105   P. M. Holt, *The Mahdist State in the Sudan,* 2nd ed., Oxford 1970, p. 54.

106 Ibn Khaldun, *Muqaddima*, ed. F. Rosenthal, II, N.Y. 1956, p. 156ff.
107 Holt, *Mahdist State*, pp. 112–3. The text of this letter can be seen in Dajjani, *Haraka*, 188–9; Ibrahim Fawzi, *Al-Sudan bayn yaday Kitshinir wa Ghurdun*, II, Cairo 1901, p. 216ff.; or Muhammad Abu Salim, *Manshurat al-Mahdi*, II, Khartum 1963, pp. 70–3. There is an English translation in Ziadeh, *Sanusiyah*, pp. 53–7.
108 Dajjani, *Haraka*, p. 190.
109 *Ibid.*, p. 191.
110 *Ibid.*, pp. 222–3; Shukri, *Sanusiya*, pp. 90–1.
111 Duveyrier, *Confrérie*, pp. 18–9.
112 *Ibid.*, p. 26; Klopfer, *Aspekte*, p. 40.
113 Duveyrier, *Confrérie*, pp. 24–31; Klopfer, *Aspekte*, pp. 40–1.
114 Duveyrier, *Confrérie*, p. 8.
115 *Ibid.*, p. 79.
116 *Ibid.*, pp. 44–5.
117 Nachtigal, *Sahara and Sudan*, pp. 63–4.
118 Duveyrier, *Confrérie*, pp. 45–6.
119 *Ibid.*
120 Ulrich Braukaemper, *Der Einfluss des Islam auf die Geschichte und Kulturentwicklung Adamauas*, Wiesbaden 1970, p. 101. It has been claimed that Mamadou Lamine (al-Hajj Muhammad al-Amin), the Soninke jihad leader of the 1880s in Senegal, was a Sanusi. He did marry a woman from Waday who was the daughter of a Sanusi leader, but he seems to have been himself an unorthodox Tijani. For comments on this question, see H. J. Fisher, "The Pilgrimage of Muhammad al-Amin," *JAH*, 11, 1970, pp. 51–69, esp. p. 57.
121 See the "geographical list" of *zawiyas* in Duveyrier, *Confrérie*, p. 57ff.
122 See the map in Evans-Pritchard, *Sanusi*, p. 15.
123 E. Rossi, *Storia di Tripoli e della Tripolitania, dalla Conquista Araba al 1911*, Rome 1968, p. 332; Ziadeh, *Sanusiyah*, p. 34; Rinn, *Marabouts*, pp. 495–6.
124 Ziadeh, *Sanusiyah*, p. 33.
125 Andre Martel, *Les Confins Saharo-Tripolitans de la Tunisie, 1881–1911*, I, Paris 1965, Chapter IV.
126 'Abdallah al-Tamimi, *Watha'iq wa buhuth*, Beirut 1971, pp. 102–3.
127 Abdurrahman Cayçi, *Büyük Sahra'da Türk-Fransiz Rekabeti (1858–1911)*, Erzerum 1970, pp. 69–70.
128 See Duveyrier, *Confrérie*, p. 41, for a typical expression of these attitudes; also Rinn, *Marabouts*, p. 495, pp. 510–1. The closeness of these two writers to French official quarters is enough to guarantee the accuracy of the views expressed.
129 René Pottier, *Un Prince Saharien Meconnu: Henri Duveyrier*, Paris 1938, *passim*.
130 Henri Duveyrier, *Exploration du Sahara; Les Touareg du Nord*, Paris 1864.
131 Paris 1884, 1886, in the publication series of the Parisian Société de Géographie.
132 For a revealing account of French activities in Senegal and Sahara, see A. S. Kanya-Forstner, *The Conquest of the Western Sudan, a Study in French Military Imperialism,* Cambridge, 1969.
133 Rossi, *Storia*, p. 339; Cayçi, *Büyük Sahra*, p. 49. See B. G. Martin, "Five Letters from the Tripoli Archives," *JHSN*, 2, 1964, pp. 350–72, particularly

Letter V, concerning the Mai or Bornu, who styles himself *"mutasarrif* of Bornu" in a communication to 'Ali Riza Pasha, Veli of Tripoli. See Rossi, *Storia,* p. 339, note 95, for a letter from the Amir of Zinder to the Veli of Tripoli c. 1870, in the *Millet Kütübhanesi,* Istanbul.

134   Rossi, *Storia,* pp. 339–40.
135   *Ibid.,* p. 340.
136   Rossi, *Storia,* p. 341. Some details of the project can also be seen in Ömer Subhi, *Trablusgarb ve Binghazi ile Sahra-yi Kebir ve Sudan merkezi,* Istanbul 1307/1889–1890.
137   See the French text of this note in Cayçi, *Büyük Sahra,* pp. 194–5.
138   See Martel, *Confins,* I, pp. 700–24, for the Morès affair.
139   The reports of weapons at Jaghbub in Duveyrier, *Confrérie,* p. 21 are hardly credible, nor the remarks of Ziadeh, *Sanusiyah,* p. 62, on the same subject.
140   Shukri, *Sanusiya,* p. 94.
141   *Ibid.,* pp. 94–5; Evans-Pritchard, *Sanusi,* pp. 22–3.
142   Evans-Pritchard, *Sanusi, passim.*

Chapter 5

1   The vocalization of this name is ambiguous. It may be either a plural or a dual. For an explanation of the phrase, see note 5 below.
2   Muhammad Mustafa Murabbih Rabbuh, *Qurrat al-'Aynayn fi karamat al-Shaykh Ma' al-'Aynayn,* ms. in the Moroccan National Library, Rabat. This compilation, written about 1930, is an indispensable source for the career of Ma' al-'Aynayn. I would like to thank Dr. H. T. Norris for giving me access to his microfilm of this manuscript, and Tom Whitcomb for obtaining photographs of it for me. Two other sons of Ma' al-'Aynayn – Muhammad Taqiallah and Sidi Buya – wrote short biographies of their father, but neither of them are accessible to me. See E. Levi-Provençal, "Ma al-'Ainain," *EI*[1], 3, and Julio Caro Baroja, "Un Santon Sahariano y su Familia," in *Estudios Saharianos,* Madrid 1955, pp. 285–335, esp. p. 294. Muhammad al-'Aqib al-Miyabi, *Majma' al-Bahrayn 'ala karamat Shaykhina Ma 'al-'Aynayn* is another manuscript source frequently quoted by Murabbih Rabbuh.
3   Rabbuh, *Qurra,* fol. 60.
4   *Ibid.,* fol. 60. P. Marty, "Les Fadelia," *RMM,* 21, 1915–6, p. 157, claims that Ma' al-'Aynayn was born between Gumbu and Walata in the "year of the comet" (1838?). I prefer the date 10 February 1831 (27 Sha'ban 1246) given by Murabbih Rabbuh.
5   H. T. Norris, "Shaykh Ma' al-'Aynayn al-Qalqami in the Folk-Literature of the Spanish Sahara," *BSOAS,* 31, 1968, pp. 113–37 and 347–76, esp. p. 116. According to Marty, "Fadelia, p. 157, she came from the Tulbat al-Ataris, "fraction maraboutique du Hodh," whereas according to Caro Baroja, "Santon," p. 293, she gave her son the name Ma' al-'Aynayn because he was her only son, and losing him to illness would be like losing the "water of her eyes" (the fluid within the eyeball) that "permits vision."
6   On the first page of his *Na't al-Bidayat wa tawsif al-Nihayat,* Cairo 1347/ 1927, Ma' al-'Aynayn cites a rhyming genealogy by al-'Alami. This sharifian family tree also appears in Baroja, "Santon," p. 288, note 6. Occasionally

useful for the career of Ma' al-'Aynayn is Angel Domenech Lafuente, "Ma el Ainin, Señor de Smara," *Africa, Revista de Tropas Coloniales,* 17, in eight or more parts, Madrid, beginning in July 1946, pp. 309–12. Much of the same material appears in the same author's book, *Algo sobre Rio de Oro,* Madrid 1946, pp. 34–44. The reference to Lamtuna ancestry appears in Section One of the article, p. 309.

7   According to this same genealogy (see note 6), Yahya al-Qalqami was nine generations away from Ma' al-'Aynayn.

8   According to P. Soleillet, *Voyages et Découvertes,* Paris 1881, p. 218, Muhammad Fadil was told by al-Hajj 'Umar, "Either you submit to me or we have a war." Fadil supposedly replied that he would never submit to anyone and would prefer to go into the Sahara and stay there, which he appears to have done in the 1860s.

9   See Marty, "Fadelia," p. 140.

10   Rabbuh, *Qurra,* fol. 60.

11   *Ibid.,* fol. 61.

12   *Ibid.*

13   Muhammad al-Mukhtar al-Susi, *Al-Mas'ul,* IV, Fadala, Morocco 1960, pp. 83–101.

14   Ma' al-'Aynayn, *Na't al-Bidayat,* pp. 190–9.

15   Rabbuh, *Qurra,* fol. 67.

16   *Ibid.,* fol. 71.

17   *Ibid.,* fols. 71–72, 86; Baroja, "Santon," p. 296.

18   Rabbuh, *Qurra,* fol. 89, says that his father had observed that the people of this region had a great "unsoundness" of belief.

19   Baroja, "Santon," pp. 296–7; Rabbuh, *Qurra,* fol. 91.

20   Susi, *Mas'ul,* IV, p. 97.

21   Camille Douls, "Cinq Mois chez les Maures Nomades du Sahara Occidentale," *Le Tour du Monde,* Paris 1888, pp. 177–224, esp. p. 202.

22   For an analysis of the descendants of Ma' al-'Aynayn, see Miguel Molina Compuzano, *Contribución al Estudio del Censo de Población del Sahara Español,* Madrid 1954, pp. 75–8.

23   Norris, "Ma' al-'Aynayn," p. 116.

24   Douls, "Cinq Mois," p. 199.

25   F. E. Trout, *Morocco's Southern Frontiers,* Geneva 1969, p. 156.

26   Douls, "Cinq Mois," p. 203.

27   Norris, "Ma al-'Aynayn," p. 369.

28   Douls, "Cinq Mois," p. 204.

29   Baroja, "Santon," p. 295.

30   D. MacKenzie, "The British Settlement at Cape Juby, Northwest Africa," *Blackwood's Edinburgh Magazine,* 146, 1889, pp. 412–21, esp. p. 412.

31   *Ibid.,* pp. 415–6.

32   E. Bonelli, "Viajes al interior del Sahara," *Boletín de la Sociedad Geográfica de Madrid,* 21, 1886, pp. 324–38.

33   The extent of al-Hasan's perturbation about these developments can be seen from his decrees about MacKenzie's and other foreigners' activities in the south; cf. Ibn Zaydan, *Ithaf A'lam al-nas bi-jamal akhbar Hadirat Miknas,* II, Rabat 1349/1930, p. 333ff.

34   Susi, *Mas'ul,* IV, p. 93.

35   Ahmad ibn Khalid al-Nasiri al-Salawi, *Al-Istiqsa' li-akhbar duwal al-Maghrib al-Aqsa',* IX, Casablanca 1956, pp. 180–2.

36 Douls, "Cinq Mois," p. 178.
37 Trout, *Frontiers*, p. 154.
38 Susi, *Mas'ul*, IV, p. 93.
39 Rabbuh, *Qurra*, fol. 93.
40 Domenech Lafuente, "Ma el Ainin," p. 312.
41 See Baroja, "Santon," pp. 304–5 for the literature of shipwrecks, etc., on this coast.
42 *Ibid.*, p. 300.
43 Rabbuh, *Qurra*, fol. 93.
44 Lafuente, "Ma el Ainin," p. 312.
45 Baroja, "Santon," p. 305, note 1.
46 Rabbuh, *Qurra*, fol. 94.
47 Susi, *Mas'ul*, IV, p. 93.
48 Rabbuh, *Qurra*, fols. 96–7. The foundation document for the Marrakish house is cited in its entirety by Rabbuh.
49 Lafuente, "Ma el Ainin," p. 311.
50 Susi, *Mas'ul*, IV, p. 93.
51 Rabbuh, *Qurra*, fol. 98.
52 *Ibid.*
53 Susi, *Mas'ul*, IV, pp. 93–5.
54 J. Asensio, in *Hesperis*, XI, Paris 1930, p. 33.
55 Norris, "Ma' al-'Aynayn," p. 376.
56 M. A. Ba, "À Propos de Smara," *L'Afrique Française*, 44, 1934, p. 96.
57 Baroja, "Santon," p. 306.
58 *Ibid.*, pp. 305–18, with plans and drawings.
59 *Ibid.*, p. 308.
60 In his *Mubsir al-Mutashawwif*, I, p. 139ff., Ma' al-'Aynayn has much to say about the *khalwa*, its uses, the length of such retreats, etc.
61 Ahmad al-Shinqiti, *Al-Wasit fi tarajim udaba al-Shinqit*, Cairo 1380/1960, pp. 365–6.
62 Ba, "Smara," p. 96.
63 Baroja, "Santon," pp. 308, 329.
64 G. Désiré-Vuillemin, *Contribution à l'histoire de la Mauritanie*, Dakar 1962, pp. 91–102.
65 *Ibid.*, p. 94.
66 *Ibid.*, p. 92.
67 *Ibid.*, p. 95.
68 See A. S. Kanya-Forstner, *The Conquest of the Western Sudan*, Cambridge 1969, for the details of French imperialism in this region.
69 Désiré-Vuillemin, *Contribution*, p. 95.
70 *Ibid.*, pp. 103, 114.
71 *Ibid.*, pp. 104, 114.
72 *Ibid.*, pp. 125–36.
73 *Ibid.*, p. 134ff.
74 Tijikja was a holy place for members of the Qudhfiya because one of their leaders was buried there. See E. Dermenghem, *Le Culte des Saints dans l'Islam Maghrebin*, Paris 1954, pp. 241–5.
75 Susi, *Mas'ul*, IV, p. 95.
76 *Ibid.*
77 *Ibid.*, pp. 95–6.
78 Edmund Burke, "The Moroccan Ulama, 1860–1912, An Introduction," in

N. Keddie (ed.), *Scholars, Saints, and Sufis,* Berkeley 1972, pp. 93–125, esp. p. 119.
79 'Allal al-Fasi, *Independence Movements in North Africa,* Washington 1954, p. 86.
80 Ibn Zaydan, *Ithaf,* I, Rabat 1928, p. 452.
81 Al Moutabassir, "Ma el Ainin ech Changuity," *RMM,* 1, 1907, pp. 343–51, esp. p. 346. For further information on this textile (*khant*) see al-Shinqiti, *Wasit,* p. 523.
82 Al Moutabassir, "Ma el Ainin," pp. 346–7.
83 *Ibid.,* pp. 347–8.
84 Marty, "Fadelia," p. 163.
85 *Ibid.,* p. 164.
86 Rabbuh, *Qurra,* fol. 114.
87 Baroja, "Santon," p. 320.
88 Norris, "Ma al-'Aynayn," p. 118.
89 Marty, "Fadelia," p. 166.
90 Rabbuh, *Qurra,* fol. 116.
91 Baroja, "Santon," p. 312; Rabbuh, *Qurra,* fols. 73–80.
92 Al-Moutabassir, "Ma el Ainin," p. 351.
93 See also Sarkis, *Mu'jam al-Matbu'at,* I, Cairo 1913, pp. 1602–6; Levi-Provencal, "Ma al-'Ainain," pp. 56–7; Zirikli, *Al-A'lam,* VIII–X, Cairo 1960, pp. 145–6; Brockelmann, *Geschichte der Arabischen Literatur,* Halle 1958.
94 See note 91 above.
95 *Hidayat al-mubtadi'yin fi'l-nahw* and *Tabyin al-Ghumud fi fann al-'arud.*
96 Rabbuh, *Qurra,* fols. 74–6; Al-Moutabassir, "Ma el Ainin," p. 350.
97 *Fatiq al-ratq,* on the margin of *Na't al-Bidayat,* Cairo 1347, p. 192.
98 *Ibid.,* p. 188.
99 *Ibid.,* p. 187.
100 *Ibid.,* pp. 132–4.
101 Ma' al-'Aynayn, *Na't al-Bidayat,* p. 20.
102 *Ibid.,* p. 200.
103 For "Anni mukhawi li-jami' al-turuq," see Al-Moutabassir, "Ma el Ainin," p. 349; Rabbuh, *Qurra,* fol. 74.
104 J. Abun-Nasr, *The Tijaniya, a Sufi Order in the Modern World,* London 1965, p. 21.
105 Ma' al-'Aynayn, *Mubsir al-mutashawwif,* II, Fez 1314, p. 176.
106 Al-Fasi, *Independence Movements,* pp. 80–1.
107 Zaydan, *Ithaf,* II, pp. 361–3.
108 *Ibid.,* pp. 359–60.
109 Ma' al-'Aynayn, *Mubsir,* II, pp. 225–6.
110 Al-Moutabassir, "Ma el Ainin," p. 347.
111 Cairo, n.d.
112 Ma' al-'Aynayn, *Madhhab,* p. 4.
113 Rabbuh, *Qurra,* fols. 33–4.
114 *Ibid.,* fols. 73–4.
115 Burke, "Ulama," p. 111.
116 Odette du Puigaudeau, "Une Nouvelle Généalogie de Cheikh Ma'-el-'Ainin u. Mamin," *Hesperis-Tamuda,* 14, 1973, pp. 157–63.

Chapter 6

1 An early draft of a part of this chapter appeared as "Muslin Resistance to Colonial Rule: Shaykh Uways b. Muhammad al-Barawi and the Qadiriya Brotherhood in East Africa," *JAH*, 10, 1969, pp. 471–86.

2 See B. G. Martin, "Arab Migrations to East Africa in Medieval Times," *IJAHS*, 7, 1974.

3 Burhan Mkelle, *Ta'rikh jaziratina Qumr al-Kubra*, fol. 41; Xerox of author's manuscript in my possession.

4 Sayyid Ahmad b. 'Abd al-Rahman, *Manaqib al-Sayyid Muhammad b. Ahmad b. Abi Bakr al-Shadhili al-Yashruti*, Cairo 1353/1934. There is an abridged French translation of this text by Paul Guy and Abdourahamane bin Cheik Amir, *La Vie et l'Oeuvre du Grand Marabout des Comores, Said Mohamed ben Ahmad al-Ma'arouf*, Tananarive 1949.

5 Lyndon Harries, "The Swahili Chronicle of Ngazija," unpublished paper, Madison, Wisconsin 1968, p. 23.

6 'Abd al-Rahman, *Manaqib*, pp. 7–8.

7 Fatima al-Yashrutiya, *Rihlat ila'l-Haqq*, Beirut n.d. (c. 1958), p. 55.

8 'Abd al-Rahman, *Manaqib*, pp. 11–14; Shaykh 'Abdallah Saleh Farsy, *Tarehe ya Imam Shafi*, Zanzibar 1944, p. 8.

9 Sultan Chouzour, *Idéologies et Institutions: L'Islam aux Comores*, Aix-en-Provence 1972, p. 61.

10 'Abd al-Rahman, *Manaqib*, pp. 14–5.

11 *Ylang-ylang* is an essential oil, made from the flowers of a small tree and used as the chemical base of many perfumes.

12 Sultan Chouzour, *Idéologies*, pp. 17, 65. Among other social reforms, Ma'ruf wished to outlaw ostentatious "*grands mariages*" among Comorians.

13 'Abd al-Rahman, *Manaqib*, p. 16. Ma'ruf was an author and poet as well as a man of great spiritual gifts. He wrote a short prose treatise on the distinction between true and false inspiration in dreams, based on certain observations by the fourteenth-century Shadhili author al-Iskandari in his *Kitab al-Hikam*. Ma'ruf's poetry is of a high standard. One of his poems deals with the close relation between the *shaykh* and his pupil; another uses the old sufi imagery of wine and intoxication to describe the relation between an advanced mystic and God.

14 'Abd al-Rahman, *Manaqib*, pp. 37–42.

15 See J. van Ess, "Die Yašrutiya" (Libanesische Miszellen, VI), *Die Welt des Islams*, XIV, Vienna.

16 'Abd al-Rahman, *Manaqib*, pp. 8–9.

17 Yashrutiya, *Rihla*, pp. 152–3.

18 *Ibid.*, pp. 257–8.

19 Sayyid Naguib al-'Attas, *Preliminary Statement on a General Theory of the Islamization of the Malay-Indonesian Archipelago*, Kuala Lumpur 1969, p. 17.

20 Shaykh 'Umar 'Abdallah, oral information, Moroni, August 1970.

21 Burhan Mkelle, *Ta'rikh*, fols. 50, 55–6.

22 M. D. D. Newitt, "Angoche, the Slave Trade, and the Portuguese, c. 1844–1910," *JAH*, 13, 1972, pp. 659–72, esp. p. 662.

23 Ernesto Jardim da Vilhena, "A Influencia Islamica na costa Oriental d'Africa," *Boletim da Sociedade de Geografica de Lisboa*, 24a, 1906, pp. 133–46, 166–80, 197–218.

24 *Ibid.*, p. 201.

25 *Ibid.*, pp. 202–3.

26 See the comments of Sayyid Najib al-'Attas, *Preliminary Statement*, pp. 25–6. Every Muslim is expected to know his own faith in its essentials, and therefore he is a potential missionary of Islam. Thus a trader or merchant can easily serve as a proselytizer.

27 Burhan Mkelle, *Ta'rikh*, fol. 55.

28 R. G. P. Lamburn, "The Yaos of Tunduru, An Essay in Missionary Anthropology," unpublished paper, Makerere University Library, n.d., quoted by E. A. Alpers, "Toward a History of the Expansion of Islam in East Africa: The Matrilineal Peoples of the Southern Interior," unpublished paper, Los Angeles 1971, p. 27.

29 See A. Oded, *Islam in Uganda, Islamization Through a Centralized State in Pre-Colonial Africa*, N.Y. 1974, p. 246, a letter written by an Arab trader for Kabaka Mutesa in 1882, to Sir John Kirk.

30 See *Akta des kaiserlichen Gouvernements von Deutsch-Ostafrika betreffend religioese Bewegungen (Islamische Bewegungen)* series G9, vol. 46 (Band 1, 1908–10), National Archives of Tanzania, Dar es-Salaam. Telegrams from Bezirksamtmann Wendt, Lindi, to von Rechenberg, Dar es-Salaam, 26 and 27 July 1908.

31 *Akta*, vol. 46, telegrams of Wendt to von Rechenberg, governor of German East Africa, and Schoen, Bezirksamtsmann Kilwa, to von Schleinitz, 3 August 1908, letter, Wendt to von Rechenberg, 19 August 1908.

32 See a new translation by me of the Mecca Letter in *Akta*, vol. 46, item 15469, in C. H. Becker, "Materials for the Understanding of Islam in East Africa," *TNR*, 1968, p. 59. 'Isa B. Ahmad was also called "al-Msujini"; see p. 157.

33 *Akta*, vol. 46, Letter, Wendt to von Rechenberg, 13 August 1908.

34 *Akta*, vol. 46, Dispatch, von Rechenberg to Reichskolonialamt, 13 August 1908.

35 Shaykh Abdallah Saleh al-Farsy, *Sayyid Said bin Sultan*, English trans. J. W. T. Allen, Zanzibar 1944, pp. 32, 38, 56. For Bushiri, see J. A. Kieran, "Abushiri and the Germans," B. A. Ogot (ed.), *Hadith*, III, Nairobi 1970, pp. 156–201.

36 For the career of Shaykh Uways, see 'Abd al-Rahman b. Shaykh 'Umar al-Qadiri, *Jala' al-'Aynayn fi manaqib al-Shaykhayn, al-Shaykh al-Wali Hajj Uways al-Qadiri wa'l-Shaykh 'Abd al-Rahman al-Zayla'i*, Cairo n.d. (c. 1954); by the same author, *Al-Jawhar al-Nafis fi khawass al-Shaykh Uways*, Cairo 1383 H./1964. There is also some material in Ibn Muhyi al-Din Qasim's *Majmu'a qasa'id fi madh Sayyid al-Anbiya' wa Sidi 'Abd al-Qadir al-Jaylani*, 3rd ed., Cairo 1374/1955.

37 'Umar al-Qadiri, *Jala'*, p. 3, *Jawhar*, pp. 8–9.

38 'Umar, al-Qadiri, *Jala'*, p. 3.

39 'Umar al-Qadiri, *Jawhar*, p. 9. For a short biography of Salman al-Jaylani (or Kaylani), see 'Abd al-Karim 'Allaf, *Baghdad al-Qadima*, Baghdad 1380/1960, pp. 198–200. For the Kaylani family in the later nineteenth century – their ties to the Ottomans – see Ibrahim al-Durubi, *Al-Baghdadiyun, akhbaruhun wa majalisuhum*, Baghdad 1377/1958, p. 5–23. Sayyid Salman bin 'Ali (1843–95), the father of Shaykh Uways' teacher, Mustafa ibn al-Sayyid Salman, was on very good terms with Sultan 'Abd al-Hamid II. Salman visited the sultan at least twice in Istanbul and was decorated with a medal

of the Mecidiye order, first class. Later, he was made *kaziasker* of Anatolia and then of Rumelia ('Allaf, *Baghdad*, p. 199). Thus it is quite conceivable that the Uwaysiya branch of the Qadiri order was open to important Pan-Islamic influences.

40   'Umar al-Qadiri, *Jala'*, pp. 3–10, *Jawhar*, pp. 9–10.
41   J. S. Trimingham, *The Sufi Orders in Islam*, Oxford 1971, pp. 114–6, 121.
42   For the Arabic text of this *qasida*, see Ibn Muhyi al-Din Qasim, *Majmu'a qasa'id*, pp. 69–70.
43   The Karramiya was a Muslim set of eastern Persia named for Abu 'Abdallah Muhammad b. Karram (d. 225/869–70). One of their doctrines stated that God had a "body"; this shocked their contemporaries. See *Shorter Encyclopedia of Islam*, Leiden 1953, pp. 223–4.
44   The Janahiya were followers of 'Abdallah b. Mu'awiya; they are also known as the Tayyariya. This minor Shi'i sect believed in reincarnation, metempsychosis, and an allegorical exposition of the *Qur'an*. See "Djanahiya," *EI¹*, 1, p. 1013.
45   'Umar al-Qadiri, *Jala'*, p. 56. Pages 52–6 of this book contain a full account of the murder of Shaykh Uways, probably by Bah Geri tribesmen, who were supporters of Muhammad 'Abdallah Hasan.
46   The fact that he called himself the "Master of the Time" suggests that Uways was concerned about millennial issues, although this point is far from conclusive.
47   E. Cerulli, "Note Sulle Movimenti Musulmani nella Somalia," *Somalia*, 1, 1957, p. 4.
48   'Umar al-Qadiri, *Jala'*, p. 51, includes two lines of a *qasida* by Shaykh Uways in the "Rahanwayniya language" (in Arabic script), in which Uways predicts his own death at the hands of the Salihiya. The *qasida* is described as being of some length. Cerulli, *Somalia*, 3, p. 37, includes the text and an Italian translation of another poem of Shaykh Uways, also written in Arabic script. Doubtless others could be recovered. For other poetry, including some about the Salihiya, see B. W. Andrzejewski and I. M. Lewis, *Somali Poetry, An Introduction*, Oxford 1964.
49   For an account of Uways' travels, see 'Umar al-Qadiri, *Jala'*, pp. 10–2. A partial list of *khalifas* created by Shaykh Uways is given in *Jawhar*, pp. 17–24; it includes one man, 'Ubud al-'Amudi, who was sent to Java. Some of the *nisbas* (names indicating geographical origins) gave some hints as to the varied ethnic backgrounds of Uways' followers: al-Barawi, al-Shashi (from a quarter in Mogadishu), al-Maqdishi, al-Gandarshi, al-Marki, al-Zanjibari, al-Hadrami, al-Oghadini, al-'Alawi, al-'Aydarus, al-Rahanwayni, al-Warshaykhi, al-Bantu'i, etc.
50   'Umar al-Qadiri, *Jawhar*, pp. 10–1.
51   'Umar al-Qadiri, *Jala'*, pp. 21–40, *Jawhar*, pp. 119–54. According to A. H. Nimtz, Jr., "The role of the Muslim Sufi Order in Political Change: An Overview and Micro-Analysis from Tanzania," unpublished Ph.D. thesis, Bloomington, Indiana 1973, p. 58, two informants (Shaykh Kassim b. Juma and Shaykh Hasan b. Umayr) claim that Barghash invited Shaykh Uways to Zanzibar in 1301/1883–84.
52   'Umar al-Qadiri, *Jala'*, p. 22.
53   *Ibid.*, pp. 3, 22. According to Nimtz, "Role," pp. 61, 73–4, 'Umar accepted a khalifaship from Uways in 1301/1883–4. His sons 'Ali and Muhammad

continued to spread the *tariqa* – particularly 'Ali, who was probably instrumental in spreading the order in the Rufiji District.

54 Shaykh Abdullah Saleh al-Farsy, *Tarehe Imam Shafi*, Zanzibar 1944. English trans. J. W. T. Allen, pp. 17–9; Swahili text, pp. 35–8.

55 One of these was doubtless the 'Aydarusiya. Another Qadiri link to East Africa is that of the Barzanji family – a group of Kurdish Qadiri (and Naqshbandi) sayyids from the village of Barzanja, near Sulaymaniya in northern Iraq. Ja'far bin Hasan b. 'Abd al-Karim al-Barzanji (1690–1764), who was the Shafi'i *mufti* of Madina, wrote a *mawlid* in verse that is still very popular along the coast. More information about this family can be had from Ahmad b. Ahmad b. Mahmud al-Barzanji, *Nafahat al-Utrujiya fi manaqib al-sadat al-Barzanjiya*, British Museum ms. or. 9571. It is not clear whether Ja'far or other Barzanjis actually visited East Africa.

56 'Umar al-Qadiri, *Jala'*, p. 22.

57 *Ibid.*, p. 27.

58 *Ibid.*, p. 30.

59 'Umar al-Qadiri, *Jawhar*, p. 24.

60 Oral information from Shaykh Hasan b. 'Umayr al-Shirazi – a prominent Qadiri leader, missionary, and Shafi'i *qadi* of Dar es-Salaam – 3 April 1968. For its movement into the Rufiji Delta, see National Archives of Tanzania, *Provincial Office, Eastern Provinces, Native Administration*, Rufiji, Morogoro P.O., File no. 61: ID 481, 486, 489–91, 492, 494; ID II, 621–2 of 1933 and 1936, about a dispute over *tariqa* flags that involved Shehe Mohammedi bin Shamte, a pupil of the Zanzibar Qadiri leader 'Ali bin 'Umar al-Qullatayn al-Barawi. I owe these references to Miss Anne Ackroyd.

61 See A. Abel, *Les Musulmans Noirs du Maniéma*, Brussels 1960; Crawford Young, "The Congo," Chapter 14 in J. Kritzeck and W. H. Lewis, *Islam in Africa*, N.Y. 1969.

62 The spread of this order is obscure. It is known in Mogadishu and on the Comoros, where its most important leader was "Ahmad Fundi" (d. 1945), whose real name was Ahmad bin Muhammad bin Khamis. Of Hadrami origin, Ahmad wrote *Al-Durrat al-samiya fi ma'rifat fada'il suluk al-tariqat al-Rifa'iya*, Cairo 1357/1937. On Anjouan, his home island, Muslims attached to other brotherhoods seem to look down on the Rifa'is and their leader. The Rifa'i practice of sticking skewers through the flesh of the neck, cheeks, and other parts of the face still continued on Anjouan in the summer of 1970.

63 *Akta*, vol. 46, J. 133, letter from Wendt, Lindi to Dar es-Salaam, 12 January 1909. In this letter, Wendt declares that "according to the *Liwali* of Lindi and Qadi Omar [a local Muslim leader], an Islamic movement, a kind of *zikri*, was taking place here about twenty years ago [1889], which died down in the von Wissmann period and then became popular again in 1901 and 1902 . . . spread by *shaykhs* from Zanzibar." Wendt also notes its appearance at Sadani about 1903 and claims that he "warned" the district officer at Bagamoyo and the government about it at that time.

64 For these events, see R. Coupland, *The Exploitation of East Africa*, London 1939, pp. 15–6, 22–3.

65 Al-Farsy, *Sayyid Said*, pp. 36–7 of translation.

66 S. B. Miles, *The Countries and Tribes of the Persian Gulf*, London 1919, pp. 418–38, gives information as to the Hinawi or Ghafiri alignment of various tribes. More information as to the origins of this split will be found

in 'Abdallah bin Humayd al-Salimi, *Tuhfat al-A'yan bi-sirat ahl 'Uman*, II,
Cairo 1347/1928–9, pp. 121–9. R. F. Burton, *Zanzibar, City, Island and
Coast*, I, London 1872, pp. 372–4, notes that in Zanzibar and 'Uman the
rivals occupied separate quarters, would not intermarry, and rarely en-
countered each other without a "faction fight." An analysis of Hamid bin
Muhammad al-Murjibi or of names and *nisbas* of the Arabs mentioned in
Tippu Tib, *Maisha Tippu Tib kwa maneno yake mwenyewe*, ed., tr. W. H.
Whitely, Nairobi 1966, would show that a majority of the traders in slaves
and ivory on the African coast and inland were of the Hinawi group.

67 Burton, *Zanzibar*, I, pp. 372–4; al-Farsy, *Sayyid Said*, pp. 36–7 of translation.
68 Miles, *Countries*, p. 428, notes the Banu Jabir as Ghafiris.
69 See B. G. Martin, "Notes on Some Members of the Learned Classes of Zanzibar and East Africa in the 19th Century," *IJAHS*, 4, 1971, pp. 525–45.
70 Al-Farsy, *Tarehe*, translation, pp. 17–9. For the court faction, see Abdallah
bin Hemedi'l-Ajjemy, *The Kilindi*, Nairobi 1963, p. 208.
71 *Uganda Journal*, 15, 1951, pp. 49–64.
72 London 1952.
73 Oliver, "British Occupation," p. 52.
74 R. Oliver, *Missionary Factor*, pp. 107–8; Tippu Tib, *Maisha*, p. 23. That
Sulayman was a member of the Qadiriya was confirmed by Shaykh Hasan
b. 'Umayr al-Shirazi, interview, Dar es-Salaam 10 April 1968. He was also
a distant relative of Abu Bakr bin Taha al-Jabri al-Barawi of Bagamoyo,
according to Shaykh Hasan. According to Nimtz, "Role," p. 60, note 1,
Sulayman b. Zahir was not a Qadiri, nor from Brava. Nimtz's Tabora informants evidently disagree with Shaykh Hasan's recollection, which I prefer, as it is better supported by documentary evidence. For further information about this Sulayman b. Zahir (or Zuhayr), see Oded, *Islam in Uganda*,
pp. 240, 243, 273. In a letter to Kabaka Mutesa, which Oded wrongly thinks
is a forgery, Sayyid Barghash warned the Kabaka to get rid of the English
and warned him too about the missionaries.
75 Oliver, *Missionary Factor*, p. 108.
76 'Umar al-Qadiri, *Jawhar*, p. 24.
77 Oliver, *Missionary Factor*, p. 108.
78 N. R. Bennett, *Arab Power*, Boston 1964, pp. 218–9; Kieran, "Abushiri,"
III, pp. 168, 178, mentions Khalifa's "secret instructions" to the insurrectionists.
79 *Akta*, vol. 46, Dispatch, von Rechenberg to Colonial Office, 12 August 1908.
80 Al-Farsy, *Sayyid Said*, pp. 19, 37 of translation.
81 I would like to thank my former colleague Dr. J. Iliffe for this oral information from his files. The informant here is Abdiswamadu Abubakari of Lindi
and the information was collected in 1966, when he was about seventy.
82 The teacher was Qadi 'Omari bin Ahmad of Kilwa, father of Jamal al-Din
bin 'Omari, author of an account of the Maji Maji war.
83 H. N. Chittick, *Annual Report for 1958*, Department of Antiquities, Tanganyika government, Dar es-Salaam 1959, pp. 28–9.
84 Al-Farsy, *Sayyid Said*, p. 38 of translation.
85 See note 79.
86 E. C. Hore, *Tanganyika*, London 1892, pp. 86–7.
87 In mid-1886, Rumaliza was obtaining help from Tippu Tib for his activities

in Uvinza and elsewhere. See Tippu Tib, *Maisha*, p. 119; Hore, *Tanganyika*, p. 273.

88   According to Kieran, "Abushiri," p. 177, it was rumored in May 1889 that both Rumaliza ("Mohammed bin Alphan") and Tippu Tib's son Tipura were coming to attack the Germans at the coast. This detail comes ultimately from the Holy Ghost Fathers Archives, Paris, C. S. Sp. 197 A 11, Zanzibar, 7 May 1889, Courmont to Emonet, Mhonda Mission Journal, 1886–93, 5 December 1888.

89   Tippu Tib, *Maisha*, p. 131.

90   *Ibid.*, pp. 119–21; R. Schmidt, *Geschichte des Araberaufstandes in Ost-Afrika*, Frankfurt/Oder 1892, pp. 184, 217.

91   Schmidt, *Geschichte*, p. 184.

92   *Deutsches Kolonial-Blatt*, 1894, p. 6; H. Brode, *Tippoo Tib, the Story of His Career in Central Africa*, London 1907, p. 238.

93   Brode, *Tippoo Tib*, p. 239; *Deutsches Kolonial-Blatt*, 1894, pp. 6–14.

94   R. Slade, *King Leopold's Congo*, London 1960, p. 113.

95   Grant and Bagenal, *Kigoma District Book*, III, 1929.

96   T. von Prince, *Gegen Araber und Wahehe*, Berlin 1913, p. 293. For more information about Mkwawa and his fort, see Alison Redmayne, "Mkwawa and the Hehe Wars," *JAH*, 9, 1968, pp. 409–36.

97   *Deutsches Kolonial-Blatt*, 1895, p. 382; Brode, *Tippoo Tib*, p. 249. For further information on Shaykh Zahir, see Nimtz, "Role," pp. 65–6.

98   See Al-Farsy, *Tarehe*, translation, p. 25 for 'Ali bin Khamis al-Barwani, a cousin of Rumaliza's, who was persecuted and mistreated by Sayyid Barghash for abandoning his Ibadi views and becoming a Sunni.

99   For the texts of some of these manifestos sent to Northern Nigeria, see *Al-Khitabat al-mutabadila bayn al-Imam al-Mahdi wa'l Shaykh Hayatu*, Khartum 1381/1962, pp. 8–13.

100   See note 78. For further discussion of the possibility of minor Qadiri involvement in the Maji Maji rising, see Nimtz, "Role," pp. 69–70.

101   For this subject, see Becker, "Materials," pp. 34–7.

102   Burton, *Zanzibar*, I, p. 466.

103   Salah al-Bakri, *Fi janub al-jazirat al-'Arabiya*, Cairo 1368/1949, p. 192.

104   Some Baluchis were members of the Qadiri brotherhood. At the village of Kaole outside Bagamoyo is the tomb of a *khalifa* of the order named Shaykh 'Abd al-Rahman bin Jalal Khan al-Balushi (d. 1351/1932). See G. S. P. Freeman-Grenville and B. G. Martin, "A preliminary handlist of the Arabic inscriptions of the Eastern African Coast," *JRAS*, 112, 1973, p. 117.

105   *Akta*, vol. 46, Bezirksamtmann Dinckelacker, Bagamoyo, to government, Dar es-Salaam, 21 August 1908; letter from A. Lorenz, a German teacher in Bagamoyo, to government, 9 March 1909.

106   *Akta*, vol. 46, A. Lorenz to government, 9 March 1909.

107   'Umar al-Qadiri, *Jawhar*, p. 24; for Zahir's rainmaking and other activities, see Herrman, Draft Report, *Akta*, vol. 46, 5 December 1908.

108   *Akta*, vol. 46, von Rechenberg to Dinckelacker, Bagamoyo, 8 March 1909. For a different view, see Nimtz, "Role," p. 68.

109   *Akta*, vol. 46, H. Brode, German consul, Zanzibar, to government, Dar es-Salaam, J. 275, 8 April 1909.

110   *Akta*, vol. 46, Wendt, Lindi, to government, Dar es-Salaam, J. 770, 2 August, 1910, von Rechenberg to Wendt, 11 October 1910; etc. The trial of the

defendants was concluded by November 1910, as von Rechenberg believed that the matter had been allowed to drag on far too long. The material on the trial itself, in Section I D/8B of the German Archives in Tanganyika, has not been recovered and may have been lost or destroyed during the peregrinations of the German colonial administration after 1915.

111 L. W. Hollingsworth, *Zanzibar Under the Foreign Office, 1890–1913,* London 1953, pp. 177–90.
112 *Ibid.,* p. 47.
113 *Ibid.,* p. 189.
114 'Ali bin Hamud to 'Abd al-Hamid II, ARC 122a, Zanzibar Archives, Istanbul, undated (c. summer 1907). My thanks are due to Mr. E. Greene for the use of his copy of this document.
115 Becker, "Materials," pp. 35, 43.
116 The discovery of files of this newspaper would do much to illuminate the Pan-Islamic movement on Zanzibar. Zanzibar Archives?
117 Ahmad bin Sumayt, *Al-Ibtihaj fi bayan istilah al-Minhaj,* Cairo 1353/1935, p. 28.
118 See R. J. Gavin, "The Bartle Frere Mission to Zanzibar, 1873," The *Historical Journal,* 5, 1962, pp. 122–48, esp. pp. 124, 145.
119 Hollingsworth, *Zanzibar,* pp. 119–30.
120 *Ibid.,* pp. 80, 93–106.
121 See note 65 above.

Chapter 7

1 For Arab settlements in Somalia, see I. M. Lewis, *The Modern History of Somaliland,* London 1965, pp. 20–7; E. Cerulli, *Somalia,* 1, 1957, *passim.*
2 Migrations of individual Persians or groups of Iranians to the East African coast were a constant factor in medieval times, particularly near the time of the Mongol invasions. One example is that of the founders of the Shashiya (or Shanshiya) Quarter of Mogadishu. This name is derived from the central Asian city of Shash (or Chach, now Tashkent). In his *Kitab al-'Ibar,* Ibn Khaldun records that the population of Chach was ordered to evacuate the town c. 604/1207–8 by the Khwarizmshah Qutb al-Din Muhammad II. Chach lay in the path of an invading army of the Khita (Qara Khitay) led by Küchlüg Khan (the Kishli Khan of the Arabic sources). Two other towns, also in the Valley of Farghana – Isfijab and Kasan – were evacuated at the same time. According to a variant reading in Ibn Khaldun, the inhabitants of the three towns dispersed into the "lands of Islam," finally reaching "Cairo, Baghdad, and Mogadishu." This passage is not included in the Beirut edition of the *'Ibar* (V, 1961, p. 228), but it appears in an otherwise unidentified edition (Bulaq?) of the *'Ibar* cited by Sharif 'Aydarus al-Nadiri al-'Alawi, *Bughyat al-Amal fi ta'rikh al-Sumai,* Mogadishu 1955, pp. 45–6, where it is cited as "vol. VI, p. 107." Sharif 'Alawi first drew attention to this point. It is also worth noting that the tombs of certain Persians near Mogadishu whose inscriptions date to the early thirteenth century (see Cerulli, *Somalia,* 1, pp. 2 and 9) are dated not long after the evacuation of the population of Chach. The *nisba* of one of these persons (al-Khurasani) accords well with the geographical area from which he may have come.
3 See Jalal Yahya, *Al-Tanafus al-Duwali fi bilad al-Sumal,* Cairo 1959, pp. 76–7, for more details.

4   I. M. Lewis, "La Communità ('Giamia') di Bardera Sulle Rive del Giuba," in *Somalia d'Oggi*, II, Mogadishu 1957, pp. 36–7. According to Lewis, Ibrahim Jabaro may have been a member of the Ahmadiya. See also L. V. Cassanelli, "Migrations, Islam, and Politics in the Somali Benaadir, 1500–1843," in H. G. Marcus and J. Hinnant (eds.), *Proceedings of the first U.S. Conference on Ethiopian Studies . . . 1973*, East Lansing 1975, pp. 101–15. Cassanelli shows that the Bardera movement might have been of Wahhabi inspiration: it opposed saint cults (p. 110), and apparently had much in common with Muhammad 'Abdullah Hasan's movement later in the century.

5   Lewis, "Communità," p. 37.

6   See Vittorio Bottego, *L'Esplorazione del Giuba, Viaggio di Scoperta nel Cuore dell' Africa*, Rome 1900, p. 24. He states that by the time of his trip via Kolonkol in 1893, the *tariqa* settlement had been sacked and destroyed by the Ethiopians. This point is quoted by R. L. Hess, "The Poor Man of God, Muhammad Abdallah Hassan," in Norman R. Bennett (ed.), *Leadership in Eastern Africa, Six Political Biographies*, Boston 1968, p. 75, note 14.

7   For a hagiography of Shaykh Zayla'i, see 'Abd al-Rahman al-Qadiri, *Jala' al-'Aynayn fi manaqib al-Shaykhayn*, Cairo n.d., Part II.

8   See 'Abd al-Rahman, *Jala'*, Part I, for the career of Shaykh Uways.

9   The founder of this suborder of the Ahmadiya, Shaykh Muhammad al-Dandarawi, was seen by Swayne in 1893 when he visited his settlement on the Tug Fafan. He was then a very old man. Swayne states that the settlement "was full of *widads* and *mullahs* from different Somali tribes," and was "as large as Hargeisa." See H. G. C. Swayne, *Seventeen Trips through Somaliland*, London 1900, pp. 240–1.

10 For the Ahmadiya itself, see the chapter "Ahmad ibn Idris and sufism," in Amin Rihani, *Muluk al-'Arab*, I, Beirut 1951, pp. 278–93; J. S. Trimingham, *The Sufi Orders in Islam*, Oxford 1971, pp. 114–21. The Rifa'iya in Somalia was largely a coastal order with centers in the ports. An important figure of the order was Salim bin Ahmad Mirwas from Daw'an in the Hadramawt (d. 1936), the owner of the Mirwas Mosque in Mogadishu. In his *Bughya*, al-'Alawi includes a chapter on Somali sufi orders, pp. 221–9.

11 Le Chatelier, *Les Confréries Musulmanes du Hejaz*, Paris 1887, pp. 92–7.

12 Rihani, *Muluk*, I, pp. 287–8.

13 Trimingham, *Sufi Orders*, pp. 114–21.

14 Le Chatelier, *Confréries*, p. 92, calls Shaykh Muhammad ibn Salih al-Rashidi a *muqaddam* of the Rashidiya. According to him, the order had four *zawiyas* in Mecca. In this book, published in 1887, there is no mention of the Salihiya.

15 See Cerulli, *Somalia*, 1, p. 190.

16 'Ali Nairobi was from a Dulbahante fraction that had migrated to the Kismayu area. See E. R. Turton, "The Impact of Muhammad Abdille Hasan in the East Africa protectorate," *JAH*, 10, 1969, pp. 641–57, esp. p. 647.

17 According to F. S. Caroselli, *Ferro e Fuoco in Somalia*, Rome 1931, p. 8, this phrase was first put into circulation by the British colonel J. Hayes Sadler, who had been fighting other "mullahs" among the Afridi tribes of the Indo-Afghan Northwest Frontier District.

18 See p. 200.

19 Lewis, *Somaliland*, p. 65; 'Abd al-Sabur Marzuq, *Tha'ir min al-Sumal, al-Mulla Muhammad 'Abdallah Hasan*, Cairo 1964, p. 14.
20 Marzuq, *Tha'ir*, p. 14, gives his dates as 1836–1913 and suggests that he was an itinerant arbitrator of tribal disputes, known for his "patience and generosity."
21 Marzuq, *Tha'ir*, p. 15, suggests that Sayyid Muhammad spent about ten years in Somalia wandering about and seeking knowledge from many *shaykhs*; also Lewis, *Somaliland*, pp. 65–6. See also Jama' 'Umar 'Isa, *Ta'rikh al-Sumal fi'l-'usur al-wusta wa'l-haditha*, Cairo 1385/1965, pp. 54–5, who mentions his love of riding and horsemanship.
22 'Isa, *Ta'rikh*, p. 55, suggests 1889 as his date of departure for the Hijaz.
23 Marzuq, *Tha'ir*, p. 16, suggests that he had with him a group of thirteen pupils and companions, whose names he lists. He also states (pp. 16–7) that the Sayyid and his thirteen friends made a secret compact at the Tomb of the Prophet in Madina to return to Somalia and start a *jihad* against the four foreign powers who occupied Somalia. He gives no sources or other evidence for these statements, the validity of which is hard to assess.
24 Marzuq, *Tha'ir*, p. 16, gives the date of his return as 20 August 1895.
25 Lewis, *Somaliland*, p. 66; Marzuq, *Tha'ir*, pp. 18–9, mentions a clash between the Sayyid and a local *qadi* that landed Muhammad 'Abdallah Hasan in prison for a short time; he also notes an episode involving one of the *'ulama* of Berbera, a chewer of *qat*, denounced by the Sayyid.
26 For the issue of *tawassul*, see p. 197.
27 Lewis, *Somaliland*, p. 66.
28 'Isa, *Ta'rikh*, p. 55.
29 *Ibid.*, p. 60.
30 *Ibid.*, pp. 60–1. A similar story, involving a misionary, appears in Marzuq, *Tha'ir*, p. 20.
31 'Isa, *Tu'rikh*, p. 64.
32 *Ibid.*, p. 63. For a study of the French arms trade, see Enid Starkie, *Arthur Rimbaud in Abyssinia*, Oxford 1937.
33 'Isa, *Ta'rikh*, p. 59; a similar text occurs in Marzuq, *Tha'ir*, p. 37.
34 The original document is reproduced in D. Jardine, *The Mad Mullah of Somaliland*, London 1923, p. 40. The Sayyid's reply is reproduced on p. 42.
35 Lewis, *Somaliland*, p. 70.
36 See Anonymous, *The Somali Peninsula, New Light on Imperial Motives*, Mogadishu and London 1962, p. 34, Appendix II.
37 Lewis, *Somaliland*, p. 71; Marzuq, *Tha'ir*, pp. 42–4.
38 Turton, "Impact," pp. 63–109; Lewis, *Somaliland*, pp. 63–91.
39 Hess, "Poor Man," pp. 63–109; Lewis, *Somaliland*, pp. 63–91.
40 For a history of the war in Somalia seen from the British side, see *Official History of the Operations in Somaliland, 1901–04*, 2 vols., London 1907; H. Moyse-Bartlett, *The King's African Rifles, A Study in the Military History of East and Central Africa, 1890–1945*, Aldershot 1956.
41 Lewis, *Somaliland*, p. 68; Moyse-Bartlett, *King's African Rifles*, p. 164.
42 Moyse-Bartlett, *King's African Rifles*, p. 178.
43 'Isa, *Ta'rikh*, p. 66.
44 For an official account of this engagement, see Moyse-Bartlett, *King's African Rifles*, pp. 178–81.
45 'Isa, *Ta'rikh*, p. 75. Marzuq, *Tha'ir*, pp. 50–1, also has an account and estimates that there were about 6,400 men on the dervish side, of which

1,400 were cavalry and the rest foot soldiers. Among them they had about 600 rifles. The rest were armed with spears, swords, etc.

46 'Isa, *Ta'rikh,* pp. 68–9.
47 See Caroselli, *Ferro,* Chapters IV and V.
48 Lewis, *Somaliland,* pp. 72–3.
49 Caroselli, *Ferro,* Chapter V, esp. pp. 88–9.
50 *Ibid.,* Chapter VI.
51 See the Arabic document reproduced in Caroselli, *Ferro,* p. 224, signed by 'Ali Sa'id Pasha at Lahj in 1917, or the same text (with some errors) in Cerulli, *Somaliya,* 3, 1957, pp. 4–5.
52 Caroselli, *Ferro,* p. 164.
53 *Ibid.,* p. 171.
54 For the best Arabic text of this work, see *Somaliya,* 3, pp. 7–26. See note 70 below.
55 Caroselli, *Ferro,* Chapter VII.
56 Jardine, *Mad Mullah,* pp. 183–6.
57 Jardine, *Mad Mullah,* pp. 184–5, includes an English translation of this letter but unfortunately does not reproduce the Arabic text. The text in 'Isa, *Ta'rikh,* pp. 97–8, is merely a retranslation of the letter from the Italian of Caroselli, *Ferro,* pp. 129–31.
58 Most of the other *khalifas* of the Salihiya in the country, according to Caroselli, *Ferro,* p. 131, opposed the Sayyid on this occasion.
59 Caroselli, *Ferro,* p. 131.
60 'Isa, *Ta'rikh,* pp. 99–104.
61 Caroselli, *Ferro,* p. 136; Lewis, *Somaliland,* p. 75.
62 Caroselli, *Ferro,* pp. 141, 143.
63 Moyse-Bartlett, *King's African Rifles,* p. 192.
64 Lewis, *Somaliland,* p. 77.
65 See the plan of the Taleh forts in Caroselli, *Ferro,* p. 264.
66 Lewis, *Somaliland,* p. 77; for another English version of this poem, see B. W. Andrzejewski and I. M. Lewis, *Somali Poetry, An Introduction,* Oxford 1964, pp. 70–4; see 'Isa, *Ta'rikh,* pp. 117–8, for an Arabic version.
67 Moyse-Bartlett, *King's African Rifles,* pp. 420–2.
68 Caroselli, *Ferro,* Chapter X.
69 *Ibid.,* pp. 222–5.
70 This poem, a *qasida* in forty-four lines, rhyming in *ha,* appears in *Somaliya,* 3 (ed. Y. O. Kenadid), 1967, pp. 28–9. It probably is dated 1334/1915–6, and it is so far the only text available.
71 Moyse-Bartlett, *King's African Rifles,* pp. 425–33.
72 See Marzuq, *Tha'ir,* p. 203, for a list of the members of this delegation.
73 Moyse-Bartlett, *King's African Rifles,* p. 431.
74 'Isa, *Ta'rikh,* p. 126, gives the Somali text and an Arabic translation, perhaps by the Sayyid. This poem was sent to 'Uthman Ghaba, the sultan of the Toba (a clan that lived near Imi), with a request for aid.
75 Andrzejewski and Lewis, *Somali Poetry,* p. 55.
76 About two-thirds of the text of the *Risalat al-Bimal* first appeared in 'Isa, *Ta'rikh,* pp. 146–65, in 1965. The text published by Shaykh Yasin Kenadid appeared in his continuing cultural and historical anthology, *Somaliya,* 3, June 1967 (pp. 7–26 at the end of the number). Here Kenadid includes the whole text. These two versions show some minor variations. In fact, they come from a single individual, Al-Hajj Muhammad Ahmad Liban. Liban

memorized the written text he was carrying with him to the Bimal from
fear that he might be captured by the Italians while he was in possession
of an incriminating document. The original he destroyed. As for the text of
the *Qam' al-Mu'anidin*, it has only appeared so far in 'Isa, *Ta'rikh*, pp. 99–
104. At the end of the text, at the bottom of p. 104, 'Isa states: "I have
attempted to get hold of the remainder of the text . . . but until now, I
have been unable to do so." However, Marzuq, *Tha'ir*, pp. 106–8, includes
an Arabic translation of a poem in Somali. This is supposedly an abridged
translation of the *Qam'*. Copies of the original were sent to Shaykh
Muhammad Salih and to the Sultan of Turkey, through Abyssinia.

77 'Isa, *Ta'rikh*, p. 100.
78 *Ibid.*, p. 104.
79 *Ibid.*, p. 101.
80 *Ibid.*, p. 99.
81 Citations here are taken from 'Isa's version of the text, except for *tawassul*
   and other points at the end of the *Risala*, where the page references apply
   to the version published by Kenadid (Somaliya, III, 1967). Marzuq, *Tha'ir*,
   refers on p. 63 to another *risala* entitled *Mubahith al-munafiqin*. This may
   be the formal title of the "Message to the Bimal."
82 'Isa, *Ta'rikh*, pp. 146–7.
83 *Ibid.*, p. 148.
84 *Ibid.*, pp. 148–9.
85 *Ibid.*, pp. 149–52.
86 *Ibid.*, p. 152.
87 *Ibid.*, pp. 152–5; the *Sayf al-Battar*, by 'Abdallah ibn 'Abd al-Bari al-Ahdal
   (from the famous Ahdal family of Zabid in Yaman), is cited in Sarkis,
   Mu'jam al-matbu'at, I, Cairo 1928, p. 495. It was published in Cairo in
   1273/1856–7 as part of a *Majmu'a*.
88 'Isa, *Ta'rikh*, pp. 156–7.
89 *Ibid.*, pp. 157–8.
90 *Ibid.*, p. 157.
91 *Ibid.*, pp. 159–60.
92 *Ibid.*, p. 161.
93 *Ibid.*
94 *Ibid.*
95 *Ibid.*, p. 162.
96 *Ibid.*, pp. 162–3.
97 Kenadid, p. 22.
98 See H. Laoust, *Les Schismes dans l'Islam*, Paris 1965, pp. 274–5.
99 Ibn Taymiya, *Qa'ida jalila fi'l-tawassul wa'l-wasila*, ed. Ṭaha al-Zayni, Cairo
   1373/1953–4, pp. 25–6, for a discussion of the two possible sorts of visits
   to tombs.
100 Laoust, *Schismes*, p. 324
101 Cerulli, Somalia, 1, pp. 187–9.
102 Two volumes in one.
103 *Al-Sikkin ai-dhabiha 'ala'l-kilab al-nabiha.*
104 *Nasr al-Mu'minin 'ala'l-marada al-mulhidin.*
105 Al-Qutbi, *Majmu'a*, I, pp. 44–6, 53–4.
106 Al-Qutbi, *Nasr*, in *Majmu'a*, I, pp. 58–9, 60–2.
107 Al-Qutbi, *Majmu'a*, pp. 59.
108 *Ibid.*, pp. 59, 61.

109   *Ibid.*, p. 73.
110   *Ibid.*, p. 70.
111   *Ibid.*, p. 72.
112   *Ibid.*
113   Cerulli, *Somalia*, 1, p. 199.
114   Al-Qutbi, *Majmu'a*, pp. 134–7.
115   See B. G. Hill, "Čat (Catha edulis Forsk)," *Journal of Ethiopian Studies*, 3, 1965, pp. 13–25; Al-Qutbi, *Majmu'a*, pp. 135–6.
116   Al-Qutbi, *Majmu'a*, pp. 137–8; Ibn Taymiya, *fatwa* or *risala* no. 13, *Kitab al-Sama' wa'l-Raqs*, in *Majmu'at Al-Rasa'il al-Kubra*, Cairo 1323/1905–6, pp. 278–315, generally opposes dancing, but the real question is the one of the dancer's motives.

Bibliography

A. Archival Materials

Akta des kaiserlichen Gouvernements von Deutsch-Ostafrika betreffend religioese Bewegungen (Islamische Bewegungen), series G9, National Archives of Tanzania.

National Archives of Tanzania, Provincial Office, Eastern Provinces, Native administration, Rufiji, Morogoro P.O., File no. 61.

B. Books and Manuscripts in Arabic, Turkish, Etc.

Abdallahi dan Fodio, *Tazyin al-Waragat*, ed. Mervyn Hiskett, Ibadan 1963.

Abu Salim, Mahammad, *Manshurat al-Mahdi*, Khartum 1963.

Ahmad ibn 'Abd al-Rahman, Sayyid, *Manaqib . . . al-Sayyid Muhammad ibn Ahmad b. Abi Bakr al-Shadhili al-Yashruti*, Cairo 1353/1934.

'Al, 'Abdallahi, *Dhikr ibtida' . . . jihad Shaykhina . . . Amir al-Mu'minin . . . 'Umar b. Sa'id*, ms., Nuru Tal Library, Dakar.

Kayfiyat al-Hajj 'Umar . . . , ms., Falke Collection, Northwestern University Library, Evanston, Iillinois.

Kitab al-Aja'ib al-qadriya . . . , ms. no. 5, Ifan Library, Dakar, Fonds Curtin.

Rihlat Shaykina ul-Hajj 'Umar, ms., Sayyid Nuru Tal Library, Dakar.

Arslan, Shakib, *Hadir al-'alam al-Islami*, Cairo 1352/1934.

al-Ashab, M. T., *Barqa al-'Arabiya ams wa'l-yawm*, Cairo 1366/1947.

al-'Azm, Sadiq al-Mu'ayyad, *Afrika sahrayi kebirinde seyahat*, Istanbul 1316/1896.

al-Bakri, Salah, *Fi janub al-jazirat al-'Arabiya*, Cairo 1368/1949.

al-Baytar, 'Abd al-Razzaq, *Hilyat al-Bashar*, III, Damascus 1961.

Behij al-Din, Mehmet, *Tarih-i-Ibn Ghalbun*, Istanbul 1284/1867.

Bello, Muhammad, *Infaq al-Maysur fi ta'rikh bilad al-Takrur*, Cairo 1383/1964.

Çayçi, A. *Büyük Sahra'da Türk-Fransiz rekabeti (1858–1911)*, Erzerum 1970.

al-Dajjani, Ahmad Sidqi, *Al-Harakat al-Sanusiya, nashatiha wa namuwwuha fi'l-qarn al-tasi' 'ashar*, Cairo 1967.

al-Farsy, Shaykh Abdallah Saleh, *Sayyid Sa'id bin Sultan*, Zanzibar 1944.

Tarehe Imam Shafi, Zanzibar 1944.

Hilmi, Shehbenderzade F. Ahmet, *Senusiler ve önüniincü asrin büyük mutefekkir-i-Islamisi Sayyid Muhammad al-Senusi*, Istanbul 1307/1908.

Ibn Abi Diyaf, *Ithaf Ahl al-Zaman*, Tunis 1960.

Ibn Muhyi al-Din Qasim, *Majmu'a qasa'id fi madh Sayyid al-Anbiya . . . wa Sidi 'Abd al-Qadir al-Jaylani*, Cairo 1374/1955.

Ibn, Taymiya, *Qaida jalila fi'l-tawassul wa'l-wasila*, ed. T. al-Zayni, Cairo 1953.

Ibn Zaydan, *Ithaf a'lam al-nas, bi-jamal akhbar Hadirat Miknas*, Rabat 1349/1930.

Iluri, Adamu 'Abdallah. *Al-Islam fi Nijiriya wa 'Uthman ibn Fudi*, Cairo 1368/1948.

'Isa, Jama' 'Umar, *Ta'rikh al-Sumal fi'l-'usur al-wusta wa'l-haditha*, Cairo 1965.

al-Jaza'iri, Muhammad ibn 'Abd al-Qadir, *Tuhfat al-za'ir fi ta'rikh al-Jaza'ir wa'l-Amir 'Abd al-Qadir*, Beirut 1384/1964.

Kamara, Shaykh Musa, *Ta'rikh al-Hajj 'Umar*, ms., Ifan Library, Dakar.

al-Madani, Muhammad Zafir, *Nur al-Sati' wa burhan al-qati'*, Istanbul 1883.

Marzuq, 'Abd al-Sabur, *Tha'ir min al-Sumal, al-Mulla Muhammad 'Abdallah Hasan*, Cairo 1964.

al-Misurati, 'Ali Mustafa, *Ghuma, faris al-Sahra'*, Tripoli 1968.

Mkelle, Burhan, *Ta'rikh jaziratina Qumr al-kubra*, Xerox of author's manuscript in my possession.

al-Nadiri al-'Alawi, Sharif 'Aydarus, *Bughyat al-Amal fi ta'rikh al-Sumal*, Mogadishu 1955.

al-Qadiri, 'Abd al-Rahman b. Shaykh 'Umar, *Jala' al-'Aynayn fi manaqib al-Shaykhayn* . . . Cairo n.d.

al-Qadiri, 'Abd al-Rahman b. Shaykh 'Umar, *Al-Jawhar al-Nafis fi khawass al-Shaykh Uways*, Cairo 1383/1964.

al-Qalqami, Ma' al-'Aynayn, *Fatiq al-Ratq*, Cairo 1347/1927 (on the margin of his *Na't al-Bidayat*).

al-Qalqami, Ma' al-'Aynayn, *Mubsir al-mutashawwif*, Fez 1314/1896.

al-Qalqami, Ma' al-'Aynayn, *Na't al-Bidayat wa tawsif al-nihayat*, Cairo 1324, 1347/1927.

al-Qutbi, Shaykh 'Abdallah, *Majmu'a al-Mubaraka*, Cairo 1919.

Rabbuh, Murabbih (Muhammad Mustafa ibn Ma' al-'Aynayn), *Qurrat al-'Aynayn fi karamat al-Shaykh Ma al-'Aynayn*, ms., National Library of Morocco, Rabat.

Rihani, Amin, *Muluk al-'Arab*, 1, Beirut 1951.

al-Salawi, Ahmad al-Nasiri, *Kitab al-Istiqsa' li-akhbar duwal al-Maghrib al-Aqsa'*, Casablanca 1956.

al-Sanusi, Muhammad 'Ali, *Al-Majmu'at al-Mukhtara*, Beirut 1388/1962.

Al-Sayyadi, Abu'l-Huda, *Da't al-Rushud li-subil al-ittihad wa'l-inqiyad*, Istanbul n.d.

Sayyid, Muhammad al-Mu'tasim, *Mahdi al-Sumal*, Cairo 1963.

al-Shinqiti, Ahmad, *Al-Wasit fi tarajim udaba al-Shinqit*, Cairo 1380/1961.

al-Shinqiti, Ibn al-Hibat, *Manaqib al-Shaykh 'Umar*, xerox of manuscript in possession of J. R. Willis.

Shukri, Muhammad Fu'ad, *Al-Sanusiya, din wa dawla*, Cairo 1948.

Subhi Ömer, *Trablusgarb ve Binghazi ile Sahra-yi kebir ve Sudan merkezi*, Istanbul 1307/1889.

Sukayrij, Ahmad, *Kashf al-hijab 'an man talaqa ma' al-Shaykh al-Tijani min al-ashab*, Fez 1332/1913.

Sumayt, Ahmad bin, *Al-Ibtihaj fi bayan istilah al-Minhaj*, Cairo 1353/1935.

al-Susi, Muhammad al-Mukhtar, *Al-Mas'ul*, IV, Fadala, Morocco 1960.

Al-Suyuti, Jalal al-Din, *Al-Kashf 'an mujawaza hadhihi'l-ummat al-alf*, ms., Loth 1031/Bijapur 85, India Office Library, London.

Tal, 'Umar, *Bayan ma waqa'a bayni wa bayn Amir Masina Ahmad bin Ahmad*, ms., 5605, BNP.

Tal, 'Umar, Letter to al-Amin al-Kanemi, ms., 5693, BNP.

Tal, 'Umar, Poems in praise of al-Kanemi, mss. Bornu 32 and 33a, Library of Ahmadu Bello University, Zaria.

Tal, 'Umar, *Rimah hizb al-rahim 'ala nuhur hizb al-rajim*, printed on the margin of 'Ali Harzihum ibn al-'Arabi al-Fasi, *Jawahir al-Ma'ani*, Cairo 1382/1962.

Tal, 'Umar, *Safinat al-Sa'ada*, ms., Nuru Tal Library, Dakar.

Tal, 'Umar, *Suyuf al-Sa'id*, ms. no. 5401, BNP.

Tal, 'Umar, *Tadhkirat al-Ghafilin 'an qabh ikhtilaf al-mu'minin*, ms. no. 5609, BNP.
Tal, 'Umar, *Tadhkirat al-Mustarshidin wa falah al-talibin*, ms. no. 5603, BNP.
Talfi, Yarki, *Tabbakiyat al-Bakka'i*, ms. no. 5697, BNP.
al-Tamimi, 'Abd al-Jahil, *Buhuth wa watha'iq fi'l-ta'rikh al-Maghribi, 1816–1871*, Tunis 1972.
al-Tijani, Muhammad al-Hafiz, *Al-Hajj 'Umar al-Futi, Sultan al-Dawlat al-Tijaniya*, Cairo 1382/1963.
Usuman dan Fodio, *Bayan wujub al-Hijra . . .* , ms. no. 193, Shahuci Judicial School, Kano, from a microfilm in the possession of Mervyn Hiskett.
Usuman dan Fodio, *Hidayat al-Tullab*, Zaria n.d.
Usuman dan Fodio, *Hisn al-Afham*, ms., Falke Collection, Northwestern University Library, Evanston, Illinois.
Usuman dan Fodio, *Ihya' al-Sunna*, Cairo 1962.
Usuman dan Fodio, *Majmu' thalatha kutub* (Litattafai uku a hade . . .), Zaria 1962.
Usuman dan Fodio, *Nasa'ih al-ummat al-Muhammadiya*, manuscript on microfilm in the possession of Mervyn Hiskett.
Usuman dan Fodio, *Shifa' al-Ghalil fima ashkala min kalam Shaykh shuyukhina Jibril*, manuscript belonging to Imam Nasir Kabara of Kano.
Usuman dan Fodio, *Wathiqat al-ikhwan*, Zaria n.d.
Yahya, J., *Al-Tanafus al-Duwali fi bilad al-Sumal*, Cairo 1959.
al-Yashrutiya, Fatima, *Rihlat ila'l-Haqq*, Beirut n.d.
al-Zawi, Tahir Ahmad, *Wulat Tarabulus min bidayat al-fath al-'Arabi ila nihayat al-'ahd al-Turki*, Tripoli 1390/1970.

C. Books, Articles, Papers, Etc., in European Languages

Abel, A., *Les Musulmans Noirs du Maniéma*, Brussels 1960.
Abun-Nasr, J. M., *The Tijaniyya, A Sufi Order in the Modern World*, Oxford 1965.
Abun-Nasr, J. M., *A History of the Maghrib*, Cambridge 1971.
Agéron, C. R., *Les Algériens Musulmans et la France (1871–1919)*, Paris 1968.
(al-'Ajami) Abdallah bin Hemedi'l-Ajjemy, *The Kilindi*, Nairobi 1963.
Ajayi, J. A., and Crowder, M., *History of West Africa*, I, London 1971.
Allworth, E. (ed.), *Central Asia, A Century of Russian Rule*, N.Y. 1967.
Andrzejewski, B. W., and Lewis, I. M., *Somali Poetry, An Introduction*, Oxford 1964.
Anonymous, *The Somali Peninsula, New Light on Imperial Motives*, Mogadishu and London 1962.
al-'Attas, Sayyid Naguib, *Preliminary Statement on a General Theory of the Islamization of the Malay-Indonesian Archipelago*, Kuala Lumpur 1969.
Ba, A. H., and Daget, J., *L'Empire Peul du Macina*, Paris 1962.
Ba, M. A., "À propos de Smara," *L'Afrique Française*, 44, 1934.
Ba, T. A., "Essai Historique sur le Rip," *BIFAN*, 19, 1957.
Barkun, M., *Disaster and the Millennium*, New Haven 1974.
Batran, A. A., "An Introductory Note on the Impact of Sidi al-Mukhtar al-Kunti (1729–1811) on W. African Islam in the 18th and 19th Centuries," unpublished paper, 1972.
Batran, A. A., "The Kunta, Sidi al-Mukhtar al-Kunti and the Office of the Shaykh al-Tariqa al-Qadiriya," in (J. R. Willis (ed.), *The Cultivators of Islam*, I, London 1976, forthcoming.

Becker, C. H., "Materials for the Understanding of Islam in East Africa," ed. B. G. Martin, *TNR*, 68, 1968.

Bennett, N. R., "The Arab Power of Tanganyika," unpublished Ph.D. thesis, Boston 1964.

Berbrugger, A., "Un Chef Kabyle en 1804," *RA*, 3, 1859.

Bivar, A. D. H., and Hiskett, Mervyn, "The Arabic Literature of Nigeria to 1804: A Provisional Account," *BSOAS*, 25, 1962.

Bottego, V., *L'Esplorazione del Giuba, Viaggio di Scoperta nel Cuore dell'Africa*, Rome 1900.

Boyer, P., "Contribution à l'Étude de la Politique Religieuse des Turcs dans la Régence d'Alger," *Revue de l'Occident Musulman et de la Méditerranée*, 1, 1966.

Brass, A., "Eine Neue Quelle zur Geschichte des Fulreiches Sokoto," *Der Islam*, 10, 1920.

Braukaemper, U., *Der Einfluss des Islam auf die Geschichte und Kulturentwicklung Adamauas*, Wiesbaden 1970.

Brode, H., *Tippoo Tib, The Story of His Career in Central Africa*, London 1907.

Brown, W. A., "The Caliphate of Hamdallahi, a Study in African History and Tradition," unpublished Ph.D. thesis, University of Wisconsin, Madison, 1969.

Burke, E., "The Moroccan 'Ulama, 1860–1912: An Introduction," in N. Keddie (ed.), *Scholars, Saints and Sufis*, Berkeley 1972.

Burton, R. F., *Zanzibar, City, Island, and Coast*, I, London 1872.

Cassanelli, L. V., "Migrations, Islam, and Politics in the Somali Benaadir, 1500–1843," in H. G. Marcus and J. Hinnant (eds.), *Proceedings of the first U.S. Conference on Ethiopian Studies . . . 1973*, East Lansing 1975.

Caro Baroja, J., "Un Santon Sahariano y su Familia," in *Estudos Saharianos*, Madrid 1955.

Caroselli, F. S., *Ferro e Fuoco in Somalia*, Rome 1931.

Carrère, F., and Holle, P., *De la Sénégambie Française*, Paris 1855.

Cerulli, E., "Note Sulle Movimenti Musulmani nella Somalia," *Somalia*, 1, 1957.

Chittick, H. N., *Annual Report for 1958*, Department of Antiquities, Tanganyika government, Dar es-Salaam, 1959.

Chouzour, Sultan, *Idéologies et Institutions: l'Islam aux Comores*, Aix-en-Provence, 1972.

Clapperton, H., *Journal of a Second Expedition into the Interior of Africa*, Philadelphia 1829.

Coupland, R., *The Exploitation of East Africa*, London 1939.

Cour, A., *L'Établissement des Dynasties des Chérifs au Maroc*, Paris 1904.

Deny, J., "Les Registres de la Solde des Janissaires Conservés a la Bibliothèque Nationale d'Alger," *RA*, 61, 1920.

Dermenghem, E., *Le Culte des Saints dans l'Islam Maghrabin*, Paris 1954.

Désiré-Vuillemin, G., *Contribution à l'Histoire de la Mauritanie, de 1900 à 1934*, Dakar 1962.

Domenech Lafuente, A., *Algo sobre Río de Oro*, Madrid 1946.

Domenech Lafuente, A., "Ma el Ainin, Señor de Smara," *Africa, Revista de Tropas Coloniales*, 17, 1946.

Douls, C., "Cinq Mois chez les Maures Nomades du Sahara Occidental," in *Le Tour du Monde*, Paris 1888.

Duveyrier, H., *Exploration du Sahara; Les Touareg du Nord*, Paris 1864.

Duveyrier, H., *La Confrérie Musulmane de Sidi Mohammed ben 'Ali es-Senoussi et sa Domaine Géographique*, Paris 1884.

Émerit, M., *L'Algérie à l'époque d'Abd el-Kader,* Paris 1951.

Émerit, M., "Un Problème de Distance Morale: la Résistance Algérienne à l'Époque d'Abd-el-Kader," *Information Historique,* July–October 1952.

Émerit, M., "L'Exploitation de Os des Musulmans pour le Raffinage du Sucre," *RHM,* 1, 1974.

Evans-Pritchard, E. E., *The Sanusi of Cyrenaica,* Oxford 1949.

al-Fasi, 'Allal, *Independence Movements in North Africa,* Washington, D.C. 1954.

Féraud. L. C., "Histoire des Villes de la Province de Constantine, *Recueil des Notices et Mémoires de la Société Archéologique . . . de la Province de Constantine,* 4, 1870.

Freeman-Grenville, G. S. P., and Martin, B. G., "A Preliminary Handlist of the Arabic Inscriptions of the Eastern African Coast," *JRAS,* 24, 1973.

Gavin, R. J., "The Bartle Frere Mission to Zanzibar, 1873," *The Historical Journal,* 5, 1962.

Goldziher, I., "Zur Charakteristik Galal el-Din us-Sujuti's und seiner literarischen Thaetigkeit," *Sitzungsberichten,* Wiener Akademis der Wissenschaften, 69, 1871.

Grant and Bagenal, *Kigoma District Book,* III, 1929.

Guilhem, R., and Toé, S., *Précis d'Histoire du Mali,* Paris n.d.

Haas, W. S., "The Zikr of the Rahmaniya Order in Algeria," *MW,* 33, 1943.

Al-Hajj, M., "The 13th century in Muslim Eschatology, Mahdist Expectations in the Sokoto Caliphate," *CADRB,* 3, 1967.

Hamilton, J., *Wanderings in North Africa,* London 1856.

Harries, Lyndon, "The Swahili Chronicle of Ngazija," unpublished paper, Madison, Wisconsin, 1968.

Hess, R. L., "The Poor Man of God, Muhammad Abdallah Hassan," in N. R. Bennett (ed.), *Leadership in Eastern Africa, Six Political Biographies,* Boston 1968.

Hill, B. G., "Čat (Catha edulis Forsk.)," *Journal of Ethiopian Studies,* 3, 1965.

Hiskett, Mervyn, "Material Relating to the State of Learning among the Fulani before their *jihad,*" *BSOAS,* 19, 1957.

Hiskett, Mervyn, "The Song of the Shehu's Miracles, a Hausa Hagiography from Sokoto," *African Language Studies,* 12, 1971.

Hiskett, Mervyn, "The Origin, Sources, and Form of Hausa Islamic Verse," *Spectrum,* 3, 1973.

Hiskett, Mervyn, *The Sword of Truth,* N.Y. 1973.

Hiskett, Mervyn, "The Nineteenth Century *jihads* in West Africa," in *Cambridge History of Africa,* V, Chapter 6, forthcoming.

Hodgkin, Thomas, "Usuman dan Fodio," unpublished paper, 1968.

Hollingsworth, L. W., *Zanzibar under the Foreign Office, 1890–1913,* London 1953.

Holt, P. M., *The Mahdist State in the Sudan,* 2nd ed., Oxford 1971.

Hore, E. C., *Tanganyika,* London 1892.

Houdas, O. V., *Le Maroc de 1631–1812 par Ezziani,* Paris 1886.

Hourani, Albert, *Arabic Thought in the Liberal Age, 1798–1939,* Oxford 1967.

Hourani, Albert, "Shaykh Khalid and the Naqshbandi Order," in *Festschrift Richard Walzer,* Oxford 1974.

Hurgronje, C. Snouck, "Eenige Arabische Strijdschriften Besproken," in *Verspreide Geschriften,* III, Leipzig 1926.

Jardím da Vilhena, E., "A Influencia Islamica na Costa Oriental d'Africa," *Boletim da Sociedade de Geografica de Lisboa,* 24a, 1906.

Jardine, D., *The Mad Mullah of Somaliland,* London 1923.

Julien, C. -A., *Histoire de l'Algérie Contemporaine* . . . *1827–1871,* Paris 1964.

Kanya-Forstner, A., *The Conquest of the Western Sudan, A study in French Military Imperialism,* Cambridge 1969.

Kanya-Forstner, A. S., "Mali-Tukolor," in M. Crowder (ed.), *West African Resistance,* London 1971.

Kasembeg, A., "De l'Ijtihad et de ses Différents Degrés," *Journal Asiatique,* 21, 1850.

Kenadid, Shaykh Yasin, *Somaliya,* Mogadishu 1965–.

Kesteloot, L., *et al., Da Monzon de Ségou, Epopée Bambara,* Paris 1972.

Kieran, J. A., "Abushiri and the Germans," *Hadith,* III, Nairobi 1970.

Klopfer, H., *Aspekte der Bewegung des Muhammad ben 'Ali al-Sanusi,* Wiesbaden 1967.

Laoust, H., *Les Schismes dans l'Islam,* Paris 1965.

Last, D. M., and al-Hajj, M., "Attempts at Defining a Muslim in 19th Century Hausaland and Bornu," *JHSN,* 2, 1965.

Last, D. M., *The Sokoto Caliphate,* London 1968.

Le Châtelier, A., *Les Confréries Musulmanes du Hedjaz,* Paris 1887.

Lévi-Provençal, E., *Les Manuscrits Arabes de Rabat,* Paris 1921.

Lévi-Provençal, E., "Ma' al-'Ainain," *EI*[1].

Lewis, B., *The Middle East and the West,* London 1968.

Lewis, I. M., "La Communità ('Giamia') di Bardera Sulle Rive del Giuba," *Somalia d'Oggi,* 2, Mogadishu 1957.

Lewis, I. M., *The Modern History of Somaliland,* London 1965.

Lovejoy, P., and Baier, S., "The Desert-Side Economy of the Central Sudan," *IJAHS,* 8, 1975.

MacKeen, A. M., "The Rise of al-Shadhili," *JAOS,* 91, 1971.

MacKenzie, D., "The British Settlement at Cape Juby, Northwest Africa," Blackwood's *Edinburgh Magazine,* 146, 1889.

Mage, Eugène, *Voyage dans le Soudan Occidentale (Sénégambie-Niger),* Paris 1868.

Maquet, Y., "Des Ikhwan al-Safa à al-Hajj 'Umar . . . ," *Arabica,* 15, 1968.

Margoliouth, D. S., "On Mahdis and Mahdism," *Proceedings of the British Academy,* 7, 1915–6.

Margoliouth, D., "Senusi," in J. Hastings (ed.), *Encyclopedia of Religion & Ethics,* XI, p. 195.

Martel, A., *Les Confins Saharo-Tripolitaines de la Tunisie, 1881–1911,* Paris 1965.

Martel, A., "La Politique Saharienne et Ottomane . . ." in *Le Sahra, rapports et contacts humaines . . . . 7ième Colloque d'Histoire . . . Aix-en-Provence,* Aix 1972.

Martin, B. G., "A Mahdist Document from Futa Jallon," *BIFAN,* 25, 1963.

Martin, B. G., "Five Letters from the Tripoli Archives," *JHSN,* 2, 1964.

Martin, B. G., "A Muslim Political Tract from Northern Nigeria: Muhammad Bello's *Usul al-Siyasa,*" *Boston University Papers on Africa,* 5, 1971.

Martin, B. G., "A Short History of the Khalwati Order of Dervishes," in N. Keddie (ed.), *Scholars, Saints, and Sufis,* Berkeley 1972.

Martin, B. G., "Arab Migrations to East Africa in Medieval Times," *IJAHS,* 7, 1974.

Marty, Paul, "Les Fadelia," *RMM,* 31, 1915–6.

Al-Masri, F. H., "The Life of Shehu dan Fodio before the Jihad," *JHSN,* 2, 1962.

Al-Masri, F. H.; Adeleye, R.; Hunwick, J. O.; and Mukoshy, I. A., "Sifofin Shehu,

An Autobiography and Character Study of 'Uthman b. Fudi in Verse,"
CADRB, 2, 1966.

Al-Masri, F. H., "A Critical Edition of Dan Fodio's *Bayan wujub al-Hijra 'ala'l-'ibad*," unpublished Ph.D. thesis, Ibadan 1968.

Miles, S. B., *The Countries and Tribes of the Persian Gulf*, London 1919.

Molina Campuzano, M., *Contribución al Estudio del Censo de Población de Sahara Español*, Madrid 1954.

Al Moutabassir, "Ma el Ainin ech Changuity," *RMM*, 1, 1907.

Moyse-Bartlett, H., *The King's African Rifles, A Study in the Military History of East and Central Africa*, Aldershot 1956.

Nachtigal, G., *Sahara and Sudan*, ed. A. G. B. Fisher and H. J. Fisher, IV, London 1971.

Nallino, C., "Le Dottrine del Fondatore della Confraternita Senussita," in *Raccolta di scritti* . . . , II, Rome 1940.

al-Naqar, 'Umar, *The Pilgrimage Tradition in West Africa*, Khartoum 1972.

Newitt, M. D. D., "Angoche, the Slave Trade, and the Portuguese, c. 1844–1910," *JAH*, 13, 1972.

Nimtz, A. H., "The Role of the Muslim Sufi Order in Political Change: An Overview and Microanalysis from Tanzania," unpublished Ph.D. thesis, Bloomington, Indiana, 1973.

Norris, H. T., "Shaykh Ma al-'Aynayn al-Qalqami in the Folk-Literature of the Spanish Sahara," *BSOAS*, 3, 1968.

Oded, A., *Islam in Uganda; Islamization through a Centralized State in Pre-Colonial Africa*, N.Y. 1974.

Olderogge, D. A., "Osman dan Fodios Aufstand und seine Bedeutung," *Akten des XXIV Orientalistenkongresses*, Muenchen 1957.

Oliver, R., "Some Factors in the British Occupation of East Africa, 1884–1894," *Uganda Journal*, 15, 1951

Oliver, R., *The Missionary Factor in East Africa*, London 1952.

Oloruntimehin, B. O., *The Segu Tokolor Empire*, London 1972.

Ouane, Ibrahim-Mamadou, *Pérégrinations Soudanaises*, Lyon n.d.

Perès, H., "Les Poésies d'Abd al-Kader Composées en Algérie et en France," *Cinquantenaire de la Faculté des Lettres d'Alger*, Algiers 1932.

Person, Y., *Samori, une Revolution Dyula*, Dakar 1968.

Pocock, D., *Social Anthropology*, London 1971.

Pottier, R., *Un Prince Saharien Méconnu: Henri Duveyrier*, Paris 1938.

von Prince, T., *Gegen Araber und Wahehe*, Berlin 1913.

Rahman, Fazlur, *Islam*, N.Y. 1968.

Reichardt, C. A. L., *A Grammar of the Fulde Language*, London 1876.

Reid, A., "Nineteenth Century Pan-Islam in Indonesia and Malaysia," *Journal of Asian Studies*, 26, 1967.

Reid, A., *The Contest for North Sumatra* . . . , Oxford 1969.

Reid, A., "Habib Abdur Rahman az-Zahir," *Indonesia*, 13, 1972.

Rinn, L., *Marabouts et Khouan*, Algiers 1884.

Robinson, David, "Legitimacy, Constituency, and Failure in the Torodbe Movement of Futa Toro," unpublished paper, New Haven, Conn. 1972.

Robinson, David, "Abdul Qadir and Shaykh 'Umar: A Continuing Tradition of Islamic Leadership in Futa Toro," *IJAHS*, 6, 1973.

Rossi, E. *Storia di Tripoli e della Tripolitania, dalla Conquista araba al 1911*, Rome 1968.

St. Martin, Y. -J., *L'Empire Toucouleur et la France, un Demi-Siècle de Relations Politiques (1846–93)*, Dakar 1967.

Salenc, Jules, "La Vie d'el Hadj Omar," *BCEHSAOF*, 1, 1918.

Savory, R. M., "The Principal Offices of the Safavid State during the Reign of Shah Isma'il," *BSOAS*, 33, 1960.

Schmidt, R., *Geschichte des Araberaufstandes in Ost-Afrika*, Frankfurt/Oder 1892.

Seydou, Christiane, "Trois Poèmes Mystiques Peuls du Futa Jalon," *REI*, 40, 1972.

Shinar, P., "Note on the Socio-Economic and Cultural Role of Sufi Brotherhoods and Marabutism in the Modern Maghrib," *Proceedings of the First International Congress of Africanists, Accra, 1962*, Evanston 1964.

Shinar, P., "'Abd al-Qadir and 'Abd al-Krim," in *Asian and African Studies*, I, Jerusalem 1965.

Sivers, Peter von, "The Disease of the Infidel: Crisis of Authority in 19th Century Muslim Algeria," unpublished paper, Los Angeles 1970.

Sivers, Peter von, "The Realm of Justice: Apocalyptic Revolts in Algeria (1849–1879)," in *Humaniora Islamica*, I, The Hague 1973.

Slade, R., *King Leopold's Congo*, London 1960.

Smith, 'Abdallahi, "The Islamic Revolutions of the 19th Century," *JHSN*, 2, 1961.

Smith, Abdallahi, review of J. S. Trimingham, *History of Islam in W. Africa*, *Ibadan Magazine*, March 1963.

Socé, Ousman, *Contes et Légendes de l'Afrique Noire*, Paris 1962.

Stanley, Lord, "Narrative of Mr. W. C. Thompson's Journey from Sierra Leone to Timbo, Capital of Futa Jallo in Western Africa," *JRGS*, 16, 1846.

Starkie, F., *Arthur Rimbaud in Abyssinia*, Oxford 1937.

Stevens, J. W., *An Historical and Geographical Account of Algiers, Comprehending Novel and Interesting Details of Events Relative to the American Captives*, Philadelphia 1797.

Subtil, E., "Histoire d'Abd el-Gelil, Sultan du Fezzan," *Revue de l'Orient*, 1844.

Suret-Canale, J., "Touba in Guinea – Holy Place of Islam," in C. Allen and R. W. Johnson (eds.), *African Perspectives*, Cambridge 1970.

Swayne, H. G. C., *Seventeen Trips through Somaliland . . .* , London 1900.

Tauxier, L., *Moeurs et Histoire des Peuls*, Paris 1937.

Tippu Tib (Hamid bin Muhammad al-Murjibi), *Maisha . . . Tippu Tib kwa maneno yake mwenyewe*, ed., tr. W. H. Whiteley, Nairobi 1966.

Toynbee, A. J., *Survey of International Affairs*, I, Oxford 1927.

Trimingham, J. S., *A History of Islam in West Africa*, Oxford 1962.

Trimingham, J. S., *The Sufi Orders in Islam*, Oxford 1971.

Trout, F. E., *Morocco's Saharan Frontiers*, Geneva 1969.

Turton, E. R., "The Impact of Muhammad Abdille Hasan in the East Africa Protectorate," *JAH*, 10, 1969.

Tyam, M. Aliou, *La Vie d'el-Hadj Omar, Qasida en Poular*, Paris 1935.

Usuman dan Fodio, *Nur al-Albab*, Arabic text and French translation by Isma'il Hamet, *RA*, 42, 1898.

Usuman dan Fodio, *Ta'lim al-Ikhwan*, ed., trans. B. G. Martin, *Middle Eastern Studies*, 4, 1967.

Valensi, L., *Le Maghreb avant la Prise d' Alger, 1790–1830*, Paris 1970.

Van Ess, J., "Die Yašrutiya: (Libanesische Miszellen, VI)," *Die Welt des Islams*, XIV, Vienna 1975.

Vaysettes, "Histoire des Derniers Beys de Constantine depuis 1793 . . . ," *RA*, 3, 1859.

Voll, J. O., "Two Biographies of Ahmad ibn Idris al-Fasi (1760–1837)," *IJAHS*, 4, 1973.

Wallace, A. F. C., *Religion, An Anthropological View*, N.Y. 1966.

War Office, London, *Official History of the Operations in Somaliland, 1901–04*, London 1907.

Wilks, Ivor, "The Saghanughu and the Spread of Maliki Law," CADRB, 2, 1966.

Wilks, Ivor, "The Transmission of Islamic Learning in the Western Sudan," in J. Goody (ed.), *Literacy in Traditional Societies*, Cambridge 1968.

Willis, J. R., "Al-Hajj 'Umar b. Sa'id al-Futi al-Turi (c. 1794–1864) and the Doctrinal Basis of His Islamic Reform Movement in the Western Sudan," unpublished Ph.D. thesis, London University 1971.

Zebadia, Abdelkader, "The Career of Ahmad al-Bakkay in the Oral Evidences and Recorded Documents," *RHM*, 3, Tunis 1975

Ziadeh, N. A., *Sanusiya, A Study of a Revivalist Movement in Islam*, Leiden 1958.

Glossary

amir
prince, local ruler, military commander

'askari
soldier

baraka
blessing, charisma

bey
Turkish military title for official in charge of a *beylik*

beylik
Turkish administrative division

dey
Turkish or Algerian military title, generally superior to a bey

dhikr
sufi ritual, "recital"

dirham
Islamic silver coin

hadra
sufi session, gathering, or ritual assembly

hajji, hadji
Muslim pilgrim

hijra
migration, removal

hujub
Muslim amulets

ijaza
usually a diploma given by a teacher to a student for reading an Arabic legal, or
    other, text

ijtihad
the principle of free legal or theological interpretation

ikhwan
"brothers," members of a sufi organization

imam
leader in prayer or head of state; in the latter meaning, equivalent to *khalifa*
    ("caliph")

jihad
"holy war" or personal struggle for self-control

khalifa
successor, head of state, or ruler

khalwa
place for sufi retreats, mystical seclusion

mahdi
"rightly guided one," Islamic messiah

makhzan
government, mostly used in North Africa

mithqal
small Islamic weight, often used for gold

mujaddid
renewer, reviver

mujahid, pl. *mujahidun*
warrior, participant in a jihad

mujtahid
person able to exercise *ijtihad* – unrestricted interpretation in legal problems

mulla, mullah
Muslim cleric

muqaddam
local official or leader in a sufi organization

muqallid
conservative juridical or theological imitator who follows precedents already
   established

murabit, marabout
local holy man, saint

murshid
spiritual guide or director

mutasarrif, müteserrif
Turkish or Arab administrator, generally of a *müteserriflik;* provincial governor

mütevelli
Turkish administrative title

qadi
Muslim judge

qiyas
analogical reasoning

qutb
chief mystic, "spiritual pole"

ribat
sufi center, frontier fort

sayyid
"master" name often used for a person claiming descent from a Muslim "holy
   family"

shari'a
sacred law of Islam

sharif, pl. *ashraf*
"noble" individual, often of a "holy family"

shaykh, sheikh
sufi leader, spiritual director

sufi
Muslim mystic

sunna
the practice of Prophet Muhammad, an accepted action

talaba, sing. *talib*
students, followers

taqlid
principle of juridical imitation, lack of originality

tariq, pl. *turuq*
Muslim mystical organization

tawassul
intercession to God through saints

'ulama, sing. *'alim*
men learned in religious law

umma
Islamic community, "nation"

veli, wali
Ottoman governor, often of a *vilayet*

wadi
dry river bed, valley

wali
governor, saint

wazir
minister, helper, aide

wifq, pl. *awfaq*
magic square, charm

wilaya
saintship

wird
sufi ritual, connection to an order

zakat
tax, income tax

zawaya
tribe, one that does not bear arms

zawiya, pl. *zawaya*
sufi center, lodge

Index